Internationalizing the Pacific

Since World War I, Wilsonian – or liberal – internationalism has been one of the most influential discourses in international politics. This is the first book to examine the ramifications of Wilsonian internationalism beyond the realm of inter-state relations in the abode of non-governmental organizations and intellectual interchange. *Internationalizing the Pacific* explores how liberal internationalists in the Asia–Pacific envisaged the international community: what their relationship was with the state from the time of the formation of the League of Nations and through the major wars in the region of the 1930s and 1940s. The Institute of Pacific Relations (1925–61) or IPR provides a unique trans-Pacific vehicle for probing the issues.

The victim of McCarthyist attack in the 1950s, the IPR was memorably accused of being a communist front organization and of being responsible for the 'fall' of China into communism. However, in the inter-war period, the IPR was a rare and unique multinational private organization. Unlike many other European-based organizations, it focused on the Asia–Pacific region, and Asian members played a significant role in articulating a Pacific vision. Its founders were inspired by Wilsonian ideas, and they regarded themselves as 'liberal internationalists'. It was a forerunner both of what we call a non-govermnental organization (NGO) in the Asia–Pacific and of a think tank in the region. Above all, it provided a high-level forum in which American, Japanese, Chinese, British, and other policy intellectuals could articulate their sometimes competing visions and approaches to the emerging Pacific region.

This book gives a fresh insight into inter-war internationalism in the non-Euro-American context in this critical period, leading to World War II and the formation of the United Nations. Examining an impressive range of documents – from the United States, Britain, Australia and Japan – it tells a coherent story of the founding and activities of the IPR and examines the development of ideas of a 'single world community'.

Tomoko Akami is Lecturer in the Faculty of Asian Studies, Australian National University.

Asia's transformations

Edited by Mark Selden
Binghamton University and Cornell University, USA

The books in this series explore the political, social, economic and cultural consequences of Asia's twentieth century transformations. The series emphasizes the tumultuous interplay of local, national, regional and global forces as Asia bids to become the hub of the world economy. While focusing on the contemporary, it also looks back to analyse the antecedents of Asia's contested rise.

This series comprises two strands:

Asia's Transformations aims to address the needs of students and teachers, and the titles will be published in hardback and paperback. Titles include:

Debating Human Rights
Critical Essays from the United States and Asia
Edited by Peter Van Ness

Hong Kong's History
State and Society under Colonial Rule
Edited by Tak-Wing Ngo

Japan's Comfort Women
Sexual slavery and prostitution during World War II and the US occupation
Yuki Tanaka

Opium, Empire and the Global Political Economy
Carl A. Trocki

Chinese Society
Change, Conflict and Resistance
Edited by Elizabeth J. Perry and Mark Selden

Mao's Children in the New China
Voices from the Red Guard Generation
Yarong Jiang and David Ashley

Remaking the Chinese State
Strategies, Society and Security
Edited by Chien-min Chao and Bruce J. Dickson

Routledge Studies in Asia's Transformations is a forum for innovative new research intended for a high-level specialist readership, and the titles will be available in hardback only. Titles include:

*Now available in paperback

Internationalizing the Pacific

The United States, Japan and the
Institute of Pacific Relations in
war and peace, 1919–45

Tomoko Akami

Routledge
Taylor & Francis Group

LONDON AND NEW YORK

First published 2002 by Routledge
11 New Fetter Lane, London EC4P 4EE

Simultaneously published in the USA and Canada
by Routledge
29 West 35th Street, New York, NY 10001

Transferred to Digital Printing 2003

Routledge is an imprint of the Taylor & Francis Group

© 2002 Tomoko Akami

Typeset in Baskerville by
Prepress Projects Ltd, Perth, Scotland
Printed and bound in Great Britain by
TJI Digital, Padstow, Cornwall

British Library Cataloguing in Publication Data
A catalogue record for this book is available from the British Library

Library of Congress Cataloging in Publication Data
Akami, Tomoko, 1959–
    Internationalizing the Pacific: the United States, Japan and the
Institute of Pacific Relations in war and peace, 1919–45/Tokomo
Akami.
    p. cm. – (Routledge studies in Asia's transformations, 3)
Includes bibliographical references and index.
    1. Institute of Pacific Relations. 2. Pan-Pacific relations.
3. Pacific Area – Foreign relations. 4. United States – Foreign
relations. 5. Japan – Foreign relations – 20th century.
6. Globalization – Political aspects. 7. World politics – 20th
century. I. Title. II. Series.

DU29.A45 2001
327′.09182′3–dc21   2001044309

ISBN 0–415–22034–3

Contents

List of figures

Foreword

The study of international history, that is, the history of international relations, has been transformed significantly in the last decade or so. Traditionally understood in the framework of 'diplomatic history', the subject has tended to focus on interactions among sovereign states, especially those that are called 'great powers'. Their foreign policies and strategies have been minutely examined to determine how these powers have dealt with one another in peace and war. The questions most frequently asked have been: How did wars begin? How were postwar settlements arrived at? How did great powers rise and fall in the international arena? These are, and remain, legitimate questions, and in many ways they provide the point of departure for any study of international affairs. To explore such questions, it is imperative to undertake empirical research, preferably in the archives of the countries that are being discussed. With the opening of more and more archives to researchers, we may expect to see the continuing publication of monographs in the traditional mode.

That is to be welcomed. At the same time, however, there has been a growing tendency among scholars, especially among the younger generation, to go beyond the traditional frameworks of diplomatic history and add new layers, propose fresh perspectives, and suggest connections that have not usually been stressed. Thanks to the efforts of these scholars, today international history is one of the most exciting sub-fields of history.

For instance, historians have been paying increasing attention to cultural issues and phenomena as vital aspects of international affairs. Traditionally, to the extent that culture comes into play in a study of diplomatic history, it has tended to be viewed as a means of enhancing a nation's effectiveness as a power. Cultural diplomacy best describes this perspective; propaganda efforts undertaken through books, movies and the like, or educational exchange programmes conceived as an instrument of foreign policy, are examples. There are, however, monographs that deal with cultural relations that have little or nothing to do with official policies or with interstate affairs. They show that cultural phenomena – such as tourism, international scholarly gatherings, or the spread of American food and fashions abroad – have a life of their own quite independent of the geopolitical 'realities', yet impinging powerfully upon them.

'Realities', too, have begun to be given fresh meaning in the recent scholarly literature. Traditionally defined by geopolitics – military power, economic resources, and the like – it has become clear that alleged 'realities' are not realities at all but exist more in the realm of ideas and imagination. How an international 'reality' has come to be imagined is itself a fascinating cultural question. Once we begin talking of imagined realities, not 'realities' as something given, the gate is opened to incorporating so many factors, cultural and other, to our study of international history.

Another remarkable development among specialists has been to pay close attention to non-state actors as well as to states as shapers of international relations. Some domestic non-state actors, such as business organizations and religious bodies, do become part of the decision-making process when the state accommodates their interests and perspectives in defining foreign policy. There are, at the same time, international non-state actors, among which the most conspicuous examples are multinational corporations and non-governmental organizations, that are not necessarily tied to a given state's policy-making processes, although at times the two also complement one another. The literature on these organizations adds significantly to our understanding of who the players are in the international arena.

Related to the above scholarly developments is the renewed interest in internationalism and cosmopolitanism. Diplomatic history and interstate affairs of necessity focus on the interplay of national interests, and nationalism is the key ingredient in any such analysis. In most studies, internationalism tends to be understood as inter-nationalism, that is, as a mechanism for mediating potentially conflicting nationalisms. Some recent works emphasize, however, that internationalism may have a life of its own, quite apart from the desires or wishes of sovereign states. Likewise, cosmopolitanism, an awareness of, and a willingness to appreciate, different cultures, which has been a popular subject of study in art history or comparative literature, has begun to claim the attention of some of the most imaginative historians of international relations. The recent revival of interest in the study of international organizations attests to this phenomenon.

Students of international history have also been paying closer attention to the 'periphery', smaller, weaker countries and peoples, not simply as pawns in the game of great-power politics but as players in their own right. It now seems to be widely accepted that, even when we examine the foreign policies of the great powers, it is imperative to examine how small countries have had their own agendas and at times have been quite successful in manipulating the great powers to get what they want.

All these trends suggest that international history is becoming more and more global in scope and perspective. It may be said that one aspect of what is called globalization is scholarly and intellectual inter-connectedness. It now seems axiomatic that it makes no sense to study United States foreign policy, for instance, without an awareness of how it is manipulated by, and attuned to, local political and cultural forces. But globalization is more than a matter of inter-state linkages; it also includes transnational movements of capital, goods, services, ideas and labour. It is promoted – but also sometimes contested – by multinational corporations, international organizations, and border-crossing scholars and students. No wonder, then, that global consciousness is beginning to inform some of the best recent works in international history.

If I have accurately noted some of the significant scholarly trends in this field, then it seems obvious that Tomoko Akami's book is truly reflective of those trends. It focuses on one important international non-governmental organization, the Institute of Pacific Relations, examines how the participants in its activities, coming from many countries, sought to define an alternative world order, explores the meaning of Wilsonian internationalism in the Asia–Pacific region, and proposes a fresh, global perspective on inter-war international relations.

Wilsonian internationalism has lately been a subject of renewed interest among historians and political scientists. This may reflect the awareness that the twentieth century was a 'Wilsonian century', to borrow from the title of a book by Frank Ninkovich. Writers ranging from Ninkovich to Henry Kissinger have tried to come to grips with the impact of Wilsonianism upon the world, but few have looked beyond the United States and Europe. Some have argued that Wilsonianism was a culmination of the Enlightenment tradition, not really a beginning of anything new. Yet if we look at the rest of the world, at Africa, the Middle East, Asia and Latin America, it is obvious that there was something uniquely twentieth century about the Wilsonian world order; it was truly global and established political, economic and cultural connections across nations and regions. At the same time, it encouraged multiculturalism; an awareness of cultural diversity in the world arena that had emerged at the turn of the century was given an institutional expression in the League of Nations and other organizations. The Institute of Pacific Relations was, as this book shows, one important example of individuals from Asia and the Pacific attempting to adapt Wilsonian internationalism to a culturally diverse region and to create a peaceful Pacific community. The efforts failed in the short run, but they are still continuing, and similar efforts are being undertaken elsewhere in the world. It would take a lifetime's study to seek to understand these developments, but Tomoko Akami's book shows one helpful way to begin the inquiry.

Akira Iriye
Harvard University

Acknowledgements

I thank William Holland for his help and for his continuing efforts to encourage scholars to reassess the Institute of Pacific Relations (IPR). As a result of this he faced criticism as well as praise. Having met him, and knowing his commitment to the IPR and his integrity, I hope that he will understand some of the critical comments I have made about the IPR. The book is an attempt to seek the meaning of the IPR in the broad framework of international politics in the twentieth century, and to argue the significance of its pioneering efforts in the Asia–Pacific region.

This book could not have been completed without the help of many people, including Holland. My deepest thanks go to the scholars who have been supportive all through the time that I was engaged in this project, especially Yamaoka Michio and Paul Hooper. They were very generous with their time and in sharing source materials which were critical to this work. Without the materials at Waseda University and the University of Hawai'i at Manoa, it would have been impossible to write this book. They also introduced me to other scholars in the field, Katagiri Nobuo, Ōshiro Jōji, Igarashi Takeshi, Lawrence Woods, Thomas Burkman, Charles Hayford and Jon Davidann. Without their support and scholarship, this book would not have come into being. I also thank Nakami Mari, Sandra Wilson, Shiozaki Hiroaki, Yui Daizaburō, Itō Takashi, Sheldon Garon, John Dower, Miles Fletcher, Stuart Macintyre, Nicholas Brown, John Legge, Douglas Craig, Diane Stone, Richard Higgott, Frank Moorhouse, David Jenkins, Warren Osmond, Dipesh Chakrabarty and many others for their suggestions and inspiring ideas at various stages of the project.

I thank Tessa Morris-Suzuki, John Caiger and Gavan McCormack for their encouragement, support and guidance. I thank Mark Elvin for making it possible to obtain the writings of William Carter, the son of Edward Carter. I thank Paul Carter, the grandson of Edward Carter, for letting me use them. I thank Ishii Yoneo and the staff of the Department of the Pacific and Asian History, Research School of Pacific and Asian Studies, Australian National University, especially those who worked there during the period 1991–6.

I thank Craig Reynolds, Aat Vervoorn, Mark Selden, Akira Iriye and Pamela Hewitt for their encouragement in the last few years. Without their support, it would have been very difficult to maintain the determination to finish the writing. I especially thank Mark Selden, Akira Iriye and Vicky Smith at Routledge for giving me the opportunity to publish this work and for their valuable comments and encouragement. I also thank Craig Fowlie for his encouragement and patience. Thanks also to Linda Poskitt and the staff of the Faculty of Asian Studies, Australia National University, for their support and understanding, especially over the last two years.

My colleagues and friends have provided me with great help all through the project and in hard times. They read drafts, commented on ideas, gave me emotional support and provided accommodation at research destinations. I thank especially Lewis Mayo, Miriam Lang, Rosemary Trott, Ann Gun, Pete van Ness, Greg Fry, Pauline Kerr, Cindy O'Hagan, Donald Denoon, Lorraine Elliot, Fiona Paisley, Leslie Holmes, Diane Stone, Iain and Heather McCalman, Michael and Debbie Thawley, Annette Clear, Andrew Leu and Denise Backhouse, but also many others. I also thank Mukaiyama Hiroshi, Yamashiro Hiromichi and Ishii Osamu for their excellent training and warm support over many years. I have gained great inspiration from these colleagues and many others. The bibliography contains only a portion of their works.

I also thank the Rockefeller Foundation, the Daiwa Bank Foundation for Asia and Oceania and the Department of the Pacific and Asian History at the Research School of Pacific and Asian Studies, Australian National University, for funding the initial research. Without these funds, this study could not have begun or have been sustained. I thank the staff of the Research School of Social Sciences, now a part of the Institute of Asia-Pacific Studies of Waseda University, the Archives of the University of Hawai'i at Manoa, the Manuscript Section of the Butler Library of Columbia University and staff of other institutions for their help.

Lastly, my sincere thanks to my family, my father, my mother and my sister, Ayako, in Japan, and to the Hammers in Australia for their warm support and love. My special thanks to Chris for his love, support, integrity, insight, discussions and patience. And Cameron. Your life is a history of my efforts to turn the manuscript into a book. You have no idea how happy your smile and laugh made me feel during the long journey of writing. I do not know where life comes from, but I know how precious it is. I hope the world you live in will not be a mean-spirited one.

Tomoko Akami
(On my birthday, 3 December 2000)
August 2001

A note on conventions

Japanese personal names throughout the book are presented in Japanese form – with the family name followed by the given name. Exceptions are made in the case of Japanese scholars who are well known. Macron marks have been used where relevant except where the word appears commonly in English without macrons. I applied the latter convention to names of Japanese cities such as Tōkyō and Kyōto, names of the period such as Taishō and Shōwa, and names of regions in Japan such as Kantō and Chūgoku. I have used Pinyin Chinese transliteration, except in cases when the names have not survived, such as Mukden and Jehol.

List of abbreviations

ACIPR	American Council of the Institute of Pacific Relations
ACLS	American Council of Learned Societies
ACNJA	American Committee for Non-Participation in Japanese Aggression
AIIA	Australian Institute of International Affairs
AP	Associated Press
APEC	Asia Pacific Economic Cooperation forum
BCRC	British Commonwealth Relations Conference
BIIA	British Institute of International Affairs
CCP	Chinese Communist Party
CFR	Council on Foreign Relations
CIC	Committee of Intellectual Cooperation
COI	Office of the Coordinator of Information
FPA	Foreign Policy Association
GJPA	Greater Japan Peace Association
IA	international authority
ICPA	International Culture Promotion Association
ILO	International Labour Organization
INGO	international non-governmental organization
IPR	Institute of Pacific Relations
IPW	Institute of Politics at Williamstown
IRAA	Imperial Rule Assistance Association
ISIPR	International Secretariat of the IPR
JARC	Japanese American Relations Committee
JCIPR	Japanese Council of the Institute of Pacific Relations
JIA	Japan International Association
LNA	League of Nations Association
NHK	Nihon hōsō kyōkai (Japan Broadcasting Cooperation)
NIEs	newly industrialized economies
OSS	Office of Strategic Services
OWI	Office of War Information
PPSC	Pan-Pacific Science Congress
PPWC	Pan-Pacific Women's Conference
SCAP	Supreme Commander of the Allied Powers
RIIA	Royal Institute of International Affairs
TIPER	Tokyo Institute of Political and Economic Research
UP	United Press
USSR	Union of Soviet Socialist Republics
YMCA	Young Men's Christian Association
YWCA	Young Women's Christian Association

Introduction

What were the dominant ideologies and institutions of international politics of the twentieth century? At the dawn of the twenty-first century, this seems a particularly appropriate question to ask. What distinguished them, what were their limitations, what was their potential, and what prospects do they hold for the new millennium?

This book focuses on Wilsonian internationalism as one of the most influential discourses in shaping these dominant ideologies and institutions.[1] Although the history of internationalism and international institutions is a well-developed field, it has focused mainly on Europe. This book extends the analysis to an important yet largely neglected region, the Asia–Pacific, during the inter-war period. Its object is to examine some crucial international issues in this period from an Asia–Pacific perspective by critically assessing the nature and implications of Wilsonian internationalism in the region. I use the case of the Institute of Pacific Relations (the IPR, 1925–61) as a vehicle for this analysis. I suggest that the issues the IPR confronted and illuminated have great relevance to contemporary discussions of international relations.

Although the observation that Wilsonian internationalism promoted and was promoted by 'liberal democracy' is not unusual, this view is problematic from a non-Euro-American perspective. Woodrow Wilson (1856–1924, President of the USA 1913–21) led the discussions on post-war reconstruction at the Paris Peace Conference in 1919. His 'New Diplomacy' defined 'new' codes and practices for international politics and the new international order in the coming years. Key players in this process, including Wilson were, however, representative of what were then known as the great powers. They were not only powerful nation-states, but also empires. The inter-war period was a period of transition from empires to nation-states. These empires' double standard was clear in the non-Euro-American periphery – 'liberal democracy' at home and colonial rule in other parts of the world. As Iriye notes, what distinguished the framework of international politics in the Asia–Pacific region in the 1920s was not nation-states as in Europe, but empires (European, American and Japanese).[2] The region was virtually filled with the colonies of the empires which won World War I. These empires negotiated and defined the post-League new international order. A young Japanese diplomat could not help feeling cynical about the new order: 'imperialism had been condemned in principle, but colonial territories other than those of a defeated Germany continued to exist'.[3]

How did those who advocated Wilsonian internationalism and the 'New Diplomacy' understand and conceptualize the Asia–Pacific in their new order? Were they conscious of the double standard? Or was it not even an issue? And what did Wilsonian internationalism mean for those who lived in the region? Were there substantial movements or institutions corresponding to Wilson's initiatives? Surely the preponderance of studies on the development of modern internationalism and international organizations in the European context is not merely the product of scholarly Eurocentricity. Still, while the number of institutions and movements and their penetration in the Asia–Pacific may not have matched the level in Europe, this does not mean that there was no attempt at institution-building in the region. Nor does it diminish the significance of these attempts. On the contrary, such efforts, because of their rarity, highlight the nature of Wilsonian internationalism.

The IPR was one of the very first non-governmental organizations in the Asia–Pacific that tried to institutionalize Wilsonian internationalism in the Asia–Pacific. Frank Atherton (1877–1945), a philanthropic businessman in Hawai'i and major promoter of the IPR, for example, demonstrated his Wilsonian view at the first IPR conference in Hawai'i in 1925:

> If one and all will approach our [IPR] meetings with a humble spirit and a real desire to learn from others of their problems and opinions, and with an earnest desire to work out a constructive plan for the future to bring about better understandings and hearty cooperation in all matters affecting the relations of man to man and nation to nation, great good is bound to result.[4]

Like Atherton, IPR members had faith in human nature and believed that they could solve problems by gathering 'scientific' information and generating 'rational' discussion. They also believed that international organizations, such as the League of Nations, were the right tool to achieve their goals. These characteristics largely accord with scholars' definition of Wilsonians.[5] Accordingly, many IPR members belonged to local associations to promote the League of Nations. For John Fairbank, an IPR member in the late 1930s, 'the IPR in its day stood almost alone as the protagonist of international integration in the Pacific area'. By 'international integration', he meant the extension of 'international stability and justice' into the region.[6] What sort of international society did IPR members, Wilsonian internationalists in the Asia–Pacific, envisage? How did they try to institutionalize it in the region? What role did the IPR, a pioneering 'private' international organization, play in this process?

The IPR was one of many 'private' international organizations that flourished in the 1920s. But as Fairbank noted, it was unique because of the regional focus. Like the League of Nations, many official and non-official international organizations were based in Europe and were mainly concerned with European affairs. In 1933 a pioneering study on 'private international organizations' described the IPR as the only organization of this kind with its headquarters located in the Pacific region.[7] Here, 'private international organizations' were the equivalent of international non-governmental organizations (INGOs), and I use both terms interchangeably.[8]

The IPR was established as a permanent institution with its headquarters, the International Secretariat of the IPR or the ISIPR, in Honolulu in 1925. National Councils of the IPR were soon founded independently in Australia, Britain, Canada, China, Japan, Korea, New Zealand, the Philippines, the United States and later in France, the Netherlands, the USSR, the Dutch (the Netherlands) East Indies, Thailand and India. The executive body, the Pacific Council, consisted of representatives from these National Councils. The ISIPR organized conferences every few years. Participants travelled to these conferences by sea. Although trans-Pacific routes and their frequencies were increasing, the journeys still took a long time. Participants needed to take extended leave from their work. If one could afford it, however, it was worth the money and time. These conferences were regarded as prestigious and influential.[9] For those who perceived the significance of the new powers in Asia, Japan and China, the conferences provided opportunities to visit, observe and gain first-hand experience that would not have been possible otherwise.

This is the first book to make extensive use of archival sources on the IPR in the United States, Japan, Australia and Britain, and to attempt to synthesize them. William Holland (Research Assistant of the ISIPR in 1928–31, Research Secretary in 1933–43 and Secretary General in 1946–61) described the IPR as like the proverbial elephant.[10] It meant different things for the people involved. The IPR's operations were widely dispersed and multi-layered. As well as coordinating the activities of various National Councils, and organizing meetings of the Pacific Councils and IPR conferences, the ISIPR launched a journal, *Pacific Affairs*, in 1927, and the American Council of the IPR (ACIPR) introduced *Far Eastern Survey* in 1932. The book focuses on the IPR's headquarters (the ISIPR) and the National Councils in Japan (Japanese Council of the IPR or the JCIPR[11]) and, to a lesser extent, the United States (the ACIPR). It also highlights the IPR's international conferences, which took place biennially between 1925 and 1933 and triennially from 1936 to 1945.[12] The United States and Japan held the key to defining the 'new' order in the region. Although the significance of the Chinese Council is recognized, its examination is left for another study.

I limit the use of the main sources to the years 1925–45 in order to illustrate the issues and intellectual paradigms as IPR members saw them in this period. This approach is particularly important in understanding the IPR, whose dominant image has been coloured and distorted by the McCarthyist attacks of the early 1950s.[13] I make extensive use of sources not only in Japan and the United States, but also in Britain and Australia. In particular, the views of the IPR's Australian members were valuable for providing insights into the regional and global politics of this period, which until now has largely been discussed from the perspective of the great powers.

The issues examined in this book are crucial to an understanding of Wilsonian internationalism in the Asia–Pacific in this period. These are American leadership, colonialism, the nation-state, non-state agencies (or INGOs), the Pacific Community and non-Euro-American powers in Asia. When referring to the powers in Asia, namely Japan and China, IPR founders in the United States often used the term the Orient or Oriental powers. Although these terms are now discredited, I reproduce them when IPR members used them. This is not because I dismiss the critical claims of Said's *Orientalism*. On the contrary, it is to highlight the unproblematized Orientalist assumptions of IPR members.

The IPR was funded by big business and philanthropic giants, which provided resources, motivations and networks beyond the boundaries of the nation-state. Criticism of the elite nature of INGOs and major foundations – their class-biased agendas, their hegemonic power, their non-accountability to the public and their 'elitist' attitudes – is valid and significant.[11] I do not, however, analyse 'class' or 'capital' as a substantive issue here. This is because I see that the most significant element which defined their activities was their relationship to the state, not necessarily their 'class' background or their relationship to 'capital'. I shall return to this point shortly in the discussion on non-governmental agency.

Wilsonian internationalism, which was dominant in the IPR, was a particularly American interpretation. It was the basis of an American vision for the Pacific region and for the world. Furthermore, this internationalism was not static, but continued to be renegotiated in the 1930s and early 1940s. For American internationalists, the new codification of international politics was part of Americanization. Yet despite Wilson's emphasis, their project initially did not encompass the entire world. In 1919, the majority decided that the League of Nations was a European affair. Their leadership in the Pacific, however, was never in question, and it was this regional leadership that defined the nature of the IPR and its two main agendas, the Pacific Community and non-state agency. Here, I avoid the term isolationism. Whatever the relevance to America's relationship with Europe, it does not accurately describe its relationship with the Asia–Pacific. In the inter-war period, at least in the economic domain, the government and certain business groups in the United States were enthusiastically engaged with the region and advocated US leadership there. This book suggests that the course which the IPR took was a manifestation of early efforts of American internationalists to define the parameters of what would emerge in the following decades as the structure and praxis of the American global order.

Although some scholars regard the IPR and other related organizations as a vehicle of Anglo-American solidarity,[15] I stress that the IPR's vision was distinctly American. In the 1920s, the IPR advocated a particular concept of the Pacific Community. It was a vision for the region held by American internationalists – an American-led regional order, independent from European politics.[16] Unlike East Asian regionalism, whose origins go beyond the last two centuries,[17] the concept of the Pacific Community was a modern regionalism, initiated and led by the United States. Whereas Arif Dirlik argues that the notion of the Pacific is a Euro-American invention,[18] the IPR's Pacific was distinctly American. What is now often termed the Asia–Pacific region was called the 'Pacific' region in the inter-war period. It was an exciting, yet ambiguous concept, and contained various competing elements. It synthesized Asia and non-Asia, and it emphasized a relationship between Asia and non-Asia, particularly the United States.[19]

This inter-war regionalism shared certain elements with more recent regionalism.[20] Some scholars stress the connection and argue that the IPR was the predecessor of later institutions, such as the Asia–Pacific Economic Cooperation forum (APEC).[21] It is indicative that the term 'the Pacific region' is still common, especially in North America, with the same focus as in the inter-war period – the Pacific rim – rather than the Pacific islands within. How did Wilsonian internationalism influence the IPR's regionalism, and what are the implications for current developments?

Wilsonian internationalism

'Liberalism': ideology, gender, class, race and nation-state

Wilsonian internationalism was not always regarded as a dominant or influential discourse of international politics in the twentieth century. This recognition is a recent phenomenon. In the past, it was often dismissed as insignificant,[22] largely as a result of the view that it 'failed' to prevent World War II. It also owes something to E.H. Carr's critical assessment, which has long been regarded as a classic, but has often been misunderstood. His work, or a simplified understanding of his work, contributed to the dominant perception of an artificial dichotomy between 'utopians' and 'realists'. Wilsonians were located at the opposite end of the spectrum to realists. They were seen as 'weak' and heavily flawed. By the end of the 1930s, they were understood to have been defeated by nationalists, and ultimately to have 'failed' to prevent the world war.

This negative interpretation seems to have changed towards the end of the Cold War. When the then American President George Bush declared the new world order at the time of the Gulf War in 1990, he seems to have coined a term for a set of already accepted and influential ideologies and institutions in international politics. Many would have vaguely associated them with the Charter of the United Nations. Scholars sought the origins of this 'new' order in an attempt to examine and define its nature. Re-evaluation of Wilsonian internationalism occurred in this process. Scholars looked back to the pre-Cold War period, and found a similar dynamic in the inter-war period. Indeed, it is easy to see a parallel between Samuel Huntington's 'Clash of Civilizations' and Toynbee's work on civilizations. 'Culture' or 'civilization', as distinct from political ideology, has again become a legitimate topic in international politics.[23] As a result, works on Wilsonian internationalism flourished in the last decade of the twentieth century. In 1993 Arthur Schlesinger Jr stated: 'We are all, more or less, Wilsonians today.'[24] Others defined Wilsonian internationalism as a significant, dominant, positive and democratic force in international politics in the twentieth century[25] and suggested that it is the core of the Charter of the United Nations, and the basis of the new world order of the post-Cold War period.

A large chunk of the twentieth century, the period between the 1930s and the end of the Cold War, however, presents a problem. The Cold War period saw the significant development of civil rights, feminist and various other democratic movements. The United Nations committed itself to human rights, the causes of the underprivileged and the 'development' of the 'third world'. Yet international politics of this period is more often described as having been dominated by 'realist' thinking and the balance of power. The late 1930s and early 1940s are even more problematic. They are pictured as dominated by nationalism and realism. It was, however, precisely this intellectual and institutional context in which the Charter of the United Nations was formed. How do we understand this crucial period? Did Wilsonian internationalism fail and decline? Was it outmanoeuvred by its opponents, but arose phoenix-like in 1945? Was the inter-war period an aberration in its otherwise smooth development? Or had the internationalism been strong throughout? This last scenario is further complicated because Wilsonian internationalism was regarded as 'liberal' and its opponents as 'illiberal' or 'reactionary'. Should we then view the late 1930s and early 1940s as a 'liberal' period?

I have suggested elsewhere that a key to understanding the nature of Wilsonian internationalists is a critical assessment of the nature of their 'liberalism'.[26] The assumption that Wilsonians were 'liberal' is very strong. It is not a coincidence that the new world order declaration and Francis Fukuyama's victorious manifestation of 'liberal democracy' occurred around the same time. 'Liberal democracy' is regarded as the core of the new world order and Wilsonian internationalism. Yet it is not an easy task to pin down what 'liberal democracy' means. It is like a phantom, or even a god. It exists in people's minds in the purest form, but it means different things and takes different forms for each person. Inter-war contemporaries certainly regarded Wilsonian internationalists as 'liberals' in opposition to nationalism and imperialism.[27] But did they really oppose the state and empire? Were they 'liberal', as often assumed, and if so in what way?

What seems to have loosely bound Wilsonian internationalists and what earned them the label 'liberal' was their adherence to a set of important but abstract notions vaguely associated with enlightenment – peace, reason, freedom, progress, tolerance and democracy. Any rigorous attempt at defining their 'liberalism' seems to land on slippery ground, because their adherence to these principles may or may not have meant commitment to any concrete causes or social movements. Furthermore, their advocacy of these ideals in an international arena may not have benefited certain underprivileged groups in their own country.[28]

It is important to remember that 'liberal democracy' after 1917 was a slogan adopted by anti-communist forces in domestic and international political arenas. Those who claimed to be 'liberal' in the 1920s and 1930s located themselves in opposition not only to 'imperialists' and 'nationalists', but also to 'socialists' or 'communists'. They were often anti-communist. This limited the extent of their 'liberalness', at least on issues of ideology and class. IPR members in the inter-war period, for example, thought of themselves as 'liberal'. Yet the IPR was a patrician organization, a gentleman's club. Its members and conference participants included many notable public figures and those who represented big business. They *knew* they belonged to the national elite. Similarly, their 'liberalness' was limited on the issue of gender. Despite the participation of small yet active female groups in international politics in this period, IPR members also *knew* that their peer group was mainly men.[29] These were the 'facts' for them, and in their mind their intolerance to communism, or their unproblematized elite status or gender bias often did not undermine their 'liberalism' in the slightest. The crucial question for this book, then, is: Was this also true of their understanding of the nation-state, 'racial' inequality and colonialism? Could these 'liberals' actually question these frameworks and hierarchies and try to change them? Before turning to this central theme, I first define and explain the key terminology.

Post-League internationalism

Although Wilsonian internationalism is the conventional scholarly term, I use the term 'post-League internationalism' for Wilsonian internationalism after the formation of the League of Nations. There are several reasons for adopting this rather cumbersome terminological distinction.[30] First, I want to make it clear that this is not a study of the idealism or ideals of Woodrow Wilson. Post-League internationalists were not necessarily the same creatures as Wilsonian idealists, if the latter ever existed in a pure form. In making this distinction, I hope that the term post-League internationalism is less burdened with the moral and ideological assumptions discussed above. Despite their clear adherence to the concepts of the enlightenment, Wilson's 'principles' themselves were limited by his political motivations and the historical context. Furthermore, post-League internationalists accepted the compromises made at the Paris Peace Conference of 1919, a point elaborated in Chapter 1.

Second, by using the term post-League internationalism, I am questioning the dominant framework of the dichotomy between Carr's two abstract antitheses, 'utopians' and 'realists'. Instead, I want to emphasize the ambiguity of post-League internationalists in the positions they adopted between these two poles. Wilsonian internationalists have been closely associated with 'utopians'. Although Carr noted that this dichotomy was artificial and hypothetical, nevertheless he still separated ideals from institutions: 'The ideal, once it is embodied in an institution, ceases to be an ideal.'[31] A similar perspective is evident in the work of later scholars. In 1993, Knock stated that the Wilsonian ideal 'is still before us'.[32] Yet from this perspective, 'ideals' were and will always be ahead of us. Perhaps what is crucial is attention to the process of *institutionalization of ideals* after 1919.

Here, I find the concept of discourse, rather than ideals, helpful. Within a certain discourse, certain ideals are institutionalized. These institutions both promote the ideals and reproduce and reinforce the current structure of dominance. As Foucault notes, discourse can reinforce dominant ideologies and power relations on which these ideologies are formed. At the same time, it can also undermine and expose this structure of dominance, planting the seeds of future challenges.[33] Post-League internationalism can be understood not only as a set of ideas or ideals, as Carr saw it, but a discourse in which its advocates and institutions operate. Post-League internationalists advocated Wilsonian principles, but they also operated in newly established *institutions* in the transitional period from empires to nation-states. Some of these institutions were governmental, such as the League of Nations and the International Labour Organization (ILO), and others were non-governmental. The IPR was one of the latter. While these institutions and their members tried to institutionalize new ideas, to a great extent, they also reinforced the structure of dominance of the day, namely the power of empires and states. Post-League internationalists were neither pure utopians nor complete cynics. They inhabited the shades of grey between the abstract poles of 'utopianism' and 'realism'. This emphasis on its ambiguity is important, not because I want to prove that it was reactionary.[34] Rather it is because a constant and critical analysis of their 'liberalism' would clarify its potential.

Internationalism versus nationalism: a false dichotomy?

Despite the claims of many 'inter-war liberals', posing a dichotomy between internationalism and nationalism is also fraught. First, internationalism does not necessarily reject the nation-state framework, but often it is based on it. In a recent discussion on international economic governance, Hirst and Thompson distinguish globalization from internationalization. The former is defined as the phenomena or activities based on transnational organizations, such as multinational corporations, whereas the latter is understood as being promoted by institutions based on the nation-state. They argue that internationalization and its institutions have dominated the twentieth century, and that transnational organizations are still rarer.[35] In further demonstration of the resilience of the nation-state, even recent leading works on transnationalism do not reject the centrality of the state. Nye and Keohane, for example, define transnational relations as 'sets of direct interactions among sub-units of different governments that are not controlled or closely guided by the policies of the cabinets or chief executives of those governments'.[36] Although some, such as Huntington, dismiss internationalism as inherently inefficient and insignificant,[37] nevertheless it remained dominant in the twentieth century. It did not erode state power or the framework of the nation-state. Quite the reverse. It often enhanced it.

Second, the dichotomy suggests an almost automatic tension between the nation/state and 'liberal' internationalists. This is particularly misleading for an analysis of post-League internationalists. Here it is important to distinguish between *laissez-faire* liberalism and New Liberalism. Carr argued that although *laissez-faire* liberalism had to be modified in domestic politics in the inter-war period, an American idealist, Wilson, transplanted it to 'the almost virgin soil of international politics'. There it soon became the dominant ideology.[38] The liberalism influential among post-League internationalists, including IPR members, however, was not exactly *laissez-faire* liberalism, as Carr claimed in 1939. Rather, it was New Liberalism of Thomas H. Green's school, according to whom:

> That philosophy could satisfy the new needs of social progress, because it refused to worship a supposed individual liberty which was proving destructive of the real liberty of the majority, and preferred to emphasise the moral well-being and betterment of the whole community.[39]

In the inter-war period, New Liberalism was influential among intellectual elites in Britain, Australia and Japan, and to an extent among New Dealers in the United States,[40] and defined the intellectual milieus to which post-League internationalists belonged. This meant that their notion of the role of the state was changing from oppressor of individual rights to guardian of the welfare of society. Post-League internationalists were not exactly utopian cosmopolitans or believers in *laissez-faire* liberalism. They were inclined to see state intervention as morally good and necessary for the welfare of society. This distinction is crucial in defining their internationalism, because it indicates their cooperative stance towards the state. Furthermore, in the inter-war period, both the nation and the state were often reified as a coherent and organic entity, and understood as identical. This conceptual framework did not easily allow a diversity of opinions and views inside the state and the state apparatus, or among various sections of society. Non-official New Liberals, especially those with a strong identification as members of the 'national' elite, could easily represent the perspective of the nation/state (which was often the empire) in the international arena without the state pressure.

Third, the dichotomy often involves a moral judgement and suggests the moral righteousness not only of 'liberal' internationalists, but also of the post-League order they supported. This was the self-image that 'liberal' internationalists both in Japan and in other countries tried to portray in the 1930s. 'Liberal' internationalists, despite their goodness, 'failed' and were 'outmanoeuvred' by their opponents, 'reactionary' nationalists.[11] The rectitude of the international order was further strengthened after the victory of the Allied forces in World War II.

Critical views of this moral righteousness, however, have always been present, albeit in a minority. Konoe Fumimaro (1890–1945, Prime Minister, 1937–9 and 1940–1), E.H. Carr, Justice Pal at the Tokyo Tribunal, and Christopher Thorne all recognized that the international order was a system to preserve the interests of the dominant powers of the time.[12] Dower's examination of the case of Yoshida Shigeru (1878–1967, Prime Minister in 1946–7 and 1948–54) further suggests a shade of grey among so-called 'liberal' internationalists in the 1920s and 1930s.[13] I want to further this critical analysis of the assumption of the moral righteousness and 'liberalness' of the post-League international order and those who supported it.

There are numerous motivations for this critical approach. In the 1930s and 1940s, Japanese militarists, intellectuals and bureaucrats challenged the international order to justify Japanese military aggression and human rights violations in the Asia–Pacific, including Japan. This critical rhetoric remains powerful among Japanese neo-conservatives who want to justify Japanese aggression during the Pacific War.[14] Questioning the legitimacy of the international order should not in any way justify aggression or atrocities. Mindful of this danger, I still argue for the importance of a critical examination of the dominant ideologies and institutions of international politics. This would expose the double standards of powerful nations, be they Japan, the United States or another country. It is this double standard of the United States in particular that lends legitimacy and appeal to neo-conservatives in the region. They attack 'Western'/American hypocrisy often with the purpose of rejecting external intervention in domestic affairs, and of legitimizing their suppression of the democratic rights of certain groups in their country. Critical scrutiny of the conduct of powerful countries could demonstrate these double standards. This would be the first step in undermining the legitimacy of these anti-democratic forces. Furthermore, such an analysis would enhance self-reflection, rather than self-congratulation, clarifying the dominant system's limitations yet furthering the boundary of its possibility. The end result, one hopes, will be greater equity and social justice both in domestic and in international arenas.

The IPR and new agendas

A specific American interpretation of post-League internationalism defined the nature of the IPR in the mid-1920s, as well as its two main agendas, the

Pacific Community and non-state agency. Did these agendas and the IPR's experiments have the potential to challenge the dominant ideologies and institutions of international politics of the day? At the second IPR conference in Honolulu in 1927, Herbert Croly, editor of *New Republic*, thought so:

> [The IPR's] function is really novel and more radical than these delegates seemed to realize. It is an experiment in the use of the understanding in elucidating and integrating political relationships. If it carries on its work with any success, it may eventually exercise an important influence on the world of affairs in the Pacific...[45]

This potential of the IPR for new approaches to international politics has not been properly evaluated until recently. This is partly because many IPR members were not conscious of this radical implication, as Croly himself noted. It is also because the IPR was demonized by the American right as a communist front organization in the late 1940s and early 1950s. Several prominent members in North America were accused of being communists and of aiding the 'fall' of China to communism in 1949. Previous works on the IPR focused mainly on assessing these charges, often with the intent of proving that they were fabricated.[46] The IPR included some communist members, but it was not an organ of socialist internationalism in the inter-war period. Most IPR members in this period were *concerned* about various political, economic and social issues, and American IPR members were generally sympathetic to Roosevelt's New Deal policies. Although many were reformist rather than revolutionary, they probably seemed like communists to some Americans in the supercharged atmosphere of the early Cold War. This will be elaborated in Chapters 8 and 9, but here the point needs to be made that the claim by the American right reflected not the nature of the IPR in the inter-war period, but the hyperbole of McCarthyism. It probably also represented antagonism or jealousy towards the IPR in the United States, which enjoyed considerable influence in policy formulation during the war period. Unlike Croly, McCarthyist attackers and defenders of the IPR alike regarded it as an American rather than an international organization. They saw its significance only in American foreign policy towards China, not in its implications for new ways of viewing and conducting international politics.

The Pacific Community: colonialism and Orientalism

The IPR's agendas had new and challenging elements to the dominant ideologies and institutions of international politics. On this point, American, not European, initiative and leadership was critical. American-led regionalism, which was embodied in the notion of the Pacific Community, challenged the Eurocentric view of the world. The core of the IPR's regionalism was not only the process and degree of political and economic regional integration. Rather, what was significant was a Pacific-centred perspective of the world, and the excitement that accompanied this new perspective. This American concept of the Pacific transformed the region from the periphery of Europe, the 'Far East', to a central stage in international politics. At the same time, the 'Far East' remained a part of the Pacific, indicating that its challenge to Eurocentricity was an ambiguous one. This new view could not have emerged without American confidence in its regional leadership. Believing in American exceptionalism, IPR members in the United States argued its manifest destiny in the Pacific. Despite their colonial possessions and interventions both in the Pacific and in the Americas, they distinguished their policy from the 'old' European colonial rules, and considered their criticism of the latter legitimate.

With the concept of the Pacific Community, the IPR's founders broke new ground. They tried to achieve a more equal partnership between Euro-American powers and non-Euro-American powers in Asia, Japan and China. This was a sore point in the League of Nations. It also challenged the dominant perceptions of the power hierarchy between 'East' and 'West'. The interaction between the powers in Asia and the 'West' does not exactly fit into the Orientalist discourse that Said defines between colonizers and the colonized (mainly the Middle East in his study). What Hall calls the discourse of the 'West and the rest' is probably more applicable. At issue here is not only formal colonial relations, but a power hierarchy in a context in which formal colonial relations did not exist.[17] Tanaka argues that a similar 'Orientalist' discourse was not peculiar to Euro-American colonizers, but was also to be found among their Japanese counterparts. Japanese bureaucrats and intellectuals constructed their own 'Orient' in order to legitimize their superior position in Asia.[18] Did IPR members support or try to overturn this power relationship between the 'West and the rest'? Did JCIPR members attempt to construct a similar dynamic between Japan and 'the rest of Asia'? Here an analysis of IPR members' rhetoric of 'culture' becomes critical. It was an effective tool to legitimize and reinforce hierarchical relationships, even in the absence of a formal colonial relationship.

The IPR founders did not challenge the colonial (European, American and Japanese) status quo in the 1920s. Rather, they sought modification of conduct. Their Pacific Community was largely a community of the powers. The USSR was regarded as a Pacific power and an integral member of the community. More significantly, the community included not only colonial powers located in the region (Japan and the United States), but also European powers with colonies in the Pacific (Britain, France and the Netherlands). Nevertheless, an anti-colonial element was not totally absent in the vision of the Pacific Community. Despite the fact that the colonies in Asia and the Pacific were largely ignored, Korea was initially included and the Philippines participated throughout the life of the IPR. Furthermore, IPR members spoke of China as a Pacific power, and IPR fora provided Chinese members with a rare venue to criticize the unequal dealings of the other powers in China, particularly Britain and Japan. Like Korean members in 1925–31, and to a lesser extent Philippine members, Chinese participants consistently challenged the IPR's support for colonialism. The seeds of anti-colonialism were, therefore, sown in the early stages. Although the sentiment against Japanese colonialism intensified in the 1930s, the position against colonialism in general only became dominant in IPR operations towards the end of World War II.

Non-state agency: the state and the New Liberals

The IPR's second agenda was to become a non-state agency in international politics. This could have been a very radical idea, as it could have challenged state authority or questioned the dominant notion of a national entity. How far did 'liberals', or more precisely 'New Liberals', at the IPR push this agenda? Here, their relationship with the state becomes crucial. By relationship with the state, I do not mean only state support, pressure or coercion. Rather, what I see as critical is the extent to which members of the IPR and major foundations that funded the IPR were embedded in the framework of the nation-state. If this extent was great, it would be rather futile to assume the opposition of 'liberal' internationalists to the state. Their status as 'non-governmental', 'non-official' or 'private' did not mean much unless one examines whom they were ultimately serving. They could *voluntarily* promote what they regarded as the interests of their nation-state (or empire) in the international arena. I use the term 'international publicists' to describe this role of post-League internationalists. It should be distinguished from what Keck and Sikkink call transnational advocacy groups, which promote certain universal causes.[49] Significantly, IPR members distanced their internationalism from pacifism in 1927.[50] Pacifists, strictly speaking, oppose all war.[51] Pacifism means a denial of the ultimate right of a nation-state to fight against other states or to defend itself. This was not a position the IPR held.

The IPR case demonstrates clearly that post-League internationalism and nationalism were not inherently incompatible, and that in certain countries post-League internationalism grew stronger, not weaker, in a time of war. The problem of incompatibility did not arise for JCIPR members before 1931. It did not even become an issue for their counterparts in the Allied countries during the Pacific War. The governments of the Allied countries 'defended' what was understood as the post-League order. IPR members in the Allied countries simultaneously became more patriotic and more 'Wilsonian' during the Pacific War. This was not the case for JCIPR members after 1931, and particularly after 1937, because the Japanese government backed military aggression in China, which was seen as a challenge to the international order. JCIPR members began to propose an alternative regional vision, the New Order in East Asia, and the JCIPR withdrew from the IPR's international research project and from IPR conferences after 1939. This was, however, not a sign of the decline of the JCIPR's internationalist activities, as is often assumed. It continued to cooperate with the ISIPR, and many of its members became more active as international publicists and in think-tanks.[52] This co-option of IPR members to the state apparatus (and that of post-League internationalist organizations in general) was also a phenomenon in the United States and other Allied countries. The process occurred with very little resistance from the IPR. Rather, as representatives of the national elite, IPR members often enthusiastically promoted this development.

Non-official expert: knowledge for state or society?

Post-League internationalists were strong promoters of the non-state agencies in international politics, which flourished in the 1920s. In 1930, Alfred Zimmern (1879–1957), professor of international politics and an ardent League supporter, noted that non-governmental experts became important in the work of the League of Nations in the 1920s: '[T]he most striking achievements in international policy in the last decade have not been due to the decisions of statesmen but to the recommendations of "experts".'[53] White also demonstrates how prominent these non-governmental expert organizations had become by 1933.[54] Despite the fact that most of them were headquartered in Europe, Americans clearly led these organizations. They had the highest per capita membership of such organizations, and they gave more money to them than any other country. This American leading role was pronounced in Asia. Organizations based in the United States tended to have stronger member representation from Asia, particularly Japan and China, than those based in Europe.[55] The IPR reflected this American strength in INGO activities in the Pacific region.

The IPR's agenda as a non-state agency did not mean setting a challenging alternative channel for state-to-state relationships, or advocating universalist causes in an international arena. Rather, the IPR aimed to become a non-state agency of experts on current affairs in Asia, initially for both society and the state. The notion of 'expert' in international politics was changing in this period. For Carr, a diplomat until his mid-forties, 'experts' meant diplomats and soldiers, and 'practice, not theory, bureaucratic training, not intellectual brilliance, [was] the school of political wisdom'.[56] In contrast, for Wilson, House, Zimmern and many post-League internationalists who were involved in the League of Nations or INGOs, 'experts' meant non-official specialists. They were mainly academics, lawyers, journalists and business people. These conflicting views caused an uneasy tension between emerging non-official experts and state bureaucrats. This was not because the former tried to undermine state authority. Non-official experts were demanding a share in policy-making that had hitherto been reserved for officials and soldiers. As the latter defended their position and influence, these new non-official experts advocated their significance, legitimizing their status and increasing their influence.

Post-League internationalists not only promoted their status as 'experts', but also pioneered new disciplines and constructed new knowledge. Their status as 'experts' depended on the authority of their 'knowledge'. In 1951, White assessed the IPR as 'one of the most interesting associations, whose contribution to scientific investigation has been outstanding'.[57] IPR members were 'experts' in international relations[58] and current affairs in Asia and the Pacific islands.[59] Their regional expertise produced the knowledge which can be seen as a forerunner of area studies – the field that was to become popular particularly in the United States during the Cold War.[60] IPR members constructed, promoted and disseminated certain 'knowledge' of the region among specialists and policy-makers in Europe, North America, Australia and New Zealand. Fairbank notes that in the 1930s and 1940s 'foreign offices, corporations, and the press took [IPR conferences] seriously, and participants were often profoundly influenced by the experience'.[61]

These 'experts' on the region at the IPR were increasingly co-opted to the state apparatus as think-tank members. This was, however, not the direction initially taken when the IPR was founded in 1925. Like other post-League internationalists, IPR founders stressed another non-state element in international relations, public opinion. Although its operations were addressed to the elite, the minds of IPR members were initially occupied by the public and its education. IPR members hoped to influence public opinion so that eventually it would indirectly influence foreign policy-making.

The IPR founders were mainly American post-League internationalists with a strong interest in the Pacific region. They pursued an American-led regional order, and advocated two major agendas: to achieve a more equal relationship with the new powers in Asia; and to promote a non-state agency in international politics. The focus of the organization was the region, and members aimed to educate public opinion, through which they hoped to influence foreign policy-making. This initial vision, however, contained various contradictory factors that were inherent in American post-League internationalism. Furthermore, IPR members in the United States and in other countries did not pursue a unanimous vision for the IPR or the regional order. Various visions existed and competed.

In the 1930s, key IPR officers, such as Edward Carter (1878–1954), who became Secretary General of the IPR in 1933, gradually shifted the scope of IPR activities from the region to the world, and made IPR operations more state-oriented. Such moves anticipated American internationalists' gradual assertion of US power and vision in global politics. They strengthened their commitment to post-League internationalism and the post-League international order. But these notions were constantly redefined in order to adjust to a new context. As IPR operations became more state-oriented, co-option of its members to the state apparatus was furthered not only in Japan, but also in other countries. The Sino-Japanese War and the Pacific War furthered this move. The United States emerged as the most important power in this newly defined international order. How did this happen? How did IPR members in other countries, especially Japan, respond to an American vision initially for the region and then for the world? How did IPR members see the region in the wider international order? How did these wars change their views? This is the story I seek to tell.

As Dower noted, constructing a history of the IPR is a formidable task[62] because of the scope of the organization and its complex politics. It is also a morally difficult task in light of the events that affected the IPR in the 1950s.[63] I hope that this book will be one step contributing to discussions and debates on key issues in the discourse of international politics of the twentieth century and beyond. The IPR is a precious window that provides us with a new perspective on matters that have long been accepted without close scrutiny.

Part I

New agendas

The East is to be opened and transformed, whether we will or no; the standards of the West are to be imposed upon it; nations and peoples which have stood still the centuries through are to be quickened, and made part of the universal world of commerce and of ideas which has so steadily been a-making by the advance of European power from age to age.

(Woodrow Wilson, 28 January 1904, cited in Knock, 1993: 10–11)

1 The Paris Peace Conference and post-League internationalism

On 14 December 1918, James Shotwell (1874–1965), professor of history at Columbia University, observed the crowd as Woodrow Wilson's carriage passed by his window at the Carillon Hotel. Shotwell was a member of the American delegation for the coming Peace Conference.

> Looking down from our windows we could see the crowds converging down the different streets into the square like a solid black stream. ... The soldiers tried to keep a single track way open for the President [Wilson] from the bridge over the Seine through the Place de la Concorde. ... But the pressure of the crowd was so great that the line of soldiers was moved in and out until the space which they were to keep clear was all indented and twisted instead of being a straight line ...[1]

Such was the popular enthusiasm for Wilson and his proposed vision for peace and a new international order. One large placard demonstrated what Wilson represented for them – 'Wilson le juste'. They had suffered bitterly, and wished for a world without war. Wilson appeared to be able to deliver what many so fervently desired.

The Paris Peace Conference (January to June 1919) was significant in defining 'new' codes and practices of international politics in the following decades, which were often termed the 'New Diplomacy'. Its core consisted of six general principles: open diplomacy, freedom of the sea, free trade, disarmament, fairer treatment of colonial subjects and the establishment of the League of Nations. Wilson set out these principles in the 'Fourteen Points' in January 1918.[2] The 'principles' themselves, however, were not free from the constrictions of the time. Furthermore, during the conference many concessions were made. Wilsonian internationalists (after the formation of the League of Nations) or post-League internationalists supported both these 'principles' and the outcome of the conference, including the League of Nations and the post-League international order.

Many contemporaries and later scholars have discredited the achievements of the Paris Conference. Socialists saw the League of Nations as a capitalist plot – a view which some scholars shared.[3] The process of the conference alarmed and alienated even those who had been strong initial supporters of Wilson's vision. Labour groups criticized as reactionary and unsatisfactory the League's handling of industrial relations. In the United States, Herbert Croly, editor of *New Republic*, who supported the 'Fourteen Points', disapproved of the way that the peace was negotiated at Versailles.[1] Seizing the political opportunity to remove the long-ruling Democrat Wilson from office, Republican internationalists joined the condemnation, arguing that the League was an organ of the imperial powers.[5] This negative reaction was also evident among some Japanese participants at the conference. Konoe Fumimaro, who was to play a significant role in Japanese diplomacy and politics in the 1930s and 1940s, attended the conference. He noted: 'I saw that the hope of many people for the reform of the world based on justice clearly betrayed at the beginning of the conference', and 'power still rules the world'.[6] Yoshida Shigeru, a young diplomat who was soon to be called a 'liberal' internationalist, was also sceptical. Having observed the conference closely, he strengthened his faith in *Realpolitik* (bilateral military agreements, secret diplomacy and concessions under duress).[7]

These descriptions give the impression that there were initial high ideals, which were compromised in the course of the conference. It would be wrong to totally dismiss the idealistic nature and the significant implications of Wilson's vision. Despite criticism, the League of Nations promoted the causes of the underprivileged or powerless – labour, women, children and ethnic minorities. Committees were set up, and organizations such as the International Labour Organization (ILO) grew from these agendas.[8] His vision also originated in a climate of social enquiry in the 1910s, and many social activists and intellectuals all over the world saw his vision as a symbol of peace and democracy.[9] Wilson himself noted in the Fourteen Points that his post-war vision was based on the principle of justice:

> An evident principle runs through the whole programme I have outlined. It is the principle of justice to all peoples and nationalities, and their right to live on equal terms of liberty and safety with one another, whether they be strong or weak.[10]

In his view, it was the only principle upon which the people in the United States could act. He was determined to stop 'new' colonial acquisitions by great powers, be they European or Japanese. This was clear in his strong opposition to the Allied powers' request for re-annexation of the Axis powers' colonies. On this point, it is fair to say that his 'anti-imperialist' principle receded in the course of the conference negotiations. At the same time, the principle in question had been limited before the negotiation took place. First, the Fourteen Points were written when the war was still being fought. They defined war ideology for the Allied forces, and provided post-war settlement conditions for the Axis powers. To him, 'imperialists' inevitably meant the Axis powers, and the colonies of the former Allied powers remained intact. Second, in the document, Wilson did not argue for the independence of the Axis powers' colonies, nor even for an equal weight for the voices of these colonial subjects. The fifth point in question read:

> A free, open-minded, and absolutely impartial adjustment of all colonial claims, based upon a strict observance of the principle that is determining all such questions of sovereignty *the interests of the populations* concerned must have equal weight with the equitable claims of the government whose title is to be determined. [emphasis added][11]

The paternalism is obvious. Wilson's principle of justice, liberty and equality applied only to certain deserving nations. As he later elaborated, he envisaged a community in which 'the strong and the great ... put their power and strength in the service of right' and protect the weak.[12] This paternalism permeated both Wilson and the representatives of European powers. It was even more obvious in their attitudes towards non-'Western' colonies. In the Fourteen Points, there was no reference to Asia or Africa in relation to self-determination. The 'principle' applied only in a European context.

The conference discussion furthered this rather blatant Orientalism. The mandate system, for example, was proposed by David Lloyd George as a compromise between the Allied powers' request for re-annexation and Wilson's strong opposition to it. Initially developed by the South African representative, Jan C. Smuts, it was a 'liberal' administration of semi-colonial rule. Although the welfare of the local population was considered a priority, a supervising government held powers similar to its imperial predecessor. Furthermore, it was argued that 'the character of the mandate must differ according to the stage of development of the people, the geographical situation of the territory, its economic conditions and other similar circumstances'. The geographical situation referred to how far they were from the 'centre of civilization'. Accordingly, South West Africa and certain islands in the South Pacific were best administered under the laws of the mandatory state because of 'their remoteness from the centre of civilization' as well as the sparseness of their population and their small size.[13] Thorne critically points out these overt and implicit assumptions of racial superiority in the making of the 'new' international order.[14]

Following Wilson's 'principles', the League's new order was based on new codes of practice, 'New Diplomacy' (open diplomacy and multilateralism), and various agendas, such as freedom of the sea, free trade and disarmament. Nevertheless, most of those involved in the conference negotiation were aware that this 'new' order was a product of a transitional period from empires to nation-states. The United States voted against entry to the League, mainly because a majority in Congress saw it as ruled by European power politics. Britain was the League's major backer. Although this can be explained by British enthusiasm for 'New Diplomacy', Birn argues that the League was peripheral in British foreign policy-making.[15] An equally plausible interpretation may be that British officials saw the League as a new type of security system to guard their imperial interests. Similarly, the Japanese government supported the League not so much because of a commitment to international justice but, rather, because it saw the League as a collective security system of the powers and felt that it was important to be a part of it. In the 1920s, the Japanese government sought a cooperative policy with the powers, and supported the League. Japan was a founding member of the Council of the League, and Nitobe Inazō (1862–1933), a leading post-League internationalist in Japan, served as one of its three Under-Secretaries General in 1920–6.

It is easy to dismiss any significant change from the 'old' *Realpolitik* to Wilson's New Diplomacy. Nevertheless, it is also clear that new factors came to light at the conference: the emergence of a non-Euro-American power, Japan; the increasing significance of non-state factors in foreign policy-making, such as non-state agencies and public opinion; and the emergence of American leadership in international politics. These were crucial in defining the outcome of the conference, and the nature of post-League internationalism and its official and non-official institutions, including the IPR. I discuss the first two factors in this chapter, and the last in the next chapter.

New powers in Asia

Along with the United States, Britain, Italy and France, Japan, the first non-Euro-American power in the twentieth century, was regarded as one of the great powers at the Paris Conference. Two representatives from the great powers made up the Council of Ten, which decided major policies in the initial stage of the conference. By March 1919, however, the decision-making power had shifted to the Council of Four, which consisted of the political leaders of the four great powers, excluding Japan. The reason for this may have been the problems caused by Japan's status as a non-Euro-American power. One such problem was the Japanese proposal to insert a racial equality clause into the Covenant of the League of Nations.[16]

The debate over this proposal was about the nature of new codes of international relations. There is no doubt that equality of 'race' was a logical consequence of the proposed new order. For many, not only for Japanese, it was reasonable to have this principle as a basis for the League of Nations, the institution on which this order was centred. In 1918, Konoe Fumimaro argued that racial and economic equality were essential to eliminate future international conflicts in the new international order.[17] In early 1919, the Japanese delegation initially proposed that the Covenant of the League of Nations would include the following clause:

> Considering the equality of a nation is the basic principle of the League of Nations, its member countries should not set any legal or other discriminations, and should give equal treatments to all the nationals of the member countries despite their races or nationalities.

After a few months of negotiation, the Japanese delegation had to water down the proposal. At last, at a meeting of the League of Nations Commission on 11 April 1919, they proposed to insert the following wording 'the endorsement of the principle of the equality of nations and the just treatment of their nationals' into the preamble of the Covenant.[18] A majority who attended this meeting thought that they could not reject this basic principle. Among the seventeen participants at the meeting, it gained eleven votes, including those of the representatives from Italy, France and China.[19]

The opposition was, however, formidable. Wilson, who presided over the meeting, overruled the proposal on the ground that it lacked unanimous support.[20] According to Edward M. House, Wilson's foreign policy adviser, Wilson was in favour of accepting it, but House persuaded him to side with the British.[21] Robert Cecil, British delegate, a Conservative politician and future head of the British League Nations Union (1923–45), led the opposition. He represented not only Britain, but also the Dominions, among whose representatives was Australian Prime Minister William (Billy) Hughes, one of the most adamant opponents of the principle.[22]

The final Wilson ruling exposed two fundamental problems of the post-League 'new' order. First, even those who supported the League and Wilson's principles felt that domestic opinion was not ready for racial equality. For those unsympathetic to Wilson's vision, such as Billy Hughes, the issue was clearer. With an election coming up in Australia, Hughes argued: 'The idea [of racial equality] was what ninety-five out of one hundred of Australian people would oppose.'[23] This was a significant consideration for a politician who was head of a national delegation from a representative democracy with an expanding national franchise. Second, the right of national sovereignty came before the principles of social justice or human rights. According to Kazumata, respect for 'domestic affairs' was formalized as one of the most significant principles of modern international law as a result of this debate on 'racial/national equality' in 1919.[24] The debate caused many conference participants to realize that the issue of 'racial equality' had significant implications for their domestic politics. 'Respect for domestic affairs' meant safeguarding the state from international intervention. Cecil said that, important as it was, 'the racial question' could not be solved 'without encroaching upon the sovereignty of States members of the League'.[25] It was also clear that, despite their denials, the Japanese delegates hoped that the clause would eventually influence various nations' immigration policies.[26]

Wilson's final ruling relieved not only those who explicitly opposed the proposal, but also North Americans who were sympathetic to the principle of 'racial equality'. They were aware of its far-reaching implications for their 'domestic' affairs. One American thought it fortunate that they did not have to oppose the proposal openly.[27] The Canadian Prime Minister noted that the ruling meant a removal of 'absolutely any danger of attempted interference by the League with these domestic questions [immigration and naturalization]'.[28] Similarly, not only critics of the League,[29] but also those who advocated the League and other related organizations, agreed that equality in international politics was a matter not of race or justice for individuals, but of nations and their power. Alfred Zimmern, a prominent British post-League internationalist, stated:

> The questions and conflicts which arise out of [race] have never admitted and never will admit of judicial determination; they are political questions … and must be handled by wise and understanding statesmanship on both sides.[30]

William H. Taft, former Republican President and a supporter of Wilson's League, proposed a safeguard clause for state sovereignty. Taft recommended to Wilson its insertion into Article XV (on disputes not submitted to arbitration) of the Covenant in mid-March 1919. This was prompted by his anxiety over the outcome of the Japanese proposal. He wanted to prevent intervention of the League's Council in the areas of immigration and tariffs.[31] Although the concept of state sovereignty, or Westphalian sovereignty, was not new, and had been assumed in international law, the Covenant of the League was the first to spell it out. Accordingly, Article XV, Section 8, would read:

> If the dispute between the parties is claimed by one of them, and is found by the Council, to arise out of a matter which by international law is solely within the domestic jurisdiction of that party, the Council shall so report, and shall make no recommendation as to its settlement.[32]

The Charter of the United Nations inherited this legacy (Article II, Section Seven). This further demonstrates the significance of the clause in international politics of the twentieth century, and the incident which prompted this formal codification.

The Japanese delegates were not so different from their opponents in their basic understanding of international politics. Some suspected that the Japanese proposal of 'racial equality' was not an embodiment of the spirit of the 'New Diplomacy', but a bargaining tool for more important territorial claims in China and the South Pacific islands.[33] This interpretation probably fails to understand the thrust of Japanese foreign policy. The Japanese government did not give an instruction to use the proposal for this purpose. The instruction read: 'In order to eliminate disadvantage of the [Japanese] empire caused by racial prejudice, we should try to secure a proper safety method as long as the circumstances allow.'[34] While the 'racial equality' proposal was presented as a matter of principle, this instruction indicates that the issue was also related to pragmatic imperial interests because 'racial equality' meant the acquisition of the rights of business and property by Japanese residents in foreign countries. More significantly, however, the proposal was an expression of not so much the principle of justice as of Japan's pride as an imperial power.[35] A few Japanese, such as Ishibashi Tanzan (1884–1973), economist and journalist at *Tōyō keizai shimpō*, criticized Japan's double standard, wanting equal status with the powers, but conducting discriminatory and imperial policies towards 'other' Asians.[36] For most Japanese, however, racial discrimination was hurtful, because Japan was treated as inferior to the powers and because Japanese were considered to be like other 'Asians'. They also felt that all the great powers were practising discriminatory policies towards what they regarded as 'lesser' peoples. If there was a double standard, therefore, it was not peculiar to the Japanese empire. Makino Nobuaki (1861–1949), who led the negotiation, expressed this pride as a power:

> the people of the countries which had advanced cultures and were eligible to become a member of the League should be treated as equal no matter what race or nationality they were.[37]

Makino's paternalism was no weaker than that of their European or American counterparts.

> [The League] will, beside providing for social reforms, also look after the welfare and interests of the less advanced peoples by entrusting their government to mandatory States. It is an attempt to regulate the conduct of nations and peoples towards one another according to a higher moral standard than has obtained in the past…[38]

For the powerful, the Japanese delegation used the rhetoric of a 'new' code of 'national' equality. But for the weak they wanted the old imperial code and annexation, as was clear in their request for the acquisition of the former German colonies of the South Pacific islands.[39] The dispute over the Japanese proposal for racial equality clarified critical elements of the post-League order. The right to claim equal treatment belonged only to citizens of a powerful nation/empire, and state sovereignty was the basis of the 'new' order. Non-Euro-American powers remained problematic in the order. Although this was a negligible issue in Europe, it was an urgent concern in the Pacific.

Non-state agency and state/empire

The Inquiry and the Round Table

Another new factor evident at the conference was the growing significance of non-governmental agencies in international politics. This was a product more of war than of peace. Non-governmental sectors were mobilized during World War I on an unprecedented scale. Inter-governmental organizations such as the War Cabinet and the Allied Forces stationed staff in various countries, and they worked alongside colleagues from other countries.

Unofficial organizations, such as the Red Cross and YMCA International, worked in a similar manner. Americans who headed these official and non-official organizations included future key IPR figures, such as Edward Carter, Chief Secretary of the YMCA with the American Expeditionary Force in France in 1917–19, Jerome Greene (1874–1959), Executive Secretary of the American Shipping Mission of the Allied Maritime Transport Council, London, in 1917, and Newton Baker (1871–1937), Secretary of War in 1916–21.

At the Paris Conference many non-official young male professionals accompanied politicians and senior government officials. Among them was a group of twenty-three Americans known as the 'Inquiry' group. It was made up of lawyers, businessmen, academics and journalists whom House had recruited to devise a post-war reconstruction plan. They drafted most of the Fourteen Points on territorial solutions.[40] The Inquiry was the first non-governmental foreign policy brains trust in American history. It was not only a product of wartime mobilization, but also reflected the views of Wilson and House.[41] Diplomats were equipped to handle daily problems, but were too busy to address long-term issues. The State Department had no time, House concluded, to draft proposals or recruit highly trained thinkers for the job.[42] James Shotwell was a principal member of the Inquiry, and he later became a founding member of the IPR. For him, the Inquiry opened up a new avenue for academics: 'never before had universities been mobilized for such a service … it called for specialists whose interests lay in a different academic world from that of undergraduate instruction.'[43] At the conference, the Inquiry had a considerably greater role than merely furnishing information. To their surprise and excitement, they were involved in the Inter-Allied Commissions, shaping the terms of the Versailles Treaty. The success of this Inquiry group inspired many NGOs in the 1920s. Government officials were not always well disposed to this development. Shotwell recorded hostility from the State Department, which regarded the Inquiry as a group of 'amateurs'.[44]

These Americans worked closely with their British counterparts. Among them were Round Table members. The Round Table, established in London in 1909, had a strong connection with the Foreign Office, but it was not part of any government department. Its origins went back to Milner's Kindergarten, a group of young Oxford graduates appointed to key administrative positions in South Africa in 1901 by Alfred Milner (1854–1925), then High Commissioner for South Africa. Soon branch offices were established in major cities of the British Commonwealth.[45] Lionel Curtis (1872–1955) and Philip Kerr (1882–1940), later Ambassador to the United States, were key members of this group. Curtis was to become a leading figure in British involvement in IPR activities between the late 1920s and the mid-1930s. Many Round Table members participated in British Commonwealth delegations at the Paris Conference. In Britain, this was partly because its members were close to the Lloyd George faction of the Liberal Party.[46] It was also because its members were rare foreign 'experts' in Britain and the

Dominions. Frederic Eggleston (1875–1954), an Australian Round Table member, participated in the conference. He would become active in post-League internationalist movements, and a key figure in the IPR in Australia. From Japan, young diplomats, such as Matsuoka Yōsuke (1880–1946), Yoshida, Arita Hachirō and Shigemitsu Mamoru, and non-officials, such as Konoe, were sent to assist senior diplomats. They were to play a crucial role in inter-war diplomacy. Matsuoka and Konoe became involved in the JCIPR. Like their counterparts in the United States and the British Commonwealth, they belonged to a modern national elite – male, university educated, often with law degrees.

These young professionals and bureaucrats were strongly influenced by the idea of democracy. Like Wilson, they were convinced of the significance of the new open diplomacy and the role of non-officials and public opinion as opposed to secret diplomacy dominated by politicians and soldiers. Japanese diplomats, such as Shigemitsu and Arita, felt the need for reform of the Ministry of Foreign Affairs so that it could adapt to this changing climate. They established the *Kakushin dōshikai* (Reformists' Association) within the Ministry.[47] More significantly, Konoe was enthusiastic about 'democratization' of foreign policy machinery, and argued the need for a good propaganda organization and national news agency. He also emphasized the importance of the input of non-official experts in policy-making. His initiatives, which originated in 1919, were crucial in the process of the co-option of the JCIPR into the state apparatus in the late 1930s and early 1940s.

Counterparts in the United States and the British Commonwealth shared views similar to Konoe's, and tried to form an Anglo-American organization of foreign experts. In Britain, this was to become the Royal Institute of International Affairs (RIIA), or Chatham House,[48] and its American counterpart was the Council on Foreign Relations (CFR) (see Chapter 2). On 30 May 1919 at the Majestic Hotel, where the British delegates stayed during the Paris Conference, thirty-three 'British' and Americans proposed a new institution.[49] The core of this group was from the Inquiry and the Round Table. Lionel Curtis initiated the move. His model was a research institution like the Royal Geographical Society. Members would study, publish and discuss issues of international affairs, and enhance communications between government and experts. He hoped that the institutes 'would form centres where [members] would converse on these subjects, just as they now conversed in the Carillon and Majestic Hotel'.[50]

Chatham House (the RIIA) and British post-League internationalists

The proposed organization recognized the significance of the two major non-official elements of international politics – non-official foreign experts and public opinion. Curtis thought that the experts who gathered at the conference constituted the most valuable factor for producing *sound* public opinion.

Right public opinion was mainly produced by a small number of people in real contact with the facts who had thought out the issues involved. ... National policy ought to be shaped by a conception of the interests of society at large; for it was in the advancement of that universal interest that the particular interest of the several nations would alone be found. It was all important, therefore, to cultivate a public opinion in the various countries of the world which kept the general interest in view.[51]

Curtis demonstrated not faith in but scepticism towards the ability of the public, reflecting dominant views among intellectual elites. The public did not have the capacity to analyse foreign affairs properly. They needed to be guided by 'experts'.[52] Foreign experts could judge what was right for the nation, and the interests of the population would somehow coincide with what experts regard as 'national' interests.

These experts' position in relation to the state was very different from that of the *laissez-faire* liberals. Key members of the Round Table, such as Curtis, Kerr and Zimmern, who also became central at the RIIA, were strongly influenced by New Liberalism.[53] On the one hand, Wilson differed from these New Liberals, as he was sceptical about strong, centralized state power. Yet Wilson, too, thought that the state needed to play a new role in a rapidly changing society.[54] Arguably, he was the first American president to believe that the state would protect minorities and satisfy the majority.[55] Wilson and British New Liberals saw the state as morally good, and regarded social reform as its moral duty.

New Liberals also emphasized the role of the state in international politics. Zimmern, for example, argued that states were the building blocks of the international community. 'The work of internationalism', he noted, 'would be more properly called the work of inter-state organization'. Furthermore, New Liberals tended to reify the nation and to identify it with the state. They believed that the state and the nation was a coherent entity and that the nation inherently supported state actions. Wilson held a similar opinion, viewing the nation/state as a human body, an organic entity. Zimmern wrote: 'It is as right and healthy for a state to have a foreign policy as for an individual to manifest its personality. A state without foreign policy is a dead state.'[56]

These views reflected a wider intellectual paradigm of the day. The framework of nation-states, as well as empires, was becoming dominant. And so was the notion of 'national culture', as well as 'civilization of an empire'. Both were strongly influenced by social Darwinism and eugenics.[57] The reification of the nation was even stronger than that of the state, and political, economic and social conditions furthered this process.[58] The franchise reached much wider populations in some industrialized countries. 'The unity of the nation', 'society as a whole' and 'social welfare' became the dominant rhetoric of bureaucrats and intellectuals,[59] particularly in anti- or counter-socialist camps. They wanted to promote a view of a unified and harmonious whole, not two divided classes. While the rhetoric was used to enhance the welfare of society and the rights of the underprivileged, it was also used to appease a discontented population, and strengthened the power of the state. Modern 'national traditions' were reinvented to construct the regime of truth and legitimize the strong social control of the state over the nation.[60] As a result, the population no longer questioned the 'existence' of the reified nation and 'national culture'. These were effective ideologies for the state to mobilize the population and make them willingly serve its economic and military activities.

Carr criticized this notion of the organic whole: 'the doctrine of the harmony of interests ... became ... the ideology of a dominant group concerned to maintain its predominance by asserting the identity of the interests with those of the community as a whole'.[61] Although he regarded the notion as a *laissez-faire* liberal concept, it was even more manifest in New Liberalism. The implication was equally significant for the 'international community'. In Carr's view, British New Liberals, such as Zimmern, used the same rhetoric of the harmonious international community to justify the domestic and international status quo.

These New Liberals also legitimized British colonial rule by adopting an Orientalist rhetoric. In 1918 Zimmern noted that the slogan 'non-annexation' was nonsense, because some places were not equipped for self-government and 'civilized' governments alone could provide this.[62] Acknowledging their contribution to the 'demolishment of prejudice against granting self-government to India', Kendle sums up the attitudes towards the 'East' among these British Round Table members, many of whom supported the League and became members of the RIIA: they argued that the superior position of the European in the world involved not a privilege but a 'special obligation to serve'.[63] Curtis defined this attitude as 'democratic imperialism', a combination of liberalism and imperialism.[64] What mattered for these 'democratic' imperialists was, as Quigley points out, not social reforms or the welfare of the society or colonies *per se*, but the preservation of declining British elite traditions and institutions. The only way to prevent this decline was to extend these traditions to the working classes and the colonies, before they were destroyed.[65] This New Liberalism was influential not only among British post-League internationalists, but also among their Dominion counterparts. Those who became active in IPR operations in these countries mainly came from this intellectual milieu.[66]

Part II
The Pacific Community

2 The Pacific Community

An American vision of the regional order

American post-League internationalism in the 1920s

Strong American leadership was evident at the Paris Peace Conference. This was the third new factor in the post-League international order. American internationalism developed not so much as part of the pacifist movement as an assertion of American leadership. American internationalists argued strongly for US involvement in World War I, not only to attain peace, but also to lead the world.[1] Many thought that the old European powers had caused the disastrous war and were discredited. The United States, untainted and fresh, could claim a strong new leadership. American internationalists believed in 'American' ideals, exceptional quality, and a special mission to the world. As Wilson put it in 1912: '[E]ver since we were born as a nation we have undertaken to be the champions of humanity and the rights of men.' Now the time had come: 'America is now going to be called out into an international position such as she never has occupied before.'[2]

There was a serious problem with this American leadership: it flew in the face of foreign policy orthodoxy, the Monroe Doctrine. According to the doctrine, the United States should exercise independent leadership, independent from European politics. For many Americans, the negotiations at the Paris Conference suggested that European powers would dominate the League of Nations. As a result, Congress voted against American entry. A Democrat President, Wilson, had initiated the League and Republicans were quick to seize on popular sentiment against involvement in European politics. Republican internationalists such as Elihu Root (1845–1939), former Secretary of State in the Theodore Roosevelt administration (1901–9), argued that the essence of the League was the old 'evil' European power politics, and that American involvement would threaten its independence.[3] The Republicans defeated Wilson in 1921 and ruled until Franklin D. Roosevelt regained the presidency for the Democrats in 1933. In the 1920s, they pursued what Smith terms 'independent internationalism'.[1] Root defended this Republican foreign policy in the first issue of *Foreign Affairs* in 1922, the journal of the Council on Foreign Relations (CFR). What mattered was not membership of the League of Nations, but 'the rights and obligations incident to the membership of the community of nations'.[5]

It was not Wilson but these succeeding Republican administrations that defined post-League internationalism in the United States. Their independent internationalism was the main force behind the Washington Conference of 1921–2 and the Pact of Paris of 1928 (General Treaty for Renunciation of War as an Instrument of National Policy). According to DeBenedetti, the latter was 'the most advanced expression of the post-war Republican goal of tying the popular dream of world peace to its partisan vision of an organizing world of law and economic cooperation free from political precommitment'.[6] These treaty frameworks, which the Republican administrations instituted outside the League of Nations, complemented the League and became a significant part of the machinery of the post-League order. The basis of the condemnation of Japanese aggression in the 1930s and 1940s, for example, was not only the Covenant of the League of Nations, but also these treaties.

The transition from Wilson to the succeeding Republican administration complicated the ideological or partisan factor of post-League internationalism. Steigerwald defines American Wilsonians as moderate liberals, and notes that they came from various political and ideological backgrounds.[7] The assumption of their 'liberalness', however, is problematic. Their adherence to concepts such as reason, liberty, peace and democracy did not automatically imply commitment to domestic reformist movements. Rather, it was more common that leaders of social movements saw American international involvement as undesirable.[8] Wilson was an exceptional Democrat at an exceptional time in history because he had a great vision for the role of the United States in the world, as well as a strong commitment to concrete reform movements. To further complicate the issue of ideology and party affiliation, the Republican Party included a strong reformist element, which split the party and contributed to the long Democrat rule in the 1910s.[9]

This ideological and partisan complexity characterized American post-League internationalists in the inter-war period. It also meant a certain continuity of foreign policy between the Wilson administration and its successors. In 1923 Root stressed the irrelevance of party affiliation to issues of the national interest and foreign policy,[10] and Republican administrations advanced one of the Fourteen Points, free trade.

The Washington Conference

The Pacific and the United States

If there was a distinguishing feature of Republican internationalism in the 1920s, it was its enthusiastic pursuit of an American order in certain regions. Isolationism meant isolation from European politics. The Monroe Doctrine defined and protected the US sphere of interest – the American continent, Asia and the Pacific – and the United States was actively involved in these regions. Senator Henry Cabot Lodge makes this point in his speech opposing the American entry to the League of Nations in 1919:

> ... I object strongly to having the politics of the United States turn upon disputes where deep feeling is aroused but in which we have no direct interests. It will all tend to delay the Americanization of our great population, and it is more important not only to the United States but to the peace of the world to make all these people good Americans than it is to determine that some piece of territory should belong to one European country rather than another. For this reason I wish to limit strictly our interference in the affairs of Europe and Africa. We have interests of our own in Asia and in the Pacific which we must guard upon our own account ... [11]

Lodge shared the notion that Americanization was the basis of world peace. Yet it was important for the United States to keep out of areas that were not regarded as its sphere. The Pacific region, Asia included, was clearly the extended frontier where the United States could pursue its manifest destiny.

The United States started late as a Pacific power, but advanced quickly, particularly after the Spanish–American War. It gained the Philippines, Guam and Samoa, and Puerto Rico in 1899, and annexed Hawai'i in 1898. Its strategic commitment to the region increased and commercial interests expanded. At the beginning of the twentieth century, Roosevelt's administration consolidated and advanced America's status as a Pacific power. [12]

As the United States advanced as a Pacific power, American professionals – traders, missionaries, journalists and academics – found new opportunities in the region. They spearheaded interaction with the region, especially China and Japan. [13] They also formed friendship associations in major cities, including the Japan Society in New York (founded in 1907). Responding to these business and tourist demands, and enhanced by the rapid development of communication and transportation technology, shipping companies increased routes and frequencies of transpacific lines. [14] Missionaries or correspondents for *Harpers* and the *Christian Science Monitor* provided American readers with new and fascinating first-hand observations. These professionals were influential in shaping knowledge of Asia and the Pacific islands. [15] Academics also contributed to constructing new knowledge. Universities began programmes on China and Japan, and the initiative on the West coast was noted. Although Chinese studies developed more quickly and on a bigger scale, lectures on Japan also began at Yale in 1906, at Stanford in 1907 and at the University of California in 1911. [16]

While Pan-Americanism was an expression of US leadership in the Americas, the Pan-Pacific movement of the 1910s was its extension in the Pacific. [17] An advocate of the movement, Alexander Hume Ford, came to

Hawai'i in 1907 and started a monthly bulletin, the *Mid-Pacific Magazine*, in 1910. His inspiration was clearly Pan-Americanism. Modelled after the Pan-American Union, he founded the Pan-Pacific Union in 1917.[18] In the 1910s and 1920s, it organized many Pan-Pacific conferences, which were attended by influential members of Pacific rim countries.[19] His desire for fame and local commercial interests – tourism, and plantations and factories in need of cheap 'coloured' labour – were probably the force behind this movement. Although local race relations were never as rosy as presented, he promoted Hawai'i as a model of racial and cultural harmony.[20]

These Pan-Pacific conferences disseminated the Pacific-centred view (see Figure 2.1), laying a good intellectual and institutional foundation for the IPR in the Pacific rim countries. Pan-Pacific Clubs were established in various countries. In Tokyo, a club was formed on Ford's second visit in 1924. Reflecting strong business enthusiasm, an Osaka branch soon followed. Diplomats, businessmen, politicians and academics, 'the leading men of all Pan-Pacific races', gathered for meetings and speeches.[21] Chambers of Commerce, Rotary Clubs, the Red Cross, Chambers of Industry and trade unions in the Pacific rim countries also took up this Pan-Pacific zeal, and held their own Pan-Pacific conferences.[22]

Japan occupied a central position in this American Pacific. In the mid-1920s, John Tilley, British ambassador to Japan in 1926–30, predicted a great American influence on Japan:

> the wide interest [was] felt along the [US] Pacific coast in things Japanese. Many had Japanese friends who passed backwards and forwards from Japan. … There is nothing strange in this, given the relative nearness of the two countries, but it brought home to me the weight of influence which America is bound to exercise on Japan as compared with England, where … practically no interest is felt in Japan except in some special circles.[23]

For Americans, with a strong regional interest, the Pacific meant growing American influence and opportunity. However, as regional interactions increased, concerns also grew. The rising power of Meiji Japan earned praise, but it was a new and unknown power in Asia, and a threat to North America's security and economy.[24] Anxiety was higher on the Pacific coast than on the East coast or Europe. The Japanese victory over Russia in 1905 convinced some Americans of its strategic potential. Even before then, Alfred T. Mahan, close confidant of Theodore Roosevelt, military strategist and popular writer, sounded the alarm. Mahan's book, *The Problem of Asia*, written in 1900, signified a new perception: Asia had become a problem for American security. He argued the strategic significance of the Pacific and the need for a proper American defence capacity on the Pacific coast and within the Pacific.[25] These concerns were echoed in Canada as a 1910 *Round Table* article warned of the

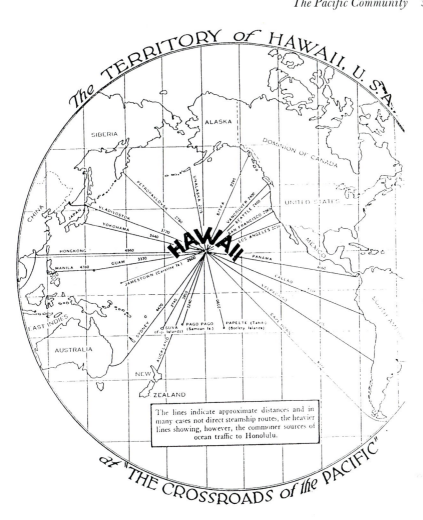

Figure 2.1 Hawai'i as the centre of the Pacific, 1922.

Source: *Pan-Pacific Union Bulletin*, 1922 (filed in A981/1/Conf 260).

threat of Japan not only to security, but also to trade and investment on the Pacific coast.[26] China was another area of possible conflict between Japan and the United States. Both governments concluded various agreements to secure each other's rights in China.[27] Significantly, the proceedings of the IPR conferences between 1927 and 1939 were published under the title *Problems of the Pacific*. The Pacific had become a problem for the United States, in which Japan was the central concern.

Japan presented a problem also for the 'Anglo-American race'. Concern on the Pacific coast was high, because this was where most of the 'Oriental' immigrants lived. Racial discrimination in California after 1882 mainly affected Japanese immigrants because those from other countries in Asia were already excluded. A class element was also apparent. While there was concern over Japanese investment on the Pacific coast, local anxiety was caused not so much by hundreds of business visitors and upper middle-class Japanese students at prestigious universities as by the 30,000 Japanese immigrant workers who had settled in the area, mostly in California.[28] The more visible Japanese entry into the labouring classes became, the more boycotts of Japanese shops and violence against Japanese were reported.[29] This escalated into a serious diplomatic issue, first in 1907 and again in 1913. In 1907 Asian students in San Francisco schools were segregated. Japan and the United States concluded a gentlemen's agreement whereby Japan voluntarily restricted emigration. The mass media promoted sensational and negative images of Asians as the 'Yellow Peril'. Popular books in both countries argued an inevitable clash between yellow and white races.[30] In 1913 California passed a law banning the acquisition, ownership or long-term lease of property by foreigners who did not have the right to naturalization. This affected Japanese farmers' ownership of land. After protests by the Japanese government, President Wilson sent the Secretary of State to persuade California to repeal the law, but without success.

The Washington Conference and the immigration dispute

The Republican administration promoted independent US leadership in the Pacific much more enthusiastically than Wilson had done. This was clear at the Washington Conference of 1921–2, led by Charles Hughes, Secretary of State in the Harding administration. It concluded the Five Power Treaty on naval disarmament, the Nine Power Treaty on China and the Four Power Treaty on the Pacific. Scholars regard these treaties as defining a new American-led and multilateral framework of stability and cooperation for the region. They complemented rather than challenged the League of Nations. They were not a total departure from old practices. These treaties did not challenge colonialism, but guaranteed the powers' interests at the expense of China.[31]

Many contemporaries in Japan and some in the British Dominions saw the Washington Treaties as an expression of Anglo-American solidarity.[32] It is more accurate to see them as an expression of a regional order led by Americans. It was not so much an assertion of American dominance as a multilateral framework of cooperation between various powers under American leadership. Not just Anglo-American cooperation, but the American–Japanese relationship, was central to this order. The Harding administration regarded US–Japan economic cooperation as an important foundation of this regional order. It was crucial for American business interests, which were strong backers of the administration.[33] As the United States intended and Britain anticipated, the Four Power Treaty superseded the Anglo-Japanese alliance (1902–21). Japan was now a 'partner' of the United States in an American-led multilateral framework of cooperation.

Although Iriye argues that this framework failed very soon after it was established, mainly because of the challenge of the USSR, the Washington Conference, nevertheless, had profound implications for the development of the concept of the Pacific in the 1920s. The notion of the Pacific as an American sphere and the idea of the 'Pacific Age' first appeared during Roosevelt's administration. What was new in the 1920s was the concept of the 'Pacific Community'. In 1927, Herbert Croly emphasized the significance of the Washington Conference for a development of this new construct of the Pacific:

> The World War brought to an end the efficacy and the authority of European domination in the Atlantic. ... It is profoundly significant that the Washington Conference of 1921, which, by dividing sea power between the British Empire and the United States, destroyed the physical basis of the traditional conception of the Atlantic Ocean as a liquid extension of Europe, looked in the direction also of a new conception of the Pacific.[34]

For Croly, this new Pacific was more than an entity: it was a community of 'political equals', signifying a new form of conduct of international politics:

> The Washington Conference treated the Pacific, for the first time, as a somewhat independent political and economic area. It even outlined a sketch of a Pacific regional community, which, if it could be realized and developed, would neutralize the Pacific highway as an instrument of predatory politics. ... The peoples of the Pacific are particularly protected in theory against any further aggression, and in this sense they are by way of forming *a community of political equals* which are obligated to consult one another about their common political and economic difficulties and policies.[35] [emphasis added]

This concept of the 'Pacific Community' was American, quite distinct from European. The impressions of British ambassador to Japan, Tilley, highlighted this point:

> at San Francisco I found, to my surprise, that the subject in the air was pan-Pacific relations. ... There were three American speeches ... pointing out that the Pacific was now the crucial region, so to speak, of the world ... I heard talk of a Pacific civilization and philosophy, which was something superior to its European counterpart. I believed this was a myth.[36]

The notion of a superior Pacific was an assertion of American superiority over Europe.

For Pacific Community advocates, the concept was an excellent framework in which they could pursue a more equal relationship with the new powers in Asia than could their European counterparts. Were these powers, China and Japan, really regarded as equal partners? How did this new Pacific civilization or philosophy deal with them? Hosoya argues that, at the governmental level, the United States tried to accommodate China as a Pacific power, almost equal to the United States, Britain and Japan. In his view, it was Japan that opposed this because of its claim of 'special interests' in Manchuria and Mongolia. Usui, on the other hand, argues that Japanese diplomacy after the Washington Conference emphasized the commercial relationship with China, and maintained a non-interventionist policy towards Chinese politics, at least until 1927. This meant respect for China as a nation-state and for its sovereignty.[37]

If indeed the Washington Treaties aimed to achieve a Pacific Community of political equals, the passing of the anti-Japanese immigration law in 1923 (the law was executed in 1924) signalled a critical failure. There were other pressing political and economic factors that contributed to the demise of the Washington system. Yet this 'failure' alarmed some American post-League internationalists, and became a direct trigger prompting their non-governmental solution, the IPR. Only one year after the conclusion of the Washington Treaties, Congress passed a law banning all Asian immigration. As this meant the virtual exclusion of Japanese immigrants, the Japanese called it *hainichi iminhō* (anti-Japanese immigration law). Official and popular Japanese protest was strong, and sensational books and articles predicted an inevitable race war.[38]

The law polarized opinions and consolidated two opposing groups in both Japan and the United States: one that felt the need for even stronger US–Japan cooperation and another that opposed this move. Certain naval strategists in Japan belonged to the latter group, presenting formidable opposition to the policy of cooperation with the United States.[39] In contrast, post-League internationalists in both countries strengthened their advocacy for a cooperative relationship. They were key figures in US–Japan relations, many of whom were to become central in the IPR. While Wilson showed sympathy towards American labourers and supported moves against Japanese land ownership in 1913, the Republican administration and business circles saw a cooperative US–Japan economic relationship as the basis of its regional vision. For them, Japan was a secure market and an important trade partner. Along with pro-Japan lawyers and religious leaders, business people became central in the lobby against anti-Japanese immigration. Many were Republicans. They had close contacts with Japan, and were often referred to in Japan as *shin nichika* (pro-Japanese people). The Japanese American Relations Committee (JARC), formed in San Francisco and New York, included Wallace Alexander, Chairperson of the Chamber of Commerce in San Francisco, Julius Rosenbald, a philanthropic Chicago businessman, Thomas Lamont (1870–1948), a partner of the J.P. Morgan Bank,[40] Elihu

Root, a Republican senator, John Mott (1865–1955), a YMCA leader of the International Student Volunteer Movement, and Henry Taft, brother of William H. Taft and Attorney General. George Wickersham (1858–1936), former Attorney General, Republican, an influential member of the CFR and strong League supporter, was so active that the movement in New York was called the 'Wickersham Movement'. Similarly, their Japanese counterparts were promoters of the cooperation with the United States, and they were referred to as pro-American (*shin beika*). Big business was well represented. They formed the Japanese branch of the JARC, many of whose members were to be involved with the JCIPR.[11]

These Americans promoted more equal race relations. In contrast, the labouring classes, particularly on the Pacific coast, felt the threat of Japanese immigration more acutely than their wealthy, worldly opponents.[12] They formed an anti-Japanese immigration coalition with other groups, centred at the California Joint Immigration Committee in San Francisco. The committee consisted of the American Legion, the State Federation of Labor, Grange (an agricultural union association) and Native Sons of the Golden West (a citizens' association representing the upper and upper middle classes). V.S. McClatchy, a proprietor of three newspapers in San Francisco, was Secretary of the Committee in 1924, and led a campaign for Japanese exclusion.[13]

A strong nativist tenor was prominent in this coalition. The nativism was concerned with the preservation of 'old-stock' Americans. By then laws barring miscegenation between 'white' and Afro-Americans already existed in twenty-eight states. In this period, these laws were either extended to other states, or extended to other 'races', such as Asians and indigenous Americans.[14] McClatchy argued that 'the long established policy of the nation has been the preservation of this country for the white race'.[15] Not only Asians, but ethnic or religious groups other than Anglo-Saxon Protestants and dissidents such as communists, socialists or anarchists, who were often associated with 'foreign' names, were discriminated against under immigration laws. The East coast tended to worry about 'Jews' and 'Germans',[16] whereas the West coast was concerned about 'Asians'. DeBenedetti notes that this nativist sentiment was evident even in the peace movement.[17]

The concepts of 'American' ideals were crucial in this debate. McClatchy advocated Japanese exclusion on the basis of protection of the American race, and accused JARC members of disloyalty to their nation. Although Sidney Gulick spent twenty-five years in Japan, and was known as a promoter of Japan to the United States, his argument against McClatchy was based on his Christian humanism, which was applicable to wider groups than Japanese immigrants. He defined American citizenship as based on Christian ideas and democratic principles, and emphasized the existing diversity within the population, including 'Negroes', American Indians, Mexicans and Chinese.[18]

In comparison, the argument of most American post-League internationalists at the JARC was limited. They applied 'racial' equality only to the Japanese, basing their argument on the high achievement of Japanese civilization. They may have believed in 'liberal' principles of equal rights, diversity and tolerance, but these were only applicable to select deserving groups, e.g. Japanese members of the JARC. Americans and Japanese members of the JARC were anxious that Japan be on an equal footing with European powers. They argued for a quota system for Japanese immigrants, as applied to Europeans, rather than repeal of the law. There was no suggestion of a similar change in the treatment of non-Japanese 'Asians'. Even so, these proposals still challenged the strong nativist climate of the time. American members often had to fight against the label 'un-American'.[49] Furthermore, their JARC activities modified the dominant view of 'Western' superiority over the 'East'. They recognized the new powers in Asia, and argued for the need to *learn* from and about them.[50] It was this attitude which was reflected among American IPR founders in 1925.

Promoting Anglo-American solidarity? the RIIA, the CFR and the Institute of Politics at Williamstown

When Lionel Curtis, a member of the Round Table, envisaged an organization of non-official experts on foreign affairs in 1919, he clearly recognized the United States as the new great power. His response was to advocate Anglo-American solidarity. He noted that 'The British and American Commonwealth are the two central pillars upon which [the peace of the world] must rest'.[51] This was not an unusual view in Britain, its Dominions and the United States. The notion of 'English-speaking countries' reflected this kind of thinking, and was promoted by institutions such as the English Speaking Union (1918), while the Rhodes Scholarship scheme emphasized the ties with Anglo-Saxon stock.[52]

Curtis also wanted an Anglo-American organization that would lead interaction among foreign affairs experts in the world. The experience of the Paris Conference further convinced Curtis, and American participants, such as Shotwell, seemed to have concurred.[53] A provisional committee was set up, and Curtis and an American, Whitney Shepardson (1890–1966), became joint secretaries. In February 1920, it was recorded: 'Practically everybody of any importance in England and America has joined.' In July the British component, the British Institute of International Affairs (BIIA soon to be the RIIA), was founded in London, and Dominion members such as Eggleston became founding members.[54]

The difficulties in founding the US counterpart, however, demonstrated that not all Americans shared Curtis's grand vision. In the United States, many, including post-League internationalists, were reluctant to be involved with European organizations. Shotwell and Shepardson, who were in charge of the organization of the American counterpart of the RIIA, admitted: 'American public opinion would not permit them to join with the British.'

They decided to form a similar, but independent organization, which soon merged with a group of bankers and lawyers initially organized by Elihu Root. The group was incorporated as the CFR on 29 July 1921.[55]

Some scholars maintain that the RIIA and the CFR promoted a vision for the world based on Anglo-American solidarity, as Curtis envisaged. In a similar way, others see the IPR, whose membership overlapped with that of the RIIA and the CFR, as part of this project.[56] The East coast establishment, to which many post-League internationalists belonged, was strongly Anglophile, and this was evident in Wilson himself.[57] The Institute of Politics at Williamstown (IPW), which started as a summer school in Williams College, Williamstown, Massachusetts, in 1921, was one of the joint projects of these Anglophile Americans and their British counterparts. Harry A. Garfield (1863–1942), President of the college and son of the twentieth American President, James Garfield, was the main force behind this project. The Round Table group was involved from its inception, and CFR members worked closely with Garfield. Garfield had strong ties with Curtis and the Round Table group from his student days at Oxford and London in the late 1880s. In the 1920s, Garfield discussed the idea of 'the first joint meeting of foreign affairs experts from the English-speaking world' with Curtis. Shepardson, Curtis and Kerr were greatly involved in it.[58] Garfield had good official connections (his brother was Secretary of the Interior in the Roosevelt administration). Well-known diplomats and politicians mainly from the United States and Europe gathered to discuss international politics, chiefly League matters, in this small town on the border of Massachusetts, Vermont and New York.[59] The event received extensive publicity.[60] Although the IPW lasted for only a decade, it was highly regarded among foreign affairs experts.

The Inquiry group at the Paris Conference was the main inspiration for the IPW, but it had its innovative side. Despite its European focus and heavy official involvement, its success and new methodology were two major factors that IPR founders found attractive. It was an organization based not on 'national' foreign affairs experts, such as the CFR and the RIIA, but on periodic international conferences. Its object was 'to educate the leaders of public opinion in the new world situation'. It targeted 'experts' – university teachers, officials in the military and State Department, business people in international banking and finance, newspaper editors and other public figures.[61]

Despite obvious links of this American project with Curtis's group in Britain, it is hard to establish whether the CFR and the IPW were promoting a vision of an international order based on Anglo-American solidarity. Continental European politicians and diplomats gathered at the IPW with different motivations and agendas. Kendle and Schulzinger, in their respective studies of the Round Table and the CFR, question Anglo-American solidarity as the coherent agenda of these organizations. They also doubt its influence on official or public thinking.[62] British post-League internationalists were mainly concerned with the preservation of the imperial framework. RIIA members were probably more enthusiastic about British cooperation with the League of Nations and the United States than were some Round Table members.[63] Nevertheless their priority was imperial relations. Curtis and Kerr, major advocates of Anglo-American solidarity in the Round Table and the RIIA, often had to fight scepticism among their colleagues, let alone officials and other foreign expert groups. They were increasingly disillusioned and alienated.[64]

No doubt Curtis hoped cooperation with the United States would invigorate the declining empire. As Carr noted, it was the consoling dream. Even Anglophile Americans did not necessarily respond without reservation.[65] Shepardson sums up the view of American post-League internationalists. A former Rhodes scholar, married to Curtis's niece, and deeply influenced by Curtis's work on the Commonwealth, he was the CFR member probably closest to Curtis. Yet even he found Curtis's view patronizing. To Shepardson, American and British values were quite distinct from each other:

> I always had the feeling about Curtis that he believes in his heart that the US is a temporary lost section of the British Commonwealth which some day ... will come back within the fold. I do not think he realises to any important degree that we have grown and developed along lines of our own and that we have here in this country a civilization essentially different from the British.[66]

Wilson's Fourteen Points were the guiding principle of the new international order, but they did not encompass non-Euro-American powers in Asia. A new order was needed in the Pacific, and the Republican administration attempted to establish it by means of the Washington Conference. Iriye argues that these governmental attempts failed to replace the European imperial system.[67] The base of this American regional order, relatively equal relationships with the new powers in Asia, also seems to have been greatly damaged when the US Congress passed the anti-Japanese immigration law. The IPR was initiated by American post-League internationalists with a strong regional interest at this precise moment. It was a non-official attempt to restore and advance the new regional order, which was embodied in the concept of the Pacific Community. It was inspired not only by Wilson, but by the Republican independent internationalism of the 1920s. The concept was embedded in its practical interests and faith in American mission and ideals. Ironically, according to contemporary critics, American ideals, particularly the frontier spirit and individualism, were rapidly losing ground in the wake of drastic social change.[68] These 'ideals', therefore, had become 'ideologies' at the moment they were launched in the international arena, and probably for that reason they were very powerful. This American regional order was not a simple assertion of its hegemony, but a multilateral framework of cooperation of the powers under the leadership of the United States. Along with Britain, Japan emerged as a significant and powerful 'partner'. This Pacific Community carried all the excitement and anxiety of a dawning new era and was to be rigorously pushed by the IPR in the mid-1920s.

3 From vision to influence

Founding the Institute of Pacific Relations

It was a rainy Sunday afternoon in New York on 22 February 1925. Around half past two, a group of men 'particularly interested in inter-racial and international questions' gathered at the Yale Club, near Grand Central Station Terminal. A Sunday during the congressional recess was chosen so that these busy public figures could attend. They came to discuss a proposal for a new institute, 'its purpose, scope and method and the nature of American participation in it'. This proposed institute was to become the IPR. The letter of invitation noted: 'Problems arising from the increasing intercourse between the Peoples of the Pacific Basin have inspired the proposal to hold at Honolulu an institute somewhat similar to the Williamstown Institute, under the auspices of an international committee made up of representatives from Australia, New Zealand, China, Japan, the Philippines, Canada and the United States'.[1] The only country missing from this list and which sent delegates to the first conference was Korea.

Invitations were sent to men considered to be opinion leaders with an interest in the Pacific. They were selected from the fields of religion, press, business, academia and education. The meeting was organized by a temporary executive committee (the New York committee), which had been discussing the institute for some time. The committee itself consisted of prominent Americans, mainly from the East coast: George Blakeslee, professor of political science and 'Far Eastern' specialist at Clark University in Worcester, Massachusetts, and organizer of the Institute of Politics at Williamstown; John Finley, Editor of the *New York Times*; John Mott, an inspirational leader of the YMCA; G.A. Johnston Ross, professor at the Union Theological Seminary, New York; Chester Rowell, an influential journalist at *World's Work Magazine*, San Francisco; James Speers, owner of a shipping company, James McCutcheon Company, New York; and Ray Wilbur (1875–1949), President of Stanford University.

This Yale Club meeting was a turning point. Two months earlier, Merle Davis, who was in charge of the organization of this project and who was to become the first General Secretary of the IPR in 1926, had predicted the significance of this planned meeting. If this group of eminent men support their proposed conference, this meant 'a great enlargement of the scope and influence of the Hawaii programme'. Their conference would exert 'both a national and international influence' in forming 'public opinion and new legislation of the first importance'.[2]

The Yale Club meeting made it clear that this greater potential was in sight. It defined the nature of the IPR in a number of important ways. First, despite the input of various Pacific rim countries in the very initial stages, and despite the institute's international structure, this meeting was entirely an American affair. Second, the meeting was dominated by East coast foreign policy or regional experts, who can be also categorized as American post-League internationalists. This suggested that the two major agendas of the project – new attitudes towards the new powers in Asia and non-state agency status – reflected these internationalists' vision for the region. Third, although its elite orientation was strongly evident, the scope of the project was not confined to policy formulation, nor was it exclusively for public enlightenment. Those who gathered at the Yale Club were optimistic about the influence of their new project both on public opinion and governmental policies.

Prelude to the Yale Club meeting

Until the Yale Club meeting, the initiative and organization for the Institute came mainly from the YMCA.[3] The initial plan had been not to found a permanent institution, but to hold a YMCA conference in Honolulu. The Christian element had been strong. The main impetus had been race relations in the Pacific, particularly disputes over Japanese immigration to the United States. In 1921, the YMCA in Honolulu proposed that representatives of the countries bordering the Pacific should meet in 1923 to discuss problems caused by race relations.

This call for a conference could only have happened following the Pan-Pacific movement centred in Hawai'i in the 1910s. It was promoted by A.H. Ford and his Pan-Pacific Union, which hosted various Pan-Pacific conferences. This had created enthusiasm for the concept of the Pacific Community among a small but influential group of people in the Pacific rim countries. Frank Atherton, a philanthropic businessman and enthusiastic YMCA member in Honolulu, assisted in the financing of the Pan-Pacific Union and the organization of these conferences.[4] He came from a prominent family that combined business with a strong missionary tradition. He was heavily involved in local religious and philanthropic activities, including the YMCA.[5] Responding to Ford's request to the Honolulu YMCA that a conference should be held,[6] at the end of 1921, the committee of the Honolulu YMCA met at the Pacific Club, a local gentlemen's club.[7] They decided to hold a conference that would aim to 'consider how [Christian ideas and principles] might be made a common basis of understanding and motivation for the Pacific peoples'.[8]

In 1922 this proposal gained the strong support of John Mott. In the same year, the matter was discussed with YMCA leaders in Asia, who expressed strong enthusiasm for the project. As a result, the 'Second World's Conference of Young Men's Christian Association Workers Among Boys' at Portschach, Austria, in May 1923, resolved that on the initiative of the YMCA in Hawai'i it would hold a Pacific YMCA conference in Honolulu in February 1925. It would invite the YMCA's National Committees of the 'nations bordering the Pacific'.[9] They chose Hawai'i because it was thought to be an ideal location for 'long time promotion of a community of interest of the people in the Pacific, and progress in the development of inter-racial understanding and goodwill'.

The central executive committee (the Honolulu group, mainly composed of Honolulu residents – six Americans, two Chinese and two Japanese) and the central committee were based in Honolulu. The latter was an international body and comprised representatives from Australia, Canada, China, Japan, Korea, New Zealand, the Philippines and the United States, as well as Hawai'i. These countries were probably selected because of their strong YMCA representation. Importantly, Korea and the Philippines were included as original members at this early stage and Hawai'i had its own representation, separate from mainland United States. Most representatives at this stage were YMCA members. The committee sent an invitation to each National Committee of the YMCA in the above-mentioned countries on 7 December 1923. Preparation for the IPR conference began in 1924, and was conducted by the YMCA National Committee in each country. Initially, the Honolulu group organized the conference and shaped the programme with the assistance of mainland members and the American YMCA. The group included Atherton, Arthur Dean, President of the University of Hawai'i, Charles Loomis, a YMCA officer from Hawai'i, and G.A. Johnston Ross and James Speers from New York.

Although the Hawai'i group remained central, developments on the mainland, especially in New York, were key to defining the nature of the IPR. This was because the organizers needed to secure funding from foundations or grant bodies that were concentrated in New York. The funding issue was critical in the subsequent development of the organization. Although some organizations depended on subscriptions or revenue from publications, money raised by this method was limited. These activities were also possible only when there was a strong organizational base. IPR organizers needed a substantial amount of money to hold a large-scale international conference. One of the few options was to approach wealthy foundations or individuals. This meant also autonomy from the state. Funding for the first conference was to come from the Honolulu group, mainly from Atherton (US$25,000), but also $10,000 from John D. Rockefeller Jr, $5,000 from the Carnegie Endowment, and some from wealthy philanthropists such as Julius Rosenwald (Sears Roebuck & Co. in Chicago), Thomas Lamont (a partner at the Morgan Bank, New York) and banking and shipping companies. For its size and membership, the IPR enjoyed a relatively big budget. This made officers rather lax about cultivating other sources in the initial stage, and possibly enhanced its elitist nature.

Support from the Rockefeller Foundation[10] and other sources was not in sight in 1924, and obtaining funding was an urgent issue for conference organizers. They needed to shape the project in such a way as to appeal to and be accepted by these respectable foundations and the academic establishment. The first major hope was the General Education Board in New York. In an application to the board in April 1924, Atherton, as a representative of the Honolulu group, described the project as a 'conference or institute closely resembling that of the Williamstown Institute of Politics, although it is narrower and more specific in its subject'. Although there were other well-known foreign affairs organizations in the United States, such as the CFR and the Foreign Policy Association (FPA), the IPW was a reasonable choice. It was a successful and well-recognized institution, and the only one that held annual international conferences. The Honolulu group argued that it would model itself after the IPW with a distinct regional focus: to solve racial conflict in the Pacific through free and frank discussion.[11]

Almost a week after Atherton's letter to the General Education Board, Johnston Ross, member of both the Honolulu group and the New York committee, met Harry Garfield, organizer of the IPW and President of Williams College, at the Century Club, New York. They were joined by Jay A. Urice, a YMCA officer in New York who worked closely with Davis. Garfield welcomed the outline of the proposed conference 'heartily', and was happy to give some tips. In his view the IPW's success could be attributed to the following four factors: finance, personnel, method and connections with the State Department.

Garfield emphasized the importance of a degree of 'academic freedom' and avoiding funds from too many sources, because they would dominate the direction of the enterprise. He also took great care 'to vary the viewpoints'. The methods of the IPW were the round table, a small group discussion led by an expert on a subject; the open round table; and public addresses on more general issues. To keep discussion open and to avoid misleading publicity, no resolutions were permitted. Garfield maintained that relations with the State Department had been cooperative. The Secretary of State, Charles Hughes, who led the Washington Conference, was enthusiastic. The Department lent maps, and staff attended the conferences unofficially. 'The State Department seemed ready to encourage such efforts as the Institute', he said.[12]

At the Century Club, Garfield introduced Urice and Ross to a person who was to become pivotal in defining the nature of the IPR – Raymond Fosdick, trustee of the Rockefeller Foundation. Urice and Ross tried to get Fosdick to participate in the conference and to advise them on their grant application.[13] A student of Garfield's at Princeton in the 1900s, and a supporter of Wilson's vision for the New Diplomacy and the League of Nations, Fosdick was Under-Secretary General at the League of Nations in 1919–20. He became a trustee (1921–36) and President (1936–48) of the Rockefeller Foundation. He was influential at the Foundation, and his support became crucial in the funding of IPR operations. The involvement of Fosdick in the IPR project started earlier than the lunch at the Century Club. Atherton had already approached him about applying to various foundations for grants, to which Fosdick replied sympathetically.[14]

Although doubtful about projects with a religious bias, Fosdick showed great interest in the idea of applying Christian principles to modern problems. The idea first came to his attention even earlier in 1922 when Edward Carter put forward his application for a project called the 'National Inquiry into the Christian Way of Life'. This came to be known as the Inquiry project, which lasted until 1932. This should not be confused with the Inquiry group organized by Edward House for the Paris Conference. Carter's project aimed to seek ways of applying Christianity to the modern problems of race, industrial and international relations through the conference method. By discussing different viewpoints, Carter believed, a solution to problems would emerge. The method was considered important in defining the format of IPR conferences.[15] Fosdick was impressed by the project and recommended generous funding.

> Personally, this is one of the most unique matters that has ever been brought to my attention. ... The question is constantly asked whether Christianity has any applicability to modern life. ... Of course the study is a venture ... but it is aimed at a real goal and it is in capable hands.[16]

Despite some reservations, Fosdick's sympathy towards the project and his faith in Carter's ability were apparent. With good funding, Carter ran the Inquiry from 129 East 52nd Street, an annex of the YMCA building at number 135, facing Lexington Avenue. It was to become the address of the ACIPR when he became Secretary in 1926, and later the International Secretariat of the IPR (ISIPR) after he was appointed as General Secretary in 1933. Carter maintained good relations with the senior staff of the Rockefeller Foundation, including Fosdick. Many of them were involved in other foundations and academic associations. This proved a great strength when Carter took charge of funding applications after 1926. The Honolulu office's lack of this ability later proved fatal.

Although the basic direction of the conference was shaped by mid-1924, a more definite step was taken in December. This coincided with the appointment of Merle Davis in November 1924 as organizer of both the conference and an American group of participants.[17] Reflecting the shift of emphasis of the proposed project, Davis possessed the attributes of being not only YMCA man, but also 'expert'. The son of an influential missionary family, he was born and grew up in Japan. There he worked for many years as General Secretary of the international YMCA before he became Director of the 'Survey of Race Relations: A Study of the Orientals on the Pacific Coast'. The project was organized in 1923 by the Institute of Social and Religious Research (located in New York) and based in San Francisco.[18] Ray Wilbur was Chairperson of the executive committee of this 'Survey'. Wilbur soon became a member of the New York committee for the proposed conference, and then was appointed as the first chairperson of the Pacific Council, the executive body of the IPR, after its first conference.

Despite his strong connections on the West coast, Davis decided that, as well as Honolulu, New York should be a pivotal point. In San Francisco, he wrote to Atherton that he would have to make New York his base for some time and that he would not head west before mid-February.[19] While keeping his job in San Francisco, Davis left for New York immediately after his appointment. He remained there until 18 December 1924, and returned to New York again on 5 January 1925. In New York, he was based at the International Committee of the YMCA at 347 Madison Avenue, and worked with its officers, including Urice. Davis was energetic and busy, as he needed to travel to many cities on the East coast and the major cities between New York and San Francisco.

The direction of the IPR project became clearer in Davis's letter to John D. Rockefeller Jr, dated 19 December 1924. Davis denied the central role of the YMCA and the Honolulu group. Instead, he emphasized the role of an international committee and the similarities between the IPW and the proposed conference. He argued that it would bring together 'men of the East and the West for a thorough discussion of racial problems'.[20] Was this new emphasis an initiative of Davis or the New York committee, and was it against the wishes of the Honolulu group? It is clear that Davis's primary loyalty and responsibility were to the Honolulu group. His letter to Atherton demonstrates his dilemma and uncertainty.

> It is somewhat difficult for me to know how far I can rightly and wisely assume responsibility and initiative. The New York Committee are leaving these to me as a representative of the Central Committee, and I am so far from you Hawaii leaders that one is in danger of going too far, or of not going far enough...[21]

Recall, however, that the Honolulu group had taken some steps in a similar direction. In early 1924 it decided to take the IPW as their project's model. The 'new direction' which Davis emphasized in the letter to J.D. Rockefeller Jr, therefore, cannot be seen as totally against Honolulu's wishes. There was a consensus among the organizers, including Davis and the Honolulu group. To secure funds and prominent participants for the conference, they needed to downplay the YMCA's influence and Christian image.

The advice of Raymond Fosdick and other figures in major foundations played a crucial role. There was no direct instruction or pressure from the Rockefeller Foundation or other foundations. Yet applicants could not ignore the views of influential trustees and advisers. Consequently, the applications to these foundations largely shaped the nature and direction of IPR operations. This informal and indirect influence occurred only because the early IPR organizers wanted the kind of prominence that the trustees considered worthwhile funding.

The failure of the application put by the Honolulu group to the General Education Board was a critical turning point. Urice and Davis heard the news on 10 December 1924. They needed to learn from this experience very quickly, and to secure other funding for the conference, which was planned for the following year. Fosdick, with insider knowledge of the board, explained the main reasons for the failure. First, an international conference was outside the board's interests. Second, Alexander Ford had given the board the impression that his Pan-Pacific Union was an advertising agency, and that the proposed conference was related to his projects. The third and 'probably the most important factor' was doubts about the YMCA's influence. It was felt that the YMCA might be promoting its own cause and that it was not a suitable convenor for such a gathering. In mid-December 1924, Davis needed to dissociate the proposed conference from the Pan-Pacific Union and to play down the role of the YMCA. To strengthen this non-religious, 'scientific' aspect, he formed an advisory board comprising various eminent specialists with no YMCA background.[22] This became a temporary executive committee (the New York committee). It was distinct from the central executive committee (the Honolulu group) and the central committee of international representatives. Whereas the last two were dominated by YMCA members, the New York committee consisted of 'experts' on Asia and race issues. As noted, the New York committee became central in organizing the Yale Club meeting.

Fosdick and the directors at the General Education Board were not alone in thinking that the project should not be built on the YMCA. Wilbur, Chairperson of the New York committee, also opposed 'any religious denominational influence' in the project. He had a strong faith in science, fact and rationality. Born into a pioneering family in the Midwest and brought up on the Californian frontier, he lectured and practised medicine before he became President of Stanford University (1916–43). He chaired the 'Survey of Race Relations'. The results of this 'scientific' research demonstrated the usefulness of Japanese agricultural labourers to the local economy and community. It also found a remarkable degree of Americanization among American-born Japanese and Chinese. Wilbur recorded that 'the survey was a new departure in American education' on race relations.[23] He argued for the importance of obtaining the 'truth' and 'facts', because, in his view, misunderstanding and ignorance were the cause of problems. For the American professional elite, like Wilbur, 'scientific' research was 'neutral', and very valuable, and Davis wanted to enlist these people for the conference.

Other advice came from the Rockefeller Foundation's Roger Greene, who also became a founding member of the IPR. Greene was born and raised in Japan in a Congregational missionary family. He was a diplomat before he took up a position at the Foundation in 1914. He was most active in its medical programme in China in 1914–35. His older brother, Jerome, was a Wall Street banker at Lee and Higginson Company. Jerome was involved in the formation of the IPR, and was to play a significant role, especially in 1929–32. Roger Greene advised Davis to diversify funding of the project beyond American sources. This, he argued, would help to emphasize the 'international' outlook of the project, and help in getting the Rockefeller grant. Rockefeller Jr would not support a project if his money constituted more than half of the finance of an enterprise. The suggestion led Davis and the New York committee to stress 'international' principles in the funding, organization and programme of the conference.[24] Wilbur agreed, insisting that no one country or religion should predominate.[25] The idea was supported at the Yale Club, and attempts were made to implement it.

The next crucial advice came from former American ambassador to Japan Roland Morris. Morris opposed public discussion of Asian immigration. He suggested to Davis that a preliminary American conference should be held, which became the Yale Club meeting. Atherton approved the idea, and John Mott strongly supported it. Mott felt that 'Morris presented a large challenge to their conference plan' and that the meeting would be a good chance to resolve the matter. Like Davis, Mott predicted that the meeting would define the nature of the planned project: if it went well, then the project would have more influence on public and official thinking and might even bring about a change in immigration legislation. If it did not, they could still hold a smaller-scale conference in Hawai'i.[26]

Morris represented the negative State Department attitude towards the proposed non-official conference. In their view, it could do more harm than good by re-igniting the debate over the so-called anti-Japanese immigration act. The State Department regarded the matter as closed. Assistant Secretary of State, John MacMurray, told Davis in January 1925 that while it was now 'far worse to attempt to stop' the conference, official cooperation, involvement and funding should not be sought. The conference was still of vital interest to the government:

> We cannot forget, and you should not forget, that the Government has a very great stake in how these matters are handled. … I would appreciate having reports sent me on the development of the conference plans.

MacMurray, however, gave positive suggestions: the conference should face up squarely to different opinions; it should choose anti-Asian immigration groups that would not embitter the discussion; and it should not overdo the publicity.[27]

The attitude of the State Department towards this conference was in sharp contrast to that towards the IPW. As Garfield detailed, the IPW enjoyed considerable support and patronage from the Department, and notable diplomats, mainly from Europe, participated along with non-official foreign experts. The IPR was not going to receive this support. This did not discourage an optimistic and confident Davis:

Mr Morris will be an able opponent but we will have present at the preliminary conference several men of equal ability like President Wilbur, Chester Rowell, Professor Wilson of Harvard and others who will put up a strong case for holding the Hawaii meeting.[28]

The conference would seek ways of dealing with the new powers in Asia.[29] Optimism and enthusiasm were to dominate the tone of the coming Yale Club meeting.

The Yale Club meeting

At the Yale Club, a morning session of core members was followed by a larger general meeting in the afternoon.[30] The morning session was attended by Davis, Wilbur, Urice, Speers, Blakeslee, Carter, Stanley Hornbeck (listed as 'Lecturer, Harvard University, and Expert on China, Washington, DC'), Archibald Coolidge of Harvard and Editor of *Foreign Affairs* (the journal of the CFR), Charles Batchelder, former Commissioner, Far Eastern Trade Bureau, and Galen Fisher, Executive Secretary of Social and Religious Research. Davis recorded that 'The morning meeting was very helpful in that it allowed the leaders to come to a uniform policy'.[31] The name Hornbeck should be noted here. Although many IPR founders saw the US–Japan relationship as the basis of the IPR, in the 1930s Hornbeck would emerge as one of the strongest advocates of sanctions against Japanese aggression in China within the State Department.

At two-thirty, the afternoon session started. The background of the participants is shown below:

Academics	15
Press: proprietors/journalists	10
Business	7
Officials	
Public service (4)	
Non-profit foundations (4)	
League of Nations (1)	9
Religious	
YMCA (5)	
Church (2)	7
Total[32]	51

Added to those who attended the morning session, participants in the afternoon session included James Shotwell of Columbia and George G. Wilson of Harvard, both of whom were experts in international relations, and Roland Morris, Sidney Gulick, John Mott and Henry Moore of the American Asiatic Association. They were male professionals all. The lack of women is conspicuous as women's groups were active in peace movements and enthusiastic about the proposed conference. Davis had appealed to women's associations, mainly female suffrage groups, to gather support.[33] They would become an important base for IPR activities, organizing public addresses and luncheons. Yet the meeting's venue suggests that women were not expected to be prominent among organizers or participants. Despite the substantial numbers of women at IPR conferences and the support of women's associations, they were not offered a role in terms of agendas and policy decisions. As a result, they began their own organizations in 1928 (see Chapter 5).

Representation of clergy and the YMCA was far weaker than in the original plan. This probably did not mean a diminished Christian influence. Those listed as other professionals may well have included those from missionary or church families. Similarly, law and medicine were not represented, although some may have had degrees in these fields. While political affiliation is hard to identify, Republicans were probably slightly more dominant at the ACIPR in the 1920s.[34]

Some prominent members of the Japanese American Relations Committee (JARC) attended the Yale Club meeting. Sidney Gulick (the Federal Council of Churches) was there but not George Wickersham or Henry Taft, both Republicans and former Attorneys General. Wickersham was a member of the CFR, but did not join the IPR. When he was approached by the ACIPR in late 1934, he was reluctant to join because of other commitments.[35] Although Gulick played no major role in the IPR in the following years, other JARC members, Frank Atherton, Chester Rowell and Wallace Alexander, Chairperson of the Chamber of Commerce at San Francisco, did. Probably because of distance, the only JARC member present at the Yale Club was Rowell.

Enthusiasm and optimism defined the meeting. Most of the participants were not leisured men but busy working professionals. To invest their time and money on Sundays, dinners at the clubs or meetings in business hours, and to take time off for travelling to conferences, they had to have a sense of duty, faith, conviction, energy and money. Excitement and enthusiasm were also crucial. Davis was most encouraged by the fact that so many notable figures shared this enthusiasm for the Honolulu project:

> Another impression was the amazing response of the greatest American experts in the different fields that we are proposing to discuss at Hawaii. … [W]ith the leadership and participation of such able men, we will be able to carry out to a successful finish a plan of large proportions.[36]

These participants felt that the proposed project was totally new, cultivating new attitudes towards the region and the state. They were advocating new relations with the new powers in Asia and a greater role for non-state agencies. While they were fascinated by the region, their enthusiasm was combined with the conviction that Americans needed an accurate knowledge of the powers in the region. The impact of immigration disputes over Japanese in California had been profound. The lesson they learned was that 'Orientals' understood Americans far more than Americans understood them.[37] At the Yale Club the view was strongly expressed. Ellsworth Huntington, professor of geography at Yale, for example, argued for the need for new attitudes towards 'Orientals':

> We have to get the Orientals to tell us what they think about us. The Orientals understand us a great deal better than we understand them. ... We have to go to the conference primarily to learn from the Orientals.

By 'Orient', Huntington meant the new powers in Asia, Japan and China. Korea was not mentioned as a possible member country at the Yale Club meeting. This is curious because Korea, along with the Philippines, had been included as a member of the proposed conference and institute. Soon after the meeting, Korea reappeared in the conference list, and a Korean group participated in the first IPR conference. There is no record explaining this temporary omission of Korea from the notes of the Yale Club meeting. It was not that the organizers regarded colonies as ineligible, for the Philippines was on the list. Japanese opposition to Korean participation is a likely reason. This may seem to be over-sensitivity towards Japanese concerns, especially as the meeting was a purely American gathering. Yet East coast 'foreign experts', who dominated this meeting, particularly those who were involved with the IPW, saw a good US–Japan relationship as fundamental to the success of the project. They opposed separate Korean participation because they felt that it might harm 'good' US–Japan relations.[38] Korea's omission may have reflected this view of organizers, such as George Blakeslee, who was very active at the IPW. Although a Korean group participated in IPR conferences in 1925 and 1927, the issue of their legitimacy lingered, and eventually led to Korea's withdrawal, to be elaborated in Chapter 5.

As well as their attitude to the new powers in Asia, the participants at the Yale Club strongly argued for non-governmental status of the conference. A cynic could point out that they had little choice. The State Department had expressed its negative view, and no assistance or cooperation could be expected. Nevertheless, the support for a non-official approach at the Yale Club was not defensive. It was very positive and enthusiastic, which was characteristic of American IPR founders. This stance towards the state can be contrasted with the view of IPR members in Britain, the Dominions and Japan as well as American IPR members in the 1930s and 1940s.

It is, however, misleading to overemphasize the difference between New Liberal post-League internationalists in the British Commonwealth and American post-League internationalists. First, the latter's enthusiasm for non-governmentality did not mean that they were challenging the nation-state framework or the authority of the state. Non-governmentality was considered valuable for state-to-state relations, not for advancement of universalist causes. Wilbur noted: 'if [the proposed non-official gathering] does not go well, we will take blame, but if it goes well, then the government will be glad'. The presence of prominent political figures who could stand strong 'against' the state, such as Wilbur, explains the IPR founders' confidence in 'non-governmentality'.[39] Wilbur's strength rested not so much upon his advocacy challenging the state, as upon his central position in Republican political circles. Soon he would serve as Secretary of the Interior in the administration of Hoover, his personal friend.

With the exception of Morris and John Abbott, Vice-President of the Continental and Commercial Bank of Chicago, a majority at the Yale Club meeting supported non-governmentality. Non-official professionals, especially academics, thought that their contribution to the society and the state – enlightening public opinion and policy-making – would be valuable to the government. This was a point Shotwell of Columbia University expressed when he was working for the 'Inquiry' project in 1917–19. They also thought the conference would be more effective because participants would be able to talk more openly. Huntington, for example, stated that his experience at the Pan-Pacific Science Conference in Australia in 1923 taught him that less official intervention would promote more and better discussion. Philip Brown, professor of international law at Princeton, also opposed official involvement: 'intelligent and democratic society would make progress on a spirit of liberality and a Christian spirit'. This optimism was further strengthened by their faith in 'science'. As Wilbur noted, they believed that 'scientific' research would discover the 'truth' and solve the problem.

To ensure unofficial status and protect speakers' freedom, they suggested that the conference avoid resolutions, political issues and excessive publicity. Yet, while they were wary of a jingoistic press, they took a more open attitude to publicity than British organizations, such as the Round Table and the RIIA, which were very strict about not revealing who said what in their meetings. This cautious attitude could easily have led to *elitism*. From its very beginnings, the IPR was concerned only with national elites. The aim of the conference was to provide these public opinion leaders with the 'facts'. It was a Platonic attitude of wise men's rule – 'knowledgable experts educating the ignorant masses' – common in foreign affairs experts' organizations. Nonetheless, participants believed that people would do the 'right' thing if they had the 'right' information. The masses were not there to be manipulated, but to be trusted as long as they benefited from good guidance. The proposed project was regarded as significant in fostering the 'right' public opinion. It would influence policy-making in the long run, rather than being closely involved in policy formulation.

The Yale Club meeting defined the nature of the IPR. It decided that the conference should not be one isolated event, and that they should aim to found a permanent institute to hold conferences periodically. Its aim was an international non-governmental organization of regional experts to influence public opinion and, indirectly, policy-making. It was funded by American philanthropic and big business money, and initiated by Americans. As we shall see, the trends and directions within IPR operations which became stronger in the 1930s were present in this initial formulation. They coexisted with other conflicting factors, and took little encouragement to come to the fore.

The IPR's Pacific Community represented the enthusiasm, hope and desire of these American post-League internationalists. Not having soiled its hands with old imperialism and free from European politics, they had a sense of mission and confidence to lead the new order with new attitudes towards the state and towards the new powers in the region.

4 The Japanese Council of the IPR in the 1920s

What did the post-League international order mean to Japan in the 1920s, and what were the implications of the IPR's Pacific Community or the American-led regional order? Who joined the Japanese Council of the IPR (JCIPR), and what role did they play in regional and domestic politics? This chapter demonstrates that JCIPR members supported the post-League order and the American-led regional order in the 1920s. Their view would become more critical in the 1930s, leading some members to advocate an alternative regional vision, the New Order in East Asia. This changing view was closely related to their growing reformist inclinations – New Liberalism in the 1920s, and statist reformism (*kakushin shugi*) in the 1930s. Like their counterparts in the United States and other countries, JCIPR members were not opposed to the state or the empire even in the 1920s. This was reflected in their two key roles as non-official post-League internationalists – international publicists and think-tank members. Their cooperative relationship with the state was accentuated in the 1930s, and their significance would increase especially after the outbreak of the Sino-Japanese War in 1937.

Supporting the dominant international order: the Versailles–Washington system

How Japanese diplomatic circles and foreign experts regarded the IPR's Pacific Community or American-led regional order depended on their views about American leadership in international politics. It is indicative that those who I term post-League internationalists in Japan were commonly referred to as the pro-Anglo-American faction (*eibeiha*) or liberal internationalists (*jiyū kokusai shugisha*). This suggests that their contemporaries understood that the international order was dominated by the United States and Britain. Accordingly, most Japanese scholars see the post-League international order as synonymous with the League of Nations and the Washington Treaties of 1922 and call it the Versailles–Washington system. This post-League order was not only understood to be dominant – it had also been endorsed by the Japanese government since its inception. In 1918 Hara Kei (Prime Minister from 1918 to 1921), one of the first strong party politicians, overcame formidable opposition within the political elite, and defined diplomatic orthodoxy for successive party-dominated governments: 'cooperation with the great powers' (*kyōchō gaikō*).[1] The policy was clearly indicated in the government's instruction to the Japanese delegation to the Paris Conference:

> although Japan should demand the rewards for its contribution during the war, it should avoid isolation from the other powers, especially Britain.[2]

At the same time, in order to promote this policy and adjust the increased bureaucratic demands flowing from the establishment of the League of Nations, Hara tried to strengthen the role and power of the Ministry of Foreign Affairs. As a result, the Ministry was expanded, and many new staff recruited. Non-official Japanese post-League internationalists ('liberal' internationalists or pro-Anglo-American faction) were aligned with government policies and what they regarded as the dominant order. They were not opposed to the state/empire, and they shared much with the young career diplomats at the Ministry, who were also called 'liberal' internationalists.

Some argue that the interpretation of the post-League order varied among those official and unofficial post-League internationalists. The dividing point was how they regarded American leadership in the post-League order. Many diplomats, including Yoshida Shigeru, were sceptical about American leadership in world politics and Wilsonian initiatives, especially the proposed 'New Diplomacy'. For them, Britain, which had been a 'traditional' and important ally since 1902, remained the most dominant power. International politics was centred in Europe, particularly London. For them, the post-League order still operated within the framework of the 'old' *Realpolitik* of secret treaties and bilateral dealings of the empires/great powers.[3] The above government instruction for the Paris Conference demonstrates the point. This cynical and negative view of the 'New Diplomacy' was dominant in political and diplomatic circles.[4]

According to scholars who emphasize this internal division among post-League internationalists, Shidehara Kijūrō (Foreign Minister in 1924–5, 1926, 1929–30 and 1931, and Prime Minister in 1945–6) belonged to a pro-American faction. He saw the United States as a new, but significant power, and was more ready to accept American leadership than some of his colleagues in the Ministry of Foreign Affairs. The views of JCIPR members were very similar to Shidehara's in the 1920s. Shidehara led the Japanese delegation at the Washington Conference of 1921–2, which can be summarized as a defining exercise of the US-led regional order. Asada sees Shidehara's leadership as the starting point of the Japanese New Diplomacy.[5]

It is important not to underestimate the significance of Shidehara's new initiative and the formidable opposition he had to face. He was positive about American initiatives, committed to peaceful means and the 'New Diplomacy' in a hostile domestic environment. Although the Nine Power Treaty on China (concluded at the Washington Conference) reconfirmed the principle of the Open Door policy and equal opportunity among the powers in China, Shidehara's insistence on respecting China's sovereignty was noteworthy. He maintained this non-intervention principle in Chinese affairs in very difficult circumstances.[6]

Yet too much emphasis on the distinction between Shidehara or the pro-American faction and pro-British faction can be misleading. It misses the point of the post-League order and Japanese cooperative diplomacy. First, the dominance of a cynical view of 'New Diplomacy' and American leadership in political and diplomatic circles did not equate to a lack of support for the League. Like the US Congress, Japanese officials saw the League as dominated by European powers but, unlike Congress, they supported the League for the same reason as their European counterparts. This support was not so much a demonstration of their commitment to international justice as of their concern with Japanese sovereignty and imperial interests. For them, the League was an institution to guarantee and protect them.

The foreign policies of Tanaka Giichi (Prime Minister and Foreign Minister in 1927–9) can be understood in this light. Tanaka sent troops to China in 1927 and 1928, an action which was labelled as 'nationalist' and 'reactionary' *Seiyūkai* policy, as against Shidehara's 'internationalist' and 'liberal' *Minseitō* policy.[7] Yet the same Tanaka cabinet signed the Pact of Paris in 1928, renouncing war as a means of solving international disputes. Scholars who emphasize the difference between pro-American and pro-British factions hold that Tanaka was pro-British and adopted the old *Realpolitik* approach, whereas Shidehara was pro-American and adopted the New Diplomacy.[8] It could be said, however, that Tanaka was keen to cooperate with the great powers, but, like other powers, he was committed to the protection and advancement of national/imperial interests in China.[9]

Second, although those who were sceptical of American leadership tended to distinguish themselves from the pro-American faction, this distinction was very weak for those who accepted American leadership more readily. Like it or not, by 1921 even sceptics had to admit that the United States was a leading power, especially in the Pacific, and had to accept the Washington Treaties.[10] After all, the Anglo-Japanese alliance had been replaced by the Four Power Treaty. At the same time, despite his faith in the principles of the New Diplomacy, Shidehara as well as his American counterparts could not ignore or dismiss *Realpolitik* elements in negotiating diplomatic deals with the powers. His cooperative policy with the powers was a 'compromise', like most diplomatic negotiations.

Third, the Washington Treaties, which Shidehara negotiated, also reflected the contradictions inherent in the post-League order and Japanese cooperative policy.[11] Colonies did not have the right to be part of the international community or to conduct the New Diplomacy. According to one leading Japanese internationalist, China also had too 'little self-governing power to take an active part in this community'.[12] It was not regarded as an equal player and did not sign the Nine Power Treaty. Rather, the treaty, which was seen a starting point of New Diplomacy, was an agreement for the empires to have fair shares in China. Nor did Shidehara deny the importance of Japanese national polity (*kokutai*), the fundamental base of the nation/empire, often identified with the emperor system. Like post-League internationalists in other countries, he did not deny Japan's national/imperial interests in China, but argued for pursuing them through economic and cooperative means.[13] In the 1920s, official and non-official post-League internationalists alike understood the post-League order as the Versailles–Washington system, and accepted American power and its leadership, particularly in the Pacific region. The Washington Treaties, especially the Nine Power Treaty on China, were regarded as a dominant framework of the order, at least until the mid-1930s.

Challenge to the post-League order: Konoe's thesis of 1918

Konoe Fumimaro articulated a position critical to what was to become the post-League order in his thesis of 1918. A brief analysis of this position is important before we move on to an examination of the implications of the IPR's Pacific Community in Japan and the nature of the JCIPR in the 1920s. It is not only that his view was shared by many bureaucrats, military cliques, politicians, intellectuals and ordinary people in Japan who were opposed to the post-League order; rather, it is because Konoe held a key to understanding JCIPR members' relations with the state and their views about the region. First, as a member of the national/imperial elite, Konoe belonged to a milieu similar to the post-League internationalists. Through common education they shared close social ties, ideas, culture and a sense of the political and intellectual dynamics of the time. Second, Konoe's vision for the international order, which he clarified in 1918 and advanced in the 1930s, was to become dominant among JCIPR members in the 1930s. Third, he saw the significance of two functions of post-League internationalists – as non-official international publicists and as experts on international affairs – and promoted their co-option into the state apparatus.

Konoe's thesis of 1918 is often regarded as a blueprint for the declaration of the New Order in East Asia (*Tōa shin chitsujo*), which he issued in 1938 (during the term of his first cabinet). This New Order is linked to the ensuing vision of the Greater East Asia Co-prosperity Sphere. Yet his thesis of 1918 could be also viewed as an expression of his hopes for Wilsonian principles. Konoe thought that they were far from being realized, but had in fact been *compromised* at the Paris Conference. His thesis reflected strong reformist thinking. Although born into a family closely related to the emperor, Konoe became critical of Japanese social structure around the time of his father's death in 1904.[14] He did not proceed to *Gakushūin* high school – the expected path for boys of aristocratic and imperial backgrounds. Instead, he took a competitive examination and was accepted by *Ichikō* (First High School). *Ichikō* was the most prestigious public high school, and there he discussed the latest social theories, literature and religion with the best, brightest and most fortunate. By the 1880s, *Ichikō* had become the preparatory school for Tokyo Imperial University. These two institutions jointly produced the national/ imperial elite, and implanted a sense of mission as members of the future leaders of Japan.[15] Konoe did not need to seek an official career, and unlike his classmates who went on to Tokyo Imperial University, he transferred to Kyoto Imperial University. There, he studied with Kawakami Hajime, a socialist economist, and Nishida Kitarō, a philosopher famous for his work *The Study of Good* (1911). Konoe was attracted to socialism – not Marxism but the socialism of Oscar Wilde. In 1914, while still at university, he translated Wilde's *The Soul of Man under Socialism*. Two issues of the journal *Shin shichō* (New Thoughts)[16] which carried this translation were banned. Although Konoe may be more appropriately described as a counter-socialist than a socialist,[17] he lived in a time when socialism captivated idealistic young minds.

This critical view of society, beginning in his childhood and nurtured during his student days, defined his world view. Before leaving for the Paris Conference as a junior member of the delegation (he was twenty-eight years old and serving an internship at the Ministry of Home Affairs), his article, 'Eibei hon'i no heiwa shugi o haisu' (Denounce pacifism which favours Britain and the United States) was published in *Nihon oyobi Nihon jin* (Japan and Japanese) in December 1918. He wrote:

> Democracy and humanitarianism are based on a sense of equality among people. This is represented domestically by the call for democratic rights [*minken jiyū ron*] and internationally, by insistence on equal living rights [*seizon ken*] among nations. ... The pacifism of Britain and the United States is a convenient peace-at-any-price principle for those who want to preserve the status quo and it has nothing to do with social justice. If Japanese intellectuals were conscious of social justice and Japan's position, they should be challenging this status quo. Instead, being indulged by beautiful words and influenced by pacifism which is convenient for Britain and the United States, they desire the League of Nations as if it were a preordained gospel. This attitude is very servile and should be denounced from the perspective of social justice. ... At the coming Peace Conference, Japan should join the League, but it should insist on the exclusion of economic imperialism and discriminatory treatment between white and yellow races. It is not only militarism which harms social justice...[18]

He still hoped that the League would achieve economic and racial equality. At Versailles, however, he was quickly disillusioned.[19] Konoe criticized the League not because he supported *Realpolitik*, but because the post-League order did not realize its potential. His faith in the significance of Wilson's vision did not seem to have waned. He committed himself to advocating what the League should have been. Soon after the formation of *Kokusai renmei kyōkai* (the League of Nations Association or LNA) in 1920, the Japanese branch of an international organization headquartered in Brussels, he became a member of its council. He urged the public to study world affairs, and criticized fanatical patriotism and militarism.[20] Konoe shared many ideas with post-League internationalists in Britain and the United States. He felt the need to reform diplomatic machinery and to recruit experts from outside the Ministry of Foreign Affairs – talent from military, business, the press and academia.[21] Like his Anglo-American counterparts, he also noted the importance of public opinion and the media in foreign policy-making. Accordingly, he argued for the establishment of a propaganda organization and a strong national agency for reporting overseas news to Japan and Japanese news overseas. He implemented these ideas later in organizations such as *Dōmei tsūshin* (national propaganda and news agency) and *Showaū kenkyūkai*, his think-tank. Younger JCIPR members, mostly graduates of *Ichikō* and the Tokyo Imperial University, shared Konoe's views and played a central role in these organizations.

Despite all these 'post-League internationalist' elements, Konoe's thesis has been understood as an expression of Asianism, a contending regional vision against the post-League order.[22] There is good ground for this argument. Although his father, Konoe Atsumaro (1863–1904), died when Konoe was only thirteen, his Asianism seems to have had a profound influence on Konoe. Atsumaro was an advocate of Asian solidarity, especially the Sino-Japanese alliance against the 'Western' powers from the late 1890s. In 1898, Atsumaro founded *Tōa dōbunkai* (East Asia Common Culture Association) (1898–1945). Konoe was committed to this organization. He became its vice-chairperson in 1922.[23] It is not, however, clear whether Konoe saw China as an equal partner. Sun Zhongshan (Sun Yat-sen), advocate of Great Asianism and Asian solidarity against the 'Western' powers, read Konoe's thesis with great interest and they met and exchanged views on Konoe's way to the Paris Conference.[24] Yet Konoe did not argue for Asian solidarity against the 'West' in 1918. 'Race' or 'culture', often seen as key factors to unite Asia, were not his central concern. Rather, the thesis focused on economic and structural inequality among independent nations, which he saw as the basis of racial inequality. Here Japan had more in common with latecomer European countries, such as Germany, than with China or colonies in Asia. Interestingly, this focus on structure, not 'culture' or 'civilization', was also evident in E.H. Carr's criticism of the post-League order.[25]

Can we call Konoe's thesis of 1918 an expression of Wilsonian ideals? It is perhaps more useful to view Konoe as sharing ideas with Wilson and his supporters. His notions were as circumscribed as those of Wilson and the post-League internationalists. Konoe's thesis did not go far enough to challenge the fundamentals of the post-League order. Equal rights, which he argued for independent nation-states, great or small, were not extended to colonies. These were the precise limitations of Wilson's vision and the post-League order. Konoe and the Japanese post-League internationalists demanded equal status for Japan with the Euro-American powers. The stronger their desire, the more contemptuous they tended to be of the colonies in Asia and even of China. With few exceptions, this desire was strong among elite groups – military officers and post-League internationalists alike.

American regional order and the JCIPR

The Pacific and the United States

JCIPR members belonged to the mainstream of post-League internationalism. First, the Pacific was the central concern of post-League internationalists in Japan. This was not the case in the United States and the British Commonwealth. There, the main focus was on European affairs. Even in the United States, where there was a consensus that American leadership should be exercised in the Pacific, IPR members belonged to a minority who were interested in and concerned with the Pacific region. Most were interested in European or Latin American affairs. Second, American leadership in international politics, particularly in the Pacific, was well accepted in Japan by the 1920s. The IPR's Pacific Community, or American-led regional order, was largely welcomed by Japanese post-League internationalists. This reaction was not typical. In Australia the IPR's concept of the Pacific was regarded as a challenge to the British imperial order. Although the British empire had a great presence in the region, faced with the emerging new power of Japan in Australia, there was a sense of insecurity about its defence capabilities, economic competence and the preservation of its 'Anglo' stock. This sense was furthered by the shift in British defence focus away from the Pacific in the face of another growing power, Germany. Most Australian post-League internationalists saw the new American regional order as another threat to the imperial order. Australian IPR members who argued for a new and more independent Australia and a region-centred view belonged to a very small minority.[26]

As had been clear at the Paris Peace Conference, non-Euro-American powers posed problems for the post-League order, and this was particularly the case in the Pacific. Understandably, many Japanese were critical of the post-League order. Japanese post-League internationalists could not dismiss this problem. Their concerns were often expressed as a criticism of the Eurocentricity of the League and its neglect of the Pacific. In 1926, leading internationalist and JCIPR member Kanzaki Kiichi pointed out this Eurocentricity. Inoue Junnosuke (1867–1932, General Director of the Bank of Japan in 1919–23 and 1927–8, Minister of Finance in 1923 and from 1929 to 1931, and Chairperson of the JCIPR from 1926 to 1929) also questioned whether the League was relevant outside Europe.[27] Similarly, Shibusawa Eiichi (1840–1931), a philanthropist, business leader and a patron of the IPR, argued the need to pay more attention to the Pacific.

While things are stabilized in Europe partly due to the League of Nations, what about the Pacific? The attention of the world has moved eastward. It seems the future issue lies in the Pacific. Japan, as the major empire in the East, should take it seriously that urgent matters have now shifted to the East.[28]

The Pacific mainly meant the United States and Japan's relations with it. Not all welcomed this new great power in the region. The issue of immigration was unresolved, and the American navy was growing in strength. The Washington Conference promoted a Republican regional vision. It emphasized cooperative relations with Japan in a multilateral framework, and Japan was elevated to the position of important 'partner'. This confidence building, however, largely collapsed when Congress passed the anti-Japanese immigration law. Opposition to the cooperative policy ambushed this opportunity, and criticism of both the post-League order and the American regional order grew in Japan.

At this critical point, non-official American post-League internationalists, who had a strong concern with the region, attempted to pursue what the Washington Conference could have achieved, the Pacific Community and a more equal relationship between the United States and Japan. The IPR was their answer. The JCIPR responded to this call enthusiastically. They were pro-American, and strong backers of Shidehara's cooperative foreign policy. For them, the Pacific Community represented a new era and new conduct. In 1928 Saitō Sōichi (1886–1960), Secretary of the Tokyo YMCA and council member of the JCIPR, thought the IPR symbolized 'The Arrival of the Pacific Age':

Once there was an age when the world centred around the Mediterranean, and then came an age of the Atlantic. ... But from now on, the world will be centred around the Pacific.

Saitō's notion of the Pacific Age was inspired not by Japanese thinkers, but by John Hay, Roosevelt's Secretary of State. It was nonetheless a reworking of the post-Washington Conference. Not the American hegemony, but the US–Japan partnership was the core of this new era.[29] JCIPR members regarded the Japanese empire as a Pacific power. Sawayanagi Masatarō (1865–1927), another JCIPR member who led the Japanese group at the IPR conferences in 1925 and 1927, noted:

The Pacific Ocean is gradually becoming the centre of the world, and Japan is firmly lodged in the thinking of internationally minded people as one of the important Pacific Powers. As such, Japan's future is inseparably linked with the slowly unfolding destiny of the great Pacific area.[30]

They considered it crucial to cooperate with other powers, especially the United States, and to fulfil their duty in maintaining the international and regional order. While accepting American leadership, they saw the Pacific Community as a US–Japan joint regional order.

How Japan, the first non-Euro-American power in the twentieth century, would fit in with the other powers was ambiguous. Since the Meiji Restoration the national elite had wanted to be a part of the powers, the 'West' (*Seiyō*). They looked to their advanced technology and economy, and their political and social systems. The 'West' represented a model to catch up with. By contrast, 'Asia' was ruled by the powers, and represented 'the past' and 'backwardness'. Zumoto Motosada (1862–1943), propietor/journalist of the *Herald of Asia*, an influential journalist and JCIPR member, identified 'Japan' strongly with the 'world', by which he meant the 'West'. Yet, in his view, Japan did not fit in the 'West' naturally, and extra effort was needed. For Zumoto, Japan assumed the martyr-like duty of harmonizer between 'East' and 'West'.[31] Similar sentiments of sacrifice and duty had been expressed at the conclusion of the Anglo-Japanese Treaty and the Versailles Treaty.[32]

In the 1920s, most JCIPR members understood that an alternative regional vision, Pan-Asianism or Asianism, represented a challenge to the Pacific Community and the cooperative relationship between the United States and Japan. The Pan-Asiatic Congress, which took place at Nagasaki in August 1926, was a part of these Asianist movements. Its resolutions challenged the European colonial status quo: improvement in the conditions of Asian races under colonial rule; abolition of unequal treaties; the revival of Asian spiritual and material civilizations; alliance of Asian races in the domains of culture, politics and economy; and promotion of Asian products and industries.[33] They saw 'Western' dominance as a temporary phenomenon, and wanted to regain past glory. Unlike dominant Japanese Asianism, which emphasized Japanese leadership over the 'rest' of Asia,[34] these resolutions argued for equal comradeship among the countries in Asia.

In contrast, JCIPR members thought that the Pacific Community accommodated non-Euro-American powers, and provided a solution to the biggest problem of the post-League order – Japanese inequality with other powers. They did not question Japan's status as an imperial power in Asia. Like 'liberal' imperialists at the Round Table and the RIIA in Britain, they advocated the need for 'enlightened' imperial rule in the colonies to strengthen the imperial order. In 1919, Sakatani Yoshirō (1863–1941), son-in-law of Shibusawa, a member of the House of Peers and later a JCIPR member, proposed a reform of Japanese military rule in Korea. In his letter to the Governor-General in Korea he argued the importance of respecting Korea's culture and language, allowing more opportunity for Koreans to fill positions in the administration.[35] Other JCIPR members, such as Sawayanagi, argued for an assimilation policy.[36] Comparatively speaking, Sakatani was very sympathetic to 'locals'. Yet, the object of this moderate policy was to appease the independence movement in Korea, which he saw as of crucial strategic importance for future imperial development.[37] Sakatani and Sawayanagi differed only in manner, not in essence, from the militarists they criticized.

In the 1920s, JCIPR members felt that Japan should cooperate with the United States and contribute to this new regional order as a Pacific power. Accordingly, they distanced themselves from 'Asia'. Zumoto, for example, dismissed its significance, describing Asianists as 'radicals' and 'adventurers'.[38] JCIPR members also felt that the promotion of Asianism (led by Japan or not) would damage the image of a democratic, peaceful and civilized 'Japan', and stressed its harmonious attitude towards other powers.

Despite this, the JCIPR initially attracted Asianist groups. Merle Davis, the first General Secretary of the International Secretariat of the IPR (ISIPR), attended the ceremony at the formation of the JCIPR on 6 April 1926. He noted that 'reactionary members such as the head of Black Dragon Society, Uchida Ryōhei, and Editor of *Kokumin* (A Nation), Tokutomi (Iichirō) were involved in the formation of the JCIPR in 1926'.[39] The Black Dragon Society refers to *Kokuryūkai* or the Amur Society (1901–45), an expansionist Asianist group. Sabey and Norman differ sharply in their evaluations of its significance in the 1920s.[40] The influence and activities of these Asianists were negligible at the JCIPR. Yet their presence indicates an overlap between two organizations, which were often located at opposite ends of the spectrum. Neither Asianists nor JCIPR members denied Japanese imperial status in the region, and Asianist sentiment was not totally absent among JCIPR members.[41] Zumoto himself was to display this at the Kyoto IPR conference in 1929. The IPR's Pacific was a synthesis of 'Asian' and 'non-Asian' elements. The presence of Asianists implied contentious regional visions for the Pacific at the JCIPR, symbolically foreshadowing future problems with the ISIPR.

In the 1920s, however, the JCIPR enthusiastically promoted cooperation with the great powers, especially the United States. Another reason for its strong support was its pro-American tendencies. Many JCIPR members were attracted to what the United States represented. For them, it was a dominant power, and the ideal embodiment of democracy. Nitobe Inazō, who was to become chairperson of the JCIPR in 1929, studied at Johns Hopkins University in 1884–6, and was one of the first to predict the dominance of the United States in international politics as early as in 1904.[42] This was not a common view in Japan at the time. He became a pioneer of American studies in Japan.[43] He wrote *Heimindō* (1919), a commoners' version of his earlier work, *Bushidō*. Whereas the latter discussed Japanese moral codes for warrior classes (*bushi*), equivalent to chivalry in Europe, the former extended this virtue to commoners, and discussed the Japanese style of citizenship and democracy. He cultivated pro-US attitudes among younger JCIPR members. Takaki Yasaka[44] (1889–1984) was Nitobe's student at *Ichikō*, and became an active JCIPR member. He was another pioneer of American studies in Japan (professor of American studies at Tokyo Imperial University). Like Nitobe,

Takaki saw the United States as an ideal democracy; adapting its democracy to Japan was his major interest.[15]

Expecting a negative view of the United States after the immigration act, in 1926 Merle Davis was pleasantly surprised to see the strong faith in the United States among the founders of the JCIPR:

> I was impressed with the faith in the goodwill and justice of the United States to which many of the Japanese leaders still cling. America was the source of their idealism, and to her they still feel that they owe their training, their point of view and much of their culture. America had been for many years a 'Star of Hope' to these men.[16]

This explains why they took the American anti-Japanese Immigration Act of 1924 so seriously. The law betrayed their ideals and expectations of the United States, and their ' "Star of Hope" was totally extinguished by the Exclusion Act'.[17] Those who were to become JCIPR members opposed the law publicly.[18] They were severely let down. Nitobe decided not to go to the United States until the law was repealed, and Shibusawa expressed his profound disappointment to American members of the JARC at the Pan Pacific Club in Tokyo.[19]

It is significant that the JCIPR was established after this incident, and that its members still strongly supported the American-led regional order. Why did this disillusionment not lead JCIPR members to question the IPR's Pacific Community? Did this incident make them realize the problem of Japanese policies towards Korea and China? Takaki's view is illuminating. He saw a great opportunity in the IPR to 'correct' the 'wrongs' of the United States.[50] In this process of rationalization – convincing themselves of the importance of the IPR even after the 'betrayal' of their 'Star of Hope' – the concept of the reified nation played a crucial role. They thought that there was still a possibility of the law being repealed if Americans understood the situation *correctly*. It was not the *real* United States that had passed the law. Shibusawa told Davis:

> We owe too much to America, we honour her and love her too much to strike back. ... The America that we know has not acted. It is another America, not the real America. We must be patient and give our friend time to reassert her best self and make right in her own time and her own way what seems to us to be an unjust and unreasonable act.[51]

The reified nation is inherently monolithic and dismisses diversity and tensions between state policies and the views of various social groups. Shibusawa's America probably consisted of the pro-Japan business people, diplomats and intellectuals with whom he dealt. They were most likely upper-middle-class white Anglo-Saxon Protestant men. The same was no doubt true for many JCIPR members. They probably had met few new immigrants, Afro-

Americans, indigenous, rural or working-class Americans.[52] They wanted to re-establish a cooperative and equal relationship with their America, and for them the IPR's Pacific was an excellent synthesis.

Supporting the dominant domestic order: the JCIPR in the 1920s

The JCIPR supported the post-League order and government foreign policy, and its members belonged to the mainstream of post-League internationalists in this period. In the domestic context, it consisted of the national elite, mainly based in Tokyo. Merle Davis proudly and happily recorded this national elite characteristic of the newly formed JCIPR in April 1926. For Davis it was not a concern, but a very positive achievement.[53] The membership of the JCIPR in 1927 demonstrates a very similar character. There were thirteen executive members, forty-five council members (three of whom were also executive members) and forty members.[54] Although distinctions and rivalries between major regional branches were strong in Australia and the United States,[55] Tokyo dominated the JCIPR, suggesting the existence of a more centralized national elite. Officials were also included in this list. Of the ninety-five members, twelve were members of the House of Peers and two were members of the House of Representatives. There were four military officers. One of them was Nomura Kichijirō, who was to play a key role in the last-minute negotiation with the United States just before the outbreak of the Pacific War. Matsuoka Yōsuke, who participated at the Paris Conference as a diplomat, was to become a JCIPR member in 1929, but was not included in the 1927 list. He was still in Manchuria with the South Manchurian Railway Company.

Academics, businessmen and other professionals dominated the JCIPR. Nineteen were university professors, of whom twelve were from Tokyo Imperial University and three from Waseda University. Four journalists/newspaper proprietors were on the list. Well-known experts on foreign affairs and internationalists, such as Yamada Sanzō, Kanzaki Kiichi and Kiyozawa Kiyoshi, were also listed. Business was by far the most dominant category, with thirty-six members (five were also members of the House of Peers). Big business – Mitsui, Mitsubishi, Sumitomo, Asano – and big banking and insurance companies were well represented. There were only two labour representatives, Suzuki Bunji, honorary chairperson of the *Nihon rōdō sōdōmei* (Japan General Federation of Labour), and Maeda Tamon (1884–1962), Japan's representative at the ILO. Suzuki represented a middle-of-the-road labour faction, and Maeda was a governmental representative of 'labour' interests.[56]

Like many post-League internationalists in other countries, JCIPR members were professionals, not necessarily hereditary members of the upper strata of society. They had achieved influential positions mainly through education, qualifications and professional activities. Most of them were graduates of *Ichikō* and Tokyo Imperial University. According to Roden, prestigious high schools drew students from 'a wider spectrum of the rural and urban middle classes', although they were 'beyond the reach of working-class families'.[57] Money or background alone did not guarantee an elite education. The entrance examination was competitive, and there were many drop-outs. *Ichikō* was most important in the intellectual and social backgrounds of JCIPR members. The younger generation of the JCIPR was almost exclusively a product of this institution.

Although businessmen did not play a significant role in the activities of the JCIPR, their dominance reflected big business support for the cooperative foreign policy. They favoured the Republican vision of the American regional order based on a good US–Japan economic relationship. From this flowed support for the IPR's Pacific Community. Chambers of Commerce, the Banking Club and the Industrial Club supported the JCIPR financially, and hosted its addresses and lectures, as they did for other internationalist organizations. Their support did not wane greatly, even in the late 1930s.

Shibusawa Eiichi fostered close ties among business circles, the JCIPR and the state. He engaged in the philanthropic activities after his retirement in 1909 (he was then 69). Inspired by the Carnegie Endowment for International Peace, in 1912 he began to give his support to the first internationalist organization in Japan, the Greater Japan Peace Association or GJPA (*Dai Nihon heiwa kyōkai*) (founded in 1906).[58] He remained a vocal and influential financial backer of internationalism until his death in 1931. Shibusawa emphasized business interests, but he also argued that business people have a duty to serve the public and the nation/state/empire as well as the world. This might have been a result of his former career as a bureaucrat in the Tokugawa *bakufu* and the Meiji government. Or it could have been due to his great concern with the promotion of a higher status for business, whose position had been low in the Tokugawa period. He worked hard promoting the professionalization of business community. When Chambers of Commerce were created, he became the first chairperson of the Tokyo chamber (founded in 1891).[59] He stressed that business people should contribute to public profit (*kōeki*), and not just pursue personal profit. He saw peace as necessary for business. His speech, 'Peace from the point of view of the business world', at a meeting of the GJPA in June 1912 linked business morality to peace. He refuted the argument that war made business prosper. Business needed international morality.[60] Good will and high ethical standards would bring peace. For him, international morality was an extension of 'public service' to the state into the 'international community'. They were compatible goals.

The strength of Christian circles (North American missionaries and Japanese Christians) was a feature of Japanese internationalist organizations from their inception. Euro-American orientation had been strong among a small but influential elite since the Meiji era. Friendship societies with European and North American diplomats, missionaries, business people and educationalists made up an important institutional base of the internationalist movement. North Americans and concern with the US–Japan relationship, however, had always been more dominant among Japanese internationalists than Europeans or European affairs. This was partially due to geographical proximity. It was also due to the strength of American and Canadian missionaries in the Meiji era, and the importance that they attached to peace.[61] The GJPA, for example, was initiated by an American missionary, Gilbert Bowles, and a good number of foreigners (84) was included among its 562 members in 1912.[62] Christian organizations such as the YMCA, in which the influence of North American missionaries was dominant, gained social acceptance and respectability, and were central in internationalist movements.

Although containing some Christian members, the JCIPR lacked one prominent feature of other internationalist organizations with strong Christian connections – significant representation of women. A few Japanese women delegates attended IPR conferences, and Christian women's organizations, such as the YWCA, the Women's International Peace Association (*Fujin kokusai heiwa kyōkai*) and the Japanese Christian Women's Temperance Union (*Nihon Kirisutokyō fujin kyōfūkai*), were strong backers of internationalism and the JCIPR's activities. They hosted addresses and lectures by JCIPR members. Despite this, no women were listed among the JCIPR's membership in 1927 and after.

Women were not always absent from internationalist organizations in Japan. Eleven members of the GJPA were women. Shibusawa also promoted the women's peace movement, arguing that peace could not be achieved by men alone.[63] Membership of the LNA in Japan grew steadily in the late 1920s from 5,000 in 1926 to 11,771 in 1932, among whom 5,652 were students and 556 were women. The women's section grew large enough to become independent in 1930.[64] As well as the franchise, anti-public prostitution and temperance, peace was a significant agenda of Christian-dominated middle-class women's organizations.[65] Like their male counterparts, these socially and politically active women also regarded themselves as leaders, and cooperated with reform-oriented bureaucrats. Garon and Suzuki suggest that their co-optive and active involvement with the formulation and promotion of social policies smoothed the way for their wartime collaboration. Ogata also points out that Christian organizations in general did not challenge the imperial framework or military actions in the 1930s.[66] This meant that these women's and Christian organizations demonstrated a similar characteristic – a cooperative attitude to the state – as other more male-dominated internationalist organizations.

The Pacific and North America were central in internationalist movements in Japan. Increasing American naval strength and the anti-Japanese immigration movement in California were their major concerns as they presented a serious challenge to the cooperative policy. Christian elements, however, declined in some internationalist organizations, and the influence of women was also waning. One of the first organizations to reflect this trend was the Japanese American Relations Committee (JARC). It was set up in Japan in 1916 to address the immigration problem in the United States. Although business people were a main component, academics were also involved. Together they analysed the issue and played the dual role of international publicists and lobbyists. This academic involvement was a significant step for internationalist organizations, which until then had been more like social clubs than serious research or lobby groups. The JARC included prominent initial members of the JCIPR: Inoue, Nitobe, Sibusawa, Sakatani, Zumoto, Anezaki Masaharu (1873–1949), professor of comparative religious studies at the Tokyo Imperial University, and Soeda Juichi (1864–1929), member of the House of Peers. They were academics and business people with a keen interest in policies, and their prominence in the JCIPR indicated an orientation towards policy matters and political influence.

The influence of the YMCA also declined in these organizations. Despite the central role of the YMCA in the initiation of the first IPR conference, YMCA members accounted for only four at the JCIPR in 1927. They included Saitō Sōichi, Secretary of the Tokyo YMCA, Ibuka Kajinosuke (1854–1940) and Nagao Hanpei (1865–1936), Chairperson of the Japanese YMCA. Nitobe Inazō did not appear in the 1927 list. This Christian educationalist and 'expert' on agriculture, colonial policy and American studies was a major figure at the Japanese YMCA, and was regarded as one of the most active and influential internationalists in inter-war Japan. In 1927, he was still serving as Under-Secretary at the League of Nations in Geneva. After returning, Nitobe became a member of the House of Peers. When Inoue resigned as Chairperson of the JCIPR after being appointed as Minister of Finance in the Hamaguchi cabinet in 1929, Nitobe took over and remained in the position until his death in 1933.

JCIPR members regarded themselves as the national elite. This meant that they could easily be anti-populists. The JCIPR was more elitist and more oriented to the state than other internationalist organizations, such as the LNA. The LNA's aim was to promote the League's cause, and its methods were propaganda and education. Its membership was more inclusive. In contrast to the JCIPR, which was heavily concentrated in Tokyo, the LNA reached local cities and appealed to a wider section of society.[67] By 1926, although its membership was only 5,000, a hundredth of that in Britain, local branches had been established in at least eleven prefectures outside Tokyo, and women and students were strong supporters.[68] The annual membership fee for the JCIPR was 10 yen, compared with 4 yen at the LNA.[69] One JCIPR member denounced the LNA's method of propaganda, and emphasized the importance of attracting strong academic foreign affairs experts.[70] This elitism and an eagerness for involvement in policy formulation was common among other National Councils of the IPR, the RIIA and the CFR.[71]

Yet, like IPR founders in the United States, some JCIPR members felt that the enlightenment of society was also important. A prominent internationalist noted that they recognized the importance of public opinion (*yoron*), and their duty was to 'educate' and guide 'intelligent and healthy' (*sōmei kenzenna*) opinion.[72] Leading JCIPR members were actively involved in the LNA and advocated their views to the interested public. The LNA, not the JCIPR, was the right vehicle for these activities. Their role as publicists, not think-tank members, is noteworthy here. The LNA published two journals, *Kokusai chishiki* (*International Knowledge*) and *Sekai to warera* (*The World and Us*), addressed mainly to intellectuals. For wider appeal, it made effective use of public lectures. Nitobe and Ishii Kikujirō (1866–1945, Minister of Foreign Affairs in 1915), who joined the JCIPR soon after his resignation from the Ministry of Foreign Affairs in 1927, went on many lecture tours to cities all over Japan for the LNA. Nitobe, then Under-Secretary at the League of Nations, was seen as the embodiment of the League spirit. He was reported to have lectured at 150 places in Japan between December 1924 and February 1925.[73] The LNA also organized study meetings for educationalists to teach the cause and spirit of the League at schools, and asked newspaper owners to publicize them. It used other mass media, such as pamphlets and movies, and started to use radio around 1926. Shibusawa was one of the first to address the cause of internationalism using the radio.[74]

The state and 'liberals': New Liberalism and *kakushin shugi*

Post-League internationalists, including JCIPR members, supported the dominant international order and the regional order led by the United States. They also supported government foreign policy, which coincided with their agenda. Given this 'conservative' position, why were they called 'liberals'? It was certainly their self-proclaimed position. Takayanagi Kenzō (1887–1967), professor of law at Tokyo Imperial University, for example, thought that JCIPR members were a part of 'the liberal element of the Pacific countries'. He may have adhered to abstract concepts associated with enlightenment, such as liberty, rationality, progress and even democracy, but, like his American counterparts, his 'liberal' position was defined not by commitment to social movements, but by his self-proclaimed opposition to imperialism and socialism.[75]

The connection between post-League internationalists and 'liberalism' was not as automatic or direct as many have assumed. A key to understanding this relationship lies in the external and domestic policies of the governments of the 1920s, which were dominated by political parties. Post-League internationalism reflected the development of domestic democratic movements. Although Hara was by no means a champion of democracy,[76] he was the first commoner Prime Minister (*heimin saishō*). He embodied the atmosphere of the late 1910s and 1920s, '*Taisho demokurashi*' (Taisho democracy). Succeeding party-dominated governments introduced universal male franchise in 1925, and various social policies in the 1920s. Hara's cooperative policy with the great powers was maintained to a great extent by these successors, and peace and disarmament were on their agendas. Their 'liberal' or 'democratic' domestic policies were associated with this cooperative foreign policy.

Those who took an active role in contemporary social movements were inspired by the idea of 'democracy' as well as socialism. Woodrow Wilson and the League of Nations were seen a part of this democratic force. Leading intellectuals of this period, such as Yoshino Sakuzō, interpreted the Meiji Constitution in the most democratic way possible, and tried to advance greater popular political participation. Despite repeated suppression, socialist movements were widespread and played a significant political role. In the 1920s, demonstrations and disputes were numerous in cities and rural areas, forcing the government to take urgent measures.[77] Women's movements also flourished, arguing a greater political role for women. Inspiration often came from their American colleagues. Among those who promoted *Suiheisha* (the Levellers Society), the organization for the liberation of *hisabetsu buraku* people from prejudice and discrimination, the Wilsonian ideal of self-determination was noted as a source of inspiration.[78]

Did these democratic movements and intellectual trends of the day result in 'liberal' domestic policies? Were these policies indeed 'liberal'? Was cooperative foreign policy inherently related to these domestic movements or to 'liberal' domestic policies? These are separate questions, each of which needs rigorous scrutiny. Numerous works have questioned how 'liberal' domestic policies in this period really were. It is true that social policies were advanced by party cabinets. Yet underprivileged groups did not see successive party governments tackle their problems. The government also saw communism and socialism as a real threat to the existing order, especially after the Russian Revolution, and severely suppressed them. The Peace Preservation Law (*Chian ijihō*) of 1925, passed at the same time as the universal male franchise bill, banned ideas and activities which challenged the national polity and private property. This was further strengthened by the introduction of the death penalty in 1928. On the other hand, the state worked closely with the moderate factions, co-opted their agendas, and counteracted more radical forces. Furthermore, as Gordon demonstrates, the development of democracy at home did not necessarily mean anti-militarism or anti-imperialism.[79] Like the Euro-American powers, the Japanese government pursued colonial expansion at the same time as it enlarged the political franchise and implemented social policies at home.

Many underprivileged groups felt that they gained little from cooperative foreign policy and disarmament, which was promoted by big business and post-League internationalists. They saw political parties as being closely linked to big business, and as being corrupt and privileged. Party leaders, big business and post-League internationalists became targets for attack. Hara was assassinated in 1921. Hamaguchi Osachi (1870–1931), whose cabinet (1929–31) promoted various social policies and disarmament as well as radical rationalization policies, was fatally wounded in an attack in 1930 and died in

1931. Inoue Junnosuke was also assassinated. Inoue was not only a prominent post-League internationalist and the first chairperson of the JCIPR, but was also responsible for the financial policies of the Hamaguchi cabinet.

Were there inherently 'liberal' elements among post-League internationalists and JCIPR members, other than their adherence to abstract notions, and their self-proclaimed opposition to socialism and imperialism? An examination of their 'New Liberalism' is critical to understanding their position regarding the state/nation/empire. New Liberalism has been largely ignored in analyses of 'liberal' internationalists and intellectuals in Japan, including JCIPR members. Liberalism (*jiyū shugi*) in inter-war Japan was mostly defined and discussed in terms of individualism and *laissez-faire* liberalism. Accordingly, Ishibashi Tanzan, whose thought was influenced more by this school of liberalism and American pragmatism than by German idealism, has been a central subject in this field.[80] The neglect probably owes much to the 'debate on liberalism' (*jiyū shugi ronsō*) in 1933–6 and its impact on later scholars. It defined the 'liberalism' of the 1920s as *laissez-faire* and individualistic, and dismissed it as the ideology of the privileged few.[81] Japanese intellectuals of this period and later scholars saw individualism and *laissez-faire* liberalism as inherently 'Western'. They assumed that 'Japan', the other of the 'West', did not possess them or was incapable of adopting them.[82] As a result, the state was regarded as an oppressor of individual rights and freedom, not a guardian of the welfare of society. Its greater intervention was seen as problematic and 'morally wrong'.

A similar framework is applied to the evaluation of nationalists and post-League internationalists in Japan. Scholars argue that two crucial 'weaknesses' of internationalists, including JCIPR members, were their nationalism and their elite status.[83] This explains why the JCIPR was unable to present alternatives to government policies, and why it was ineffective in conveying its views to society at large. Yet the assumption is that they *failed* to become 'true' and 'morally right' internationalists. Instead they became or remained 'reactionary' and 'morally wrong' nationalists. This implies the moral righteousness of the existing international order, and an automatic opposition of 'liberals' to the state. Yet, in times of economic hardship, nationalists, especially those who deployed a national socialistic rhetoric, had enormous appeal to the underprivileged. Like these 'nationalists', New Liberals argued that the state was the provider of the welfare for society and morally good. They were prone to being statist and strong advocates of colonialism, although their rhetoric emphasized not the exploitation, but the welfare of colonies.

An emphasis on the failure of Japanese internationalists suggests that their counterparts in Western Europe and North America succeeded, and their failure was due to a peculiar 'weakness'. In other words, their problem was seen as the incompleteness of modernization, Westernization or Americanization[84] – progress towards the complete realization of various ideals that was understood as having been achieved in the 'West' or the United

States. Yet, as Cohen indicates, similar problems were apparent in organizations in the United States.[85]

Garon's works on social bureaucrats and their cooperation with non-state reformists in the 1930s and 1940s is useful in analysing Japanese post-League internationalists.[86] These social bureaucrats, who pushed statist reformism, overlapped considerably with what Itō Takashi calls *kakushin* bureaucrats. Although there was great diversity among *kakushin* groups, I define *kakushin shugi* as statist reformism and *kakushinha* as statist reformists.[87] This reformism can be located as a further statist position of New Liberalism, and very close to national socialism. I prefer the term statist reformism to national socialism, because of the latter's close association with Nazism. Despite left-leaning rhetoric and ideas, those categorized as *kakushinha* were often anti- or counter-socialists. Like many intellectuals in Europe at that time, advocates of *kakushin shugi* argued that capitalism, liberalism and individualism were bankrupt, and new systems and new philosophies were needed. Utilizing socialist rhetoric, they promoted a strong statism, and argued for a greater and stronger role for the state and the significance of the national polity. A positive evaluation of *kakushin shugi* as the vanguard of the underprivileged is dangerous because it could easily lead to a justification of their other agenda, Japanese rule in Asia.[88] *Kakushinha* saw a clear and strong connection between their domestic vision and their visions for Asia.[89] Careful examination, however, is needed to understand the views of the world and the region that were held by Japanese post-League internationalists, and to understand their relationship with the state and the nature of their liberalism.

The influence of New Liberalism was evident in the works of major JCIPR members in the 1920s, and that of *kakushin shugi* in the 1930s and 1940s. Matsuzawa argues that Rōyama Masamichi (1895–1965), a leading figure among the younger generation of JCIPR members, was influenced by New Liberalism.[90] This younger generation of the JCIPR was more aware of the problems of the current system and the need for a greater state intervention. They became increasingly close to *kakushin shugi* and Konoe Fumimaro, who was to emerge as a leader of *kakushinha* in the 1930s.

The state and the JCIPR in the 1920s

What was the relationship between the state and post-League internationalists, including JCIPR members, in the 1920s? As indicated, successive party-dominated governments and the Ministry of Foreign Affairs had a large stake in a cooperative relationship with the powers. They wanted to promote a relatively equal relationship with the powers, particularly the United States. Their backer, big business, had a profitable relationship with its US counterparts. Disarmament was high on their agenda. In this context, the crisis provoked by the anti-Japanese immigration law was a blow, and they welcomed the IPR's non-official attempt to restore a good relationship with the United States. Hence, the government was interested in the IPR and the JCIPR from the beginning.

Inoue and Shibusawa were conduits between the JCIPR and the government.[91] Paradoxically, as Wilbur's presence strengthened the ACIPR's posture towards the state, these influential figures in political circles ensured a certain autonomy for the JCIPR. As much as the government made use of these men, they could afford to be vocally critical of official policies. This was demonstrated in Inoue's conduct, especially at the 1929 conference (see Chapter 6). Their deaths in the early 1930s meant a loss of this dimension to the JCIPR.

The greater the official involvement, the harder it was for JCIPR members to critically assess official policies and propose alternative policies. It was customary for the JCIPR to notify the Ministry of Foreign Affairs of its meetings; occasionally officials attended, which limited critical discussion of policies. Yet it was not only official pressure that made the JCIPR prone to adopt a cooperative position towards the state – JCIPR members willingly acted as non-official officials, and this was the case well before the Manchurian Incident (1931). A major reason for this willingness was that they saw support for the League of Nations and loyalty to the Japanese state/empire as compatible. In 1926, for example, JCIPR members attended a meeting of League supporters, and emphasized the compatibility of *kokka shugi* (nationalism, or more precisely statism) and *kokusai shugi* (internationalism). Sawayanagi Masatarō maintained: 'In order to complete *kokka shugi*, we have to incorporate internationalism.' JCIPR members Sakatani Yoshirō and Zumoto Motosada also argued that the League spirit and military preparation were not in conflict.[92] They were not alone. Others defined 'internationalism' as based on the nation-state, and argued that it should not be confused with cosmopolitanism or the world federation movement.[93]

Despite the strong representation of big business among its membership, academics dominated the JCIPR's activities.[94] This reflected a key object of the IPR, defined in 1927, as conducting research on issues related to the Pacific.[95] The academic dominance could have enhanced the autonomy of the JCIPR from the state. Like its predecessor, the JARC, however, the JCIPR attracted academics who were interested in politics and policies. As members of the national elite, they had a strong sense of loyalty and public duty to the nation/state/empire. They operated within a dominant framework of the time, reifying the nation, national character, national culture and national interests and identifying the nation with the state. This effectively precluded them from adopting an autonomous or critical role. The lack of tension between the JCIPR and the state is more significant because the IPR advocated its role as a non-governmental agency. What mattered was not so much their unofficial status, but the aims towards which these non-official agencies were working. As later chapters demonstrate, this cooperative attitude towards the state was not peculiar to the JCIPR, and it became increasingly evident in other IPR operations in the 1930s.

The Japanese government saw the IPR as both significant and useful in the mid-1920s. Foreign Minister Shidehara took the initial step in organizing a Japanese group. In March 1925, Shidehara sent his right-hand man, Saburi Toshio, Director General of the Bureau of Trade Affairs (*Tsūshō kyoku*), to Shibusawa, and asked him to organize the Japanese delegation for the first IPR conference.[96] This also indicates that the main concern of US–Japan relations was then trade. The official communication was initiated by the Honolulu organizers (which became the ISIPR after the first conference), not the Japanese government. Usually the Honolulu office used the local YMCA headquarters until a National Council was formed. Perhaps the familiarity of Merle Davis, the conference organizer, with Japanese officials was the reason. In general, Davis was eager to acquire support from various governments.[97] As a member of a notable American missionary family in Japan, he was well connected and well respected among high officials and in other influential circles.[98] The JARC connection between the Honolulu organizers and some Japanese diplomats might have been another reason for this unusual practice. Frank Atherton, based in Hawai'i, a member of the JARC and an organizer of the first IPR conference, contacted Japanese Ambassador Hanihara in Hawai'i and Shibusawa in Japan in mid-1924. He explained that the conference was to consider human relations in the Pacific and urged Japan to send a delegation of 'influential and leading men'.[99] At this stage the most important conference agenda was the American anti-Japanese immigration act of 1924. Atherton knew Japanese JARC members, such as Shibusawa and Hanihara. Hanihara reported the development in detail to the Foreign Minister.

Still, if the government had not regarded the proposed conference as important or useful, it could have easily failed to act on the approaches. By the time a Japanese group needed to be organized for the first conference, Shidehara was well informed, had recognized its significance and took the initiative. This was in marked contrast to the scepticism displayed by the American and Australian governments, boh of which preferred not to discuss the immigration issue at a non-official international conference and ruled out their involvement.[100]

The Japanese government's high regard for the IPR and the JCIPR was demonstrated by its enthusiastic reaction particularly to the first two IPR conferences, its close involvement with the JCIPR and its generous financial aid. After taking the initiative in organizing a Japanese group, the government hosted farewell and welcome parties for participants and donated money to support their travel. Of the 30,000 yen budget for the first IPR conference in 1925, the Ministry of Foreign Affairs paid 20,000 yen. The rest was collected by big business. Mitsui and Iwasaki each contributed 5,000 yen, and Shibusawa 1,000 yen. Another 4,000 yen was allocated to eight JARC members.[101]

More important, party-dominated governments consistently supported not only the JCIPR, but also other internationalist organizations. Despite differences over policies towards China, Shidehara and Tanaka Giichi were both strong backers. The LNA enjoyed the full support of Prime Minister Hara from its inception. Hara encouraged business contributions, and initial contributions to the LNA mainly came from big business. In 1923, however, the government matched private contributions of 23,000 yen with 20,000 yen, a sum soon to be greatly surpassed.[102] The LNA became the core of the post-League internationalist movement in the 1920s, and the GJPA merged with it in 1925. The Tanaka cabinet, known for its aggressive policy in China, maintained this support, acknowledging its importance. It contributed 70,000 yen in both 1927 and 1928. In 1931 the Wakatsuki cabinet (Shidehara was Foreign Minister) gave 50,000 yen of total donations of 80,000 yen.[103] Strong official backing meant prestige, but also self-censorship on the part of internationalist organizations.

Precisely in this period, the Ministry of Foreign Affairs began to co-opt the international activities of non-official organizations, particularly their international publicist activities. This could be seen as an adjustment to the 'New Diplomacy'. The move started not with American- or European-oriented organizations, such as the JCIPR, but with organizations which mainly focused on China. Despite a strong Euro-American orientation and opposition to Asianism, Japanese post-League internationalists did not dismiss the significance of 'Asia', especially China. Key JCIPR members, such as Shibusawa and Sakatani, promoted friendship associations with various countries in Asia and financial aid for Chinese students. Shibusawa saw China as a crucial business opportunity.[104] They regarded cooperation between China and Japan as the basis for stability and security in East Asia. *Nikka gakkai* (The Japan–China Study Association) was founded in 1918 with Shibusawa's help. The LNA, too, not only focused on European issues, but cooperated with student counterpart organizations in China.[105] Makino Nobuaki (the Japanese delegate at the Paris Conference and leading post-League internationalist) and Konoe Fumimaro, both active at the LNA, were executive members of *Tōa dōbunkai* (East Asia Common Culture Association).

The view was shared by the state, and it began a systematic co-option of non-official organizations with links to China. The move was soon to be extended to Euro-American-oriented organizations, such as the JCIPR. The Ministry of Education contributed money to *Nikka gakkai* and *Tōa dōbunkai* from 1921. More significantly, in 1923, the Ministry of Foreign Affairs set up the Office of Cultural Affairs regarding China (*Taishi bunka jimukyoku*), and the activities of *Tōa dōbunkai* and other 'non-governmental' agencies came under its supervision. Legislation was enacted, and a special official account for 'cultural' activities between Japan and China was created. Publicly, this co-option was explained as accidental: greater official involvement was due to a temporary loss of facilities for Chinese students because of the Great Kanto Earthquake. Nevertheless, although 1923 marked increased state intervention, it was not a new policy. Neither was it a one-off incident. The trend steadily increased in the following years. Official contributions to these China-oriented organizations, mainly consisting of aid for Chinese students, accounted for a large sum, 285,692 yen in 1921–37.[106]

In the early 1920s, various ministries, particularly the Ministry of Foreign Affairs, realized the effectiveness of utilizing 'cultural' or 'non-official' activities to improve diplomatic relations, especially in difficult times. It was considered a good means of appeasing strong anti-Japanese sentiment in China. As Shibasaki notes, it was also an excellent way to demonstrate the superiority and maturity of the Japanese empire compared with the Chinese people and Euro-American powers. It is reasonable to assume that Konoe, as an executive member at *Tōa dōbunkai*, and someone very concerned with the prestige and status of the Japanese empire, actively promoted these moves. In 1927 the 'Office of Cultural Affairs regarding China' became the Department of Cultural Affairs. In the 1930s it further co-opted post-League internationalist organizations, including the JCIPR.

A reified notion of nation played a significant role in diplomacy,[107] and this was especially evident in this co-option of non-official 'cultural' activities. The government was quick to see the importance of utilizing the 'cultural' activities of non-governmental organizations to construct a favourable image of Japan. *Nikka gakkai* was founded not only to assist Chinese students studying in Japan, but also to foster a 'correct' understanding of Japan among these students, who, they hoped, would cultivate goodwill towards Japan.[108] It was an ideal organization for government backing. These reified images of the nation were inevitably monolithic, mainly defined by the national elite of senior bureaucrats and policy-oriented intellectuals with a specific agenda to promote.

Post-League internationalists with a Euro-American orientation used a similar rhetoric. This was true of the GJPA, the first internationalist organization in Japan, and inherited by later post-League internationalist organizations, including the JCIPR. The GJPA's role was as a voluntary international publicist for the Japanese state/empire to 'correctly' represent a 'national' voice to the 'world'. Despite their recognition of the significance of China, Japanese internationalists often identified the 'world' with Europe and North America. The GJPA's journal targeted 'Euro-American' or 'Anglo-American' readers. Although it was initially published in Japanese during 1912–17, it then switched into English. By using English, the GJPA stated that 'it could contribute to making [their] national character understood correctly and convincing the countries of the world that Japanese were not bellicose'.[109] This spirit was evident among later post-League organizations. One of the objectives of the LNA, for example, was to 'secure national interests', and to 'maintain world peace and contribute to the welfare of human beings at the same time'.[110] Just as they reified the United States, JCIPR members also felt the need to present the 'correct' image of Japan. This was an urgent issue especially when US–Japan diplomatic relations were at a low point. They felt a mission to present Japan not as an aggressor, but as a liberal, democratic and peace-loving nation. As the national elite, they felt a stronger mission to 'get it right' for overseas audiences. As later chapters demonstrate, this was even more evident in times of war. They also had much more contact with elite groups outside Japan, and were influential in shaping their image of Japan.

Reformist criticism of the dominant order

Nitobe as reformer

Nitobe Inazō bridged the gap between *laissez-faire* liberals and New Liberals in the JCIPR. In 1906–13, well before the formation of the JCIPR, he was principal of the ultimate elite institution, *Ichikō*. There he cultivated a moderate reformist orientation. His disciples became key post-League internationalists and founding members of the JCIPR. Nakami notes that one of his strong influences was Wilsonian idealism.[111] Nitobe worked as Under-Secretary at the League in Geneva in 1920–6, a job which he described as his vocation. He promoted the League to the public in Japan and throughout the world.[112]

His distinctive notion of the 'Christian gentleman' as a reformed version of the Meiji elite was another crucial factor in cultivating younger JCIPR members. As a result, they developed a particular reformist inclination. As principal of *Ichikō*, Nitobe tried to mould an alternative model of the national elite, the mannered gentleman. Before his arrival, a mentality of masculine barbarism (*bankara*) prevailed at the school, especially in the athletic clubs. Nitobe tried to build a healthy and cultured community. His inspiration clearly came from British elite institutions. Before he took up the position, Nitobe asked the Minister of Education, Makino Nobuaki, to send him to Britain to study Eton, Rugby and Harrow. At *Ichikō* he tried to introduce the modern British public school idea of the 'Christian gentleman', and he wanted to be remembered among students as Dr Arnold.[113]

Not all students were enthusiastic about Nitobe's reforms. Some rebelled against them in 1909. They asserted that Nitobe's promotion of *sociality* (*shakōsei*) was a disguised form of egalitarianism. They claimed that 'the Western custom of showing respect to women was at the expense of their masculinity', and that would lead them down 'the path of degeneracy'. Akutagawa Ryūnosuke, a student at that time, was contemptuous of Nitobe, describing him as obsessed with superficial mannerisms.[114] Nevertheless, Nitobe's sociality was far from egalitarianism. It was based on a firm sense of social rank. He aimed to modify the form, not the essence, of the Meiji elite. The rebellion suggests that even this superficial reform caused much opposition.

On the other hand, his concern with the concepts of 'sociality' and 'social service' (*shakai hōshi*) indicated a transition from *laissez-faire* liberalism to New

Liberalism. Maeda Tamon, one of Nitobe's disciples and founding JCIPR member, recorded that the word *shakai*, which Nitobe used often, was forbidden among certain conservative groups because of its association with socialism (*shakai shugi*).[115] Nitobe clearly noted the influence of T.H. Green on his concept of society.

> As Thomas Hill Green said, 'no individual has an ability to create consciousness; society is needed to create this consciousness'.[116]

Like Green, Nitobe regarded society as a moral being, and the state had a role to ensure that this moral element of society found full expression. While he emphasized the individual as the basis of the collective, not the collective itself, he was aware of the need for individual service to the whole.[117] This position was different from that of some JCIPR members of his generation, such as Ishii Kikujirō. Ishii took a *laissez-faire* approach to social issues. For Ishii, self-help (*jijo*), not social welfare, was all-important and little sense of social service was evident in his writing.[118]

Nitobe's sense of being 'social' came mainly from two sources: Christian humanitarianism based on his Quaker beliefs; and a sense of public service as the Meiji national elite (but a 'civilized' and 'gentlemanly' version). As noted, Christian leaders initiated various social and reform movements, including 'peace' movements. Ibuka, Saitō and Nagao Hanpei were involved with the JCIPR through the YMCA connections. Ibuka advocated reform of marital relationships, emphasizing a more equal partnership between husband and wife, and Nagao led temperance movements.[119] Loyalty to the nation/empire among these Christian leaders was also strong, and Nagao shared a sense of public service to the state/empire with Nitobe. He became close to Nitobe while they were colonial bureaucrats in Taiwan. Nitobe believed in the imperial system, the Japanese empire and the social order within the empire. He argued for the idea of 'Greater Japan' and its duty to serve *backward* countries, such as Korea and the South Pacific islands.[120] He promoted these ideas at *Ichikō* and Tokyo Imperial University, where he taught colonial policy.[121] While cultivating social manners and 'liberal' ideals, he moulded the minds and manners of future national and colonial administrators.

Gotō Shimpei (1857–1929, Minister for Home Affairs in 1916–18 and 1923–4) influenced Nitobe and his disciples, who subsequently became central at the JCIPR. Gotō was not involved with the JCIPR. Politically, he sided with those who wished to challenge the post-League order and the American regional order. Gotō urged that Japan should ally itself with Russia to balance American aggression in China, and advocated a more interventionist military policy. The association between Gotō and Nitobe began when he recruited Nitobe as a colonial administrator in Taiwan in 1901. They both came from Iwate prefecture, which provided an initial link, and later they became close friends.

On the surface it was an odd match, but on issues of social reform and colonial administration, they had much in common. Gotō was initially a medical doctor, and was very concerned with the health and hygiene systems in Japan and the colonies. As colonial administrator in Taiwan, president of the South Manchurian Railway, Tokyo mayor and Minister of Home Affairs he conducted various social reforms in health insurance policy and city planning. Gotō reified the nation as a biological and organic entity, and was concerned with its well-being.[122] His welfare policies aimed to strengthen the health of the population so as to provide competent human resources for industry and the military in the service of the state/empire. Like New Liberals, he saw state intervention as morally good. His connections with the JCIPR were mainly through Nitobe, but he became interested in Christian movements. Nagao, who worked under Gotō in Taiwan, introduced him to the YMCA.[123] Gotō often helped the careers of Nitobe's disciples, who were to become JCIPR members. Among them, a sense of service to the state/empire was strong.

Nitobe's idea of 'social service' was clear in his activities as a publicist. He wrote for many journals and newspapers and gave public lectures. He realized the importance of addressing the public, which to an extent demonstrated his faith in their abilities. He was probably motivated by fame and power, or a sense of duty as a public servant to the state/empire. For a semi-official figure, the role of publicist involved the risk of becoming a government mouthpiece. Nakami contrasts this compromised nature of Nitobe and other JCIPR members with that of other intellectuals, such as Yoshino Sakuzō, Kiyozawa Kiyoshi and Ishibashi Tanzan. She sees this group of intellectuals as independent public intellectuals, and more consistent in their criticism of Japanese military aggression in China.[124]

Stronger reformist sentiment

Not all Nitobe's students who became major post-League internationalists were happy with the role of publicist. Takaki seems to have been uncomfortable with it.[125] In contrast, younger members of the JCIPR who were influenced by Nitobe and Gotō had a strong tendency to pursue careers as state/colonial bureaucrats and publicists. They included Tsurumi Yūsuke (1885–1973), Maeda Tamon and Iwanaga Yūkichi (1883–1939), all of whom started their careers as state/colonial bureaucrats. Maeda was a bureaucrat and an official representative of 'labour interests' at the ILO in 1923. At *Ichikō*, he was fascinated by Nitobe's speeches and, along with Tsurumi, he became an enthusiastic follower. According to Maeda, Nitobe suggested that he become a social educationalist (*shakai kyōikuka*), and this idea shaped his career.[126]

Tsurumi was another enthusiastic follower of Nitobe, who also helped with his marriage to a daughter of Gotō Shimpei. Tsurumi was fascinated by Wilsonian ideals and formed the *Uiruson kurabu* (Wilson Club) in 1915. The core of this club consisted of students and old boys from the debating club at *Ichikō*. Speakers at the club's meetings included many who were to become JCIPR members, such as Iwanaga, Matsuoka Yōsuke and Rōyama Masamichi. Although these post-League internationalists had two major functions as think-tank 'experts' and as international publicists, Tsurumi was more a publicist. Since his *Ichikō* days, his eloquence had been famous. He was confident and had a manner that enabled him to socialize easily with Americans and British, at occasions such as IPR conferences.

Tsurumi's proposal for New Liberalism (*shin jiyū shugi*) in 1924 furthered Nitobe's reformist inclinations. He formed a new political party called *Meiseikai* and the New Liberalism Association (*Shin jiyū shugi kyōkai*) (founded in 1928), of which Nitobe became chairperson. Tsurumi urged the need to establish liberalism in Japan, which he defined as a middle-of-the-road ideology between conservative and communist forces. Tsurumi clearly stated that his was the New Liberalism of T.H. Green.[127] He argued the importance of the individual, but insisted that individuals should contribute to society as a whole.[128] In his view, New Liberalism was close to socialism, because it recognized the importance of state intervention in protecting working-class interests.[129] New Liberalism reflected the emerging political consciousness among the working classes and women, and the universal male franchise law of 1925 was one manifestation of this trend.[130]

Tsurumi was, however, counter-socialist. His main object was less to advance democracy than to protect and strengthen the nation-state against the dangers of these democratic forces:

> Reforms reflecting the needs of the society are the best way to protect the nation. A healthy movement to challenge the status quo is the only way to preserve the life of the nation. The [recent] prevailing mentality in Japan to challenge the status quo is the expression of the self-defence instinct of the Japanese nation.[131]

He wrote this in 1928, the year of the first general election based on the universal male franchise, when he was elected to the Diet as a *Meiseikai* member. Tsurumi's logic was very similar to that of the liberal imperialists at the Round Table. Similarly, for him, universal female franchise was needed, because it would foster a sense of duty to the nation among women, half of the population.[132]

The implication of his New Liberalism in international politics was significant. It marked a turning point for Japanese post-League internationalists in their attitude towards the international order. Tsurumi began to question the dominant international order, just as he questioned the domestic one. As early as 1927, he argued that great powers should not oppress small countries.[133] Race, or the inequality between Caucasian and coloured races, was central to his argument.[134] His criticism of the international order and the League of Nations became stronger after

Japan's withdrawal from the League of Nations in 1933. He argued that peace for Britain, the United States, the USSR and France meant that they would preserve their privilege. 'Real' peace, he continued, would not come until Japan achieved 'justice' by abolishing these countries' racial discrimination and unfair tariffs.[135] Tsurumi's perspective comes very close to Konoe's thesis of 1918.

Iwanaga Yūkichi was another JCIPR member of this generation. His connection with Nitobe is indirect, and his career was shaped more by a close association with Gotō, and later Konoe. In his *Ichikō* days he knew Tsurumi and Maeda. Through them he met Nitobe while he was at Kyoto Imperial University. He worked at the South Manchurian Railway under Gotō in 1911–17, and at the Ministry of Railways in 1917–18, before he established his news agency in 1920. He became very close to Konoe through university and family connections.[136] His role of liaising between JCIPR members and Konoe and his action in establishing a 'national' news agency in the 1930s will be elaborated in Chapter 8. Here it should be noted his sense of mission as a member of the national elite and a post-League internationalist inspired the establishment of this national news agency. He felt that he should 'present a Japanese perspective' to the world.

Nitobe's emphasis on social reform was in no way radical, and his disciples promoted moderate views of social reform. This was in line with the intellectual trends of the day. *Laissez-faire* liberalism was being discredited, and a greater state role in the welfare of society was seen not only as inevitable but also as morally good. Nitobe also emphasized the public duty of the national elite to the state/empire as well as to the international community. These were compatible goals, as Nitobe demonstrated in his service to the League of Nations in the 1920s. All these strengthened the discourse centred on the nation-state. Whether one was official or non-official made little difference. The stronger the sense of reform Nitobe's disciples developed, the more critical they became of the post-League international order. They were increasingly drawn to statist reformism (*kakushin shugi*) and to Konoe's visions of the world, a New Order in East Asia, an alternative regional vision to the Pacific Community. Before turning to the views of younger JCIPR members in the 1930s, we now examine how the initial agendas of the IPR were institutionalized at the first two IPR conferences.

5   The Pacific Community and the experiment of the IPR in 1925-7

The concept of the Pacific Community, an American-led regional order, was crucial to the foundation of the IPR in 1925. There were, however, other contending visions among IPR members, and the IPR's direction was continually renegotiated. We now examine this negotiation process by focusing on the ISIPR, the headquarters of the IPR, and IPR conferences, which took place every two to three years. What were these visions, and what became the dominant one? Did the process reinforce the state-centricity, colonial assumptions and Orientalist attitudes of IPR operations, or did it undermine them? How were these visions reflected in the IPR's response to crucial events in the region – the Manchurian crisis, the Sino-Japanese War and the Pacific War? What were the impacts of these events on IPR operations? I examine these questions in five major phases until the end of World War II: 1925–7, 1927–32, 1933–5, 1936–9 and 1940–5.

Visions and experiments: the first two conferences

The Pacific Community

The concept of the Pacific Community was very much alive at the first two IPR conferences in 1925 and 1927. It reflected the potential, dynamism and excitement of a new era. Herbert Croly, editor of *New Republic*, articulated it best at the second conference. Recent works on regional integration emphasize the role of 'middle powers' (such as Australia and Canada), instead of the hegemony of a superpower.[1] Similarly, in the mid-1920s, Croly saw an end to the hegemony of European global powers. His community of equal partners did not deny American leadership. It was the American-initiated Washington Conference that inspired the concept of the Pacific as a new 'independent political and economic area', not an extension of Europe. Now one could '[look] in the direction ... of a new conception of the Pacific' by 'dividing sea power between the British empire and the United States'.[2] In Croly's mind, the Pacific was independent from British hegemony, which came under American influence.

Yet what distinguished this Pacific was not American hegemony, but the community of 'political equals'.

> [The Washington Conference]... outlined the sketch of a Pacific regional community, which, if it could be realized and developed, would neutralize the Pacific highway as an instrument of predatory politics. ... The people of the Pacific are partially protected in theory against any further aggression, and in this sense they were by way of forming a community of political equals which are obligated to consult one another about their common political and economic difficulties and policies.[3]

Furthermore, this concept of the Pacific challenged Eurocentricity. It indicated a Pacific-centred world view. It looked at the Pacific from the inside, not the outside. This was clear in the map attached to the proceedings of the second conference (see Figure 5.1). Unlike most world maps available at the time, which were centred on the Atlantic, it located the Pacific at the centre. Japan and China were not in the 'Far East', but in the West, and Europe was too distant to appear.

At the same time, Europe was not totally out of sight. Croly's Pacific was not isolated from Europe. In his mind, the Washington Conference 'internationalized the Pacific' as the region was now more closely bound by international agreements and institutions. The autonomy and distinctiveness of the Pacific was couched in a framework of international codes of practice. It was the framework which the Republican administration pursued in the 1920s – independent from the League of Nations and European politics, but complementary to the League system. Croly's Pacific also accepted the post-League colonial status quo:

> No doubt powerful maritime nations, such as the United States, Japan, and Great Britain, would continue to possess legal rights in the territory of Pacific islands and in Eastern Asia, which derived from predatory expeditions of the past, and the beneficiaries of these pockets of imperialistic politics would have an interest in contesting the future development of a Pacific society of nations.

In 1927, the Pacific Community was one of political equals. It included Russia, China, the United States, Japan and also the British Dominions (represented separately from Great Britain) on the Pacific rim. It also included European powers which had colonies in the region. The first European member, a British group, joined the IPR in 1927 without any questioning of its right to do so. The American organizers of the first conference had not included Britain in the scope of their project, nor did they, including Croly, initiate British participation. It was the British Dominions' request (particularly Australia and New Zealand). The Dominions did not have discretion in foreign policy,[1] and their members felt that they

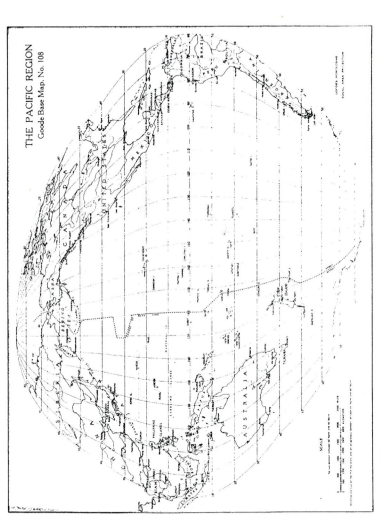

Figure 5.1 Pacific-centred view, 1927.

Source: Condliffe, J.B., ed, *Problems of the Pacific: Proceedings of the Second Conference of the Institute of Pacific Relations*, Honolulu, Hawaii, July 15 to 29, 1927, Chicago: University of Chicago Press, 1928.

could not comment on foreign policy issues independently or on British foreign policy on China – the latter was heavily criticized by the Chinese group in 1925. As a result, Dominion groups urged British representation.[5] There was little opposition in the United States. Key Americans favoured British representation because they thought that it would make higher level discussion possible.[6]

A British group was invited to the second IPR conference. This invitation was organized by Canadian members, not the ISIPR, although the ISIPR fully endorsed the decision.[7] On 12 March 1926, John Nelson (1873–1936), leader of the Canadian group in 1925, sent an invitation to the BIIA, soon to be renamed the RIIA (Chatham House).[8] The choice of the RIIA is not surprising. It had close connections with foreign affairs experts' organizations in the Dominions and the United States. Canadian IPR members belonged to a Canadian branch of the RIIA. They were much less sceptical towards American leadership in the region than their Australian counterparts. A few were even reluctant to include the British group in the IPR, and Nelson had to persuade them. This is not hard to understand as they would have shared similar security concerns, and more readily accepted cooperation with the United States.[9]

RIIA members were not overly enthusiastic about involvement with the IPR. Lionel Curtis, an ardent promoter of Anglo-American cooperation, was one of the very few who showed a great interest in the IPR enterprise. He had to persuade his reluctant or indifferent colleagues to secure one or two participants for the second conference. Those who came to IPR conferences, therefore, may not have represented mainstream RIIA. Still, their views were noteworthy. Frederick Whyte, former president of the National Indian Legislative Assembly and leader of the British group in 1927, described the Pacific and the role of Britain in the Pacific:

> It has become a commonplace in recent times to say that the future of peace and war lies in the Pacific. ... [I]t would be truer to say that whereas Europe hitherto been the center of the world and still remains its most important political area, the Eastern Hemisphere has emerged to challenge the predominance of the West, and that the world of international affairs now revolves upon the two poles of Orient and Occident. ... Now, the United States of America, in virtue of their geographical position, their immense resources, and their political power, and the British Commonwealth, in virtue of its world-wide character, stand in a position of peculiar influence and responsibility. These two, above all other nations, can influence and are influenced by every current that passes between the two poles of East and West, and their policy ... may well prove to be the decisive factor in establishing a true equilibrium.[10]

For him, the Pacific meant the 'East', not a synthesis of Asia and non-Asia as Americans tended to see it. Croly saw the Pacific as an American sphere of influence, clearly separate from British dominance. In contrast, for Whyte, the United States would assume a leadership role alongside the British Commonwealth, not only in the region, but also in the world. The nature of this global order was defined by the balance of power between the United States and the British empire, not a new concept of a community or new codes of conduct.

How did participants from Australia and New Zealand see American regional leadership? Some Australians and New Zealanders were impressed by the ability of American IPR members, and felt that American regional leadership was justified to an extent. This was a reflection of their criticism of British conduct in the region. Frederic Eggleston was central to IPR activities in Australia. He led the Australian group at the second and third IPR conferences, and was a member of the Pacific Council in 1927–39. A man with a strong regionalist view, he had been a vocal critic of London-centred imperial policies, especially on security issues, as early as 1912.[11] In 1927 he noted:

> There is no doubt ... that the Americans have an art of getting it over with Eastern races that the British have not. ... Americans have superior ability, [and are] socially miles ahead.[12]

It was not only a matter of social skill, but after another two years' observation he concluded that British lacked genuine interest in the 'East':

> The cardinal defect of the British psychology towards Eastern races is a lack of real interest in them. The days when the Westerner could come to the East, and rule it the better because he was indifferent to local quarrels and movements, are gone. At Hong Kong, the average Britisher is as ignorant of and indifferent to events in China as we are in Melbourne. All he wants to do is to make it a little bit of England. But the East is self-conscious, jealous, and moving with a premonition of vast power in the future. She demands attention and study.[13]

These comments, however, did not mean a full endorsement of the American regional leadership. Australian and New Zealand members were very anxious, even nervous, that the British might 'misunderstand' the meaning of their participation in IPR conferences. Australian IPR members represented a very small minority. A majority of Australians regarded the IPR and its proposed American regional order as a threat to the British imperial order. Even Eggleston was careful to state that they were not seeking a new affiliation with the United States.[14]

For Croly, the Pacific Community was more than American hegemony – it was a multilateral framework of cooperation. But it was still embryonic. To realize the vision, the commitment of the 'Pacific people', not states, was critical. Unofficial agencies such as the IPR would play a significant role:

> [Governments] are inevitably more preoccupied by their existing legal rights than by revolutionary visions of experimental community of nations. If ... the work of filling in the sketch is to be carried on, unofficial agencies which will act, not in opposition to existing governments, but wholly independent of declared national policies, will have to do it.

The IPR had 'elected itself to this position', and its political and intellectual implications were far reaching:

> [The IPR's] object is to give reality to the vision of the Pacific as an area of positive political association among the inhabitants of its shores, and in this respect it is ... a political novelty. It is not only attempting to bring into existence a new political community bound together by an internationalized body of water, but it is forced by its own nature to invoke for its purposes a method exclusively of inquiry, study, and consultation which heretofore has never been employed successfully in order to create a going political concern.[15]

The Pacific Community was a community of people, not states, and the IPR was to promote the formation of this community. Its purpose was analysis and consultation. For Croly, involvement in policy-making would jeopardize the IPR's novel and significant experiment. As early as 1927, he recognized that participants were seduced by political power. He repeatedly warned that involvement in policy-making would 'compromise the thoroughness of its inquisition' and make the IPR 'propagandist'. The merit of the IPR would lie in conducting 'a dispassionate, an exhaustive, and a continuing study' of crucial issues in the region, not in producing practical policy solutions for concerned states. Although the effects of these studies may not be direct or immediate, their potential would be great. It was because this 'may and should help to create the inquisitive public opinion in the various countries of the Pacific which may prevent the precipitation' of international disputes.

While Croly defined the people who gathered for the IPR as 'liberal', he also emphasized the IPR's 'realism':

> [The IPR] will guard its conduct from being unreal, not by trying to contribute to practical political solutions, but by keeping, no matter what happens, the lamp of disinterested and thorough inquiry ablaze.[16]

For him the IPR was an 'entirely realistic experiment in unrealistic politics', and involvement in policy-making, not IPR's visions, would make it unrealistic.

Its experiments were visionary, but they would be effective as long as those who conducted them remained committed to the role of non-official expert, and were not tempted by political power. He stressed the importance of critical analysis of concrete issues over ideological or abstract rhetoric.

Few of the participants at the first two IPR conferences were as articulate or cautious as Croly. In Honolulu in 1925 and 1927, participants embraced the possibility of new ways of conducting international affairs with great enthusiasm and optimism, and Croly shared this mood. The opening session of the first IPR conference on 30 June 1925 was attended by over 100 participants, and was filled with this optimism. Frank Atherton, philanthropic Honolulu businessman and soon to become Treasurer of the IPR, addressed the participants:

> There must be a growing consciousness of responsibility for the progress and *welfare* of all nations. Those living in a community have come to recognize that each man has his contribution to make to the *whole*. ... Thus it seems logical to maintain that each nation has its contribution to make to the family of nations and each should take an active and constructive part in working out that plan which shall be for the *welfare of all*.[17] [emphasis added]

The emphasized words here echoed key concepts of New Liberalism which were shared by British post-League internationalists. Nations were spoken of as organic beings. Atherton extended the idea of the welfare beyond national boundaries, and argued for the welfare of the international community. He also stressed the public duty of individuals, and argued that it should not be confined to government officials.[18]

The optimism was enhanced by their faith in 'enlightenment' and 'science'. Participants believed in the importance of *facts* and *scientific* and *objective* analysis. In 1925, Hessel Duncan-Hall (1891–1976), tutor at the University of Sydney and an author on the British Commonwealth, stated:

> [The] biggest contribution of the IPR is discovering that the most controversial questions of international relations in the Pacific can be discussed fruitfully by people of the most diverse races. They can unite together in scientific inquiry as to what the facts really were.[19]

Did participants from Australia, China, Canada, Korea, Japan, New Zealand, the Philippines, the United States and Britain (from 1927) have a sense of a community of 'political equals'? Through discussions and lectures, and also the physical environment of the first two conferences, these participants were exposed to a new and rare experience. The laboratory was the Punahou School, located at Manoa Valley, five minutes by car from Waikiki Beach. The school's facilities and seventy-acre campus were made available for the conferences. Participants stayed in dormitories during each two-week conference. One of them recalled fondly that it was like student life. There was a bell at seven o'clock to get up, and they went to the dining room to eat breakfast. They were encouraged to sit next to someone they had not yet met.[20] The quality of service was more than students could expect. They had access to messengers and automobiles, there were fresh flowers and daily newspapers in each room and entertainment was generously provided.[21]

Participants mixed and talked during discussions and meals, or excursions around the island. These personal contacts were valuable. These experiences had the potential to break the dichotomy between East and West. Harada Tasuku (1863–1940), former president of Dōshisha University in Kyoto and professor of Japanese history and literature of the University of Hawai'i,[22] recorded his experience at the first two conferences:

> An Australian at the [first] conference told me later that he had never spoken to Japanese people frankly before the conference. He had thought that Orientals had a totally different mentality from Occidentals, but found after frank talks with them that there was not much difference and that they were the same human beings with the same mentality...[23]

Photographs taken at the first conference show a striking commonality among the participants regardless of gender, race or nationality (Figure 5.2). Their clothes marked social class. Men wore single-breasted summer linen jackets and small neat collars, often accompanied by Panama hats. They may have brought dinner jackets for formal receptions and dinners. While some Japanese women wore kimonos, others wore low-waisted summer dresses, popular in the 1920s, as did Americans. It was genteel society. Eggleston wrote about participants from Asia:

> They were, of course, well to do. Their behaviour was perfect and they looked very nice people ... they conversed with the visitors in quite a well bred way.[24]

A return sea voyage to Honolulu from Yokohama, Sydney or San Francisco took almost two weeks, and the conference lasted two weeks. Only a minority could afford the time and money. They were not officials, but 'a small select group of people of influence in forming public opinion'.[25]

Although in the late 1940s and early 1950s the IPR was accused of having a communist connection, it remained largely a patrician organization in the inter-war period, funded mainly by big business and American philanthropic giants. It was commonly seen as a 'capitalist and imperialist organization'. Critics often described IPR conferences as a social chit-chat club of a privileged few.[26] Indeed, reflecting the Republican regional vision, the IPR was well representative of big business in the 1920s. Traders, ship owners and bankers shared an enthusiasm to promote internationalism. The American steamship owner Robert Dollar told Merle Davis, the first general secretary of the ISIPR

Figure 5.2 Members, associates and Secretarial Staff, Institute of Pacific Relations, Honolulu session, 1925.

Source: IPR, ed., *Institute of Pacific Relations: Honolulu session, June 30 to July 14, 1925: History, Organization, Proceedings, Discussions and Addresses*, Honolulu: IPR, 1925.

(1926–30), that 'the Institute worked on the same principle as his company did', as both promoted better understanding and peace in the region.[27] Jerome Greene, trustee of the Rockefeller Foundation, executive member of the American Council of the IPR (ACIPR) and a Wall Street banker, also presented a paper on 'The role of the banker in international relations' at the second conference: 'The wide distribution of bonds' tended to promote 'a more liberal and sympathetic attitude toward each other's national characteristics and aspirations'.[28]

The IPR did not exclude labour interests. In selecting participants for the second conference in early 1927, Edward Carter, Secretary of the ACIPR in 1926–32, made it clear that it should recruit participants with interests as diverse as possible, including 'capital and labor'.[29] When British participation was decided, Carter also demanded that participants should include Labour Party sympathizers.[30] As well as the League of Nations, the ILO sent observers and provided materials. Other representatives of labour organizations included Paul Scharrenberg (American), Secretary and Treasurer of the California State Federation of Labor, and Suzuki Bunji (Japanese), President of the General Federation of Labour in Japan. They were mainly middle-of-the-road labour activists. Like Scharrenberg, they often defended the interests of 'national' labourers against foreign ones, rather than advocating the international solidarity of the working class.[31]

The IPR tried to secure the participation of the USSR from the very beginning. This was because it was seen as an important Pacific power, not because of the ideological commitment of key IPR figures. Frank Atherton visited the USSR to negotiate its involvement with the IPR in 1927, Merle Davis at the end of 1927 and Edward Carter (General Secretary in 1933–46) in 1934 and 1936. Although the IPR contained some radical elements and later some communists were involved, it never took a Comintern line. As contemporary observers portrayed, the IPR's patrician identity was problematic in generating interest in the USSR.[32]

Another feature of the first two IPR conferences was the relatively large representation of women. This differed from the gentleman's club atmosphere of other organizations made up of foreign experts, such as the CFR (New York) or the RIIA (London), and conference-based organizations, such as the Institute of Politics at Williamstown (IPW). Many women who participated in IPR conferences independently or as a spouse of a participant were leaders of movements for peace or female franchise.[33] The National Councils of the IPR received enthusiastic support from various women's organizations. They often sponsored public lectures or luncheons for IPR members. Many male participants were supportive of issues such as female franchise.[34]

By linking common interests beyond the nation-state boundaries, business, labour and female representatives had the opportunity to form alternative networks, and to advocate their universalist causes. This, however, did not become a major feature of IPR operations. While feminist elements felt that women's issues and feminist concerns were important for better mutual understanding and peace in the region, they realized that they were not discussed at IPR conferences. Dissatisfied, these women organized a more issues-centred forum, the Pan-Pacific Women's Conference (PPWC), in 1928. Relations with the IPR remained cordial. Merle Davis gave a warm opening address to the first conference in Honolulu in 1928,[35] and the conference continues to the present day.[36]

There is no doubt that the IPR attracted a certain type of person, which might have limited the potential of its experiment. In Japan, language was a key. It was important to be able to function in English. Only a minority of the population with certain aptitudes, background, education and experience could be involved. Interestingly, in contrast to the eloquence of the Chinese, the poor English of the Japanese was noted.[37] This had been noticed at earlier major international conferences, such as the Paris Conference and the Washington Conference, and was believed to be a disadvantage for Japanese diplomacy.[38] Tsurumi, a relatively young JCIPR member (forty-two years old in 1927), was one of the very few who felt confident. Although his English was reported to have been not particularly good,[39] as an ex-member of the debating club at *Ichikō*, he had the required skill, confidence and manner.[40] Other Japanese participants were more reserved, or less confident using English.

There were very few people in Japan who could operate in a foreign language environment, and those who could were much in demand by the government and private corporations.[41]

Some saw that the choice of language at the conference limited the diversity of ideas and perspectives. A Japanese participant at the second conference noted that in China there were:

> … two sets of leaders, one communicating with Japanese leaders in the Chinese or Japanese language, and the other coming in contact with the rest of the powers through the medium of English.

The issue concerned not only language, but the aptitude and thinking of those who use a particular language.[42] The IPR's use of English was not contested. At organizations based in Europe, including the League of Nations, French was as important as English. Other Pacific-based multinational conferences, such as the Pan-Pacific Science Congress (PPSC), debated whether French should also be considered as a conference language.[43] The absence of this kind of debate at the IPR can be explained by the dominance of America and other English-speaking countries, and an initial lack of participation by continental European powers and their colonies. American IPR founders argued for an equal relationship with China and Japan, but the use of non-European languages as a conference language was probably beyond them.

Colonialism, Orientalism and reified nation

Colonialism

Did the concept of the Pacific Community challenge the dominant institutions and ideologies of international politics of the day? 'Political equals' largely meant equality among colonial powers. Colonialism was not the prerogative of great powers. An Australian member, Eggleston, stressed Australia's 'duty' and 'responsibility' for its mandates in the Pacific Islands, which it had gained at the Paris Peace Conference. He argued that the IPR should not concentrate on Asia, but should look more towards the Pacific component of the region.[44] This was an assertion of Australia's semi-imperial status, and indicates that non-great powers also operated within the dominant colonial framework.

Anti-colonial voices were not totally absent in IPR operations. The Chinese group consistently argued for a more equal relationship between China and the powers all through the IPR conferences in the inter-war period. They were most concerned with tariff autonomy and extra-territoriality. Their criticism was initially addressed to the British, although the focus later shifted to another colonial power, Japan. At the first conference, L.T. Chen, an officer representing China at the YMCA in Shanghai, criticized the British handling of recent industrial strikes in Shanghai. In doing this, he was criticizing the semi-colonial relationship between China and Britain.[45]

A more serious challenge to colonialism came from two colonies in the region, Korea and the Philippines. The selection of these two colonies as a part of the Pacific Community in 1925 is significant. Even Croly did not specifically mention colonies when he was advocating the IPR's 'radical' experiment. The only possible reasons for their inclusion were the initial YMCA's role in organizing the first conference, and its strength in these two countries. An international conference was initially proposed by the YMCA in 1919, and a letter was sent by the Honolulu committee in December 1924 to the national YMCA offices in Australia, Canada, China, Japan, Korea, New Zealand, the Philippines and the United States. The Yale Club discussions, which accentuated the departure from the original YMCA project, left Korea out of the first conference. Yet Korea was soon included again, and Korean members attended the first two conferences (seven members in the early conferences and three in 1927). The influence of Christians and the YMCA among these members was evident.

The Korean delegates tried to realize the potential of the IPR's principles of non-governmentality and individual participation to a full extent. Although they did not mention independence, an anti-imperial tone was clear. In 1925, Hugh Cynn, General Secretary of the YMCA for Korea based at Seoul, stated:

> To us [the Japanese policy of assimilation] means the ignoring of our history and culture and the deathknell of our individuality. ... Material prosperity has no meaning for us, if that prosperity spells the one-sided

advantage to those who control prosperity and to us only the losing of our own identity.[46]

He criticized the rhetoric deployed by Japanese colonial officers that Japanizing Koreans meant 'promotion of [Korean people's] welfare'. Under Japanese colonial rule, banking and major industries were controlled by Japanese, and Japanese agricultural immigration was jeopardizing the conditions of Korean peasants. A similar criticism was also made in 1927 by Helen K. Kim, Dean of Ewha College in Seoul. She pointed to the hardship of peasants in Korea, and suggested that the damage had been done by the Japanese agrarian immigration policy.

Her argument was significant because she was exploring the potential of the IPR's principle – a gathering of individuals for the well-being of the people in the Pacific area. For her, this principle made Korean participation possible in the first place. 'The new world of peace' was waiting for the IPR to 'initiate the usage of the ethical standard into all international relations'. By stressing Korea's non-military stance, she implicitly criticized Japanese aggression and indicated that it did not accord with the spirit of the IPR.[47]

The Japanese government was not pleased with these public comments. Japanese officials carefully watched and reported on the activities of Korean representatives during the conferences.[48] Some JCIPR members expressed the view that Korea belonged to the Japanese empire, and objected to its separate representation. Opinion among North Americans was divided. Although there was support for Korean representation,[49] an American 'expert group', many of whom were involved in the IPW, opposed Korean inclusion. They regarded the US–Japan relationship as a key to the success of the IPR, and were concerned about the impact of Korean participation.[50]

The two colonial groups responded differently to the IPR's framework and concept of the Pacific Community. Under the IPR's constitution, which was formalized during the second conference, membership was composed of national units. Section 2 of Article III, however, stated that the IPR would also include:

> any sovereign or autonomous state lying within or bordering the Pacific Ocean or having dominions, colonies, dependencies, territories, mandated or otherwise, in the Pacific area, subject to its being approved and admitted to membership, by the Pacific Council. ... With the approval of the Pacific Council, independent Local Groups may be organized in an eligible country which has not created a National Council.

And then there was Section 3:

> To encourage at Conferences of the Institute the fullest self-expression of distinct racial or territorial groups existing within an eligible country as defined in Section 2 of this Article, the Pacific Council and the

Secretariat may, *with the assent of the National Council of such country*, enter into direct relations with such groups ... [51] [emphasis added]

The constitution was relatively democratic in the sense that it opened a door to colonies, a practice unusual among INGOs in this period.[52] It was important for the colonies, but even more important for the Hawai'i group, a strong local group within the United States. The group had been central in initiating the first conference, and insisted on sending separate representation from the mainland. It was also relevant to countries with British Dominion status. On the other hand, the constitution confirmed a colonial/nation-state framework. It clearly included as member units European powers that had colonies in the region. By the time the constitution was formulated, British membership was well accepted. This British participation was prompted by criticism of British 'colonialism' in China at the first conference. The British group joined the IPR precisely to defend British interests and conduct in China.[53] No strong opposition was recorded on the inclusion of the British, or other European powers. French and Dutch groups followed the precedent and joined the IPR without controversy from 1933.

'Local' or 'ethnic' groups within a nation/empire were accepted, subject to conditions. European powers needed only the approval of the Pacific Council, the executive body of the IPR. Local groups, however, needed to go though a few more steps. First, they had to accept that they belonged to a nation-state/empire, and second they needed their sovereign power's accord. Then the representation of a local group had to be accepted by the Pacific Council, which was initially composed of representatives of 'independent' countries. It included British Dominions, but not colonies. The council had power over policy-making and amendment of the constitution. The Korean group pursued separate representation outside the Japanese imperial framework, and alteration of the constitution to make this possible. They withdrew in1931, when they decided that their wish would not be met. Their participation did not resume until 1942.

The Philippine group did not take the same course. It participated in all conferences except the tenth at Stratford-on-Avon in 1942. Unlike Korea, the question of Philippine independence was not whether it should be granted, but when and how. The Commonwealth of the Philippines was to be established in November 1935, and the date for independence was set for 1945. Although these dates had not yet been announced in the mid-1920s, it wa clear that independence was imminent. This probably made the framework of the IPR more acceptable to the Philippine group. This did not mean that they were not vocal about their desire for independence. In 1925, Conrado Benitez, attorney and former technical adviser in the Philippine Mission to the United States, strongly advocated independence. While praising American institutions and heritage, he denounced the benevolent imperialistic tendency of some Americans who emphasized the 'native incapacity' of the Filipinos:

Only a few days ago, a member of the American Congress who spent a few days in and about Manila, stated in this city that he found the Filipinos not only incapable of independence, but in his opinion, they will never be capable of it. Would he and his type be more charitable toward other people's capacity and develop intellectual humility if we reminded them of what Roosevelt wrote about the danger of civilization felt by the Greeks and the Romans only a few hundred years ago on account of the invasions by the barbarians of Northern Europe – the ancestors of these same men who today actually claim to be the exclusive possessors of all the human virtues and, in the garb of world trotters, pass judgment on the past, present and future capacities of the 'natives' of Oriental countries?[54]

At the second conference, however, 'the view from the Philippines' was given by an American colonial officer. He reiterated this 'native incapability' thesis as well as the unpreparedness of the infrastructure and political and economic conditions for immediate independence.[55] Key American IPR officers were probably more positive about independence and thought it inevitable. Yet they shared a similar benevolent attitude. They argued the significance of the American input in infrastructure in the Philippines, and favoured a gradual, not an immediate, shift to self-governance and independence. Ray Wilbur, President of Stanford University and Chairperson of the Pacific Council, stated in 1927:

> ... the ultimate aim of the American people, viewed as a whole, is not imperialistic. There is a faith in the democratic ideal and a faith that the American form of government and of general education will lead other countries to those advances which have meant so much in the life of America.[56]

The United States possessed superior ideals and infrastructure, and had a duty to 'offer some form of world-service as its contribution to human welfare'.[57] Wilbur tried to dampen the criticism of American colonialism in the Philippines.

Orientalism

In the IPR context, the Orient meant the 'Oriental' powers. The dynamics between these powers and the 'West', Euro-American powers, does not fit within the discourse which Said terms Orientalism. To Said, Orientalism is mainly about the relationship between the colonizer and the colonized.[58] The IPR's Pacific Community included not only American and European great powers, but also powers in Asia, the Euro-American non-great powers and two colonies. No doubt, colonialism was the structure which originated, reproduced and reinforced Orientalism. Yet if we see Orientalism as operating on two levels (essentialization of the concepts of West and East, and reinforcement of the perception of the dichotomy) and justification and enhancement of the domination of the 'West' over the 'East', it could occur outside a formal colonial relationship.

Despite the absence of formal colonial relationships, the Orientalist discourse was evident at the first two conferences. A Japanese participant pointed out that:

> [Circumstances in China] are often unduly simplified by our Western friends to correspond with their preconceived ideas.[59]

Over-simplification and stereotyping of the 'Orient' were the characteristics of Orientalism. The speaker was, however, not free from Orientalism. He argued that the situation was too complex for people in the 'West' to understand. He essentialized the 'East', and tried to justify Japanese intervention in China and exclude external intervention.

Nevertheless, JCIPR members saw a Pacific Community of 'political equals' as an opportunity to resolve the issue of inequality for 'Orientals'. Takaki Yasaka expressed this hope:

> The IPR might be a natural product of modern civilization called the Pacific Age ... We have to recognize the very fact of the awakening of racial consciousness all over the world. We have to deal with it with justice and wisdom ... I am one who believes that the aim of the institute is that of the greatest enterprise, and that it will make the most useful contribution to human civilization at the most appropriate time.[60]

As had happened at the Paris Conference of 1919, the JCIPR's concern was the equality of the Japanese. Sawayanagi Masatarō, leader of the Japanese group in 1925 and 1927, stressed Japan's role as a Pacific power and a harmonizer between East and West.[61] Yet to most observers, JCIPR members demonstrated their desire to be identified as a part of the West. Duncan-Hall, an Australian, felt that they insisted on being perceived as 'Occidental', not 'Oriental'.[62] The identification with the 'West' was their assertion of imperial power and national prestige. Japanese intellectuals and bureaucrats created their Orient, *Tōyō*. It was the other or the 'rest' of Asia, subordinate to Japan.[63] JCIPR members demonstrated an Orientalist attitude to Korea and China, similar to that of European and American colonialists. They stressed 'native' incapability and legitimized Japanese intervention.[64]

Although participants in the first two conferences saw the world through the framework of the dichotomy between East and West, they did not always assume the supremacy of the 'West'. Two points are crucial here: recognition of the diversity within the 'West', especially between Europe and the United States; and the realization of certain errors which had been made in Europe and North America. However, concepts which indicated power and moral superiority, such as modernity, progress or democracy, were attached to the West and were seen as absent from the East. This was evident in a paper, 'Eastern and Western civilizations', presented in 1925 by Anezaki Masaharu, professor of religion at Tokyo Imperial University:

> In the present time the West represents the progressive side of humanity. The western people are active and aggressive. The chief banner of the West is "Progress". ... The Occidentals find expression in progress and take pleasure in making haste. The Orientals are changing many of their ways and adopting things from the West, but still their attitude toward life is one of contemplation.

Anezaki, however, did not see the absolute superiority of the 'West'. For him, advancement was not inherently 'Western', and the word 'progress' itself only began to be used in the eighteenth century. Neither did he see differences between 'East' and 'West' as absolute. Various religions expressed fundamentally the same thing. '[T]he antagonism between the West and the East, between activity and passivity, is not fundamental.'[65]

Some participants respected the 'East', and this often reflected their self-criticism of the 'West'. The views of Dominion members were illuminating in this regard. Eggleston detailed the beauty and courtesy of women from Asia, although he was unimpressed by their imitation of 'Western' hair styles. He admired the way government and society in Japan tackled the difficulties of population and industrialization.[66] He pointed out a tendency of foreigners in Asia to dismiss the vices and idealize the virtues of their home countries:

> To hear the foreigner in Shanghai talking, one would think that there was no political incompetence in the West, no corruption in Chicago, no hold-ups in Melbourne...[67]

Eggleston's strength and originality was based on this critical self-reflection, not self-congratulation, as well as his compassion for the people in Japan and China. He urged his fellow Australians to pay more attention to this dynamically changing region. Although he pointed to the great prospects for economic activities for Australians, especially in the Pacific, he also saw a great threat from Asia, especially Japan. As a result, this foreseeing regionalist defended the White Australian Policy and tariff protection. For him, a key was not 'race'. The idea of 'White' racial superiority, which Sawayanagi saw as a base for discriminatory immigration acts against Asians,[68] was perceived to be 'incorrect' at IPR conferences. 'Scientific' research findings, such as those carried out by the 'the Survey of Race Relations', challenged the stereotype that Asians did not assimilate the democratic system of 'Western' values.[69] Eggleston, too, complied with this code.

Eggleston, however, saw a great distinction between the East and the West in terms of 'culture'. The difference in living standards, culture and 'democratic' ideals made the assimilation of Asian immigrants impossible in the short term. For him, shared ideas of democracy and political methods were essential for the governance of society without conflict.[70] This argument indicated that the people in the 'West' and the 'East' did not inherently share these ideas. Eggleston's Australia was more independent from Britain and more region-conscious. But this Australia did not accommodate Asians nor, implicitly, local indigenous groups. Tsurumi felt that discriminatory immigration and tariff policies were the basis of democracy in Australia.[71]

Americans were also critical of the supreme position of the 'West'. Like Eggleston, Charles Batchelder, former US Trade Commissioner to India, felt that the 'Orient' needed serious attention. It was important as a market and raw materials supplier for the United States. More significantly, he feared that the failure of economic development in Asia would lead to a global communist revolution. It was important to get it right, and Batchelder did not see the 'Western' model as perfect or ideal for Asia. The 'Orient' must:

> not make the mistakes of the Occident, and must avoid the sweat shop and the slum, long hours, and the exploitation of women and children, of the weak and the poor, underfeeding, bad housing and working conditions.[72]

He saw the faults in the path taken by US and European powers, and suggested modified capitalism as a better way of managing the economy in Asia. After pointing out the deficiencies of the capitalist system, in which workers had little power, he argued that a modified capitalism, cooperative production and distribution, might be a good path for Asia. Interestingly, he had seen that this model was successful in the United States.[73]

In 1925 and 1927, Anezaki, Eggleston and Batchelder critically assessed what they termed the 'Western' paths of development and industrialization. They saw the system of the West failing, and seriously sought alternative approaches. At the same time, the notion of the dichotomy between East and West was further strengthened. The distinction was made on the basis not of 'race', but of 'culture', especially 'national culture'.

Reifying the nation and politicizing the 'national culture'

Reification of the nation and national culture, a common practice in this period, had great implications for both domestic and international politics.[74] The latter was well demonstrated at IPR conferences. While contemporaries and later scholars argued that the IPR shifted its orientation from 'culture' to 'politics' around 1929, 'culture' was politically charged in IPR operations from the beginning. In particular, 'national culture' was deliberately constructed by participants to serve their own agendas, including justification of their government's policies. Furthermore, this reification contributed to essentializing the notion of the East/West.

Political agendas behind the making of 'national culture' or 'national image' varied. Japanese participants tried to promote cooperative relations with the powers, particularly the United States, by stressing an image of a liberal and peace-loving Japan. They argued that militarism was dying, and that liberalism and democratic movements were the trend. Sawayanagi stated at the first conference:

> I have already referred to the growth of a strong, liberal tendency in the educational world of Japan. Such a tendency, however, is by no means confined to educational circles; it is observable in all fields of activity. In politics, for instance, a universal manhood suffrage bill was passed finally this spring after twenty years of hard and constant fighting. As regards our foreign affairs, a new generation of diplomats with a fresh and broader outlook on the requirements of international life is rapidly coming to the front. On all hands, I notice unmistakable signs of the triumph of liberalism over the forces of reactionary conservatism.[75]

JCIPR members played a significant role as non-official, voluntary international publicists for the Japanese nation/state/empire. They had exceptional qualifications and skills as international publicists, and it was not only at IPR conferences that they contributed to the presentation of a liberal Japan. Tsurumi went on an eighteen-month lecture tour of North America from August 1924. Starting at the IPW, he gave almost 150 lectures at universities, conferences and various other institutions. In these lectures, like Sawayanagi, he promoted an image of 'liberal' Japan. One famous lecture was called 'The rising tide of liberalism in Japan', and he repeated it so many times that he almost memorized it. He tried to argue against what he termed anti-Japanese groups on occasion, such as a public lecture at the Foreign Policy Association in New York.[76] It is likely that the Japanese government at least partially funded Tsurumi's tour. It certainly contributed to the international activities of the JCIPR. JCIPR members, non-official, skilled in foreign languages, well-mannered, cultivated and well connected to North American members, were useful and effective for the government to tame the criticism of aggressive Japanese militarism. When the anti-Japanese immigration law was passed, US–Japan diplomatic relations reached a low point. It made good sense for the government to utilize them. The government was not coercive. Rather, 'non-official' post-League internationalists at the JCIPR were enthusiastic in promoting abroad these images in support of the Japanese cooperative foreign policy and counteracting 'anti-Japan' sentiment. Their role was to ensure a 'correct' understanding of the 'Japanese perspective'. They pursued this goal with a sense of mission as the national elite.

IPR conferences were an excellent platform for national image making. Participants at IPR conferences formed personal friendships, yet they often reconstructed their image not so much of individuals as of nations. Duncan-

Hall was particularly impressed with this new image of liberal Japan.[77] The manner and class of JCIPR members were effective in promoting an image of a 'liberal' and sophisticated Japan. Eggleston also noted:

> They don't at all give one the impression of a conquering militant race. ... Some of the nicest and most gentlemanly members of the conference are Japanese.[78]

Although most participants were impressed with this new image of Japan, some were more cautious. Merle Davis was born and brought up in Kyoto, and had spent much of his life in Japan before he became involved with the IPR. In 1927, he warned the first Research Secretary of the IPR, John Condliffe, former professor of economics at Canterbury University College at Christchurch, New Zealand:

> there were other currents of Japanese thought that were hostile and unapproachable – the military and naval groups and the great mass of nationalists. We are dealing only with a small English-speaking group of scholars, merchants, bankers and officials, most of whom had been educated in England and America. They were for the time being in power but were aware of their precarious situation and anxious that we should not misunderstand it or press them too hard.[79]

An image of 'liberal' Japan, which JCIPR members were eager to promote, contributed to this perception of a very clear division between liberal and reactionary factions. The view became dominant among post-League internationalists who gathered for IPR conferences.

The construction of a 'national culture' was not a peculiar practice of JCIPR members. Other members did the same thing, with different political agendas. Ray Wilbur emphasized the moral superiority of American 'national character' and justified its 'temporary' possession of the Philippines and its leadership in the region.[80] Participants from the Dominions also used IPR conferences to define their 'national cultures'. Their countries had recently acquired a more independent status, and they felt the need to construct a new 'national' identity. At the same time, this was an effective justification for their governmental policies, particularly anti-Asian immigration. They spent much time describing the history of their countries, emphasizing their Anglo-European 'traditions' and distinguishing their 'national character' from the other, Asia. Despite the use of the word of tradition, 'national characters' of the Dominions had not yet 'emerged', but needed to be created and built up. In their view, Asian immigration threatened this process. Canadian John Nelson argued in 1925:

> Canada is forced to proceed [in immigration] with caution because in addition to the lack of a national background of considerable age, her

basic population is not homogeneous, and her national type not standardized. ... The Canadian attitude is one of anxiety that the influx of Orientals shall never reach proportions that will endanger the national type which they are seeking to establish in the Dominion.[81]

A similar view was repeated by Arthur Currie, leader of the Canadian group for the second conference, in 1927.[82] Until November 1925, Nelson published the *Daily World* in Vancouver, where Asian immigration was hotly discussed. His involvement in the public debate and the 'Survey of Race Relations' project, and his active role in the YMCA movement, brought him to the first IPR conference.[83] He was, therefore, in no way an unenlightened person on race relations. He would have refuted the theory of racial superiority. But this did not lead him to support Asian immigration in Canada in 1925. By detailing the Canadian national type in the Anglo-European tradition, he justified the discriminatory immigration law. Woods suggests that this may have reflected his position as a leader of the Canadian group.[84] The process of defining 'national character' or 'national culture' was a deliberate, selective and political process. It was also closely tied to the Orientalist and state-centred nature of IPR operations. Various identities – ideology, gender, social classes and even 'race'/'culture' – were ultimately subjugated to the notion of the nation-state.

Non-state agency

As Croly noted in 1927, the merit of the IPR rested on its unofficial character. The discussion at the Yale Club and the first IPR conference emphasized the individual capacity of participants. This unofficial status was thought to be important: first, to prevent IPR conferences from becoming a stage for national groups to defend their governmental policies; and, second, to encourage individual discussion as free as possible from official constraints. Efforts were made to safeguard this unofficial character. Words such as 'delegates' were avoided at the first conference because they implied 'national' representation.[85]

This agenda was, however, seriously undermined by the dominant notion of the nation-state among IPR members. Croly had already warned of the danger of becoming involved in policy matters and policy formulation. Explaining the situation of a nation and 'national' policy and presenting 'insider' knowledge need not amount to a justification of government policies. If one reifies the nation, and identifies it with the state, however, the distinction between representing the nation as an individual and the state as an official becomes ambiguous. In this context, government policies were often seen as national expressions. 'National' representatives tend to defend their government's policies voluntarily. The case of John Nelson, for example, suggests that, despite this banner of 'unofficialness', the IPR's setting made him exercise self-censorship and not contradict governmental policies. The diverse views within a nation, which may have opposed these policies, tended to be ignored, and it was regarded as 'natural' for participants to defend their governments' policy.

The ambiguity of this 'unofficial' nature, and the close link between nation and state was furthered by the structure of the IPR. It was firmly based on 'national' units, National Councils. The IPR constitution, Article III stated:

> 1. Subject to the provisions hereof the Institute of Pacific Relations is constituted by the national units the name of whose representatives are appended to this Constitution...
> 2. A national unit ... shall be a National Council organized for the purpose of the Institute, or organization of similar purposes. ... Each constituent country shall have one National Council or equivalent organization ... [86]

There was no reference to the unofficial nature of the organization. Among INGOs in the 1920s, this structure, based on national units, was much more dominant than the direct membership of individuals to a world body.[87] White noted in 1933: 'Not only do national organizations seem to form a satisfactory basis for most international organizations, but international organizations tend to develop and strengthen national organizations.' In White's view, this was not ideal, but many organizations found it satisfactory.[88]

IPR members had to be a 'representative' of a nation and reside in the nation. Between 1925 and 1931, the regulation of nationality in national groups was, however, relatively loose. Chinese, Japanese and Koreans residents in Honolulu participated in the first conference as members of their 'home' countries, and a few American missionaries resident in Japan were included among Japanese members.[89] Duncan-Hall participated as an Australian member in 1927 while he was at Syracuse University in New York State. Harada Tasuku and Akagi Hidemichi were among a few JCIPR members who lived outside Japan. Harada was resident in Honolulu, and Akagi was based in New York as General Secretary of the Japanese Students' Christian Association in North America. Harada participated in the first two IPR conferences as a Japanese member and the third as an American member before he returned to Japan in 1932. The JCIPR had a few conference secretaries with English names for the conferences in 1929 and 1931. This was not the case for the Chinese group. Around the early 1930s, national groups consisted, more or less, of those with nationality of and residency in the nation.

IPR operations, including conferences, were based on national units, which reinforced the reification of the nation and strengthened the state-centricity of IPR operations. The conference of 1925, for example, opened with statements by the leaders of 'national' groups, presenting an Australian or Canadian view. Although some noted that there were competing views in their own countries, they tended to generalize, creating the illusion of a coherent and monolithic national character, opinion or view. Personifying nation-states was a part of this reification of the nation/state, and it was common practice among participants at IPR conferences. The name of the country was usually a reference to its government. No doubt this practice gave participants a sense of power, excitement and importance. Discussing inter-state issues was a privilege given to a very few high officials or politicians. The practice enhanced the quasi-diplomatic atmosphere. Croly commented on the dangers:

> [The IPR's] members will constantly be tempted to believe that it is capable of some salutary intervention in a critical dilemma. ... Sooner or later it will probably yield to one of these temptations or solicitations and undertake to place its authority as a research institute behind some piece of practical political advice. But I hope not. If it does commit itself to particular policies it can hardly fail to become propagandist, and it will measurably disqualify itself for the more permanently important task which no other organized body is in a position to perform.[90]

While some were more academically oriented, most participants were attracted by and aspired to power. They wanted to implement their ideas or desired self-promotion. This tendency was almost inevitable, given the selection of conference participants. The IPR aimed at the 'influential' few, not the mass. Political orientation in the IPR was, therefore, not caused by any sudden shift of focus to political topics, such as the Manchuria issue. Rather, it was inherent in the very nature of the people who gathered at IPR conferences and its National Councils, and in their assumptions about nation and state.

Between the state and society

Implications for public opinions and policies

Did the IPR influence public opinion and policy-making in this period? If the IPR guarded its principle of non-involvement in policy-making as Croly wished, its conferences would not influence foreign policy directly or immediately. Rather, they would have aimed at a longer-term effect on the views of concerned officials and the public.

In this regard, the first two IPR conferences achieved success in the limited, but influential circles that the IPR targeted. They were well received by participants and the press, and this was reported to officials. Although not front page news, IPR conferences were widely covered. The Commissioner for Australia in the United States reported that from August to October 1925 more than 350 US papers, magazines and journals carried articles relating to the institute, and that 195 public addresses on the IPR were delivered by American participants.[91] They included favourable articles by notable figures, such as Chester Rowell, a distinguished Republican commentator from Berkeley, and Wilbur, another influential Republican in California. On the East coast, the *New York Sun* praised the IPR as a new type of organization.[92] Similar publicity occurred in Japan. JCIPR members publicized the IPR's functions and aims by writing articles and giving public lectures. These articles appeared in journals for the Industry Club (*Kōgyō kurabu*), diplomatic circles, academic circles and women's associations.[93] In this way, they reached the audience they targeted and stimulated discussion on regional issues.

What of government involvement in National Councils? Initially, the US State Department was not favourably disposed towards IPR conferences, because the first conference focused on immigration policy, a sensitive issue best avoided. American IPR founders argued the significance of non-governmentality, stressing the potential and merits of discussion unconstrained by official policies. Duncan-Hall reported to the Australian government that the IPR conference in 1925 was 'one of the most important incidents after the Washington Conference'.[94] The Prime Minister's Department, which dealt with external affairs before a separate department was established in 1934, however, feared the IPR conferences' effect on immigration policies and imperial arrangements. As a result, the Australian government maintained a policy of non-involvement with the IPR.[95] In contrast, the Japanese government saw the IPR as an important and effective venue for unofficial diplomacy where a favourable outcome might be produced in relation to American immigration policy and the US–Japan relationship. The Ministry of Foreign Affairs initiated the organization of the Japanese group for the first conference and maintained close ties with the JCIPR after it was organized in 1926. It made substantial financial contributions to it, and participated in functions, meetings and discussions on activities and conferences. The case of the JCIPR suggests that greater government involvement did not mean greater influence of the JCIPR on policy-making. Rather, the close ties meant that the JCIPR was constrained in presenting critical policy alternatives, and tended to justify government agendas.

Immigration policy

When Merle Davis was organizing the first conference in late 1924 and early 1925, amendment or even repeal of the immigration act of 1924 was seen as a possible goal. This was totally abandoned at the first conference, the objective of which was noted as being to 'bring together accurate information' on the conditions which would mould opinion and feeling towards other people, and to discuss them; and to 'point the way to right actions' leading to 'understanding and peace in the Pacific'.[96] Clearly, research, not lobbying, was seen as a major function of the IPR.

A new approach to international politics was outlined in the context of discussion of immigration policy. In 1925 Chinese and Japanese participants questioned the dominant view that immigration was a domestic political issue falling under the aegis of national sovereignty. Ta Chen, professor of sociology at Qinghua (Tsinghua) College in Beijing (Peking), argued that human beings had a natural right to move and choose where to live.[97] Takayanagi Kenzō, professor of law at Tokyo Imperial University, also pointed out the historicity of the concept of national sovereignty and argued for the need for modifying it in a new context:

> [I]f we conceive of sovereignty as absolute and unlimited, just as eighteenth and nineteenth century jurists thought of private property ... international life would become unbearable and no sound international cooperation in the cause of world civilization would be possible.[98]

Tsurumi Yūsuke also argued that the notion of absolute national sovereignty was at odds with world trends. He pointed out that the core of the new movement of the twentieth century was:

> [T]o make the privileged positions monopolized by force by a minority of modern nations and races available for the common welfare of humankind as a whole, and to establish the international principles for achieving this goal, based on the might of justice and reason, not force.[99]

The welfare of the world should be sought, even at some expense to national sovereignty. Duncan-Hall, who was a member of the League of Nations Union in Australia and later himself worked for the League, found this point most interesting.[100] As a result, experts on international relations, such as Duncan-Hall, Quincy Wright of University of Chicago and Jerome Greene, discussed immigration not as a domestic political issue, but as a question of international agreements.[101]

Despite this broader potential, the issue was political and specific, and concerned mainly with American discrimination against Japanese immigration. The discussion illuminated the nature of IPR operations. The Pacific Community was an American-led regional order which envisaged a more equal relationship with the powers in Asia. Equality for colonies was not within the terms of the discussion. Chinese immigration and discrimination against Chinese overseas was a great concern for the Chinese group, but the more urgent issues were tariff autonomy and extraterritoriality. It was the Japanese group which rigorously pursued concern with discriminatory immigration policy as a sticking point for equal relationships.

The focus of Japanese members was almost exclusively American immigration policy. Duncan-Hall was puzzled that they were not concerned with discriminatory immigration policies in other countries.[102] For Japanese members, Pacific relations meant the US–Japan relationship. They seemed unaware of their inconsistency in questioning American policy while accepting Japanese imperial status in Korea or its privileged rights in China. Like the Japanese delegates at the Paris Conference in 1919, Takayanagi and Tsurumi, who enthusiastically argued for new codes of conduct in international politics, used the rhetoric of 'New Diplomacy' to negotiate the best interests of the Japanese state/empire.

There was no discussion of repeal of the law on the basis of general principle.[103] Takayanagi demanded 'enlightened' administration of the law so that 'the feelings and sensibilities of other nations or races would not be unduly injured by too vigorous an assertion of so-called "sovereign rights" '.[104] Treatment of immigrants of Japanese origin should be the same as for immigrants from European countries, and the same quota system should be adopted for Japanese immigrants as for Europeans.

The first two conferences did not result in any change to American immigration policy. A quota system was not applied to Japanese immigrants, and the article articulating discrimination based on race was not repealed. Any influence remained in the domain of public opinion. Participants reconsidered the implications of immigration, and some modified their opinions of opponents of Japanese or 'Oriental' immigration.[105]

The Pact of Paris

The General Treaty for Renunciation of War as an Instrument of National Policy, commonly known as the Pact of Paris, was another policy area discussed at the 1927 IPR conference. The pact was first proposed as a security treaty between France and the United States. Its general principle was extended, and finally it was signed by all but five independent countries in the world in August 1928. It was the first international treaty to outlaw war as a means of solving inter-governmental disputes. Interpretations of its significance differ greatly. For some, including Robert Ferrell, who wrote a history of the pact, *Peace in Their Time*, in 1952, it was 'an illusion and deception' and did very little to prevent World War II. These scholars certainly do not see it as a breakthrough in American foreign policy or international relations.[106] A recent work, however, re-evaluates its significance as 'the most advanced expression of the post-war Republican goal for peace, law and economic cooperation'.[107] Despite its low profile, its implications were enduring. Because of its 'abstract' nature, along with the Covenant of the League of Nations and the Washington Treaties, the pact was regarded as the legal base for condemning Japanese aggression in China not only during the Manchurian crisis, but also during the Tokyo Tribunal after World War II. The Tanaka cabinet, which concluded this pact in 1928, would not have anticipated such an outcome.

The IPR's involvement in this treaty was multilayered. First, James Shotwell, professor of history at Columbia University, who presented one of the most important drafts of the Pact of Paris, was an instigator of the IPR. He was present at the Yale Club meeting and, although he did not attend the first conference, he played an important role in the second and third conferences. He was the first chairperson of the IPR's International Research Committee. In addition to being an inspirational figure at the ACIPR and the IPR, he represented what he called 'action intellectuals' – academics who were positively involved in 'public affairs' or policy formulation. He was a member of the Inquiry group at the time of the Paris Peace Conference, and involved in discussions about the machinery of peace, in the 1920s.

His draft treaty was presented at the second conference in 1927, and attracted considerable attention. It was titled a 'draft treaty of permanent peace between the US and other countries'. It was co-written with his university colleague, Joseph P. Chamberlain, in response to a proposal by the French Foreign Minister, M. Briand. Shotwell stated that its aim was to embody 'all the mutual obligations which the adaptation of the principle of Locarno to America would imply'.[108] The draft closely resembled the Pact of Paris of 1928.

This draft treaty was often called the American Locarno, and closely followed the Locarno Treaty of 1925, a regional treaty for European countries. Shotwell noted that part one of the draft treaty, which dealt with renunciation of war, was 'taken literally from the Treaty'.[109] This regional focus is worth stressing. It was why the draft treaty was taken up at the Round Table on 'Diplomatic relations in the Pacific' at the second IPR conference.

The topic, diplomatic relations in the Pacific, was an ongoing theme from the first conference. The critical points in this discussion were the nature of the security system in the Pacific and the relationship between the Pacific Community and the international community. Participants emphasized the peculiarities of the region, which were both advantageous and disadvantageous for creating a secure and peaceful regional machinery. The Pacific had definite advantages. Unlike in Europe, countries were divided by sea, and did not share close land borders. The problems were, however, more pronounced. Unlike Europe, the region lacked adequate diplomatic machinery. The League of Nations did not operate efficiently in the Pacific because of the absence of the major Pacific powers, the USSR, the United States and China. The League was far from the Pacific and was mainly occupied with European affairs. British Dominions lacked discretion in foreign affairs. The barriers of language and social organization between 'East' and 'West' were also thought to prevent better understanding.

In the mid-1920s, these difficulties did not lead participants to advocate strengthening the worldwide framework. Rather, they favoured regional, not worldwide, institutions and agreements. The Washington Treaties were not enough,[110] but some new regional machineries were needed:

> Such [regional] developments in the Pacific, not necessarily within the League ... might contribute largely to the separation of the essentially world aspects of international cooperation from the more definitely European commitments which the League inherits from the circumstances of its origin.

Criticism of the League's Eurocentricity probably reflected American 'independent internationalism'. The Republican administration had been formulating a general framework of multilateral cooperation among the powers. The idea of possible independence of a regional arrangement from the League's framework is, therefore, not entirely radical or surprising. There remained, however, a strong wariness about any regional arrangement completely independent from the League.

> There is no possibility of isolating the Pacific as a region for specific agreement out of relation to general international affairs. ... It is not possible ... to regard the Washington machinery as an alternative exclusive of the League and of European diplomacy. The Pacific needs Locarno; but it needs also that its Locarno shall be in harmony and constructive relationship with the developing organs of international government at Geneva.[111]

The cooperation with the League was already evident in IPR operations in 1927. The League and the ILO regarded the IPR positively and sent observers and materials to assist with the conference.[112]

Shotwell and Chamberlain proposed an American Locarno to complement the League system in the Pacific region and work within the framework of the League. A certain autonomy and regional particularity was assumed. It was a loose but important collective security measure for the United States, a non-League member, which held a leadership position in the Pacific.

Although it originated as a security treaty between the United States and France, this draft treaty was clearly aimed at Japan at the IPR conference. Takaki Yasaka and Aoki Setsuichi (a diplomat and Director of the Tokyo branch of the League of Nations who attended the IPR conference as a League observer) pointed out that the US–Japan relationship was a major concern of Shotwell when he drafted the treaty.[113] Shotwell indicated that Japanese entry to this treaty would enhance its effectiveness:

> [the draft treaty] provides against the use of war as an instrument of policy, and if adopted by the United States and the other powers, including Japan, would so extend over the world the spirit of Locarno as to insure, not only effective measures of disarmament, but world-peace in so far as it is possible to guarantee peace by such measures of international insurance.[114]

In 1927 and 1928 Japanese experts on foreign affairs debated this draft treaty not as a multinational treaty for peace, but as a bilateral US–Japan security treaty. They were unanimous over the need for such a treaty with the United States because it was not a member of the League of Nations and welcomed the draft proposal. Nevertheless, they criticized the draft as too American-centred. As Shotwell noted, it involved 'no real departure from American settled policies', including the Monroe Doctrine, and 'carefully safeguarded American sovereignty'. Japanese participants and foreign experts critically assessed the implications of the Monroe Doctrine. This is noteworthy because it demonstrates that the JCIPR supported the American-led regional order, but not without reservations.

Rōyama Masamichi (1895–1965), then assistant professor of political science at Tokyo Imperial University, articulated the criticism among Japanese specialists. He made his first appearance at IPR conferences in 1927. He criticized the draft treaty at the round table discussion along with Takayanagi, Takaki and Tsurumi, and further clarified his points in 1928. In his view, the draft treaty lacked a clear definition of aggressive war, and of 'security' measures against aggressive parties. He also pointed out the hypocrisy of American diplomacy: what defined it was 'not idealistic humanitarianism, but contradictory diplomacy which pursued Monroeism, sovereignty and international peace'. The view was widely shared among Japanese foreign experts, including JCIPR members.[115]

Rōyama's view also revealed that, despite the fact that these experts welcomed a general concept of collective secrecy, they interpreted critically the American regional order, the League of Nations and the post-League order. It is important that this criticism was expressed well before the outbreak of the Manchurian Incident in 1931. JCIPR members supported the League and the cooperative policy of successive governments since the Hara cabinet (1918–21). This was not exactly support for new principles or ideals. Rōyama, for example, understood that 'diplomacy of the League of Nations was not based on pacifism', but 'collective diplomacy to secure national interests beyond national boundaries, to achieve mutual security and preserve the [international] status quo'. He used British diplomacy towards Egypt as an example of League diplomacy, and argued that Japanese diplomacy also 'tried to secure [Japanese] rule of Manchuria'. Japan needed the League to maintain the order in the Orient (*Tōyō*). This meant the preservation of Japanese interests in the region, which Rōyama saw as being threatened by the intervention of the United States and the rise of Chinese power.[116]

This view of the League was dominant among senior diplomats and politicians in the party governments who argued for cooperation with the great powers and international organizations. Despite military intervention in China in 1927 and 1928, or because of the criticism this aggressive policy aroused, the Tanaka cabinet was keen to restore its image of 'cooperative diplomacy'. The conclusion of the proposed Pact of Paris seemed an effective means of tempering the anxiety of the great powers, including the United States. The Tanaka cabinet felt that Japanese rights in Manchuria and Inner Mongolia should be safeguarded. Yet it also thought that signing the pact was a general gesture of agreeing with the principles of a 'civilized and modern' empire.[117] In the 1930s, many post-League internationalists, such as Takaki, were to regret not so much that Japan did not stick to the pact; rather, they regretted that they had not made enough effort to insert this safeguard clause on Japanese 'special' rights in Manchuria and Inner Mongolia in the same way that the United States had insisted on Monroeism.

It is hard to measure how much influence the JCIPR had on the Japanese government's ratification of the Pact. It welcomed a general framework, and stirred public discussion, although criticism was also strong. Debuchi Katsuji, ambassador to the United States in mid-1929, also viewed Shotwell and the IPR favourably.[118] He was the son-in-law of Tanaka, but also a main promoter of the Shidehara cooperative diplomacy with the United States. His high evaluation of the IPR might have influenced the Tanaka cabinet's favourable attitude. Yet, not because of but despite JCIPR members' debates and views, the government probably concluded the Pact for its own reasons.

Ironically, 'progressive' or 'liberal' Diet members, including JCIPR member Tsurumi, opposed the pact. The issue was not collective security or world peace, but political opportunism. The Tanaka cabinet brought the pact to the Diet for approval in early 1929; the opposition parties seized upon it to attack the *Seiyūkai* government. The *Seiyūkai* was the 'conservative' party with a strong rural voting base. Those who opposed ratification of the pact were members of the main opposition party, *Minseitō*, and other minor parties. They included many who were called 'progressives', such as Ozaki Yukio, a major advocate of universal male franchise, Abe Isoo, a socialist reformer, and Nishio Suehiro, a labour activist. Two JCIPR members were also among them, Suzuki Bunji, a labour activist, who attended the second, third and fourth IPR conferences, and Tsurumi Yūsuke. Tsurumi was one of the founders of *Meiseikai*, a new political party based on New Liberalism.[119]

The basis for the opposition of these 'progressives' to the 'conservative' government's ratification of the pact was in no way 'progressive'. They argued that the wording of the treaty violated the sovereignty of the Emperor. The preamble to the pact embodied a democratic spirit, and stated that it would be concluded in the name of the people (*jinmin*). The opposition argued that this was unconstitutional because under the Meiji constitution, sovereignty resided with the Emperor, not the people.[120] The issue had been brought to the government's attention at an earlier stage of negotiation, and the Japanese government had unsuccessfully negotiated to erase the phrase. In July 1928, the US government suggested that it meant 'on behalf of the people', not 'by the people', and that this would not violate the sovereignty of the Emperor. The government decided to go ahead, overriding opposition. Later it resolved the problem by issuing a notice to the public in June 1929 that under the constitution, the phrase would not apply to the Japanese empire. The opposition to the ratification was motivated by several factors. They wanted to destabilize the Tanaka cabinet to gain power and implement their reform policies. Their argument, however, was based not on the spirit of democracy, but on an imperial framework and the Meiji constitution which legitimized it.

The connection between the IPR and the Pact of Paris was mainly the fact that an influential member of the IPR was regarded as one of the principal drafters. While the draft was discussed extensively as one significant mechanism to secure regional stability, its interpretation varied among IPR members. One cannot deny the excitement of Shotwell and his supporters at the IPR, but as an early attempt to outlaw war the Pact of Paris was not exactly a triumph of pacifism. Various governments signed it for specific political reasons, and there were reservations. The regional implication of Shotwell's draft treaty also demonstrated the ambiguity of the Pacific Community in the post-League order. One significant area which the IPR contributed to was building popular public support for the pact to an extent. It is probably safe to say that the IPR contributed to public discussion of the pact and in this way may have assisted in making governments' job of concluding the Pact easier.

Foreign experts between the state and society

Dominance of 'experts' over YMCA men

Despite success in educating and enlightening the concerned public, each step in the institutionalization of the IPR pushed its role as a foreign policy think-tank. There was an increasing dominance of 'experts' over YMCA men in IPR operations. Downplaying the YMCA element began in late 1924. Furthermore, this push came not only from those with no YMCA background, but from prominent YMCA men. Merle Davis led a substantial reduction in the YMCA element to gain the support of 'influential' circles. The YMCA element did not vanish immediately. At the first conference, two distinct camps existed in almost every national group: religious professionals with YMCA connections; and 'experts' on Asia and the Pacific islands, including academics, business people and journalists. This was because in 1925, national groups were mainly organized by the national YMCA headquarters in each country, which had been preparing for the conference based on materials sent from the central committee (an international body based in Honolulu) several months earlier. The Australian and New Zealand groups for the first conference, for example, were selected by the respective national secretariats of the YMCA. Among them few were 'experts': John Condliffe out of eleven New Zealanders; H. Duncan-Hall and Stephen Roberts (1901–70), lecturer at the University of Melbourne, out of six Australians; and the others were YMCA-related people. In contrast, National Councils of the IPR, which were organized in each country after the first conference, were mostly dominated by 'expert' groups.

Tension between the YMCA camp and the 'expert' camp manifested itself in 1925 as a dispute over the observance of after-breakfast prayers at the Punahou School, where conference participants lodged. The practice was introduced by Australian and New Zealand groups, who were dominated by YMCA members and who arrived in Honolulu before other participants. 'Expert' groups from the American mainland, particularly those involved in the IPW, arrived shortly afterwards and strongly objected to the practice. While it was eventually modified and secularized, the dispute signified a power shift from the YMCA group to the experts.[121] As a result, George Blakeslee, a 'Far East' expert at Clark University, took charge. He had been a leading figure at annual summer meetings of the IPW for the previous four years, and he had also became central in the New York Committee for the organization of the first IPR conference. Soon after his arrival at Honolulu, he established the formula and structure of the IPR conference, closely following those of the IPW. The conferences consisted of forums for general discussion, a Round Table of a smaller number of experts on specific issues, and public addresses.

This YMCA's 'withdrawal' resulted in a rapid disappearance of religion as a conference topic. At the first conference, six out of twenty-seven topics were on religion.[122] Religion was totally dropped from the third conference. Key IPR figures were keen to overcome the legacies of the YMCA and to portray the IPR as *modern* and *scientific*.[123] This did not mean a decline of Christian faith among IPR figures. Although the number of participants with a YMCA background was substantially reduced at the second conference, many key North American IPR members came from a missionary background. Christian faith did not necessarily conflict with the emphasis on science. What bothered them was the philanthropic outlook of a friendly association, which lacked 'scientific' credibility, and appeal to 'influential' groups, including major foundations. Legacies of their YMCA origins were also strong in National Councils of the IPR in Asia, where Christians were disproportionately represented. This was especially noticeable among the Chinese participants. Eggleston recorded in 1927 that all the delegates from China were Christian.[124] To a much lesser extent, this was the case among Japanese participants. Christians in Japan and China were exposed to foreigners, their customs and language.[125] They had often studied in the United States, and they were more likely to be fluent in English than the rest of the society.

The international secretariat of the IPR (ISIPR)

Between the first two conferences, key figures formed and defined the IPR as a permanent organization. They aimed to make it modern, scientific and credible. Although they emphasized the enlightenment of public opinion, a think-tank role was gradually gaining a force. Between 1925 and 1927, an emphasis on an 'expert' organization with a strong research capability emerged. At the first conference, a committee on establishing a permanent organization was appointed. It had the objectives of creating a Pacific Council (the executive body of the IPR); establishing a headquarters; employing a secretariat; fundraising; and preparing for a second conference. The Pacific Council was duly established. Its members were to be the representatives of National Councils once they were organized. Wilbur became its Chairperson, Atherton, Treasurer, Inoue Junnosuke (Japan), first Vice-Chairperson, and David Yui (China), second Vice-Chairperson. The other members were Mungo

MacCallum (Australia), Robert Boden (Canada) and James Allen (New Zealand). To this list, a British representative, Lionel Curtis, was added from 1927. Despite American dominance in staffing and funding, the council secured multinational representation. It, however, initially did not include representatives of colonial groups (Korea and the Philippines). Unlike some INGOs of the day, the weight of members' votes did not vary according to the contribution of their National Councils. Each vote carried equal weight. Consultation with National Councils was not neglected, and a meeting was held just before each biennial conference.[126]

By January 1926, some critical decisions were made: inviting British participation for the second conference; making Honolulu the headquarters for the next five-year period; appointing Merle Davis General Secretary and Charles Loomis Associate General Secretary; raising a budget of $90,000 for the second conference in Honolulu; having the secretariat visit the participating countries to prepare; and securing a research secretary as soon as feasible.[127] A priority on research was clear.

The decision-making body was the Pacific Council, not the ISIPR. Honolulu was also not a permanent arrangement for the ISIPR. Its expenditure was US$24,500 in 1926 and stayed at a similar level until 1933.[128] Its responsibilities were administration and coordination: to prepare for and conduct the conferences; to promote research; to exchange information; and to liaise between National Councils.[129] It was not until around 1939 that the ISIPR would emerge as central in policy-making. The YMCA element was strong among its original nine staff. Davis and Loomis were YMCA men, and Atherton's family had long been patrons of local YMCA activities.

Although the main communication methods were letters and cables, the IPR emphasized the need for personal visits to make this multinational organization work. This meant sea travel, a very time-consuming practice. Key ISIPR office holders travelled extensively. Davis, the first general secretary, spent almost six months or more travelling.[130] Although Carter was critical of the expense of Davis's trips,[131] he found himself following this practice as General Secretary. The Pacific Council decided in 1929 that 'it was no longer desirable for senior secretaries to visit national units ... for the purpose of promotion', but it still recognized the necessity for these officers to keep in close touch with members in various countries.[132] Carter believed one had to visit countries in order to understand them, especially those in Asia.[133] Davis also felt that Loomis, Condliffe and William Holland, Research Assistant at the ISIPR, needed to go to Japan and China, not only for the coordination of conferences and research programmes, but also to acquire a feel for the countries.[134]

The ISIPR in Honolulu, which represented a strong YMCA element, was under constant pressure from those who wanted a more 'scientific' and 'expert' organization. The strongest pressure came from the British group, or more precisely Curtis. He was to pursue this agenda much more rigorously in 1927–9 (see also Chapter 6). In mid-May 1926, the ISIPR confirmed to the RIIA its strong support for British involvement. Yet, a month later, Curtis asked Blakeslee if the IPR could send a formal invitation, as if this had not occurred.[135] Curtis's lack of acknowledgment of the ISIPR was deliberate. He was convinced of the importance of the IPR, but he was not sure about the quality of ISIPR staff. He preferred to correspond, not through the ISIPR, but privately to ACIPR members on the East coast, such as Carter (then Secretary of the ACIPR), Blakeslee and Jerome Greene. Curtis knew them well, and he continued to do so in 1927–9. These East coast members were key figures of the ACIPR, which headquarters was located in New York. Davis and Wilbur helped to organize the ACIPR after the first conference, and they tried to make it more *national*. Wilbur, based on the West coast, replaced three East coast members with non-East coast members on the executive board in mid-1926.[136] The dominance of the East coast, especially its foreign experts, however, was an unmistakable feature at ACIPR headquarters.

How do we interpret Curtis's pressure on the ISIPR in Honolulu? Shiozaki suggests that Curtis, along with East coast ACIPR members, particularly Carter, tried to use the IPR a tool for realizing an international order based on Anglo-American solidarity. Carter's connection with Curtis went back to the time when Carter was a secretary of the YMCA in India in 1902–8 and 1911–17. When he was stationed as a YMCA officer in France during World War I and in London soon after the war, they were in close touch.[137] Their tie became stronger when Carter's secretary in France married Curtis. Around the time of the IPR organization in 1924 and 1925, however, Carter does not seem to have been greatly involved in discussions on the IPR with Curtis. Curtis's involvement in the IPR came not from Carter, but from the Canadian group under instruction from the ISIPR.

Carter was no doubt significant in the IPR, although his prominence did not emerge until 1926 when he became Secretary of the ACIPR. Carter attended the Yale Club meeting, but he did not go to the first IPR conference. Between 1922 and 1926, he seems to have devoted his time to another YMCA-related project, the 'Inquiry into the Christian Way of Life' (1922–32).[138] Significantly, his salary as Secretary of the ACIPR came from this Inquiry project before he was appointed as General Secretary of the ISIPR in 1933. By mid-1926, however, Carter was fully involved with the ACIPR. His office address for the 'Inquiry' became the address of the ACIPR, and he was in charge of the IPR's application for a grant to the Rockefeller Foundation. Carter stressed that the conference method which he promoted in the 'Inquiry' would be fruitful for IPR conferences: 'The whole technique of the discussion cultivated the frank expression of varying points of view, induced an attitude of search and inquiry and a common pooling of all possible resources of fact and opinion.'[139]

Despite Carter's importance, there is little evidence that Carter and Curtis had a joint plan for the IPR. Their correspondence about British participation in the IPR began only in early 1927, after a British group had been invited through other channels. If they shared a plan for the IPR, an almost accidental reopening of their correspondence at this late stage is rather odd. Curtis may have supported Carter's 'Inquiry', but he was also often dismissive of YMCA activities. The connection between the objects of the 'Inquiry' and Curtis's vision of a world order based on Anglo-American solidarity is also unclear. Carter seems to have had a distinct vision for the IPR, not a joint plan with Curtis (see Chapter 7).

British participation was formally granted after the second conference, and the Pacific Council, not the ISIPR, invited the RIIA to become a national unit for Britain and to be represented at the Pacific Council. The process was delayed again because Curtis was not sure about the 'quality' of the ISIPR. Curtis took the IPR seriously. He felt it important for the RIIA to become a national unit of the IPR, and organized a Far Eastern Group in the RIIA, which dealt with IPR matters. Finally, in January 1928, Curtis sent a note to Carter, telling him that the RIIA had decided to ratify the IPR's constitution.

> [W]e might take our courage in our hand and join, and as full members exercise such influence from inside as belongs to a member in helping on the creation of a Secretariat with the qualifications and experience which in our view is needed for so delicate and responsible a task.[110]

Even at this stage, Curtis clearly did not recognize the ISIPR. The British group would join and influence in 'creating' the new secretariat of the IPR. Ratification was completed soon, and Curtis became a member of the Pacific Council. Until he became preoccupied with the idea of Shanghai Municipal reform, he devoted his energy to reorganizing the ISIPR.

Experts and state and society

British participation was significant, not because of Curtis's vision of Anglo-American solidarity, but because it pushed the IPR towards greater state orientation. The British group requested a change in the conference programme so that it would be more policy-oriented. At the first conference, British 'colonial' dealings in China had been strongly criticized. At the second, the British group (the 'Far Eastern group' of the RIIA) wanted to establish 'their' case. Their concern was British policies in China. Japanese diplomats remarked that Americans from the mainland and Canadians supported the British proposal: 'They insisted that it is most appropriate to discuss urgent current affairs, such as issues in China, not religion, education and social institutions in general. The conference agendas were suddenly altered.'[111] The change occurred not only because of the British push, but because 'expert' groups in North America also agreed with this political focus.

This political inclination was exactly the point which Croly thought would jeopardize the IPR. A quasi-diplomatic role, however, excited some participants. Rather than being alarmed, the Japanese participant, Tsurumi Yūsuke, was fascinated by the change:

> What I felt, when the nature of the conference changed, was the political skill of the British participants. ... The addition of the British changed the nature of the conference. It is because although the United States is a great power, it still is relatively unused to international conferences, and tends to prefer academic discussion to politics. In contrast, Britain is skilled in international negotiations, and its way of thinking is completely political. Britain selected participants with political inclinations and, at the conference, their dealings were political and their interests in discussion were political. The international tradition of the great British empire gave them a superior position [at the conference].[142]

The British group opposed publicity about the conference. According to the RIIA constitution, the contents of talks and names of speakers at meetings were to be kept secret from the press, and the minutes recorded speakers anonymously. American participants in general were in favour of publicity. Eggleston recorded: 'Evening was stormy as Curtis objected to publicity.'[143] Curtis dismissed a propagandist role, as he felt the IPR should aim to be an institution in which 'leaders of public opinion' studied and analysed ever-changing foreign relations.[144] This was his main idea when he founded the RIIA, and his view had not changed. An American participant thought otherwise and stressed a great need to stimulate people's minds in relation to international affairs, especially in the United States where the general public was so far uninterested.

This debate over publicity illuminates the IPR's position in relation to the state and society. The IPR had three alternatives. One was to make it more like the League of Nations Associations, which concentrated on education of society (propaganda). The second was to become a purely academic research organization without much input either to society or the state. The third was to become a think-tank with input mainly to the state. The British anti-publicity position reflected the nature of the RIIA, whose object was to produce analysis and information for selected experts and policy-makers. In the IPR, other trends existed. Especially in 1925 it agreed on the priority given to wide and impartial publicity, and the education of society through publicity.[145]

The decision made at the second conference shifted the emphasis slightly, and defined the position of the IPR as straddling state and society. It concluded that the IPR was a research organization, not an unofficial diplomatic organization or an educational organization.[146] The elitist and secretive nature of IPR conferences was, however, latent from the beginning in its focus on a selected few influential people. Although this was furthered by British participation, an emphasis on education and society was not totally abandoned.

The decision was that the Institute would collect the *facts*, and interpret them, but avoid offering solutions. IPR conferences would not suggest concrete policies for government. In other words, it aimed to be a research organization with limited input to society and the state, and it would avoid direct involvement in policy-making. Curtis still hoped that IPR materials would be utilized by policy-makers. After 1927, the IPR strengthened this research emphasis, and while its educational emphasis remained a major issue, its think-tank role was to be strengthened. Although the British group did not win, as a result of this dispute, the second conference had much stricter regulation of the press than the first. This tendency was more marked at the third conference in Kyoto. An American journalist complained about this closed nature of the IPR and blamed the British.[147]

The Pacific Community meant an American-led regional order. It was a new experiment in a new context. There were other visions for the IPR and the regional order. Great ambiguity existed in 1925 and 1927, and this was a source of the dynamics within the Pacific Community. Although colonialism was supported in general, critical voices were not absent. The dichotomy of the essentialized East and West was not questioned, but participants were less sure about the absolute superiority of the West. New modes of development and new attitudes towards the powers in Asia were sought. The IPR's advocacy of non-state agency and its insistence on 'individual' not 'national' representation at the conference in 1925 was noteworthy. Despite its focus on the elite, it addressed the public/society as well as the state. The nation-state framework, however, was too dominant in the discourse of IPR operations for the potential of this advocacy of non-governmentality to be realized. Nation and 'national culture' were reified and identified with the state. This was not only used to justify state policies. It also reinforced the essentialization of 'nations' in terms of East or West. For many IPR members, the merit of a non-state agency was to contribute to the relationship between states, rather than promoting specific universal causes. The IPR's basic structure was set by the end of the second conference, and certain directions and trends, which were latent in the original setting and which coexisted with other factors, were becoming explicit. British participation furthered some of these trends, which were soon to challenge the very concept which produced the IPR in 1925, the Pacific Community.

Part III

Transition

6   From the Pacific to the Atlantic, 1928–32

The concept of the Pacific Community defined the initial setting of the IPR, and the basic structure and directions of the IPR were in place by the end of the second conference. Contending visions for the IPR and the regional order, however, had not diminished. The period between 1928 and 1932 was transitional. This spanned the latter half of Merle Davis's term as General Secretary to the period when Jerome Greene was caretaker of the ISIPR as Chairperson of the Pacific Council (1930–2). Lionel Curtis, leading figure of the IPR group at the RIIA, or Chatham House, and British representative at the Pacific Council, presented the strongest alternative vision in this period. For some, he challenged the initial concept of the Pacific Community, the IPR's structure, personnel, direction and functions, which they saw as a major factor contributing to Davis's resignation. Most key IPR figures – Davis, Atherton, Greene and Carter – opposed Curtis's reform plan. Nevertheless, Curtis's challenge prompted them to scrutinize their own visions. Almost every step they took in 1927–9 can be seen as a reaction to this challenge. In this process, the nature and directions of the IPR were renegotiated and redefined, and certain latent elements in the initial setting of 1925–7 became clearer. As a result, IPR operations displayed the very characteristics that Herbert Croly had warned against in 1927 – more state orientation and more direct involvement in foreign policy-making. They were also diverging from a regional-centred view of the world.

Loss of a Pacific sense, 1928–9

On the ship from Honolulu to San Francisco after the second conference in 1927, Curtis publicly criticized Davis to key IPR figures on board. Among them were Greene, Carter, Atherton and Wilbur. Curtis had a different vision for the IPR, and Davis did not fit into it. Although the IPR's Pacific Community included European powers, Curtis still argued that the IPR should be more world-oriented than region-specific, and more state-oriented than oriented towards the public. He felt the current ISIPR staff, especially Davis, was a major obstacle to the IPR's realizing this potential. His letter to Carter, then Secretary of the ACIPR, in January 1928 was blunt:

> [The ISIPR] was dependent on YMCA staff which ... has not the exact
> kind of training which fits them for work which has more in common
> with that of the Secretariat of the League of Nations than that to which
> the staff of the YMCA are accustomed.[1]

Curtis's view probably echoed a scepticism towards the YMCA in the East
coast academic establishment. But it was not necessarily a representative
view among experts on INGOs in this period. White described the World
Alliance of YMCA as 'the first true international non-governmental
organization to be established in the modern movement'.[2] Curtis also seems
to have ignored the fact that his old friend Carter had built his career entirely
through the YMCA. In any event, Curtis wanted to have a 'world' class General
Secretary, and Davis fell short of this calibre.[3] Curtis pursued his vision and
developed a radical reform plan for the IPR in late 1928. The conspiracy
between Curtis and Carter was not evident, and Carter did not display any
interest in the post at this stage. On the contrary, Carter became critical of
Curtis's reform plan.

Davis's vision

At his office at the ISIPR in Honolulu, Davis was kept in the dark until early
1929 about this reform plan. He was, however, well aware of Curtis's criticism
in 1927. Atherton informed him about it soon after he heard it.[4] Davis was
hurt by this criticism, as it attacked his qualities as a leader. He even
contemplated resignation. Atherton and Wilbur dissuaded him. Davis agreed
to stay on in the post, at least for the next two years.[5] Davis became more
committed to the concept of the Pacific Community. He had a strong ally in
Atherton. In autumn of 1927, Atherton met officers of the League of Nations
at its headquarters in Geneva. This convinced him the merit of their 'original'
IPR. He and Davis had a duty to prevent Curtis from turning the IPR into a
quasi-diplomatic body:

> I do not think it would be right for us to allow the English influence ... as
> some of the delegates clearly state they are primarily interested in the
> political aspect of the Institute. ... I feel that much of the strength of the
> Institute is due to the fact that we have not emphasized the political side
> of many of our Pacific problems. ... As I view the Institute from this
> distance, I feel personally more convinced that we have proceeded in the
> right way, and that because of the attitude and spirit shown by the
> secretariat ... we have won the respect and confidence of the various
> national groups. ... I should be very loath to see any change along the
> lines that Mr Curtis recommends.[6]

Davis agreed that they should not give up the original 'point of view and
philosophy of international relations'. At the same time, Davis realized

'perhaps for the first time, the wider out-reach and political implication and influence which the Institute possesses'.[7] Although Davis felt ill-prepared for this development, between 1927 and the third conference in Kyoto in 1929 he devoted himself to the IPR, trying to prove his worth, and to realize what he regarded as the original spirit of the IPR. He sailed to the United States, assisted in organization of branches, published the proceedings of the second conference through Chicago University Press and worked on fundraising in New York. Then he crossed the Atlantic and visited Geneva and London.[8]

Davis's vision of the Pacific Community was one of political equals. Although he would later attempt to prevent the Korean group from withdrawing from the IPR, the equal status of Japan and China, the new powers in Asia, was of prime importance. He tried to realize this during his general secretaryship, well before Curtis criticized him. His commitment was strengthened after he became aware of the criticism. When Wilbur resigned from the chair of the Pacific Council in 1929, Davis felt it important that a Chinese or Japanese member should succeed him.[9] This materialized only briefly. The council appointed David Z.T. Yui from China as a tentative successor. Meanwhile, Greene succeeded Wilbur's position of chair of the ACIPR and became the American representative at the Pacific Council. Soon after the Kyoto conference, the post of Chairperson of the Pacific Council went to Greene. As Greene supported another plan of Davis to recruit senior Japanese and Chinese staff at the ISIPR, it is hard to see this as an act to prevent Davis's vision of equal partnership. Greene's appointment probably represented views of members of the council, including the Japanese member.

Davis had the idea of recruiting senior Japanese and Chinese staff for the ISIPR in early 1927.[10] This was also important for 'internationalizing' the ISIPR, which was often criticized as dominated by Americans. The recruitment negotiations for two staff in Japan and China involved much energy, tact and time. Terminology was important in recruiting a person of substance. The original position, Deputy Secretary, was replaced by Associate Secretary after Davis learned that in Chinese 'Deputy' meant inferior.[11] After lengthy discussions, in April 1929 the JCIPR reported that it had selected a former diplomat, Yamasaki Keiichi. The JCIPR dismissed Davis's concerns about his official connections, although the Japanese Ministry of Foreign Affairs had clearly been involved in the selection.[12]

These appointments were symbols of Davis's vision, and the failure of this project became a direct cause of his subsequent resignation. Before the Kyoto conference, the two Japanese and Chinese secretaries had already started working at the ISIPR, and the budget needed to be increased to pay their salaries. Key American IPR members, such as Wilbur and Greene, had backed these appointments.[13] Greene, then Treasurer of the American Council, in particular, thought it important. Carter also tried to raise the funds to employ the additional staff. On the second day of the conference at Kyoto, 29 October 1929, the New York stock market crashed, beginning the era of the Great

Depression. This extinguished hopes for raising funds. Davis had to drop the appointments of these new associate secretaries in which he had invested such energy.[14] Humiliated, frustrated and feeling powerless, he submitted his resignation at the meeting of the Pacific Council in Kyoto on 7 November. The council decided that Davis would hold office until his successor was appointed, and that a committee comprising Greene and three others (one American and two Canadians) be appointed to seek a successor.[15]

Curtis's vision and response

What was Curtis's reform plan? How challenging was his vision to the notion of the Pacific Community? How was his action related to Davis's resignation? And how did other key figures, such as Greene and Carter, respond to his plan? Having criticized Davis first in 1927, Curtis did not disclose his reform plan of the IPR until it was presented in his letter to Greene in November 1928. Curtis wrote it on the Atlantic when he was returning from the ACIPR meeting in New York. The main issue was the reorganization of the ISIPR. His communication pattern was typical. He preferred writing to his friends in New York to direct communication with the ISIPR in Honolulu. Curiously, only a small number of New Yorkers – Greene and Carter and, to a lesser extent, Charles Howland and James Shotwell (the last two were involved in the IPR's International Research Committee) – discussed this letter. It was a decision made by Carter and Greene: the matter would be handled by this small group, and the result reported to Wilbur, Chairperson of the Pacific Council.[16] It meant bypassing Davis and the ISIPR in Honolulu. Davis only found out about the matter in early 1929, which made him and other ISIPR staff in Honolulu think that there was a conspiracy between New York members and the British group.

Despite his decision to confine the matter to a few New Yorkers, Greene was aware of the danger of being seen as a conspirator. He warned Curtis:

[A]ny suggestions from London looking toward the alteration of the policies of the Institute and destined for consideration by the other groups would perhaps better be sent directly, either formally to Wilbur or informally to him and the various constituent groups, including ourselves, rather than to use us, another Anglo Saxon group, as a channel for getting your ideas before the others.[17]

Clearly the ISIPR did not have any authority in IPR policy matters. The role resided with the Pacific Council. This executive body, however, was something of an imaginary committee, whose members lived in different countries and only came together at the time of a conference. Wilbur, the chairperson, was often the *de facto* Pacific Council. Greene may have decided not to tell the ISIPR about the plan at this stage out of consideration for Davis's delicate position. In any event, the ISIPR was left out of the discussion of the reorganization. The ACIPR, led by Greene and Carter, emerged as a strong and independent body, not an Anglophile follower of Curtis. They began a serious quest to build a 'truly international' ISIPR.

'Internationality' of the IPR

Curtis's reform plan included a few major changes to IPR operations. First, he was critical of American dominance of IPR research funds. For him, this meant American control over research, as it would diminish its 'international' quality. Second, he thought that the size and expenses of the ISIPR should be reduced. It should not have a permanent base, but should be shifted every two years to the location of the coming conference. This implied a rotation of headquarters among National Councils. Third, the IPR should concentrate on holding successful conferences, not conducting research programmes. The latter should, he argued, be left to each National Council.[18] Davis described the plan in early 1929: 'He was out to build a new kind of organization.'[19] Davis saw Curtis totally reorganizing the IPR, its conference techniques, research, information exchanges, publicity and emphasis.

Curtis wanted more power and autonomy for national units in administration, research projects and funding. This was an attempt to diminish the American dominance of the IPR. It also suggested the enhancement of each unit's autonomy and a federated structure for IPR operations. National Councils would take over most of the work carried out by the ISIPR, such as organizing conferences, preparing data papers and organizing and conducting research projects. As a result, a large component of the ISIPR, including the International Research Committee and its secretariat, would become redundant. The IPR would resemble the Institute of Politics at Williamstown (IPW), whose main function was an international conference of informal meetings of diplomats and experts – something Davis and Atherton termed a quasi-diplomatic organization.

Curtis's plan gained little support from Greene, Carter, Shotwell and Howland. Although he recognized its merit for future consideration, Carter disagreed strongly with Curtis. He pointed out mistakes in Curtis's understanding of the budget increases, and stressed the already existing high level of 'internationality' in the IPR's structure and projects:

> While we may not be able to achieve international mutuality in financing, I do believe that we may be able to achieve a high measure of international mutuality in the conduct of research if the American Council continues to be willing to place American funds fully at the disposal of the Institute for its international research programme…

For Carter, '[t]he aims of the Pacific Council are clearly … international'.[20] What mattered was how the research funds were used, not where they came from. Greene wrote to Curtis: 'Carter differs with you more or less radically' and 'my own position is sympathetic with yours in principle'.[21] Yet, Greene's vision for the IPR also differed substantially from that of Curtis. First, like Carter, Greene pointed out Curtis misunderstood the cost increases. They were due to the two new appointments at the ISIPR, not to increased research projects, as Curtis claimed. Second, Greene strongly supported Davis's plan for the appointments of Japanese and Chinese staff. He felt that the 'internationality' of the secretariat should be attained not by alternating its location between the 'Orient' and 'Occident', but by recruiting people of diverse backgrounds to the secretariat:

> Up to this time, [the staff at the ISIPR] has been wholly Anglo Saxon, and with the exception of Condliffe, wholly American. At best we have a heavy handicap of racial bias to overcome in the history of the inception of the Institute, its American leadership ... and in its financial support. The only feasible way to lessen this bias is to add Japanese and Chinese secretaries and to make that addition as a real one, not mere "scenery". The men selected must be of such calibre as to make them a real factor in the work of the Secretariat and to inspire the confidence of the oriental members of the Institute.[22]

Third, while Curtis envisaged the ISIPR as a General Secretary living out of a suitcase, Greene emphasized the importance of a strong headquarters: 'The integrity of the Secretariat as an international instrument is the *sine qua non* of its usefulness.' To strengthen this integrity and retain its international character, Greene proposed allocating a quota of the budget of the ISIPR to each National Council. In his view, the addition of prominent Japanese and Chinese staff might secure substantial financial contributions from these countries.

Fourth, Greene had a different view on research projects. Curtis emphasized conferences and a quasi-diplomatic function of the IPR. In contrast, Greene argued strongly that research should be given a priority. Research on the 'Far East' had been neglected, but it was valuable for international relations. This thinking was well supported by ACIPR members and dominated the decisions of the Pacific Council at the first two conferences. Knowing the 'facts' would contribute to understanding and solving problems in the Pacific, and a major function of the IPR should be research. The International Research Committee had been set up, and in late 1926, Davis had recruited Condliffe as Research Secretary of this committee.

Fifth, like Carter, Greene refuted Curtis's concern with the dominance and control of American money. He argued that the funds of the Carnegie Endowment for Peace, the Laura Spelman Rockefeller Memorial[23] and the Social Science Research Council (based in New York) were international, because their purpose was to 'promote the well-being of mankind throughout the world'. He stressed that the Rockefeller Foundation recognized the IPR as:

an international body of a character and competence which make it an appropriate agency for undertaking research on certain important topics within the Pacific area.[24]

Greene reached the same conclusion as Carter: 'it makes comparatively little difference where the money comes from.'[25] More important was an efficient and competent research committee to supervise in an unbiased manner. Greene's position was most likely in line with these establishment members who controlled research funds. Greene, Carter, Howland and Shotwell were involved with various foundations and research councils, and familiar with their operations. Greene was a trustee of the Rockefeller Foundation in 1913–17, and again in 1928–39. Shotwell was involved with the Carnegie Endowment for Peace and the Social Science Research Council.

In contrast, Curtis's idea of 'internationality' was more strictly based on the nation-state. For him, 'international' research meant a collection of research produced by 'national' institutions, with their funds coming from that nation. In a letter to the Carnegie Endowment for Peace in 1925, Curtis stressed that studies on international relations, especially war, should be conducted by:

> research institutions which must be national in character, but with international relations with like institutions. ... My own conviction is that if such institutes are really to be national, the bulk of their funds must also be national.[26]

Each national unit should carry out independent research rather than one international research institution with a sub-structure of national branches. In his view, a frank exchange of opinions was only possible among those with the same nationality. 'The discussions of a cosmopolitan gathering become unreal.'[27]

International research projects: Condliffe and his regionalist perspective

While Curtis was developing his reform plan, Research Secretary Condliffe had the international research project well under way. Condliffe, a New Zealander, who had impressed many at the first conference, was recruited as Research Secretary in 1926. He arrived in Honolulu in February 1927. He was then thirty-four years old.[28] Unaware of Curtis's plan, which implied the abolition of the international research programme, Condliffe developed initial research projects according to his understanding of the IPR's original spirit. Organizing multinational research projects from scratch was no small task. Condliffe's first duty was to go to the United States to report to the Chairperson of the Pacific Council, Wilbur. He also wanted to consult with scholars in the United States who were interested in the Pacific. He started in California where Davis had contacts through the 'The Survey of Race Relations', and went on to Oregon, Washington, Chicago and New York.

Condliffe's principle was regionalism; and the fact that he came from a non-great power within the Pacific and that he was an economist were crucial. He was less concerned with political ideology, and was unsympathetic to Marxism. His stance was not anti-colonial. Rather, he tried to diversify the views expressed. He felt that most American 'Far East' specialists at the first conference had been pro-China and against the colonial powers, Japan and Britain, and he sought out those with other views.[29] His expertise and interests inevitably influenced the projects. They were heavily focused on Japan and China and economic topics, such as land utilization, land and labour, and standard of living, prevailed.

His loyalties may have been to the British empire, like many New Zealanders of his generation with his education, and it is likely that he resented American dominance. Or perhaps it was that he was young, enthusiastic, anti-establishment and had casual manners. For whatever reason, he gave the impression of arrogance to Wilbur, Shotwell, Curtis and Carter,[30] and tension developed, particularly with Carter. Condliffe thought Carter was ambitious, eager, self-sacrificing and seldom relaxed enough to try the obvious simple course.[31] This evaluation was coloured by bitter experience, but it was probably not totally groundless. Carter's correspondence gives one the impression that he held strong opinions and was slightly manipulative.

Their clash was more than personal. It was about the control of research funds, which meant, in effect, control over the IPR. The IPR relied heavily on the Rockefeller Foundation for its resources. Its evaluation determined the nature of the IPR. The Foundation saw research as crucial to IPR operations, and valued the IPR's original contribution to research and to the creation of 'mutual understanding' in the Pacific.[32] The IPR's heavy reliance on the Foundation also meant that those who controlled the grant application, namely Carter and a few other New Yorkers, had the power to control the IPR. They realized that formal and informal close ties with officers and executives at the foundation were important, and made efforts to maintain them. With hindsight, Condliffe argued that lack of control over funds was the critical weakness of Davis and the ISIPR in Honolulu.[33] The Honolulu staff did not realize this at first. The role of fundraising was mainly left to the ACIPR in New York. Davis did not include fundraising as one of main functions of the ISIPR in 1927.[34] Atherton, a loyal supporter of Davis, did not realize the implications of this omission either. In 1927 he proposed to leave fundraising to Carter and Greene, so that Davis could concentrate on issues such as conference organization.[35]

Condliffe shared one common view with Curtis, the man who wanted to demolish his position. Condliffe was suspicious of American dominance of research projects. He suspected that Carter wanted American scholars to control the research programmes.[36] Although Condliffe gained control of the research grant after a meeting with officers at the Rockefeller Foundation, he remained critical of Carter:

> The almost unconscious assumption of superiority by so many in the United States who had access to funds was to be a constant problem in organizing a truly effective research programme.[37]

Condliffe consciously tried to counterbalance American dominance in research projects in terms of agent, method and topic. By doing so, he presented a strong case for Carter and Greene against Curtis – American funds were used in such a way that American dominance was not perpetuated. He provided the impetus and encouraged independence for Japanese and Chinese scholars. He utilized National Councils, and local institutions when it was more practical. These projects were initially supported by a grant from the IPR allocated by Condliffe and carried out by local researchers.

In Japan, arrangements were relatively easy. Research projects were carried out by the research committee of the highly centralized JCIPR, headed by Nitobe Inazō. Most academics on the research committee were from Tokyo Imperial University. The prestige of the IPR was high because of the prominence of JCIPR members and the respect commanded by Davis and Greene, both of whom were from well-regarded missionary families. Accordingly, Condliffe lodged at the Imperial Hotel and was invited to functions with influential people.

In contrast, the branches of the Chinese Council of the IPR were geographically distant, and the National Council was not yet centralized. Condliffe made use of various local institutions, universities and YMCA contacts. Although civil war was thought to be imminent, he travelled extensively. He went to Tianjin (Tientsin) and allocated research funds to Nankai University, where young Chinese economists were engaged in primary studies on prices and industrialization. In between, he even managed to attend the wedding of Jiang Jieshi (Chiang Kai-shek), soon to be the leader of the Guomindang (Kuomintang). Earlier in the year, in April 1927, Jiang had tried to suppress communist forces and had established the capital in Nanjing (Nanking). The YMCA groups and Chinese IPR members with whom Condliffe had contact were very close to Jiang and the Guomindang. Many of these Chinese members were graduates of American or British universities. Condliffe set up research projects with these local academics and foreign researchers resident in China.[38]

Although he relied on National Councils for organization, especially in Japan, this was not because he took a similar view to Curtis. Curtis argued that research on 'national' issues should be carried out by its nationals, not by 'outsiders'. Condliffe's reliance on the National Council was more pragmatic. He was not against the idea of 'foreigners' undertaking research. In fact he brought in specialists from the United States and Britain to China and Japan. They produced works including H.G. Moulton's *Japan: An Economic and Financial Appraisal* (1931) (in collaboration with Inoue Junnosuke), John Lossing Buck's *Chinese Farm Economy* (1930) and R.H. Tawney's *Land Utilization in China* (1937).

Unaware of these efforts of Condliffe, Curtis pursued the reorganization plan at the Kyoto Conference. It was presented as a British plan, although it is not clear whether his view was representative of RIIA members'. Curtis was one of the very few at the RIIA who were enthusiastic about the IPR. He could push his ideas as the British view without much internal opposition. Condliffe recorded: 'A few weeks before the conference, the RIIA submitted a proposal to reduce the [ISIPR] in view of the deficit (then about $170,000) by eliminating practically all the staff, including the Research Secretary.'[39] This proposal, however, does not appear in the records of the IPR. Contrary to the views of Davis, Atherton and Eggleston, British participants themselves felt their prominence declined at the Kyoto conference.[10] Nevertheless, the financial position of the ISIPR and its officers remained precarious, a situation accentuated by the stock market crash. Feeling uncertain about his position, Condliffe was to take up a post with the League of Nations.

Loss of the Pacific sense

Davis's resignation indicated the future direction of the IPR. But this was not a total departure. It makes more sense to view the incident as accentuating some factors which were inherent in the initial concept. The move was not only due to Curtis's challenge, but also to the events of the day. Nevertheless, some members saw this resignation a symbol that the initial dynamism had been lost. They felt that the original regionalist vision or a Pacific-centred perspective had gone, along with the new attitude towards the new powers in Asia. This was how Davis saw the whole event. In July 1930, just before his departure for Geneva, where he was to take up a position at the League of Nations, Davis wrote to Greene giving three reasons for his resignation: the change in emphasis from cultural and economic topics to political ones at IPR conferences, the lack of support for the General Secretary from the Pacific Council, and the General Secretary's lack of control over finances. Davis warned that there was a danger of losing the original IPR's components 'mutual confidence and respect ... which East and West have been building together ... during the last hundred years'. In Davis's view, the British brought in problems. He hoped that the IPR would not become 'an Atlantic Institute of Pacific Relations', and that it would not be ruled by the 'old' order:

> Men of the Pacific area formed this Institute to put into practice their ideals and to solve their peculiar problems. ... [I]f the Councils of the institute are dominated by the point of view of the old order they cannot succeed in meeting the needs of the new community of the Pacific.[11]

His view was supported by major IPR members in Honolulu, Australia and New Zealand – non-great powers or local groups located *within* the Pacific. Frederic Eggleston, a central figure of the IPR in Australia, was most vocal. Although Eggleston thought that the real influence came not from London, but New York, he shared Davis's view. He wrote to Greene that there was a danger in shifting the emphasis from culture to politics.[12] This implied a shift in IPR orientation from the society/public to the state. Greene and Curtis dismissed the claims of Davis and Eggleston. For Greene: 'Matters of political controversy endangering international relations are subjects for study and discussion par excellence.' The importance lay not in the topic, but in the manner of 'scientific inquiry'.[13] Curtis was more forthright. He argued that politics should be always the centre of IPR conferences, otherwise the British would never have attended conferences.[14]

When Davis emphasized the dichotomy between 'new' and 'old' thinking, he seems to have forgotten that in 1924–5 he himself tried to reduce the influence of the YMCA in order to present the IPR as something similar to the IPW. To be fair, however, Davis had been unsure about direction. His vision for the IPR largely remained an organization for promoting goodwill and world 'brotherhood'. Although this was still important, many IPR members, as well as the major foundations in the United States, increasingly saw this type of organization as insufficiently 'serious' or 'professional'.

As Condliffe rightly pointed out, Davis's main weakness was his lack of control over funds. Davis's views on and skills in fundraising were also problematic. His application for the grant of the Rockefeller Foundation was a contrast to Carter's. The latter was clearer, more persuasive, and attuned to the requirements of the guidelines of the Foundation.[15] Davis largely relied on wealthy contributors. Those in charge of fundraising, such as Greene, were finding this method increasingly limited and difficult:

> It is proving to be extraordinarily difficult to paint the picture of the institute to the rich man in the [Wall] Street in such a way as to win anything better than his indulgent approval of what he regards as a well meant but somewhat visionary enterprise.[16]

Nevertheless, Davis embodied the initial regionalist zeal, the Pacific-centred view and the concept of the Pacific Community. Eggleston was an enthusiastic supporter of this notion, and it is now declining because of the influence of 'outsiders':

> We go further to say that delegates from regions which do not border on the Pacific, should be particularly careful to understand the point of view of those who do. They may possess interests, but not understand. I have always ... [been] keen on preserving the character of the Institute ... well defined by Mr Davis.[17]

Furthermore, with this decline of a regional sense, experiments in a new attitude towards the powers in Asia were failing. Ian Allen, a New Zealander, questioned:

> Is there any possible development by American and British members which would be likely to create feeling between East and West? Should this be so, I feel the main principle of the institute would be jeopardized.[48]

Eggleston also worried about the danger of the undesirable emergence of a British bloc or an Anglo Saxon bloc at the IPR.[49] These observations demonstrate that despite the fact that the concept of the Pacific Community was an expression of the American-led regional order, those from the periphery of mainland America saw greater possibility in realizing a regional community among equals. In their view, the effort to establish equal relationships with the powers of Asia had been successful, but was marred by a series of incidents, culminating in Davis's resignation.

Those from non-great powers located within the Pacific were probably more equipped with a regional as opposed to a 'global' perspective. They were more attuned to thinking in terms of 'political equals', not a hegemonic superpower, and they felt greater urgency about resolving regional unrest. Davis was well aware of their significance. Australia and New Zealand 'held the balance of power in the Pacific Council on the important matters of policy'.[50]

Non-great powers' readiness to imagine the regional community seems to be well illuminated also in Eggleston's regional disarmament plan. At the IPR conference in 1929, he argued that it was easier to achieve disarmament in the Pacific. There was more space and less imperial competition than in Europe. The plan, however, failed to attract support especially among the great powers, the British and the American group.[51] Eggleston felt that the British 'put their weight against any regional consideration, or regional conference'. The concept of the Pacific as an independent entity especially under American leadership was dangerous for the British empire. It challenged its imperial order. The Australian government, as well as most Australian post-League internationalists, shared this view.[52] But why could Eggleston not get support among Americans? Did they think that regional disarmament meant a stronger defence responsibility, which they neither wanted nor thought they were ready for? The Republican administration's new regional order was mainly based on strong economic ties. The Four Power Treaty, which superseded the Anglo-Japanese Alliance, was a general framework of cooperation without a specific defence commitment.[53] Or did they think disarmament could not be achieved at a regional level. After the Washington Conference, Coolidge and Hoover both pursued disarmament mainly on a worldwide scale.

Whereas IPR members from Hawai'i, Australia and New Zealand thought Davis's resignation reflected a loss of a region-centred view, Japanese members did not seem to have seen any profound implications. Despite Davis's efforts, the JCIPR did not regard the incident as a failed attempt to achieve equality between the powers in Asia and other powers. Sawada Setsuzō, Consul General of New York, reported his meeting with Greene to Foreign Minister Shidehara. With reservations, Greene presented a slightly negative view of Davis, and Sawada seemed to have agreed with him.[54]

Why was the JCIPR so indifferent? The answer seems to lie in the expectations of the IPR among the JCIPR and the Japanese government. Both certainly saw the IPR a new regional experiment, but the IPR's merit lay mainly in its publicist function. They accepted the colonialism and power hierarchy implicit in IPR operations. Even after it realized that nothing could be done about the American immigration act of 1924, the Japanese government continued its involvement with the JCIPR and IPR operations. This suggests that the government saw the IPR as a useful organ which could be utilized for cultivating a favourable image of Japan, an underpinning of the cooperative policy towards the powers. JCIPR members also wanted to be identified with the 'Occident' not the 'Orient'. They were concerned with equality as a great power. This thinking might have explained their seeming indifference to Davis's efforts. Furthermore, a far more significant issue – conflict in Manchuria – occupied the government and JCIPR members, and this was to dominate the discussion at the IPR conference in 1929. Accordingly, Davis's resignation and its implications for the IPR's initial visions and experiments had little impact on them.

Davis, Atherton, Eggleston and Allen were not immune from an Orientalist view. They saw the world through the dichotomy of an essentialized East and West. Their respect for the powers in Asia was based on their recognition of the 'difference'. Yet their enthusiasm for regional initiative was noteworthy. In 1929, Eggleston noted:

> Something is needed which gives Pacific nations the feeling that they are meeting and discussing their own problems and deciding them free from the dominance of Western ideas and interests.[55]

This pluralistic, yet essentialized view reflected his weak sense of a single and powerful moral centre. The view also implied a tension between the Pacific and the world – the issue which was crucial in discussions of the problem of Manchuria at IPR conferences.

The Kyoto Conference in 1929

The third conference was held from 28 October to 9 November at Kyoto, the ancient Japanese capital, resplendent with autumn leaves. Kyoto was a significant place for Greene and Davis, both of whom had spent their childhoods there. At the opening session of the conference, Greene made a speech about his warm memories in what newspapers reported as fluent Japanese. This was met with applause from participants.[56] Several days earlier, the Pacific Council held meetings at Nara, another ancient capital near Kyoto. Officers and council members were hosted at the elegant Nara Hotel, which was closed to the public for the exclusive use of the IPR.

Ironically, at the same time as some detected a decline in a sense of the Pacific in office politics of the ISIPR, the Kyoto conference fostered an upsurge in regionalist enthusiasm among IPR members in 1928–9. This was particularly the case on the West coast of the United States. According to John Tilley, British ambassador to Japan, the Kyoto conference was the most discussed issue in 1928, when he attended a few meetings in California. He heard Americans arguing that the Pacific had become the crucial region of the world, and that 'a Pacific civilization and philosophy' was 'superior to its European counterpart'.[57] The view reflected American confidence in its leadership in the region in the late 1920s.

Not only on the West coast, but also in the Pacific rim countries in general, the Kyoto conference attracted great attention. There were some 220 conference participants, including observers and secretaries, who also brought their families and friends. It was a bigger event than the first two conferences. This invited criticism about the effectiveness and management of the conference.[58] Accordingly, the next few conferences confined numbers to the original size of 150 or fewer. Despite an anti-publicity policy for round table discussions, the conference also achieved extensive newspaper coverage in the Pacific rim countries. Major American papers, such as the *New York Times*, *Christian Science Monitor*, *Washington Post*, *San Francisco Chronicle* and *Los Angeles Times*, reported the conference as well as local newspapers in Honolulu, Seattle, Oakland and Portland. In Australia, Eggleston wrote a series of feature stories on the conference, and his experiences and impressions of Japan and China for Melbourne newspapers.[59] These reports were generally favourable towards the IPR, emphasizing the merit of non-official discussion of urgent political issues, and its educational role in understanding international affairs. The participation of notable figures was probably one reason for this publicity. On 25 October 1929, the *Herald Tribune* printed an article titled, 'Pacific institute in Japan draws world leaders'. A conference topic, Manchuria, one of the most contentious issues in the region at the time, was another reason for this publicity.

The Japanese press treated the Kyoto conference as a significant political event. Major newspapers *Tokyo nichinichi*, *Osaka asahi*, *Osaka mainichi* and *Tokyo asahi* reported the opening of the conference as a front page story the next day, 29 October 1929, and they filed details of conference discussions. Other papers, such as *Jiji shimpō* and *Kokumin shimbun*, also took note of the conference. The opening session was indeed a great event. Telegrams from the American President, the Prime Ministers of Australia, New Zealand and Canada were read, and Japan's new Prime Minister, Hamaguchi Osachi, made a speech. Hamaguchi's sympathy to the IPR was clear. Welcoming participants and wishing the conference success, he characterized Japan as a successful combination of 'Eastern' and 'Western' civilizations and Kyoto as a symbol of ancient culture and a peaceful environment. He emphasized his cabinet's commitment to disarmament, cooperative international relationship and world peace: 'the IPR had the most profound sympathy of the Japanese government'.[60] Hamaguchi appointed Inoue Junnosuke, the first chairperson of the JCIPR, as Minister of Finance, and Shidehara Kijūrō as Minister of Foreign Affairs. Shidehara dealt with JCIPR matters from its inception, and JCIPR members endorsed Shidehara's pro-American and cooperative foreign policies. The Hamaguchi *Minseitō* cabinet pursued this disarmament agenda at the London Naval Conference in 1930. This caused very strong opposition in the navy and among 'right wing' radicals, and eventually cost his life. (He was attacked in 1930, and died in 1931.)

Curtis's vision and the Pacific Council

The Kyoto conference was marked by several major developments. The resolutions of the Pacific Council indicate that it rejected Curtis's vision for the IPR in principle, but co-opted some of his points. First, Curtis was against much publicity, and wanted the IPR to produce materials for the state and policy-makers. The Pacific Council took his point, and decided that the round table discussions at the conference would be closed to the press. On the other hand, it also stressed the need to appeal to the public, not only policy-makers. It argued that the IPR's primary purpose was to promote better understanding of international issues, and knowledge should be shared with 'hundreds of millions' of people. Accordingly, it decided that cordial and generous cooperation with the press should be sought, and the IPR would make every effort to provide information to the press.[61] The IPR, therefore, did not abandon its role of 'educating' society.

Second and most significantly, while Curtis tried to minimize the control of the International Research Committee over IPR research projects, the Pacific Council reaffirmed its significance. It thought that the committee and its secretary were necessary, and accordingly the committee strengthened its control. During the 1929 conference, the International Research Committee spelled out what the IPR regarded as priority research areas. A regional focus was retained. Research topics should be connoted by terms such as 'Pacific' and 'relations', and should have some immediate bearing on international relations in the Pacific region. A new priority was, however, clear. Priority was to be given to topics of 'fundamental importance', or with 'the likelihood of international controversy, especially in the political field'.[62] Although this could be understood as the Research Committee co-opting Curtis's point that the IPR should engage in political issues, this view had become the consensus among key IPR members, including Greene. As a result, IPR research strengthened its orientation towards the state and policy analysis.

Colonial framework

The IPR's colonial framework became more evident in 1929 over the issue of Korean representation. The Korean group was not sure whether they could attend the Kyoto conference under the constitution formalized in 1927. Davis tried to facilitate colonial group participation. This could be seen as another of his efforts to achieve his vision of the Pacific Community. Davis's main concern was Japan and China. Yet he believed that Korea was an integral part of the Pacific Community, and enthusiastically sought a way to preserve Korean representation. This was not an anti-colonial stance, because Davis thought Korean representation could be achieved within the colonial framework with only a slight compromise on the part of colonial powers. The constitution noted that a colonial group should first communicate with the National Council of the country where sovereignty lay. To this end, Davis first wanted to establish direct communication between the Philippine group and the Pacific Council and the ISIPR in order to establish a precedent for a Korean case. This required the agreement of the ACIPR. Carter, Secretary of the ACIPR, and Wilbur, Chairperson of the Pacific Council, responded favourably to Davis in the autumn of 1928.[63] Davis was further encouraged by the positive attitude of Henry Stimson. Stimson was Governor-General of the Philippines in 1927–9, and had been appointed Secretary of State for the new Hoover administration. On 14 March 1929, only ten days after the administration took over, Davis, Atherton and Loomis met Stimson, who was passing through Honolulu on his way to Washington, DC. Stimson said that he favoured self-rule, not independence, but that it would be valuable for the Philippines to participate independently at the IPR conference.[64]

Having established a precedent for direct communication between a colony group (the Philippines) and the ISIPR and the Pacific Council, Davis wrote to the Korean group on 17 September 1929. He invited them to send a Korean representative as a local/ethnic group of the Japanese Council, but suggested they communicate directly with the Pacific Council and the ISIPR (bypassing the JCIPR). Significantly, Davis noted that this arrangement had been approved by the JCIPR. The Korean group sent a reply on 19 October. It requested an amendment of Article III, Section 2, of the constitution, to confer on them full autonomous status as a distinct 'racial' group. For them, Davis's effort was unsatisfactory because it still operated in a colonial framework.

The criticism of the Korean group indicated the full potential of the original agenda of the IPR – representation of non-official individuals. To them, the IPR gave Korean members the right to participate in its operations because it emphasized non-governmentality and the individual capacity of participants. They also pursued the notion of 'political equals' of the Pacific Community to an extent which questioned the colonial status quo. Their letter argued: 'If the IPR intended to remain a non-political organization for the purpose of study and understanding of the Pacific people, not to become another League of Nations, 'why [did] it set up an artificial standard of membership?'[65] On this point, the Korean group indicated that the lack of representation of colonies on the Pacific Council was also highly unsatisfactory.

On 25 October 1929, the Pacific Council decided to send a telegram inviting the Korean group under the conditions defined in the constitution. The group attended the Pacific Council meeting on 4 November to present their case. They confirmed that their main aim was to secure independent status in the IPR, not membership of the Pacific Council. The meeting came very close to accepting the amendment proposed by the Korean group. Greene proposed it and Nitobe Inazō supported it. Nitobe was now Chairperson of the JCIPR after Inoue's resignation, and was in charge of the Kyoto conference. Full agreement was not reached, and the matter was set aside for further study.[66] Yet they did not discuss the matter further, at least in Kyoto. The last Pacific Council meeting at Kyoto on 9 November referred only to the case of Philippine representation. Curiously, the conference proceedings, published in 1930 noted: 'After full consideration of the amendment to Article III, Section 2, desired by the Koreans, having in mind its possible implications affecting not only one national council but others as well, the Pacific Council rejected the amendment.'[67] It is unclear how and when this decision was made.

The only conclusion one can deduce from available records is that although the proposal mainly concerned Japan, it had significant implications for other colonial powers. The Pacific Council felt that the colonial framework should be protected. Although some key IPR members supported representation of colonies, this was within the colonial framework.

Furthermore, even this limited support was not unanimous in Japan, Britain or the United States. Davis contacted Saitō Sōichi, Secretary of the JCIPR and General Secretary of the Tokyo YMCA, and Takaki Yasaka, professor of American studies at Tokyo Imperial University, and they approved the method Davis proposed.[68] As indicated above, Nitobe also favoured it. As a result, Saitō responded to Davis that the JCIPR agreed that the Korean group would have separate representation and communicate with the ISIPR and the Pacific Council directly. Later this evoked strong opposition from other JCIPR members, let alone other sections of society. Zumoto Motosada and Soejima Masaomi, both JCIPR members, for example, dismissed the Korean proposal for separate representation in outrage. Zumoto argued that he represented a majority view at the JCIPR, and claimed that the Pacific Council had ignored it.[69] Nor was support for colonial representation unanimous among American IPR members. Zumoto recorded that some IPR members in the United States and Britain opposed both Korean and Philippine participation.[70]

The difference of opinion among JCIPR members was not about the colonial status quo, but about the Japanese empire's conduct and management. In an opening statement at the Kyoto conference, Nitobe noted that there had been some faults in past Japanese conduct in China and Russia. This created great resentment among Japanese who were regarded as 'ultranationalists' or 'Asianists', as well as some JCIPR members, such as

Zumoto and Soejima. Although Zumoto dismissed the 'Asianist' movement in 1926, his sentiments were in fact very close. Ōkawa Shūmei, one of the most influential Asianist advocates in this period, called Nitobe and his supporters 'slaves blindly admiring Euro-American powers' and 'un-Japanese'.[71] For them, Nitobe and his supporters accepted a subordinate position to the powers. The concern of these 'Asianists' was Japanese rights and prestige as an independent state and an empire, rather than equal rights for all 'Asians'. It was this group that strongly argued against Korean participation in IPR conferences, and for Japanese rule in Manchuria. They stressed that Japanese dealings in Manchuria were no worse than those of the Americans in Nicaragua or Mexico, or the British in Southern China.

Despite their bitter enmity, the difference between the arguments of these 'Asianists' and post-League internationalists was much slighter than often assumed. Saitō, Takaki and Nitobe did not challenge the status of the Japanese empire. Rather, they supported a more 'liberal' method of colonial administration. Rōyama Masamichi was associate professor specializing in public policy at Tokyo Imperial University, and one of the leading post-League internationalists at the JCIPR. Like 'Asianists', he argued the legitimacy of Japanese rule in Manchuria as equivalent to that of other colonial powers, even before the outbreak of the Manchurian Incident in 1931.[72]

The Pacific Council noted in 1929 that it would encourage direct communication with colonial groups. Its dealing with new colonial member groups, such as North Borneo and the Netherlands East Indies, however, were through the colonial authorities. The argument to encourage colonial participation was double-edged, and it reinforced a colonial framework. In 1930, Greene argued for the participation of a colonial power and a colony by the same logic.[73] Rejecting this framework, the Korean group would finally decide to withdraw from IPR activities in 1931, while the Philippine group accepted it. As a result, in 1931, Greene wrote an awkward explanation to Nitobe: 'Korea was an integral part of the Japanese Empire, and the Philippines were possessions of the US, but the people did not hold its citizenship.'[74]

The only other anti-colonial stance came from Chinese participants. As at the conferences of 1925 and 1927, the Chinese group pursued their case against the powers' rights in China, especially extraterritoriality and tariff rights. Although the case had the potential to be an anti-colonial claim, at Kyoto it was discussed not so much in terms of colonial powers in general or British colonialism as it had been in 1925 and 1927. Rather, it was against Japanese rights in Manchuria, to be elaborated shortly.

Non-state agency

In 1929, the IPR's merit as a non-state agency was emphasized over and over again. Wilbur, Chairperson of the Pacific Council, upheld the principle of non-governmentality, and resigned the position in 1929 when he was appointed

Secretary of Interior in the new administration of his personal friend Herbert Hoover. Greene was also a firm believer in this principle. Born and brought up in a notable American missionary family in Japan, he was aware that Japanese members were under governmental pressure. In his view, however, the Kyoto conference would be a great opportunity to show the Japanese government that discussions on policies free from official pressures were not only harmless, but productive.[75] Key JCIPR members seem to have concurred. Following the precedent of Wilbur, Inoue Junnosuke resigned from the chair of the JCIPR when he was appointed Minister of Finance in July 1929. A former diplomat and soon-to-be JCIPR member, Matsuoka Yōsuke, also argued: IPR conferences provide an opportunity 'like a *zadankai* where one can discuss various issues without reservation and try to understand others' point of view'. It was useful, he continued, only if this type of discussion were not carried out by professionals such as diplomats.[76] Another argued that their discussions might not influence policy-making immediately, but that they would contribute to psychological disarmament, and might influence policies in the long run.[77]

Nitobe, who succeeded Inoue as Chairperson of the JCIPR, also stressed the non-official status of the IPR in his opening speech at the Kyoto conference. He worked as Under-Secretary at the League of Nations in Geneva in the first half of the 1920s before he returned to Japan. According to Nitobe, the IPR which 'manifested' the League's spirit of international cooperation, had two distinct merits. One was its regional focus. It would compensate for the weakness of the League, and contribute to more informed discussion of regional issues. The more significant element, however, was its non-governmentality. He stated:

> If Geneva can boast of constellations of the political world in its assembly halls, we can, with better reason, be proud of having on the floor great leaders in science and business. If the League calls for action, the Institute appeals to reason.

Although the world needed both, in his view, non-governmental bodies should have priority because members of these organizations were specialized, and well informed, and 'their opinions and judgements [were] respected and even courted by governments'. They became advisory bodies, eventually to be co-opted into governmental organs.[78] This point is significant because he argued that the ultimate goal and merit of non-governmental bodies was not so much the advocacy of specific universalist causes, as the contribution to the state and state-to-state relations.

Nitobe's commitment to 'international cooperation' was strong; he emphasized 'the international mind' and criticized 'national egotism'. While he stressed 'liberal' notions, such as 'fairness,' 'impartiality,' 'objectivity' and a scientific approach, he also made it clear that:

> [t]he international mind is not the antonym of a national mind. Nor is it a synonym for a cosmopolitan mind, which lacks a national basis. The international mind is the expansion of the national ... [which] should begin at home. A truly international mind should include patriotism and vice versa. The antithesis of the international mind is neither patriotism nor exophilism, but chauvinism and xenophobia. ... We meet here under circumstances which I hope will not strain our patriotism over overtax our piety.[79]

This articulated the very nature of post-League internationalism. Nitobe was representative of views of not only Japanese internationalists, but also internationalists at the League, where he had worked for the past several years. His idea of 'experts' reflected that of another influential post-League internationalist, Alfred Zimmern.[80] To them, internationalism was based on the nation-state, and loyalty to the international community was compatible with loyalty to one's nation.

An emphasis on this compatibility, not only non-governmentality, was important for Nitobe and his fellow post-League internationalists. The harsh criticism of these post-League internationalists has often led many to understand that there was a dichotomy between 'nationalists' and 'internationalists'. Yet clearly, these internationalists' ideas, ideologies and framework did not challenge the nation-state or the empire, and they shared common grounds with their 'opponents'. What divided them was the degree of loyalty to the nation-state/empire, and the manner of its expression. These post-League internationalists also praised the merit of the IPR's non-governmental status without criticising the heavy government involvement. So great was its official mobilization at the time of the Kyoto conference, it makes one wonder how overseas conference participants, including key IPR figures, could have been unaware of it. Did they turn a blind eye, or did they simply regard it as the 'Japanese way'? In any case, their silence makes JCIPR members and other advocates of non-state agencies guilty of a double standard. The double standard to which I refer is not between nationalism and internationalism, but their acceptance of heavy state intervention in what they argued was a non-state agency.

Government involvement in Japan had been evident since 1925, and this continued, regardless of whether the *Seiyūkai* or the *Minseitō* was in power. Since 1925, the government had regarded the IPR highly, and acknowledged its practical value and significance. Although there were changes in cabinet composition, personnel at the Ministry of Foreign Affairs did not change dramatically in the period 1925–30. Shidehara was Foreign Minister except when Tanaka Giichi of *Seiyūkai* was both Prime Minister and Foreign Minister (April 1927 – July 1929). Diplomats who dealt with IPR issues remained in important posts despite changes of government. Debuchi Katsuji was Shidehara's right-hand man. He was also the son-in-law of Tanaka, and was ambassador to the United States in 1928–32. Keen on a close and smooth

US–Japan relationship, he saw the role of the IPR as significant, and conveyed this view to the government.[81]

Although government involvement in the JCIPR had always been strong, its extent was extraordinary at the time of the Kyoto conference. Both the Tanaka and the Hamaguchi (*Minseitō*) cabinets gave substantial financial support, and were heavily involved with the organization of the conference. Like the ratification of the Pact of Paris of 1928, this demonstrated that the Tanaka cabinet, known for its military intervention in China, pursued a 'cooperative policy' with the great powers. In May 1929 (still the Tanaka cabinet), Inoue Junnosuke (still Chairperson of the JCIPR) asked the Ministry of Foreign Affairs for 30,000 yen out of a 100,000 yen budget for the conference.[82] A further 40,000 yen were collected from Mitsui, Mitsubishi and Sumitomo, and the South Manchurian Railway Company.[83] The government also provided foreign participants with a streamlined custom service and free railway tickets in Japan, which was extended to Manchuria and Korea on the JCIPR's request. In this, the government followed the practice established by the Pan-Pacific Science Congress (PPSC) held in Tokyo in 1926. The arrangement was not unique. The Australian government had given similar travel concessions to PPSC participants when it was held in Australia in 1923. The PPSC, which began in 1920, however, did not claim to be unofficial, and invitations, organization and finance were all arranged through official channels.[84] The Japanese government made no distinction between an IPR conference and the PPSC, and this was not questioned by the JCIPR or other IPR members.

Security control was very tight in Kyoto. This was probably common practice for major international events in Japan, and it was also partly because Manchuria was a main topic of the Kyoto conference. The situation in north-eastern China was volatile. For some time, its virtual rulers had been warlords, not the central governments in Beijing or Nanjing. The region had been also the setting for conflicting interests among Japan, China and Russia since the beginning of the century, especially over the right to own and protect the railway line. In the 1920s, there were numerous disputes between the Chinese and the Japanese – involving soldiers and civilian settlers – over what they saw as their rights. The security situation was deteriorating, and an anti-Japanese sentiment was growing. This reached a peak in July 1928, when the Japanese Guandong (Kuantung) army assassinated Zhang Zuolin (Chang Tso-lin), a warlord in North China, with whom the Guandong army was competing for control of the region. While the army initially denied involvement in this assassination, an official Japanese investigation had proved otherwise already in October 1928. Nevertheless, the army insisted on their non-involvement, and the public was not informed about this finding. Prime Minister Tanaka was pressured by the Emperor to punish those responsible. The case had been an extremely important political and diplomatic matter. In July 1929, the Tanaka cabinet would resign over the mishandling of this case.

In 1928–9, the Japanese government was highly sensitive about criticism of its conduct over the incident as well as of the legitimacy of Japanese rights in Manchuria. The Kyoto conference became a significant concern. Japanese embassies and consulates in China sent numerous detailed reports on local developments as part of conference preparations, in particular research papers on Manchuria. The government also collected newspaper articles about the conference in the United States and China through 1928 and 1929. At the time of the conference, the authorities in port prefectures in Japan reported the comings and goings of participants from other countries. Their activities in Japan were reported to the Ministry of Home Affairs and the Ministry of Foreign Affairs. The mayor of Kyoto also reported details of the conference to these ministries.

Did official involvement extend to the JCIPR's research activities, or did the JCIPR maintain its autonomy? In 1927 the Japanese Consul General in Honolulu, Kuwashima, had noted that IPR conferences would focus on current political issues, and urged Foreign Minister Tanaka to send a strong team to the next conference.[85] Despite this warning, however, the JCIPR seem to have maintained autonomy in choosing and conducting research projects and selecting delegates. The government would have been loath to see the Manchurian issue openly discussed, particularly by Chinese. The decision to make it a major topic item for the Kyoto conference clearly ran counter to official wishes. Condliffe recorded how this happened. After the second conference, he travelled to Japan and China to initiate research projects and data papers for the third conference. In Japan, JCIPR members told him that Manchuria should not be a topic at the Kyoto conference, and asked whether he could convey this message to their Chinese counterparts. He was sensitive enough to the JCIPR to rule out research projects on Korea. Yet he did not follow their request blindly. In China, David Yui, Secretary General of the Chinese YMCA in Shanghai and Chairperson of the Chinese Council of the IPR, told him that the only worthwhile subject at the next conference was Manchuria, and urged him to go north and find Chinese scholars to prepare data papers.

Three Japanese figures were crucial in accepting Manchuria as a conference topic. One was Matsuoka Yōsuke, a diplomat until 1921 and then Vice-President of the South Manchurian Railway Company. Condliffe met him in Dalian (Dairen) in Manchuria and told him that the Chinese group would prepare papers on political, legal and economic aspects of Manchuria for the coming IPR conference. Matsuoka, known as 'the American' because of his US education and his manner, responded characteristically that 'he could handle them'. Back from China in Tokyo, Condliffe sensed a negative reaction on the part of JCIPR members. But Saitō Sōichi, Secretary of the JCIPR, helped Condliffe. He invited Inoue Junnosuke, Chairperson of the JCIPR, to the meeting. Like Matsuoka, Inoue's attitude was confident. Condliffe recorded:

Inoue listened to my report quietly and to the mingled relief and dismay of the professors decided to accept the challenge, but he asked me to work with the Japanese committee on a research programme to outdo the Chinese. This I did.[86]

There was no official intervention at this stage. The government was informed about this decision later in April 1928 through a diplomat in Honolulu. Condliffe relayed the decision to him. Interestingly, then Condliffe indicated that Inoue had not made this decision willingly.[87] Matsuoka and Inoue had strong personalities, and were influential in political circles. While they were closely involved with the JCIPR, their understanding of the post-League order differed greatly. Even after resigning from the chair of the JCIPR, Inoue maintained his commitment to the post-League order. As Minister of Finance, he tried to restore the Japanese economy to the post-League economic order by readopting the gold standard. He also conducted a radical rationalization policy. These policies coincided with the world depression, with devastating effects, especially in the rural economy. Popular resentment against his policies culminated in his assassination in 1932. Matsuoka played a significant role at the Kyoto conference. His experience of hardship as a student in the United States meant that he had seen a different America from the image held by many Japanese post-League internationalists. In contrast to Inoue, he became a very vocal critic of the League. Known for his eloquence in Japanese and English, he became a *Seiyūkai* politician, criticizing Shidehara's diplomacy. Later as a diplomat and Foreign Minister, he played a critical role in almost every step of Japanese diplomacy leading the empire into the Pacific War. As a consequence, he was charged as a war criminal and died in the Sugamo prison in 1946. Yet it is important to note that Matsuoka remained a JCIPR member at least until 1932, and maintained close relationships with younger JCIPR members in the late 1930s and early 1940s.

The second episode which demonstrates the autonomy of the JCIPR in 1928–9 was that it initiated research on Manchuria. Soon after Inoue's decision to take up the topic of Manchuria as a main theme of the Kyoto conference, the JCIPR held a research committee meeting in November 1927. In January 1928, it decided to meet twice a month. Rōyama was nominated as a member of the research group on law and politics, and he soon took charge of research on Manchuria. In March, Rōyama sent a letter to Takaki Yasaka, arguing that the JCIPR needed to commence research soon, even without ISIPR funds. Well informed about research development in China and the United States through IPR correspondence, Rōyama suggested that the JCIPR should utilize the documents available at the Ministry of Foreign Affairs and the South Manchurian Railway Company. He further argued that it should also think about alternative research funding. Instead of official aid, he suggested using publishers' advances for JCIPR research publications, such as Nihon hyōronsha or Iwanami shoten.[88] This indicates that the JCIPR tried to finance research projects without official funds. It also meant that although the contact between the JCIPR and the Ministry of Foreign Affairs was evidently close, it was the JCIPR that initiated the use of official sources.

Rōyama took an active role in establishing a solid foundation for research on Manchuria free from government intervention. According to a note from a Japanese diplomat in Guangzhou (Canton) in June 1929, in November 1928 Rōyama had proposed collaborative research on Manchurian issues with an American scholar, Henry C. Brownell, at Lingnan University in Guangzhou.[89] This was based on his belief that the Japanese and Chinese groups should have some common ground to discuss the issue. He sent a draft which listed a few main points for discussion – the responsibility for security defined by treaties, international conflict over the rights of railway lines, the economic potential for international trade, and the immigration situation and the impact of contact among various ethnic groups.[90] The draft was exchanged, and data papers were developed by Chinese groups in Guangzhou and Jilin (Kirin) province in Manchuria.[91] Rōyama prepared Japanese data papers along similar lines. By the time the JCIPR established the special committee on Manchurian problems in February 1929, he had collected and reprinted materials on political, economic and social conditions of Manchuria, as well as official declarations, treaties and Japanese 'legal' justifications of its rights in Manchuria.[92]

The government's intervention in the JCIPR's research schemes was not obvious until mid-1929. Until June, it was unaware of Rōyama's initiation of collaborative research with Chinese groups. When it found out, it was deeply concerned. A Japanese diplomat in Guangzhou stated that Rōyama's proposal for Chinese groups had very serious implications and could lead to misunderstanding and further anti-Japan sentiment in China. It urged the government to warn Rōyama about this danger.[93] The message was conveyed to the JCIPR, to which Takaki replied that the JCIPR would handle the issue very carefully and maintain close communication with the Ministry of Foreign Affairs. He added that Rōyama could explain the situation if necessary.[94] Despite this strong official pressure, Rōyama maintained the position that open discussion was the best way to make the powers accept Japanese rights in Manchuria.[95] Although this suggests Rōyama's strong stance on non-governmentality, the difference of opinion between him and the government was not over Japanese national/imperial rights, but how to convince the other powers of their legitimacy.

Around the same time, two Japanese diplomats in the United States urged the government to intervene in the JCIPR's organization of the Kyoto conference. On 7 May, Debuchi sent a letter to the Secretary of the Ministry of Foreign Affairs informing him that there would be thorough and critical discussion of Sino-Japanese relations in Manchuria at the conference. He suggested that Arita Hachirō, Director-General of the Asia Bureau of the Ministry, should meet a British academic who had been working on the topic.

Debuchi also urged the government to guide the discussion at the Kyoto conference, and to alert Inoue and other JCIPR members about this government intention.[96] Another Japanese diplomat in New York warned on 19 June that the Kyoto conference could damage Sino-Japanese diplomatic relations which were, in his view, improving. He argued that the government needed to 'instruct the discussions at the conference to remain merely academic'.[97] As a result, after June, just before the resignation of the Tanaka cabinet, communications between the JCIPR and the Ministry of Foreign Affairs became intense.[98]

The conflict between Japan and China only strengthened existing trends within IPR operations. The assassination of Zhang Zuolin was a looming political and diplomatic issue for the Japanese government. The Emperor notified Tanaka of his discontent over the handling of the matter. This eventually led to the resignation of the Tanaka cabinet. The official investigation had already proved that Japanese army officers committed the assassination. These officers were charged and dealt with, but the public had not been apprised of these facts in the autumn of 1929. At the Kyoto conference, the Chinese delegation accused the Japanese army of the murder. Matsuoka Yōsuke, recently resigned from the post of Vice-President of the South Manchurian Railway Company and ambitious for a political career, refuted the claim in his eloquent English. Matsuoka spoke the language of post-League internationalists, and he was convincing to the participants.[99] Praising the non-official status of the IPR, he did not see any problem in justifying Japanese policies and army activities in Manchuria at the IPR conference. Government pressure was not obvious, and his action appeared voluntary. He must have calculated that this was a good vote-catching strategy, given the publicity the event received in the mainstream Japanese press.

There were some upshots from the fierce debate between him and the Chinese representatives. Japanese, Chinese and American newspapers reported the event, and many, including the *New York Times*, praised the merit of 'frank and individual' discussions which contributed to the 'better understanding' of the issue. It is ironic because despite the frankness, Matsuoka, deliberately or not, misled the audience. The debate also emphasized that the conflict between China and Japan in Manchuria strengthened an existing trend at IPR conferences, rather than initiating a new trend. Although Japanese and Chinese participants were in the spotlight, defending or justifying national policies had been common practice from the first conference.

Rōyama's paper on Manchuria demonstrated that this practice continued. In 1929, this almost seventy-page document was probably one of the most thorough arguments for Japanese rights in Manchuria. After discussing Japanese relations with Manchuria in geographical, historical, legal, economic and cultural spheres, he concluded that 'Japanese relations with Manchuria' were 'of vital importance to her own strategy and imperial organization'. The aim of Rōyama's paper was to clarify the 'accomplished fact' of Japanese presence and to argue the 'special' aspects of the region in a framework of international law and conventions.

As a post-League internationalist, he was interpreting the Japanese case in a language and framework which were accepted and understood by his counterparts in the Euro-American powers, and possibly in China. He felt that many notions which were taken for granted in Japan were not understood properly outside Japan. He was aware that this was a formidable task, and noted that he would need a new concept of security.[100] The government was acutely conscious of the need for good 'explanations'. Japanese diplomats in Manchuria were finding it increasingly difficult to defend Japanese rights in the face of strong and detailed Chinese research. On 7 October 1929, the Consul General of Mukden (now called Shenyang) asked Foreign Minister, Shidehara, whether he knew of any research that provided grounds for the Japanese right to station its army along the railway apart from the Beijing (Peking) Treaty (or Sino-Japanese Treaty) of 1915.[101] The treaty was imposed on the Chinese government towards the end of World War I, and its validity had been criticized by both China and the powers. Rōyama's paper was the perfect document to justify Japanese rights.

The merit of his paper was not its 'nationalistic,' but its 'internationalist' aspect. He addressed his papers to those in diplomatic circles, particularly in the United States, by using concepts and frameworks familiar to them. For him, it was important that the issue was discussed thoroughly in an open forum, and that Japanese 'national/imperial' interests, like those of other countries, be understood by the powers. His method was not force or coercion, but open and 'scientific' discussion. In this spirit, Rōyama was soon to present a plan to solve the coming Manchurian crisis in 1931–2.

Greene's administration, 1929–32

Greene's vision for the IPR

Although Condliffe claimed that Carter dominated IPR decision-making in 1927–9,[102] it was Greene who held the helm of the ISIPR in 1927–32. He was already prominent in 1927, when he was still Treasurer of the ACIPR. His prominence grew after the Kyoto conference. On paper Davis's term as General Secretary was meant to continue until November 1930. After he announced his resignation at the Kyoto conference, Charles Loomis, who had been Associate General Secretary, became Acting General Secretary. The day-to-day administration and various policy issues, however, fell to Greene, who became Chairperson of the Pacific Council after the conference. While policy-making was still a function of the Pacific Council, not the ISIPR, he took more active charge than Wilbur had. Loomis provided support in the practical arrangements for conference organization. Greene conducted IPR business from the offices of Lee and Higginson, an investment bank in Manhattan where he was a partner. This meant that he had to juggle two demanding jobs with little or no money from the IPR. The situation lasted until he took up the Woodrow Wilson chair of International Relations at the University College of Wales, Aberystwyth, in September 1932, courtesy of Curtis's connections.[103]

His administration can be seen as transitional. Despite the criticism of Davis and others, Greene shared the IPR's initial principles and spirit, and maintained much of IPR operations intact. His vision differed from that of Davis, Carter or Curtis, and accordingly he initiated a few changes. None of the changes was drastic, nor in line with Curtis's reorganization plan. In retrospect, however, these changes appeared to have smoothed a path for the succeeding Carter's administration.

Greene had great faith in the IPR. Just before the third conference in Kyoto, he wrote to the Rockefeller Foundation:

> [T]he thing we are trying to accomplish is so vastly worth accomplishing that any money given to us from whatever source will be amply justified as a contribution to world peace.[104]

The Foundation shared the view.[105] In a financially difficult time between 1929 and 1931, it remained loyal and valued the activities of the IPR under Greene's helm: 'The value of the work of the Institute and its importance both as a research organization and as an instrument for promoting international goodwill cannot be questioned.'[106] Greene's commitment was clearly demonstrated by the energy, time and money (his personal contribution was US$5,000 per year) he devoted. His leadership was widely acknowledged, especially at the time of the fourth conference in China in 1931.[107]

Although he concentrated on tackling pragmatic issues – organization of the conference, the ISIPR deficit and the selection of the next general secretary, his handling of these matters reflected his vision for the IPR. His vision was well articulated in his response to Curtis's reform plan in 1928. This seems to have remained unchanged even after he resumed full responsibility after the Kyoto conference. His method was consultative. He wrote to members of the Pacific Council to ask their opinions on the previous conference at Kyoto, in preparation for the fourth conference.[108] Representatives from Canada, China, Britain, Japan, New Zealand, Australia and the United States attended a meeting of the programme committee at New York on 29–30 November 1930. The report was sent to the members of the Pacific Council and secretaries of National Councils.[109]

Greene shared the IPR's initial principles and spirit. Unlike Curtis, he believed that the integrity of the headquarters, the ISIPR, was crucial for the IPR's successful operation. Its deficit was, therefore, a great concern and he tried to solve it. He followed his principle of a two-budget policy, dividing it into one for research, and the other for administration of the ISIPR in Honolulu. This structure was not seriously questioned until Carter's 'Inquiry' project on the Sino-Japanese War extended the functions of the ISIPR into research projects. The research section had been well-off because of the Rockefeller Foundation grant. The problem was the ISIPR. Greene disapproved of the Honolulu office's method of using research funds to cover its deficits. The cost should be covered by contributions from National Councils, and in this way the 'international' character of the IPR headquarters would be enhanced. This was problematic. Contributions from National Councils to the administrative costs, other than those from American sources, remained very low. The way these amounts were decided is unclear, but correspondence suggests that the Pacific Council determined them according to the suggestions of National Councils. In 1929, against the American contribution (US$55,275 from the mainland and $13,200 from Hawai'i), the pledged quota for each country was $5,000 for Canada, and $20,000 for Japan (all in US dollars). They were £1,000 (US$5,000) for Britain, £250 for Australia and £100 for New Zealand. The quota for Japan was large because of the cost of the conference that year, but other quotas were extremely small. Except for the doubled Chinese contribution in 1933, non-American contributions largely declined in the early 1930s,[110] and later the situation deteriorated further. The British group failed to increase its contribution, allowing the American dominance of funding.

To make ends meet, Atherton, Treasurer of the Pacific Council, noted that he borrowed $50,000 annually in 1929–31 from a bank in Honolulu on his own account. To his letter of request for more contributions, each National Council explained their difficulty as a result of the Depression. Although convinced of the importance of the IPR, Eggleston wrote about the hardship of Australian economy. Paying even its quota of one per cent of the budget was hard for them. Comparing this to the amount raised in Hawai'i alone, Atherton began to question whether this small contribution reflected other councils' evaluation of IPR activities.[111] By January 1931, before the fourth conference, the deficit was $10,750.[112]

Like Atherton, Greene could have urged National Councils to increase their contributions. But this implied certain changes to the structure of each councils, increasing membership, or increasing membership and subscription fees. He had already made efforts to raise more funds in the United States, although he was finding it increasingly hard. Few options were left. Greene sought to cut the expenses of *Pacific Affairs*, the journal of the IPR, which was edited at the Honolulu office. It evolved from a newsletter, the (IPR) *News Bulletin* (1927–8), and was renamed *Pacific Affairs* in May 1928. Subscribers increased from 1,200 in 1927 to 2,000 in 1929. The subscription fee was US$2, and publication costs did not justify its monthly format. Greene proposed to the Pacific Council that it appear quarterly until the problems were resolved.[113] It is noteworthy that he did not suggest any change in editorial style. It continued to carry the section 'Views from the East', leaving the legacy of the spirit of regionalism and the flavour of the newsletter intact.

Cutting staff at the ISIPR in Honolulu did not seem to have been on Greene's agenda. He believed in the significance of the strength of the ISIPR.

He relied on Looms for the practical organization of the fourth conference, and Looms spent some time in China for its preparation. Unlike Curtis, Greene greatly valued the IPR's research function, which was organized by Research Secretary Condliffe. Condliffe's resignation, therefore, was not at Greene's urging. Condliffe felt the need to have a secure post after the Kyoto conference. He accepted the job of writing the first World Economic Survey for the League of Nations in the manner of Arnold Toynbee's annual *Survey of International Affairs*. He organized a transitional one-year arrangement with the University of Michigan, spending one-third of his time on IPR work.[114] A year later, Condliffe and his family left Honolulu for Geneva. Greene regretted Condliffe's move, but agreed that the IPR did not have the resources to keep him. Atherton also felt that the salary of the Research Secretary was not secure.[115]

The direction of the research programmes, however, did not change immediately after Condliffe's departure. Nor did Greene make any changes. The legacy of Condliffe's commitment to regional initiatives against American domination lingered. The programmes Condliffe initiated were long term. They were carried out independently by local researchers in various member countries, and their findings were gradually published. It is also important to note that Condliffe's new research assistant from New Zealand, William Holland, followed his agenda. Holland was only twenty-one years old when he joined the ISIPR in 1928. Inspired by John Mott and active in the YMCA international student movement, he was one of Condliffe's students at Canterbury University College. Condliffe, who was then Research Secretary at the ISIPR, offered him an assistant's job at US$35 a week. Holland jumped at the opportunity, and borrowed the money for the steamer fare to Honolulu.[116] Holland recorded that Condliffe's opposition to American domination and promotion of initiatives by Asian scholars 'made a deep impression on him ... and influenced his own attitudes and actions after he himself became Research Secretary (1933–43)'.[117]

Despite these 'unchanges', Greene was also smoothing the path for Carter. Unlike Davis, but like Carter and Curtis, he believed that urgent political issues should be discussed at IPR conferences. He saw the Manchurian issue in this light. Although he was aware of the criticism of the IPR's 'overly political' tendencies, he felt it should be discussed at the conference in China in 1931. This would definitely strengthen IPR's state orientation – the trend which was accentuated after Carter's time.

Unlike Carter, Greene did not concern himself with ISIPR staffing or location. Yet one episode indicated that Greene and Carter had some ideas in common – a move away from the vision of the Pacific Community. It emerged in the choice of candidates for the succeeding General Secretary of the ISIPR. Greene was in charge of this selection, at least until September 1932. Various candidates were considered before Carter's appointment at the fifth conference in 1933. The list suggests that key IPR figures were looking for someone of a calibre equivalent to Secretary General of the League of Nations. Interestingly, when Carter was appointed, the Pacific Council asked him to use the term Secretary General, not the term previously used, General Secretary.[118] The list of candidates included prominent post-League internationalists: Frederick Whyte (former British president of the National Indian Legislative Assembly), Arthur Salter (British, and Director of the Economic and Finance Section at the League in 1919–20 and 1922–31), Dwight Morrow (American banker and diplomat), Henry Hodgkin (British educator with missionary experience in China), Vincent Massey (Canadian diplomat), Alanzo Tayler (American academic specializing in food and population at Stanford University), Robert Borden (Prime Minister of Canada in 1911–20, and Chancellor of Queen's University in 1924–30), Owen Lattimore (American business traveller and writer) and Jerome Greene. Carter's name only appeared in April 1933. Although Greene was looking for another career after the reorganization of his investment bank, he did not consider himself as a candidate. Instead, he took up an academic position in Wales.

A Pacific-centred perspective is hardly evident in this list. Expert knowledge of and experiences in countries in Asia and the Pacific islands were a consideration, but not thought essential.[119] Except for Maeda Tamon, there was no serious consideration of candidates from Japan, China, Hawai'i, Australia, New Zealand or the Philippines. The people mentioned in the list were from the Atlantic side of North America or Britain, with a few exceptions. What was valued most was the candidate's prestige and calibre, and the ability to conduct appropriate government-level relations.[120] Female candidates were never suggested, despite active and enthusiastic support for the IPR among women's organizations.

Otherwise open and consultative, Greene conducted rather a secretive process. It was discussed among a small group in North America and Britain. Eggleston's correspondence indicated that progress was not reported, even to members of the Pacific Council.[121] This may have reflected the difficulty of attracting people for the post. Not many were keen on the job. The reason for this difficulty suggested in correspondence was financial. Persons who were approached were highly paid. It was a common view that a suitable person would not be attracted without an adequate salary, and Greene estimated the salary of a candidate such as Arthur Salter to be US$15,000–20,000.[122] There was, however, another significant undercurrent – the prestige and credibility of the IPR, and a lack of interest in or commitment to the issues of Asia and the Pacific among those approached. The research output of the IPR was regarded highly, but only in limited specialist circles, and the IPR had yet to earn prestige in Europe. Few were interested in international affairs, and among them, interest in current affairs in Asia and the Pacific islands was rare. The region was, for example, seen as of secondary importance to the peace movement in the United States.[123] Curtis had a hard time convincing the RIIA of the significance of the IPR. After his interest drifted, very few RIIA members took a positive interest in the IPR. Rather, many criticized contributing money to the IPR in 1933.[121] Indifference to the region was characteristic among post-League internationalists in Europe, and to a lesser extent on the East coast of North America.

The Manchurian Incident: a challenge to the regional order?

The Shanghai Conference of 1931

On the night of 18 September 1931, just before the fourth IPR conference, originally planned to take place in Hangzhou (Hangchow), China, there was an explosion on the South Manchurian Railway line near Mukden. Mukden was one of the biggest cities in Manchuria, and the northern base of the Japanese railway company. Following the explosion, the Japanese Guandong army attacked the army of Zhang Xueliang (Chang Hsueh-liang). Zhang was the son of the warlord, Zhang Zuolin, who had been assassinated by the Guandong army in 1928. Mukden was his base, although he was then staying in Beijing. This Mukden Incident or *Ryūjōko jiken* was the beginning of Manchurian crisis or what was called *Manshū jihen* (Manchurian Incident) in Japan. The Guandong army argued that it acted to defend its rights along the railway and to protect the security of Japanese residents. Its ambitions became clear in the next few months, however. It occupied major cities in Manchuria far from the railway – Mukden, Jilin, Changchun (Chungchun), Tsitsihar and Jinzhou (Chinchou). The region virtually came under the control of the Guandong army, and a puppet regime, Manchuguo (Manchukuo), was created in March 1932.

This series of incidents in Manchuria in 1931–3 had a great impact on the League of Nations and the post-League international order. This inevitably affected IPR operations. First, most post-League internationalists, including some Japanese, saw it a 'crisis' of the League and the post-League order. On 21 September 1931, the Chinese government, based in Nanjing, rejected direct negotiations with the Japanese government, which appeared unable to stop the aggression. It lodged an appeal with the League of Nations. On 30 September 1931, the Council of the League passed a unanimous resolution to urge the speedy withdrawal of the Japanese army to their old status quo along the railway. The aggression continued, contradicting the promises of the Japanese government. Upon government instruction, the Japanese representative at the Council, Yoshizawa Kenkichi (1874–1965), tried to veto an attempt to set a deadline for withdrawal. No clear and quick solution was in sight. How the League would solve the matter now amounted to a test case of its validity and effectiveness in the region. Second, this 'crisis' virtually brought the United States, still a non-League member, into the League mechanism. The American government was invited to the Council as an observer in order to deal with the Manchurian crisis. Until that point, Republican internationalism had been establishing a general framework of international cooperation, independent from, but complementary to the League. Now it virtually became a part of the League machinery.

Third, as would become more evident in the mid- to late 1930s, the crisis (or the Manchurian Incident) eroded the power base of political parties which had been promoting a cooperative policy towards the powers. From the time of the Hara cabinet (1918–21) at least until the Wakatsuki cabinet (April to December 1931) the government pursued this policy (often termed Shidehara diplomacy), and supported the post-League international order – the League of Nations and the Washington Treaties. In 1928, even the Tanaka cabinet, which conducted three army interventions in Shandong (Shantung) province, signed the Pact of Paris to demonstrate its cooperative attitude towards the powers. After the Tanaka cabinet, Shidehara as Foreign Minister once again tried to maintain a cooperative policy, but it was under severe criticism by an unsatisfied populace and opportunistic politicians, bureaucrats and military officers. Especially after the Inukai cabinet (December 1931 to May 1932), which was crushed by the May 15 Incident in 1932, political parties lost dominance in politics, and the government was less committed to disarmament or cooperative diplomacy. Now it endorsed the actions of the Guandong army, no longer merely turning a blind eye or simply accepting them.[125]

The Council of the League condemned Japanese aggression, and contemporary post-League internationalists and later scholars saw the Manchurian incident as morally wrong. The powers, however, did not condemn colonialism in general. They were not concerned with the Japanese colonial status quo before 1931, nor did they address their criticism towards their own colonial holdings. As Thorne notes, the dominant powers condemned Japanese action because Japanese 'vital interests' challenged theirs' which had been guaranteed by the post-League order.[126] Japanese post-League internationalists, including Yoshizawa, the Japanese representative at the Council, and Shidehara, the Foreign Minister, were to exploit this double standard in their initial dealings with the League.

Many Council members shared concerns over the rights of their empires in China, and were not unsympathetic to Japanese claims. They were reluctant to impose economic sanctions on Japan as argued by the Chinese delegates. The United States also ruled out the option of sanctions despite a strong push by the Far Eastern section of the State Department, especially an old IPR member, Stanley Hornbeck. As a means of breaking the deadlock, the League proposed sending an inquiry mission to China. The Council unanimously endorsed this in December 1931. Yoshizawa supported this move. He insisted that this mission should consist of members from the great powers, not small countries, and that the scope of the inquiry should be China in general. Yoshizawa hoped that in this way the mission would point out the general problem of internal security of China, and other colonial powers would realize that their interests were also at stake. They would, he hoped, see the rationale for Japanese actions.[127]

Even in early January 1932, common interests of Japan and other Council members of the League were evident. The Guandong army planned to attack Jinzhou in the first week of January 1932. It was the last unoccupied administrative centre in the region. Zhang Xueliang, realizing the difficulty of fighting the Japanese army with little support from the central government, decided to evacuate the city before the attack. This meant not only a bloodless occupation of Jinzhou by the Japanese army, but control of the entire region. The incident caused an immediate reaction from US Secretary of State, Stimson. On 7 January, he declared non-recognition of the Japanese actions and of agreements which violated the Nine Power Treaty and the Pact of Paris. It was later termed the Stimson Doctrine. The British and French governments, both treaty powers, however, did not follow Stimson. The situation changed only after a fierce fight took place between Japan and China in Shanghai in late January. Colonial powers had far greater interests in Shanghai, and they saw Japanese aggression as a liability. The League moved quickly to take a stronger stand against Japan, this time leaving the option of economic sanctions open.

The League's mission, the Lytton Commission, began an examination in February in 1932. While it was done under the very difficult circumstances of strict surveillance by the Japanese army and the police of newly founded Manchuguo, they managed to put together a report later in the year. It included two major points: actions of the Japanese army during the Mukden Incident and after could not be regarded as self-defence; and Manchuguo was not founded on the genuine desires of the residents there, but was planned and administered by the Japanese army. It proposed returning to the pre-Mukden Incident situation. The report did not recognize Manchuguo and, in reply, the Japanese government decided to withdraw from the League.

This 'Manchurian Incident' was seen as a watershed for Japanese post-League internationalists. Contemporaries and many later scholars argued their 'shift' from internationalism to nationalism in 1931.[128] To be sure, many so-called 'liberal internationalists' or 'moderate intellectuals' defended Japanese actions in Manchuria.[129] The incident, however, did not prompt a dramatic departure from the past, because the nation-state/empire had always been an integral part of their internationalism. As Rōyama's argument demonstrated in 1929, they respected international law and conciliation, and had been arguing the legitimacy of Japanese national/imperial interests in Manchuria and Inner Mongolia well before the incident.

In late 1931, the decline of political parties was not dramatic enough to affect the activities of post-League internationalists or the JCIPR. Shidehara was still Foreign Minister. Most JCIPR members did not criticize government inaction in the face of army aggression, or its acquiescence. Rather, as they had done in the 1920s, they argued the legality of Japanese army actions within a framework of international laws and treaties, such as the Covenant of the League of Nations, the Nine Power Treaty and the Pact of Paris. These 'internationalists' included Tachi Sakutarō (1874–1943), professor of international law at Tokyo Imperial University, and Shinobu Jumpei (1871–1962), former diplomat and professor of law at Waseda University. Both were on the JCIPR's executive committee. Tachi and Shinobu argued that Japanese army action constituted self-defence, and did not violate the Pact of Paris. Yoshizawa used the same rhetoric at the League's assembly,[130] and a similar argument was heard at the fourth IPR conference in China.

The Shanghai conference was held only a month after the Mukden Incident (21 October to 2 November 1931). Sino-Japanese relations were very tense, and pressure from the League and the powers was mounting. The Japanese government was deeply concerned about how the conference would unfold. Correspondence between the ISIPR and the JCIPR was forwarded to the Ministry of Foreign Affairs in Japan and the Ministry discussed the conference extensively with Japanese diplomats in China. It closely followed preparations for the conference, provided confidential material for JCIPR members and contributed financially.[131]

The conference almost fell apart, which probably would have come as a relief to the Japanese government. The security of JCIPR members was a concern, and even after the members had left for the conference key figures at the IPR were considering cancellation. It was Greene who pushed ahead. While Chinese and other National Councils' opposition to Japanese action was strong, he proposed that a modified conference be held in the relative safety of Shanghai. Having gained the support of representatives from all councils, Greene held the Pacific Council meeting at the Cathay Hotel in Shanghai on 13 October 1931. It decided to hold a proper conference in Shanghai on the condition that the conference would not adopt Manchuria as a main topic. Hu Shuxi (Hu Shuhsi), professor of political science at Yenching University, Beiping (Peiping), and conference convenor, opened the conference on 21 October:

> [T]he opening of this conference ... will be remembered ... as having set up a splendid precedent that all those who in peaceful times pride themselves as being internationally-minded must not desert the ideal of calm thinking, patient research, and open-minded discussions at a time when folly reigns and passions carry the day...[132]

Although the conference tried to avoid Manchurian issues and focus on trade relations, Manchuria hardly escaped the participants' minds. Takayanagi spoke as a representative of the JCIPR. Stressing 'liberal' nature of IPR participants and their 'natural' concern with peace, he noted the 'complexity' of Manchurian problem. Like Tachi and Shinobu, he argued that Japan was not defying the League. He deployed Orientalist rhetoric when he maintained that China was not yet a sovereign state, and justified the rights of the Japanese army in acting for the 'security' of their nationals.[133] It is worth noting that the line of argument was used by British members when they argued for their rights in China at the second IPR conference.

In contrast, Hu, representative of the Chinese group, put a straightforward case for China. He did not need twists of logic, and it was easily argued within the framework of international law and the League of Nations. For him, 'the majority of the several hundred cases that [were] pending between China and Japan, with the exception of a few relating to railways, [were] either Japanese cases against China arising from the question of lease by negotiation, or Chinese cases against Japan arising from the question of Japanese armed forces in Manchuria'. The former depended on the validity of the Beijing Treaty, and questions of equity and justice. Japanese positions and interests were 'no more special than any other foreign economic interests in China'. On the issue of Chinese sovereignty, he cynically pointed out: 'perhaps in speaking of Chinese aspirations to sovereignty, Professor Takayanagi [had] in mind Chinese aspirations for the recovery of lost rights.'[134]

Greene and other IPR members believed in the merit of 'unofficial' discussion of urgent political issues. The above exchange between the 'national representatives' of Japan and China, however, demonstrated how hard it was to realize this principle. The same difficulty was also evident in a round table discussion, 'The diplomatic machinery of the Pacific'. The topic was proposed by Eggleston in early 1931.[135] Then Manchuria was not part of the proposed scope, and his main concern was regional disarmament which he had already proposed in 1929. At Shanghai, however, it provided an opportunity for participants to discuss the general framework of collective security in the region, which inevitably included the issue of Manchuria.

As an introduction to this round table noted, it aimed to achieve the principle of 'unofficial' discussion of urgent political issues. It emphasized the 'private' nature of the IPR, and suggested a critical stance in relation to official policies. The conference did 'not serve the purposes of official diplomacy'. It tried to explain that the problems in the 'Far Eastern situation' were due to 'the limitations of political intercourse between two great nations to the established methods of diplomatic negotiation'.[136] This was hard to achieve. Japanese participants in this session were Nitobe, Saitō, Tsurumi, Shinobu, Takayanagi, Matsumoto Shigeharu (1899–1989) and Yokota Kisaburō (1896–1993), professor of international law at Tokyo Imperial University. Here, Japanese post-League internationalists tried to justify Japanese actions in Manchuria within the framework of international laws and existing treaties. While Rōyama took a leading role in research on Manchuria for the Kyoto conference, Yokota, Takayanagi and Takaki were central to the activity at the JCIPR at the time of Manchurian crisis in 1931–3.

Yokota was regarded as one of the strongest critics of Japanese actions in Manchuria. He refuted the self-defence argument of the Japanese army, especially in regard to its aggression after the initial Mukden Incident. Unlike many other post-League internationalists, including Rōyama, who stressed the 'special' aspect of Manchuria, he took a universalist stance. He argued that the matter should be dealt with by the League, and that Japan should not resort to armed force. Accordingly, he evaluated the Stimson Doctrine highly.[137]

Yokota, however, did not maintain this critical stance at the Shanghai conference. He was under government and peer pressure. On 22 October 1931, Foreign Minister Shidehara sent a note to the Consul General in Shanghai to ask him to convey a message to Yokota, who was attending the conference. The note said: as his articles and lectures had earlier caused some controversy in Japan, senior members at his university wished him to be very careful about what he would say on Manchurian issues.[138] The detailed record of the round table discussion of diplomatic machinery, where the issue of Manchuria was discussed, shows that Yokota indeed took a similar line to Tachi and Shinobu, who were also present. Yokota argued that Japanese actions did not violate the Covenant of the League of Nations.[139]

Government pressure seems to have been greater in an international context, as Yokota could insert a subtle critical nuance when he wrote his 'summary' of this discussion in the Japanese version of the conference proceedings. He noted that the fault of the League was not its lack of the knowledge about the 'Far East', or the 'special' aspects of the region, but its distance from the region. A proposal for a League regional office, he continued, had gained strong support among participants. He recorded that JCIPR members contributed to furthering the understanding that the Manchurian issue was a complex one and that Japan had a great interest in the region. Nevertheless, he doubted that Japanese military action was accepted by participants, because it was also clear that China's stake in the region was much greater. He reserved his judgement about whether Japanese military action was legal or constituted self-defence. He argued that the issue was not an abstract legal one, but required fair third-party examination of actual events. He also noted that Japanese participants stressed that Japan did not neglect or dismiss the Covenant of the League, and concluded that participants agreed that the best solution was investigation by the League.[140] Here, although taking the form of a summary, he did not justify Japanese military action or emphasize the 'special' nature of the region. He was supportive of the League's intervention.

Participants in general were supportive of the League's intervention, but argued that it had to modify its Eurocentricity. Despite their conflicting views on Manchuria, Japanese and Chinese participants agreed on this point. They saw that complementary mechanisms, such as a regional office of the League, located either in Shanghai or Tokyo, would be desirable. Takayanagi noted: 'A permanent body, either a part of the League or an independent unit affiliated with the League, and with America and Russia cooperating, is highly desirable for dealing, not only with the Manchurian question, but with questions relating to the whole international situation in the Orient.' Although Hu emphasized the need to apply a universal code to the Manchurian case, he also agreed that: 'the League of Nations might be supplemented by some machinery to deal with the daily problems of the Pacific, especially in the Far East.'[141]

When Takayanagi supported the intervention of a more regionally concerned third party which might or might not be affiliated with the League, he was not opposing government policy. Yoshizawa, the Japanese delegation at the League, and Shidehara, the Foreign Minister, were happy to countenance the League's intervention. They supported its mission (consisting of members from the great powers) to examine the case. They thought these great powers would become more understanding of Japanese actions through this means. With Japanese support, the Council of the League decided upon sending the inquiry mission, a few days before the Inukai cabinet took over on 13 December 1931.

Through these discussions, participants were redefining the regional order. The vision of the Pacific Community had receded in this period. As in 1929, they largely rejected the idea of regional disarmament. Saitō Sōichi and Jerome Greene thought it was impossible to consider 'regional' disarmament without worldwide disarmament.[142] Yet some still clung to the notion of the Pacific as a synthesis of non-Asia and Asia. Discussing the League's handling of the 'Far East' critically, many participants, including Japanese, still saw the issue of security in the framework of the Pacific. 'The concept of the Pacific area' was seen as much more useful for security in the region than one of the 'Far East' or 'the Northwest Pacific'.

> It would insure that questions of both a permanent and a transitory kind, in so far as they not only involved the countries of the Far East immediately concerned but assumed a world-character would be dealt with by interested countries, not too distant to lack knowledge, and yet sufficiently varied in their economic and political relations with the Far East to provide a background of neutrality and world-opinion.[143]

A new development was, however, evident. While the Pacific remained an important concept, what made it significant was not its distinct nature as an entity. Instead, the benefit of the concept was to allow 'neutral' and 'world' powers to intervene in the otherwise closed area of the 'Far East'. Even in the original notion of the 'Pacific Community', European powers were included as 'Pacific' powers. Yet in the mid- to late 1920s, there was a push to see the world centred on the Pacific, and the excitement with the distinct, and even superior nature of the regional entity in contrast to Europe. This seems to have disappeared in 1931. In the face of a confrontation between two powers in Asia, the IPR was shifting its emphasis more and more to the Pacific in the world, not the Pacific on its own. An increasing focus on the 'Far East' also was a challenge to an integral, harmonious and confident American regional order, which was symbolized by the Pacific Community in the 1920s.

Visions for the region: the Lytton Commission and the JCIPR

What was the role of the JCIPR in Japan during the Manchurian crisis, and how did JCIPR members respond to the Lytton Commission report? What was their regional vision of Manchuria and Inner Mongolia? Rōyama was one of JCIPR members who took the lead in this discussion. He led a group of experts, who presented a rare unofficial version of a Manchurian solution (to be detailed shortly). Rōyama did not take an active role in the IPR conferences in 1931–3. His base was his university and *Tokyo seiji keizai kenkyūsho* (Tokyo Institute of Political and Economic Research, or TIPER), not the JCIPR. Membership of these organizations, however, overlapped. After the Kyoto conference, having felt impelled to study the Manchurian issue further, Rōyama founded the TIPER in March 1930. It included a few key young JCIPR members, such as Matsumoto, Matsukata Saburō and Uramatsu Samitarō. They were in their late twenties or early thirties – a younger generation of the JCIPR with statist reformist (*kakushin*) inclinations. It was also one prototype of a think-tank organization on foreign policy. Its aim was to research international issues concerning Japan, including Manchuria. Around 1933, Rōyama also became a member of another research organization, later known as *Showa kenkyūkai* (1936–40).[111] Its initiator was Gotō Ryūnosuke, a close friend of Konoe. Its object was to examine and formulate national policies for a 'new' Japan, and to function as a brains trust for the time when Konoe would head Japanese politics. As well as Rōyama, some TIPER and JCIPR members were to be absorbed into this think-tank of Konoe.

Rōyama was central in the TIPER. He was inspiring and he represented a dominant view of a new generation at the JCIPR. A leading light of the academic establishment by 1930, he was professor at Tokyo Imperial University at thirty-four, and was already known as an international authority on Manchurian issues. Strong statism, and a left leaning, yet non- or anti-Marxist stance seems to be a key to him and younger JCIPR members at the TIPER. Rōyama was ten years younger than Tsurumi Yūsuke, an advocate of New Liberalism, with whom he was acquainted through the old boys' network of the Debating Club of *Ichikō*. Rōyama was involved with the *Shinjinkai* [the New People's Society] (founded in 1918), an elite students' organization that H.D. Smith called 'Japan's first student radicals'. Whereas Marxism–Leninism was increasingly dominant in *Shinjinkai* in the 1920s, Rōyama was more inspired by English social democracy and guild socialism, and he opposed revolutionary violence.[115]

Matsumoto, who was only a few years younger than Rōyama, shared many of Rōyama's ideological inclinations. Matsumoto had studied at Yale University after graduating from Tokyo Imperial University, and hoped to become an 'international journalist'. Back in Japan, he was doing postgraduate work with Takaki when he joined the JCIPR on the secretarial staff of the Kyoto conference in 1929. Although Matsumoto joined the TIPER soon after the Kyoto conference, his connection with Rōyama was not only through the JCIPR, but more through *Shakai shisōsha* (Social Thought Association). He noted that most TIPER members came from this association. It was a faction of *Shinjinkai* in which Rōyama was active – the faction which emphasized research and enlightenment, not actions advocated by the mainstream Marxists.[116] They were not only counter-Marxist reformists, but also statists. It was a logical progression from the New Liberalism and social democratic ideas which inspired them. Rōyama saw the need for greater state intervention in the interests of social welfare. For him, the state was not inherently evil, but a crucial instrument of radical reform, especially in times of crisis. This view inevitably influenced their relationship with the state, predisposing them for membership of Konoe's think-tank.

In 1932, Rōyama and JCIPR members at the TIPER presented a solution not entirely uncritical of the Japanese government policy towards Manchuria. While some of them were also involved in the translation of the Lytton report when it was publicly presented in October 1932,[117] the most significant document this group produced was not this translation, but their own plans for a solution to the Manchurian problem. When the Lytton Commission was sent to Japan and China, the group worked hard to present their ideas to the commission.[118] They produced a booklet of 136 pages, printed in June 1932. According to Matsumoto, it was distributed among academics and business people in Japan, translated into English and sent to the Lytton Commission before it made its report public.[119] The booklet was titled 'Manshū mondai kaiketsu an (Proposals for the solution of the Manchurian problem)', marked confidential and included the names of the authors – Rōyama, Yokota, Matsumoto, Matsukata and Yamanaka Atsutarō.[150]

There is no official record of this document or its influence on the final Lytton report. The authors definitely had occasion to meet and exchange views with the commission in Tokyo on 5 March 1932 when the JCIPR held a meeting at the Tokyo Club. The JCIPR also entertained an old friend of the IPR, George Blakeslee, who was a member of the commission, at the Imperial Hotel on 10 March.[151] The booklet contained two plans for a solution, both designed to gain the powers' recognition of Manchuguo. Whereas the second plan argued for the independence of Manchuria as a nation-state, Rōyama's influence was evident in the first plan. It argued for the creation of a transitional state of self-rule, with the agreement of the Council of the League of Nations and the United States. Although it was a virtual recognition of Manchuguo by the great powers, it emphasized the significance of an international body. A regional office of the League would administer and develop the territory, and the Tokyo office of the League would be strengthened for that purpose. Matsumoto notes that a majority of the writers of the booklet supported this plan, although Yokota was still opposed to recognition of Manchuguo. The plan was inspired by the idea of the British Commonwealth, and they felt it would obtain British support.[152]

There was some overlap between the Lytton report and Rōyama's group's plan (the first plan). Although the Lytton report did not endorse Manchuguo, as Nish points out, it did not dismiss, but upheld Japanese colonial interests.[153]

The report and Rōyama's group's plan both proposed a kind of self-rule in the area under the supervision of an international body. The Lytton report suggested relatively autonomous self-government under Chinese sovereignty and the supervision of foreign consultants appointed by the League; maintenance of security by a special police force assisted by the League; and concluding a treaty of non-intervention and mutual assistance between China and Japan. The difference was the Lytton report's recognition of Chinese sovereignty and Rōyama's group's emphasis on a strong role for Japan in this international body. Rōyama's group felt that under the 'international' supervision, endorsed by the great powers, Japanese interests would be protected in a peaceful manner.

Major political leaders, senior diplomats and army officers in Japan, however, did not take up their plan.[154] In late August 1932, Foreign Minister Uchida stated in the Diet that Japan should insist on recognition of Manchuguo even if Japanese territory was 'scorched'. The government was ready to recognize Manchuguo without the approval of the great powers. Rōyama publicly warned against this. His group's plan argued that the issue should be solved through an international body in which Japan could take the leadership. He thought the proposed government policy would lead to eventual confrontation with the powers. He noted: 'it was regrettable that the government had not listened to the arguments and criticism offered by some able people in the nation'.[155] In mid-June, the Lower House hurriedly decided to recognize Manchuguo without the approval of the powers, and this was formalized in the Japan–Manchuguo agreement in September 1932.

JCIPR members, including Rōyama, Yokota and Takaki, continued their efforts to 'explain' the Japanese case to the powers within a post-League framework, and to solve the Manchurian problem in cooperation with the powers. This continued even after Japanese withdrawal from the League of Nations in 1933.[156] The vision of the Pacific Community was disappearing in IPR operations, and Japanese aggression was condemned, not only for its imperial ambitions, but more because of its challenge to the post-League status quo. Soon the ISIPR under Carter was to emerge as a strong defender of the post-League order.

Part IV

The American world order

7 Carter's vision, 1933–5

The new Secretary General of the IPR, Edward Carter, took office in 1933, and remained in the post until 1946. This was the heyday of the IPR. Carter had a strong personality, and was a very able INGO officer. Born the son of a minister in Lawrence, Massachusetts, in 1878, his involvement with the international YMCA student movement began when he was at Harvard College in 1900. His first overseas post was Secretary of the YMCA in Calcutta in 1902, and he continued to be active in international YMCA activities in Asia, Europe and the United States. He was a founding member of the IPR, Secretary of the ACIPR in 1926–33 and Secretary General of the ISIPR in 1933–46. Between 1926 and 1946, for twenty of the thirty-six-year history of the IPR, he was a central figure at the ACIPR and the ISIPR. In the late 1940s, Carter became a target of criticism for his conduct at the ISIPR during World War II, which was followed by a McCarthyist attack. Despite this prominence and publicity, Carter remains an obscure figure. There is no biography, except for an account of his activities as Chief Secretary of the YMCA's American Expeditionary Force in Paris in 1917–19 (during World War I) and a brief entry in *Biographical Dictionary of Internationalists*.[1]

Was he a communist sympathizer? Was his ideological commitment the driving force for his visions for the IPR, the regional and the world order, as was often assumed in the late 1940s and early 1950s? The following three chapters examine Carter's visions and policies in three stages: 1933–5, 1936–9 and 1941–5. Two major wars, the Sino-Japanese War and the Pacific War, greatly affected IPR operations in this period. A key to understanding Carter's visions and policies was his globalist inclination and his great ambition for the IPR as a non-official agency in international politics. First, he was not a regionalist, in the sense that he did not see the Pacific as an insider nor did he see the world as centred in the Pacific. During two major wars in the region, the ISIPR strengthened its commitment to the post-League internationalism and the post-League order. Internationalism and the international order, however, had been redefined, and now, in Carter's view, the United States should take the leading role not only in the region, but also in the world. This shift from the region to the world reflected, or even anticipated the mood of his fellow American internationalists. Second, Carter had big ambitions for the IPR, and strengthened its policy relevance. This meant a push for its orientation towards the state, rather than the public. Although all these trends had been evident since the late 1920s, they were accelerated by Carter's determination and two major wars in the region. Under his leadership, the ISIPR became almost synonymous with the headquarters of the ACIPR in New York. It emerged as a central policy-making body, and rigorously pushed a new globalist agenda.

Carter's visions and policies

1933 and Carter's appointment

The year 1933 was marked by significant incidents in both the region and the world. The world Depression continued, and the seeming success of the Soviet experiment made many think that a socialist revolution was a possible or even desirable alternative. In this crisis period, the role of the state was expanded, and the state often sought counter-socialist schemes to neutralize popular discontent. In 1933, Hitler's National Socialist Party won the election in Germany. In the United States, after a decade of Republican rule, Democrat Franklin Roosevelt took over in the White House and started the New Deal schemes. In Britain, Ramsay MacDonald of the Labour Party formed a national coalition government. In Japan, the May 15 incident, an attempted military *coup d'état* in 1932, ended the already declining dominance of political parties. Saitō Makoto (1858–1936), Navy Admiral and former Governor General of Korea, formed the new 'national unity' (*kyokoku icchi*) government. The power of the bureaucracy and the military became stronger, and national mobilization proceeded on a greater scale than before.[2]

The post-League order remained in crisis. The USSR continued with its communist experiment, challenging the post-League order. Fascist forces in Germany and Italy were gaining power, challenging the post-League status quo in Europe. In Asia, the 'Far Eastern' crisis unfolded. Manchuguo was established, and Japan recognized its legitimacy without the approval of the other powers. This was not the end of Japan's ambitions. On New Year's Day 1933, the Japanese Guandong army attacked Shanhaiguan. The city was of strategic importance, for it was the gateway to Jehol province, right next to Mongolia. Jehol was the only province in north-east China not under the control of the Japanese army. It indicated Japanese ambitions for Inner Mongolia. This was not surprising as Japanese, and possibly many Chinese, regarded Manchuria and Inner Mongolia (*uchi Mōko*) as a coherent region, *Manmō* (Manchuria and Mongolia).

When this renewed attack took place in the 'Far East', Matsuoka Yōsuke was in the middle of the last-minute negotiations with the League of Nations in Geneva as the leader of the Japanese delegation. Even at this late stage, up until the attack, there was still room for Matsuoka to exploit the double standard of the colonial powers. Like the Lytton report, the British Foreign

Minister was sympathetic to Japanese claims. He expressed similar concerns about British colonial interests in China and security problems under Chinese authority. The American ambassador in Tokyo, Joseph Grew, who remained in the post even after Roosevelt took over, held a similar view. Patient respect for Japanese colonial rights and moral pressure rather than condemnation or sanctions would lead to an eventual solution to the problem.[3] The Japanese aggression in Jehol, however, hardened the atmosphere in the negotiations and in this context the League made its final recommendation in accordance with the Lytton report. Although the report was highly respectful of Japanese colonial claims, it nevertheless rejected the legitimacy of Manchuguo. The Japanese government did not accept this, and on 20 February 1933 it decided to withdraw from the League. Four days later, at the Assembly of the League, the Lytton recommendation was accepted by forty-two votes against one opposition vote, Japan, and one abstention by Siam (Thailand). Matsuoka made a final speech on Japanese withdrawal, rose and left the Assembly room, followed by the other Japanese delegates. One month later the Japanese government formally withdrew from the League of Nations.

The fifth IPR conference was held at Banff Spring Hotel, Banff, Canada, on 14–26 August 1933, only five months after this event. During the conference, Carter was appointed as the new secretary general. By then the only names not yet eliminated from the candidates' list were Owen Lattimore and Carter. Lattimore was only thirty-three years old with no definite post at a reputable institution. But his works on Mongolia, *Desert Road to Turkestan* (1929), *High Tartary* (1930) and *Manchuria: Cradle of Conflict* (1932), all of which were based on first-hand experience, demonstrated his unusual language skills and exceptional insights into this significant yet little-known area. By 1933, these works had earned him a solid reputation in Britain, and had greatly impressed Curtis.[4] Although born to American parents in Washington, DC, in 1900, Lattimore had close connections with Britain.[5] His first book, published in England, brought him to the attention of British literary and academic circles. A British journalist resident in Shanghai attended the IPR conference in 1933, and strongly recommended him for the position of Editor of *Pacific Affairs*.[6] Probably with Curtis's enthusiastic support, Lattimore was appointed.

Carter's appointment seems to have been simply because no other suitable candidate had been found. Carter's name first appeared only in April 1933, in a letter by Newton Baker.[7] Baker was an influential Democrat whose political career had suffered as a result of his commitment to American entry to the League of Nations.[8] In 1933 he was Chairperson of the ACIPR and the Pacific Council, and he was a strong Carter supporter. In contrast to young Lattimore, as Secretary of the ACIPR in 1926–33, Carter had proved his excellence as an able INGO administrator. The decision to appoint him was popular.[9] His salary was fixed at US$12,000, a sum a little lower than the anticipated US$15,000–20,000, and almost equivalent to the salary of the Deputy Secretary General of the League of Nations.[10] Upon his appointment,

Carter did not express surprise or enthusiasm.[11] Rather a British member of the RIIA at the conference thought that Carter showed 'considerable hesitation' because of the financial difficulties of the ISIPR.[12] Carter, however, seems to have had a clear vision of the IPR, and was ready for the job.

Redefining the American world order

Carter's policies can be summarized as follows: making the IPR a more 'world'-oriented organization by emphasizing the region's impact in world politics, and by urging the further involvement of European powers and the USSR; centralizing IPR operations in New York, by moving the headquarters (the ISIPR) from Honolulu to New York and expanding its power; strengthening the National Councils, particularly the ACIPR; and increasing the IPR's role as a think-tank. He reinforced existing trends of the Atlantic orientation and state orientation, and these trends were further accelerated by the following two wars.

Global ambition

The preface to the proceedings of the Banff conference clearly indicates Carter's vision for the IPR. It stresses the importance of the 'wider' context. Focusing on the fact that the conference was the first held on the American continent, it argued:

> ... disturbances of helpful international relations in the Pacific ... have their origin as much in the western as in the eastern hemisphere. ... [T]he setting of the conference made yet another valuable contribution to a more balanced understanding of the Pacific problems: the peace and beauty of the immediate scene invited attention to larger perspectives ... and larger problems of human welfare.[13]

The contrast between the American continent and Shanghai, the site of the previous conference was marked. Unlike many Americans who used the term 'western hemisphere' when referring to the Pacific, Carter counterpoised the 'West' with the 'Far East'. A similar emphasis was introduced in the revamped *Pacific Affairs*, the flagship journal of the IPR. It stated that it would focus on the Pacific region, but 'in relation to world affairs'.[11] Carter wanted the IPR to achieve greater worldwide prestige as a think-tank on regional affairs, and its journal to play a part. The new *Pacific Affairs* was clearly modelled after *Foreign Affairs*, the organ of the CFR in New York. Although the CFR's membership overlapped with that of the IPR, the CFR was better known. International relations experts in Western Europe as well as in North America regarded *Foreign Affairs* highly. Carter knew these Europeans well,[15] and probably wanted their recognition and readership. Part of the revamp involved dumping the old newsletter section, 'Views from the East'. Although the editorial claimed that it would aim at a wider public, *Pacific Affairs* looked as if it was designed for experts in foreign relations.

Carter also sought worldwide recognition and prestige by expanding membership in Europe. This was by no means Carter's original idea. The initial concept of the Pacific Community included European colonial powers, and 'naturally' Davis sought their participation. He visited Europe in early 1928 for that purpose.[16] In mid-1930, Condliffe obtained a favourable reply from the French.[17] Preparations for increased participation by European groups was, therefore, in progress before they took part in the 1933 IPR conference. Carter pursued the agenda rigorously, and greater European participation was achieved during his term.

Carter's eagerness to involve the USSR can be also understood in this regard, rather than ideological sympathy with communism or Soviet-style internationalism. Again, the initiative did not originate with Carter. The USSR, located on the Pacific rim, had been regarded as a Pacific power among IPR members from the very beginning. Many thought it 'natural' for the ISIPR to seek its involvement in the IPR. Davis visited Moscow at the end of 1927 for that purpose. There, he realized that like labour organizations in Europe, foreign experts in the USSR regarded the IPR as an imperialistic, capitalist organization. In 1930, Condliffe sought the participation of the USSR in the coming IPR conference and obtained their commitment.[18] Carter also felt the need for Soviet representation to make discussions at IPR conferences more politically useful and relevant. Carter was determined to make this happen.[19] He went to Moscow in 1934, and, as a result, the Pacific Ocean Institute, a branch of the Soviet Academy of Sciences, became the Soviet unit for the IPR. The fact that it was a government bureau did not bother him much. In 1936, he visited the USSR again to urge them to participate in the sixth IPR conference at Yosemite. As a result, the USSR sent two delegates to the conference, the first and last Soviet participation. The USSR members remained sceptical about the IPR, and their contribution was minimal. They criticized the imperialistic nature of the IPR and *Pacific Affairs*, which, they argued, defended Japanese actions in China.[20] Yet for Carter, Soviet involvement meant an extended institutional base, one step closer to a 'global' IPR.

'That small town' in the Pacific and New York

Carter liked the strong, centralized headquarters of the ISIPR in his base city, New York, and he gradually shifted ISIPR functions from Honolulu to New York in 1933–6. This was a part of his design to make the IPR a world organization. Honolulu had a symbolic meaning for IPR members in Hawai'i, Australia and New Zealand. They had already observed a decline in the Pacific-centred perspective at the time of Davis's resignation in 1929, and it was important to prevent any further decline. In contrast, many, including Carter and Curtis, deplored Honolulu's shortcomings as the site for the ISIPR. Carter especially did not care for its claim to be the 'Geneva of the Pacific'. For him it was just a 'small town'. He noted in 1930:

> I doubt whether in our lifetime Honolulu will ever have the world news daily. ... [T]he stimulus that comes through the almost daily visits of able minds from all over the world is something that will not be achieved in Honolulu in our lifetime.[21]

Although quite a few IPR members understood Honolulu to be the permanent location of the ISIPR, it was officially designated as a temporary location in 1927.[22] During Greene's administration, no attempt was made to change the arrangement. Although Greene conducted IPR matters from his company in New York, administrative work and conference arrangements were made by Charles Loomis, Acting General Secretary, based in Honolulu. Meanwhile, the idea of locating the headquarters in Asia constantly came up. Tokyo and Shanghai were two strong contenders.[23]

The Pacific Council meeting in 1933 concluded that Honolulu would remain the headquarters until the next conference, but made no decision about a new site. Most members of the Pacific Council assumed that Carter would move to Honolulu, for they estimated his moving costs at US$1,500.[24] Carter, however, had no such intention. It seemed he wanted to be a travelling head of the ISIPR. He told his wife not to move the furniture to Honolulu. He would visit National Councils and stay in a furnished cottage in Honolulu between trips.[25] Initially, he insisted on having no central headquarters and strengthening the National Councils.[26] This was doubtless a ploy to undermine the Honolulu ISIPR, not a denial of the need for a strong and centralized ISIPR. While the ISIPR was still located in Honolulu, Carter needed to stress the significance of each National Council, particularly the ACIPR in New York. He continued to be based at 129 East 52nd Street, New York. It was his office from 1922, when he started the YMCA-related project, the Inquiry, and it became the address of the ACIPR when he was Secretary (1926–33). From 1933 to 1945 it was the address of both the ISIPR and the ACIPR, which became virtually one entity.

Carter wanted the ISIPR in New York. He carefully planned to undermine the importance of the Honolulu office. In the beginning he flattered Honolulu, using terms he disliked, such as the 'Geneva of the Pacific', and put the term 'temporary' before his office address on the letterhead.[27] At the same time, he intended to make Honolulu a 'local' office. In 1933 as new Secretary General, Carter proposed a scheme with Loomis in charge to help make Hawai'i 'a model community of race relations'. Later he argued that the Honolulu office had increased its local emphasis from 1934, and that therefore it could not claim a budget as the headquarters as well as a salary for Loomis as headquarters' staff.[28]

One by one, Carter removed functions from the Honolulu office, and this became clear by the mid-1930s. Those who objected to this move were

Atherton, Treasurer of the Pacific Council, based in Honolulu, and to a lesser extent, members on the Pacific coast. For Atherton, Carter's move meant the loss of the Pacific-centred perspective and the IPR's 'original' spirit,[29] and he resisted it by not approving the Pacific Council budget. Similarly, IPR members on the Pacific coast opposed Carter's moves to shift the ISIPR to New York. Communication and trade across the Pacific were much denser on the Pacific than on the East coast. Academics, business people and various professionals were interested in the IPR. Leading figures formed the Bay Region branch in San Francisco in 1928, in which the Chamber of Commerce took a central role. Since 1926, Ray Wilbur, Chairperson of the Pacific Council in 1927–9 and President of Stanford University, had been trying to counterbalance the East coast dominance on the executive board of the ACIPR, and ensure a Pacific coast representation.[30] In 1929, he noted that the headquarters should be on the Pacific coast.[31] Alarmed by Carter's move in the mid-1930s, he advocated decentralization.[32] Wallace Alexander, head of the San Francisco Bay group of the ACIPR, also maintained that the ISIPR should be kept at least on the Pacific coast, if not in Honolulu, in order to retain the Pacific centrality of the IPR.

Although these were voices of prominent figures, the West coast remained weak within the ACIPR. There were reasons other than Carter's determination to centralize power in New York. Distance was one. Initially, the Honolulu group was keen to strengthen the Pacific coast group, which Davis wished to incorporate under the Honolulu group. Wilbur did not like the idea, insisting that the Pacific coast group should be under the ACIPR.[33] The headquarters of the ACIPR, however, was far away, and the staff were busy. The New York office decided in 1928 that action to promote the IPR on the Pacific coast should be postponed until 1929. It was the conference year, which would make fundraising easier.[34] Yet still in 1933, Atherton was criticizing Carter for his lack of promotion of the IPR on the Pacific coast.[35] In 1935 Carter and Frederick Field (Secretary of the ACIPR, 1934–40) undertook a serious fundraising campaign on the Pacific coast. In 1936, Charles Loomis was assigned the task of promoting the IPR in West coast cities other than San Francisco and raising US$15,000 before the sixth conference at Yosemite. Carter argued that Loomis's salary should be paid mostly by the Bay Region group. The proposition was reluctantly accepted.[36] Loomis conducted fundraising successfully through prestigious social clubs, such as the Commonwealth and Bohemian Clubs, and Chambers of Commerce in Los Angeles, Portland and Seattle. The Bay Region group decided to engage him to strengthen the group's standing on the Pacific coast for a few more months in 1937, again without financial support from the ISIPR.[37]

Other than centralizing the ISIPR's functions in New York, the object of Carter's policies can be understood as an attempt to reduce the ISIPR's deficit. It was more than US$10,000 in the mid-1930s, and Carter had to cut expenses as well as raising more funds. Making the Honolulu and Bay Region offices self-sufficient with local funds was important. Although Loomis remained on the staff of the ISIPR, his salary was now shared by the Honolulu and San Francisco groups.

At the same time, Carter successfully made Honolulu a 'local' office. At the sixth conference at Yosemite in 1936, the Pacific Council decided to have no headquarters, and Honolulu lost its claim.[38] Although it still voted that headquarters should be somewhere on the Pacific coast, and should be decided at the next conference, this never materialized. Carter remained in New York, and soon the Sino-Japanese War began. When Carter requested to transfer the research account from Honolulu in late 1935, Atherton, Treasurer of the ISIPR, tendered his resignation.[39] This represented the completion of the ISIPR's transfer to New York.

The move was not Carter's idea alone. Many others supported it. Australian delegates felt that there was a strong consensus at the Pacific Council to settle the headquarters in New York.[40] For a majority of key figures of the IPR, there was no question that New York was a crucial location for raising funds because of the existence of major foundations. Funds from the Rockefeller Foundation alone accounted for almost half of IPR revenues in 1933.[41] Other institutions, such as research centres, publishing companies and major academic associations, were also much stronger on the East coast than on the Pacific coast in this period. Chairpersons of the American Council and the Pacific Council both felt it essential for IPR operations that Carter stay in New York.[42]

The shift of headquarters to New York meant not only an Atlantic orientation, but also a stronger official and state orientation in IPR operations. New York was closer to Washington. Atherton and Alexander suggested that the ISIPR's move to New York would result in a substantial loss of private support. Alexander and Atherton predicted that local business contribution to the IPR, which had been substantial, would decline dramatically.[43] Atherton also thought that Carter did not appeal to the business community sufficiently, and he let their interest and donations dwindle.[44]

Nation-state and strong centre

In 1933, Carter stated that strengthening the National Councils was one of his major goals. This rhetoric served several objectives. First, it was a strategy to undermine the significance of the ISIPR in Honolulu, to bolster that of the ACIPR, and shift the ISIPR eventually to New York. Second, it was to achieve financial self-sufficiency for each unit without assistance from the ISIPR. Third, it could have been a way to draw greater contributions from the National Councils to the ISIPR. Carter's visits to the National Councils, however, did not result in an increase in their donations. In 1935, Britain contributed US$3,000 (£600), Japan US$850 (3,000 yen) and Australia US$600; a big contrast to Hawai'i's contribution of US$10,000.[45] Nor is there much evidence that Carter urged the National Councils to donate more.

Yet, even after he had achieved the transfer of the ISIPR to New York, in a report to the Pacific Council in 1936, Carter still stressed the need for strong National Councils: 'there can be little permanent strength in an International Secretariat which represents weak National Councils. A principal task of the Secretariat has therefore been to aid in building up the chain of National Councils.'[16] Did this mean he wanted a federation of strong National Councils – an idea very similar to that of Curtis? No doubt Carter's internationalism was based on a national unit, and was not transnational. By 1933, most National Councils also emerged as cohesive *national* bodies.

Carter, however, differed from Curtis fundamentally on two crucial points: his willingness to give greater power to the American Council, and endorsement of its centrality in 'international' activities. Carter maintained in 1936:

> The American Council is the strongest of all the Councils formed for the regional study of the Pacific. It has served as a stimulus to most of the other Councils. … It is the only Council that has established the precedent of securing the service on its staff, for long periods, of scholars of other nationalities. If the Secretariat of the American Council develops along this line, it may be that in addition to being a national center for the study of international affairs it will also become, in a modest way, an international center of the study of international affairs.[17]

Carter justified the central position of the American Council in the study of international affairs. For him, being 'American' was not in conflict with being 'international'. This thinking was evident in an increasing overlap between the American Council and the ISIPR during his period. William Holland (Research Secretary in 1934–44 and Secretary General in 1946–60) argues in his memoirs that Carter made an effort to draw a clear line between the ISIPR and the ACIPR. Indeed the phrase 'joint projects of the Pacific Council and the ACIPR' was used deliberately.[18] Nevertheless, he admits that in practice there was a great deal of overlap.[19] In Carter's mind, this was well rationalized, and he did not see any contradiction of being American and 'international'.

The rhetoric of strengthening the National Councils was useful for Carter's agenda of achieving 'truly international staff'.[50] To that end, he proposed the staff interchange scheme in 1933. Because the ISIPR was still in Honolulu then, the scheme was carried out between the American Council in New York and other councils. On his visit to Tokyo in 1934, Carter arranged for a few JCIPR members to be stationed at the New York office. Three came to New York in 1935, and this arrangement continued at least until mid-1941. In a similar manner, young staff from other National Councils were sent to New York during Carter's period.[51] The Rockefeller grants supported the scheme directly and indirectly. Jack Shepherd, National Secretary of the Australian Institute of International Affairs (AIIA), for example, arranged in 1938 to station himself at the ACIPR to undertake research partially supported by the Rockefeller grant.[52] His research on Australian foreign policy was included in the IPR's Inquiry series.

Unlike Davis, who tried to attract senior people from Japan and China in 1927–9, Carter tended to recruit young men and women, often soon after graduation. This was the case also at the ACIPR. In this way, he gained enthusiastic and competent talent at a relatively low cost. In exchange, the IPR provided a quasi-diplomatic experience, with opportunities for research and travel. Carter's method was probably necessary for a non-profit organization such as the IPR. In 1928 Condliffe too had secured high-quality, low-cost young talent. Holland was first employed at US$1,900 per annum when he was twenty-one. Some Americans were appalled by this low salary, and it was raised to $2,400 in 1929.[53] Greene contributed a large sum to the IPR, rather than being paid for chairing the Pacific Council and the ACIPR. In the 1930s, only a few major positions such as Secretary General, at US$12,000 per year, Editor of *Pacific Affairs*, at $6,500–7,000 per year, and Research Secretary, at around $5,500 per year, were well paid, whereas clerical secretaries at the ISIPR were paid around $1,500 per year. This might reflect the IPR's philanthropic rather than professional mentality. The IPR remained a place of opportunity and excitement, a stepping stone rather than a secure career with a good income.

Critical counter-forces

Regionalist initiatives

Although Carter advanced certain agendas, this did not mean that the IPR operations headed in one coherent direction. Contending counter-forces did not disappear, nor did Carter suppress opposing forces. He even cultivated elements which had the potential to become forces critical to his own directions. While centralizing the ISIPR in New York, and strengthening the power of the ACIPR, Carter saw locating important ISIPR staff in Asia as a part of the strengthening of the National Councils.[54] Although this was probably part of the rhetoric to undermine the centrality of Honolulu office, officers posted to Asia had a strong region-centred (or regionalist) perspective. This was most evident in the case of the new editor of *Pacific Affairs*, Owen Lattimore. On his appointment, Lattimore made a request to edit *Pacific Affairs* from Beijing by correspondence, so that he could continue his fieldwork and research. Carter accepted this, and Lattimore was based there until 1937, just before the Sino-Japanese War broke out.[55]

William Holland was another regionalist. He followed the principle of Condliffe, who had insisted on the importance of local initiatives, not American dominance. A new series of IPR projects in 1933–6 was largely initiated in this spirit.[56] He had travelled to and been stationed in China when he was Research Assistant in 1928–9, and then acting Research

Secretary in 1930–3. When he was appointed Research Secretary in 1933, he asked Carter if he could move the office to Tokyo. Holland thought that it would 'strengthen East–West ties within the Institute' and that Tokyo had 'greater stability and better facilities for printing than Shanghai', a contested alternative.[57] This was granted, and the office opened in spring 1934. With the help of an American officer from New York, and the cooperation of the JCIPR members, Holland conducted his work in Tokyo as Research Secretary and Associate Editor of *Pacific Affairs* for almost a year.

The joint editorial of the first issue of the new *Pacific Affairs* in 1934, probably written by Lattimore, emphasized a regionalist perspective:

[T]he Pacific ... is not a sufficiently well-integrated region to warrant exclusive regional consideration of its problems. Yet a large part of the world still thinks of East and West, of Orient and Occident, as natural antithesis, as if the world were in fact centred on the Atlantic, and as if the Pacific and the farther East were mere horizons of expansion. Such a view of the world has a historic validity of its own, but nevertheless it must be called eccentric, for an even larger part of the world posits the continent of Asia as the centre of the universe, with the West as mere external shell pushing down upon it. Such concepts, and such antithesis can be largely corrected by intensifying our consciousness of the Pacific as the region from which both the common interests and the mutual antipathies of two major universes ... can best be understood.[58]

Lattimore's statement is significant, for it challenged the dominant concept of 'the West and the rest', and saw the notion as Eurocentric. In contrast, his Pacific was a synthesis. His experience nurtured this view. He had been brought up and worked in China, and saw himself as an 'insider' in a way very different from most of his 'white' contemporaries. He was fluent in Mongolian and Chinese, and he communicated with local people, understanding their demands and aspirations, and gaining their trust. In his mind, he was not a superior colonial 'outsider', and he insisted on travelling like the locals without servants.

The editorial goes on to argue the importance of regional arrangements in international politics, and the important role that the IPR had to play:

International affairs can no longer be classified as concerning either the world as a whole or the restricted relations of definite national zones. They affect ... groups ... larger than the nations and smaller than the whole community of nations. The Institute of Pacific Relations is an outgrowth less of the instinct for creating international organs with arbitrary functions, than of the need for extra-national communication between national groups which have international interests. It is an organ for promoting information and understanding, not so much between nations as between groups or individuals within nations, and on a plane which is exactly international, but which transcends the national and does not attempt the universal.[59]

The editorial restated, and even extended, the original agendas of the IPR, which Herbert Croly had articulated in 1927. It argued for a regionalist perspective, the need for new attitudes towards Asia, the non-governmental and individual capacity of IPR members.

These regionalist forces were undermined not only because of Carter's pressure, but also because of political developments in Japan and the outbreak of the Sino-Japanese War. In May 1935, JCIPR members asked Holland to leave. They gave no reasons, but he surmised that they were under strong government or military pressure.[60] A major military coup was attempted in May 1932, and the last political party cabinet was taken over by the national unity cabinet. Military aggression continued in Manchuria, and the general sentiment in Japan was against the League. Already in the beginning of 1933, the Chief of Metropolitan Police in Tokyo described the JCIPR as an enemy sympathizer – 'providing information on the request of foreigners'.[61] Although this explains the pressure on the JCIPR not to be closely associated with foreigners, it is odd when one considers that Holland was allowed to work in 1934, and that he stayed for a year.

Why did the pressure intensify in mid-1935? It seems to be related to the government's move to co-opt various non- or semi-official internationalist organizations, a crucial process for the JCIPR, as we shall see. This incident in May coincided with the decision to absorb the JCIPR into the Japan International Association (*Kokusai Kyōkai*) or the JIA. This was a new name for the former Japanese League of Nations Association or the LNA.[62] The JCIPR called this reorganization *gappei* (merger), although it was more appropriate to call it as an absorption. While the JCIPR retained its organizational autonomy to an extent, it became one section within the JIA, and a new arrangement of secretariat and office was negotiated. This 'merger' took place at the end of 1935, and JCIPR members probably thought or were pressured to think that Holland's presence was a stumbling block in the process. As a result, Holland left Tokyo and established a new IPR publication office in Shanghai in early 1937. He soon, however, had to evacuate after the outbreak of war.[63]

Countering state centricity

Although the editorial of 1934 emphasized interactions among individuals, the nation-state framework was perpetuated. The same editorial emphasized the need for 'a feeling for the imponderables of national psychology'. By 1936 Lattimore found this 'national' framework a serious problem in editing *Pacific Affairs*. In his view, the National Council could act 'intermittently as a censor instead of as a source of supply':

Should the articles appearing in *Pacific Affairs* be regarded purely as individual expressions of opinion or should each article before final acceptance by the editor be endorsed by the approval of a national council or be subject to the veto of a national council?[64]

He warned that a structure based on the National Councils would lead *Pacific Affairs* to become a source of conflict, and he urged the Pacific Council to formulate a clear editorial policy. For Lattimore, the idea of *individual* articles was incompatible with the fact that National Councils acted as sub-editors or, more precisely, censors. They had a 'natural' tendency towards national self-censorship. The editor should have discretion in establishing the journal as a free forum for opinions, including criticism of the writers' own countries. He acknowledged that this policy would be very difficult because collecting articles and contacting authors was impossible without the help of the National Councils. Yet, reliance on the National Councils as the basic units, in his view, would lead to an 'inevitable change in the whole character of *Pacific Affairs*':

> In spite of the wordings which define the Institute of Pacific Relations as an international association of national bodies, each of which is non-official in its own country and is designed to express as many as possible of the elements of public opinion in its own country, but not official government opinion, such an arrangement would convert *Pacific Affairs* into an organ for the expression of semi-official views.[65]

Although Lattimore used the word 'convert', the original structure, based on national units, contained the danger he referred to. The problem was only amplified as conflicts between nations intensified. As Lattimore warned, *Pacific Affairs* soon became embroiled in bitter debates over Japanese policies in China. He refrained from commenting on controversial articles and instead invited responses from readers.[66] Carter backed Lattimore's handling of this issue.[67] Did Carter share Lattimore's concern with the 'national' censorship? He did not provide any editorial instruction, and the editorial policy for *Pacific Affairs* did not change. The Inquiry series which Carter soon would initiate, however, focused on the most controversial issue, the Sino-Japanese War, and interestingly, editorial control of the ISIPR was strengthened, to be elaborated in the next chapter.

Two strong regionalists, Lattimore and Holland, advocated contrasting approaches to the role of National Councils. Lattimore argued for a stronger central editorial board to 'transcend' the nation-state-centred structure of *Pacific Affairs* and to make it 'unofficial' and 'individual'. On the other hand, Holland, as Research Secretary of the ISIPR, argued against strong central control, stressing the need for attention to the interests of each National Council. He thought the universalist approach of the IPR's international research projects was flawed:

it is impossible to choose any one subject that will evoke the enthusiastic cooperation of all the groups. ... An absolutely identical method of treatment is almost never possible without greatly impairing the local or national value of a given study.[68]

This statement is significant. First, unlike those who doubted whether the 'West' represented an ideal and superior model for the 'East' in the 1925–7, in the mid-1930s, Holland felt that 'many Western national councils' assumed 'that Western civilization and economic organization were both desirable and inevitable for the East'. Second, this emphasis on 'national values' could be easily utilized by each National Council to justify its nation's official policy. This was the case at the previous IPR conferences. Using this rhetoric, in 1925–7, Canadian and Australian members justified their anti-Asian immigration policies, in 1927, American members the colonial possession of the Philippines and, since 1929, Japanese members Japan's 'special' rights in North China. Holland further reinforced the nation/state-centred framework of IPR operations. He stressed 'sensitivity to local initiatives', and argued for the need to strengthen the National Councils. The IPR should help National Councils become 'national' centres of research on international affairs in each country. He also advocated using works commissioned by National Councils rather than research by other bodies.[69] By assisting 'nationalizing' and centralizing research organizations in a country, the National Council could easily become a means of suppressing diverse opinions critical of one's own national/state policies. This was precisely what Lattimore warned of in 1936.

Carter did not seem to have pressured Holland on this point. Nor did it appear that Holland intended to make the IPR's international research projects more official or political. Despite the emphasis on the political immediacy of IPR research projects after 1929, until 1936 IPR's research concerned mainly with relatively uncontroversial and economic topics. It was only in 1937 that the IPR launched its research into the political arena, and it was Carter, not Holland, who initiated this project, the Inquiry on the Sino-Japanese War.

Education scheme: between state and society

Carter policies indicated his strong preference for a state orientation for IPR operations. He hoped that National Councils would become a think-tank in each country and influence policy-making. This became increasingly evident in the late 1930s. The move suggested that the IPR would become an even more elite (and elitist) organization. Yet the education scheme that Carter pushed presents a slightly complex picture. It was an American affair, organized by the ACIPR and the ISIPR, and it was promoted exclusively within the United States. The scheme was two pronged. On one level, it was as an attempt at democratizing the IPR, and making it more relevant to society in general. This was in line with the IPR's initial emphasis on public education. On another level, however, the schemes was closely linked to the strategic needs of the state (see Chapter 9). Here, I concentrate on their implications for the 'democratic' nature of the IPR.

Like many other Carter policies, the scheme had financial motivations. One way to increase IPR funding was to appeal to a wider audience. This meant increasing sales of IPR publications and journals, more donations and a broader membership. The original constitution of the ACIPR restricted membership to 600 in order to preserve 'quality'. In 1936, the constitution was amended,[70] and membership expanded from 475 in 1935 to 1,300 in 1942.

The scheme was also a reply to his critics. Atherton thought that the IPR under Carter was oriented to a small circle of experts. In 1936, he accused the IPR of becoming too academic and research oriented and recommended that the results of IPR research should serve a wider public.[71] Atherton did not have a more democratic organization in mind. By a 'wider public' he meant influential people in business and public office. Although Carter emphasized research, this in no sense conflicted with the search for influential people as participants. Rather Carter, too, wanted to appeal to these people, although Carter was probably more concerned with policy-makers than business people. The democratization of the IPR was an issue in other countries. Public support for the IPR did not increase across the board in the 1930s. In Australia, for example, Eggleston reported the failure of the AIIA to increase public interest in 1935.[72] Membership was restricted to expert circles and steps to expand membership were blocked.[73] The situation was similar in other countries.

The American world order: the IPR in 1933–5

Anglo-American solidarity or American order?

Around the time of Davis's resignation, some IPR members suspected that there was a conspiracy between the British group and New York members, especially Carter. Later scholars also argued this connection.[74] The previous chapter demonstrated that this was not the case in 1927–9, as key IPR figures, including Carter, did not support Curtis's reform plan. At the same time, it also suggested that by responding to Curtis's plan, each key officer co-opted his plan to an extent. After 1933, Carter, the new Secretary General, wanted the IPR to be more 'world' oriented and more relevant to policy-making. Did Curtis influence Carter's vision, and did Carter want to make the IPR more like the CFR and the RIIA, a country-based expert organization, not a multinational organization? Did Carter see the IPR as a means to promote an international order based on Anglo-American solidarity?

Carter's connection to Curtis and his groups at the Round Table and the RIIA originated in 1902, when he visited Oxford on the way to his first foreign mission in India, still under the rule of the British empire. In Oxford, 'he met what was to become the famous Round Table group'. A key figure in this group was Lionel Curtis. From that time, the two remained close. William Carter, Carter's son, thought this first encounter influenced the twenty-four-year-old Carter: 'E.C.C.'s [Edward Carter] discussions with this group had much influence on his later liberal approaches in India.'[75] 'Liberal' attitudes meant what Curtis called 'democratic imperialism'.[76] Carter did not impose what he thought of as the 'right' customs on the Indians. He encouraged them to keep their own. Carter, for example, arranged for a Sikh member of the Royal Flying Corps to wear a turban during his service.[77] He accepted differences when colonial subjects served the common good, the empire. He also made efforts for Indians to be treated on an equal basis with British citizens. He pleaded for Indian soldiers to be awarded the King's Commission, not the Viceroy's Commission, for their achievements during World War I. Carter was keen on the idea of self-rule in India, but for the purpose of strengthening the British empire. Curtis was impressed by Carter's achievement in India, as well as his wartime relief activities at the YMCA in France during World War I. In 1919 in the middle of the Paris Conference, Curtis suggested to Phillip Kerr, then Lloyd George's Secretary, that Carter be appointed Viceroy of India to promote the proposed constitutional reforms to widen self-rule in India.[78] This was more Curtis's acknowledgment of Carter's ability than a serious suggestion. Carter was, after all, American. Nonetheless, it demonstrates that Curtis and Carter agreed substantially on the handling of colonial issues.

How important was this 'democratic imperialist' attitude in Carter's handling of non-Euro-Americans at IPR operations, and for his vision of the international order? Was he against colonialism, and was his attitude towards the powers and colonies in the region 'Orientalist'? Carter's position on colonialism can be seen in his handling of the Philippine group's request for autonomy in 1929–31. According to the resolution of the Pacific Council, the ACIPR asked J.P. Chamberlain, a colleague of Shotwell at Columbia University, to prepare a statement on the constitutional status of the Philippines. He completed it in January 1931. Based on that note, with the caveat that the final vote on the issue would be decided at the next conference of the Pacific Council in China, Carter stated:

> [The executive committee of the ACIPR] considered the purpose of Section 2 and 3 of Article III of the Pacific Council [sic] in the light of the constitutional legislative and organic development of the Philippines and the repeatedly avowed intention of the United States to recognize their rights to independence and sovereignty. The Executive Committee, therefore, ... did regard the Philippines as possessing sufficient autonomy within the meaning of the two sections just mentioned, to entitle them to membership in the Pacific Council.[79]

The decision was not an acknowledgment of a fully autonomous position.

Section 3 of the constitution encouraged the self-expression of distinct racial or territorial groups 'within' a member country. The Korean group had rejected this colonial framework in 1931. Nevertheless, the ACIPR voted that Philippine group 'may be treated as a national unit'. This soon materialized, as the group was represented at the Pacific Council in 1933. This treatment as a *de facto* national group reflected the dominant, if not unanimous, view among ACIPR members: the Philippines should be granted independence in the very near future.[80]

There was another reason for this treatment. In the 1930s, National Councils became more structured, and a 'national unit' defined IPR operations more than in the 1920s. The selection of a 'national' group became more rigid. Eleanor Hinder, an Australian expatriate in China, for example, had a hard time in joining an Australian group in 1931 because of her residence.[81] This would not have been the case in the mid-1920s. The British group strongly supported this stricter framework.[82] Already in the proceedings of the 1929 conference, the Hawai'i group was no longer listed separately, but was incorporated within the US group, and no distinction was made in the proceedings of later conferences. The trend, coupled with the development and consolidation of each National Council in this period, furthered a nation-state framework of IPR operations. For the Philippine group, the reduced emphasis on sub-groups within a nation worked well, as this meant either pressure on a sub-unit, such as Hawai'i, to be totally integrated under a national group, or willingness to treat a unit as a 'national' group. As a result, the Philippine group was treated virtually as a National Council before achieving independence.

Whether this can be seen as Carter's opposition to colonialism is, however, doubtful. European colonial powers, France and the Netherlands, also joined the Pacific Council during his time. Members were often former or current colonial officers, and the latter specifically represented the 'Netherlands East Indies'. Although Carter and the IPR became very critical of Japanese aggression in China in the 1930s, their opposition to colonialism in general became evident only in 1942 (see Chapter 9).

What was Carter's attitude towards 'race' and Asia? Did he hold different attitudes towards the powers in Asia and colonies in the region? Carter was concerned with the issue of race relations, and his project, 'Inquiry into the Christian Way of Life' (1922–32) sought a solution for the conflicts of race, industrial and international relations by applying the Christian faith. His concern grew after he became Secretary of the ACIPR. In 1927, he wrote an enthusiastic letter to Greene:

> We [the American group] need imagination in finding new trails for experimentation and discovery in human relations. ... We need to learn how to enter into such a full relationship of mutuality with the Chinese and the Japanese ... in research, in resource, in imagination, and avoid the danger of America's dominating the Chinese and Japanese Group by

the sheer force of money and personnel. ... Throughout our membership, it is necessary for us to discover how we can get away from our feeling that we have superior wisdom to contribute to the Orient and instead induce a genuine recognition of the fact that we are in a great need of Chinese and Japanese help and that the deeper problems of the future can only be solved by joint study and effort.[83]

The tone is paternalistic. Yet here Carter demonstrates his strong commitment to achieving 'mutuality'. This is surprising as in the same period Condliffe suspected Carter of promoting American domination. Carter's main concern was 'Oriental powers', not colonies in the region. Issues of 'race' resurfaced in 1929, when the ACIPR discussed the inclusion of 'black' members in the American group for the Kyoto conference. Carter argued strongly for it. Here, the issue was not civil rights, but smoothing dealings with the powers in Europe and Asia:

For several years, Chinese, Japanese, and Europeans have told me that they did not feel that Americans could adjust themselves to a full understanding of the American attitude to the Orient until they had a new attitude to the American Negro. Until we have, as a matter of course, a competent Negro entering into our American Council program and attending the biennial Conferences, I do not think that we are availing ourselves of the full data and experience that we need, if we wish to take a long time to look at the question of race implication and cultural conflict across the Pacific.[84]

Although Carter may have supported the principle of dealing with the powers in Asia on a more equal footing, his manner was problematic. Younger Japanese, confident in English, such as Tsurumi Yūsuke, admired his ability,[85] but Atherton heard many complaints from older Japanese and Chinese participants at conferences.

I feel that [Carter] does not fully comprehend or appreciate the psychology of the Orientals. The Japanese, particularly the older ones and those who have not mixed a great deal with Americans, think slowly and desire ample time to weigh matters carefully before reaching a decision. One has to have great patience and tact in dealing with them. Mr Carter is so eager to see things accomplished that I have found at times he does not recognize this trait of the Orientals and forces things through with the result that he hurts the feelings of many of them. ... I know this personally from statements made to me directly in the past by several of my Oriental friends.[86]

Clearly it was Atherton or even Japanese participants who demonstrated Orientalist attitudes. They assumed distinct characters and traits particular to 'Orientals'. They argued for differentiated dealings for them. The issue is not so much Carter's Orientalist attitude, but his lack of sensitivity and patience. His forcefulness was not directed only to Chinese or Japanese. Atherton himself soon had to resist Carter's single-mindedness over the location of the ISIPR.

Carter was conscientious and enlightened about 'race' issues. This did not, however, negate his apparent strong sense of fellowship with 'Anglo-Saxons'.[87] It was very much the way Curtis looked at Americans, as comrades with common values and beliefs to constitute the British–American Commonwealth. This Anglophile sentiment was very common among ACIPR members and American post-League internationalists, especially among the East coast elite. Personal and institutional networks were close-knit. The RIIA had official connections with the CFR to which some ACIPR members also belonged. Jerome Greene, Carter, Shotwell, Blakeslee and other key IPR figures knew Curtis and his groups well.[88] They often used terms such as 'this or that side' of the Atlantic.

Could this Anglophile sentiment among certain groups of the Anglo-American establishment be influential in foreign policy-making? Quigley suggests that was the case.[89] Yet even CFR members, which had closer connections with the RIIA, often did not support the views of their British counterparts.[90] Similarly, Anglophile attachments did not seem to play a big part in organizational issues at the ACIPR. Greene was careful not to create a perception of an Anglo-Saxon bloc. Carter was also critical of Curtis's reorganization plan because he knew Curtis too well:

> Both you [Greene] and I, who have lived several years in London, know how faulty Lionel's conception in this matter [finance] is.[91]

Carter's plan to move the ISIPR to the Atlantic was supported not only by the British, but also by many Americans, and Canadians and other Europeans.[92] They agreed that it was important for Carter to be based in New York for fundraising and research purposes. More significantly, for Carter, the centre of international politics was in New York, not on the 'other side' of the Atlantic.

One development in 1933 which suggests that the attention of the British group was diverted from the IPR was the foundation of the British Commonwealth Relations Conference (BCRC). Although its institutional base was the network of the RIIA and its Dominion branches, it was a by-product of IPR conferences. It emerged through the network and methods developed at IPR conferences.[93] It followed the same format, and took the approach of an unofficial conference attended by 'leaders of public opinion'. Its main agenda was to survey and improve the relations of the members of the British Commonwealth.[94] The first BCRC was held in Toronto in 1933 soon after the IPR conference at Banff, and both were attended by almost the same members. They were so similar that Herbert Samuel, Leader of the British Liberal Party, who led the British group in 1933, read the opening speech for the BCRC at the IPR conference, creating a rather bemused puzzlement among participants.[95] For British Commonwealth countries, the BCRC was an alternative forum for similar discussions. They continued to send delegates to IPR conferences, and research collaboration and personnel exchanges were maintained. It is, however, indicative that the journal, the *Round Table*, which had reported enthusiastically the previous IPR conferences, did not refer to them after 1933.[96] Although Curtis regarded the IPR as a means to promote the Anglo-American Commonwealth in 1927, now the BCRC pursued a stronger worldwide imperial bloc. 'Oriental' powers were still regarded as 'outsiders'. Although some Australians, including Eggleston, argued the importance of Japan as a trade partner,[97] theirs was a minority voice within Australia and the Commonwealth. Most regarded Japan as an object to fear, and eventually to fight (see Figure 7.1).

This development of the BCRC probably contributed to further strengthening American leadership within the IPR. Carter was not an advocate of the concept of the Pacific Community or the American regional order. Instead, he was promoting the American global order, which was not centred in Geneva or London, but in New York and Washington. Yet, in his international order, Europe and the USSR were crucial. The Pacific region was important not so much as a distinct entity as for its relevance to the 'world'.

Japanese withdrawal from the League of Nations in 1933: continuity and co-option of the JCIPR

Japanese withdrawal from the League of Nations in 1933 had great implications for its foreign policy machinery and post-League internationalist organizations. Although the Manchurian Incident, which caused this withdrawal, was seen as a watershed for Japanese post-League inter-nationalists in their shift to nationalism, the previous chapter demonstrated that the event did not prompt JCIPR members to challenge the League of Nations or the post-League order. Instead, they continued to work hard to reconcile the Japanese case within the post-League treaty framework. Their loyalty to the Japanese state/empire remained unchanged, and although becoming more critical of the League they did not immediately abandon the pursuit of cooperation with the powers. A major role of these internationalists was to explain the 'Japanese perspective' to the 'world', and this remained the case after 1933.

The perspective of two opposing poles of 'liberal' intellectuals and the oppressive and militaristic state is neither accurate nor helpful in understanding either government policies or the JCIPR during this period. The decision to withdraw from the League of Nations was very popular, and criticism of the League was growing in Japan. The military was gaining power, and Shidehara's cooperative policy and non-intervention principle in China

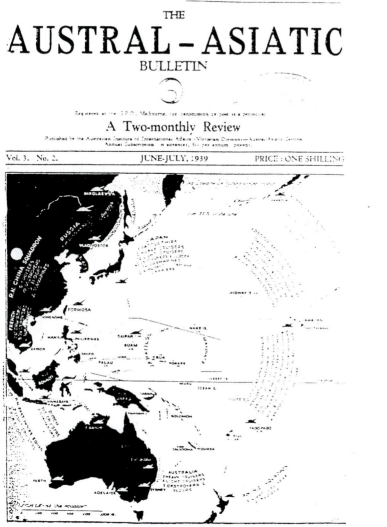

Figure 7.1 Strategic view of the Pacific in Australia, 1939.

Source: *The Austral-Asiatic Bulletin*. vol. 3, no. 2, June–July, 1939.

was under severe attack. Some in authority regarded JCIPR and IPR conferences with suspicion. Yet the withdrawal from the League did not suddenly make the Japanese government hostile towards the powers, the League of Nations and non-governmental post-League internationalist organizations such as the LNA and the JCIPR. The government did not cut its ties with the League completely. Committee members were sent to the League, and communications continued until 1938.[98] Nor did the Japanese government abandon the agenda of promoting mutual understanding and a cooperative attitude towards the powers.

The government was concerned with Japan's deteriorating international image. To justify Japanese rule in Manchuria, it was felt that a sophisticated and civilized image of Japan should be promoted. In this context, the activities of post-League internationalist organizations, such as the JCIPR, were regarded as significant and useful. The government increasingly co-opted these 'non-official' agencies and their 'non-governmental' international activities, and utilized them to make Japanese policies understood 'correctly' and to legitimize their activities in the region. JCIPR members often volunteered to undertake these tasks, and this had been the case even before 1933. Furthermore, many post-League internationalists did not oppose greater state intervention. Faced with domestic and international crisis, JCIPR members wanted the government to pursue necessary and drastic reforms. They became increasingly close to statist reformist (*kakushin*) groups and Konoe Fumimaro's circle.

Although official intervention in the activities of the JCIPR had been evident from the beginning, it gradually became more systematic and direct after 1933. This coincided with a wider restructuring of the government and ministries, especially at the Ministry of Foreign Affairs. When the Manchurian crisis was developing, certain groups at the Ministry began to argue for a new policy and for restructuring official and non-official international machinery. Early in 1933, a Diet member, closely connected to the Ministry, advocated a new 'cultural diplomacy' (*bunka gaikō*), and argued the need for the establishment of an organization for international cultural exchange.[99] The importance of this new initiative intensified after the Japanese withdrawal from the League. Those who had supported the League for the advancement of Japanese national/imperial interests needed to find a new framework.

The Department of Cultural Affairs (*Bunka jigyōbu*) within the Ministry (founded in 1927) played a key role in this newly initiated 'cultural diplomacy'. Major practitioners of this diplomacy were not officials, but 'non-official' post-League internationalists. They had been active in the LNA and another League-related organization, the Committee of Intellectual Cooperation (CIC) (*Gakugei kyōryoku iinkai*). An 'unofficial' body, the International Culture Promotion Association (ICPA) (*Kokusai bunka shinkō kai*), was established in 1934. The government explained that they could not found a new department within the Ministry because of insufficient funds. Shibasaki, however, points out that strong opposition to 'cultural diplomacy' within the government was the reason for their decision. It is also likely that bureaucrats at the Ministry and non-official post-League internationalists thought a non-governmental facade would make their activities more effective and flexible. By then, the LNA was renamed the JIA (*Nihon kokusai kyōkai*), and its objective changed from 'promoting the spirit of the League of Nations' to 'promoting friendly relations and cooperation among nations, and to contribute to the establishment of international justice and the realization of international peace'. This 'non-change' clearly suggested the continuity of the activities of post-League internationalists. The ICPA was virtually an official body. Funds came from the Ministry. The Foreign Minister appointed its executive members, including the chairperson, Konoe Fumimaro. Konoe remained in the post until his death in 1945.[100]

The initiative and corresponding restructuring within the Ministry prepared the ground for the co-option of JCIPR members (as international publicists and think-tank members) into the state apparatus, and the state began to oversee the JCIPR more systematically. JCIPR members were at the centre of the interlocking networks of post-League internationalists. Nitobe, Chairperson of the JCIPR since 1929, for example, had been a central figure at the LNA and the CIC until his death in October 1933. The JCIPR was to come under the umbrella of the JIA in 1935, and its involvement in the activities of the ICPA was a natural progression.

Despite formidable opposition within the government, this 'cultural diplomacy' gained support not only among a minority within the Ministry, but also from its top mainstream members, particularly Hirota Kōki and Arita Hachirō (see also Chapter 8). Furthermore, cultural diplomacy was not necessarily an alternative to military aggression in China.[101] Rather it was a strategy for the Ministry to protect, or even further its influence in foreign policy-making after 1933. A similar objective was evident in the proposal for *Kōsabu* in May 1932. This was proposed by so-called *kakushin kanryō* (reformist bureaucrats), headed by Shiratori Toshio. They wanted to found *Kōsabu*, a department which would focus on analysis and formulation of foreign policies. The military was gaining power in foreign policy-making as the Manchurian crisis developed, and they felt an urge to protect and advance the influence of the Ministry. There was, however, another motivation. Shiratori drew together diplomats who were frustrated by slow promotion or the lack of it, and who felt the need for a drastic restructuring of the Ministry.[102] Although their proposal met with strong opposition, the idea of founding a section of foreign policy analysis was taken up. As a result, the Department of Research (*Chōsabu*) was established at the end of 1933.

It is likely that the establishment of these new departments, the Department of Cultural Affairs (*Bunka jigyōbu*) and the Department of Research, redefined the nature and structure of the Department of Information (*Jōhōbu*) (founded in 1921) within the Ministry. Although its initial role was collecting and controlling 'information' relating to Japanese foreign policy, it became a main channel for non-official post-League internationalist organizations. In the early days of the JCIPR, Debuchi Katsuji had been Director-General of the department. He was succeeded by two others before the post was taken by Shiratori in 1930. Shiratori was in the post from October 1930 to June 1933. This suggested the strength of *kakushin* bureaucrats in the department,[103] and the influence of their thinking in relation to the JCIPR in this critical period. When Amō Eiji was appointed to the post in June 1933, he oversaw greater intervention in JCIPR activities, to be detailed shortly.

The 1933 Banff Conference and the JCIPR

For officials who promoted 'cultural diplomacy' and who argued the significance of propaganda and analysis of international affairs, the IPR and IPR conferences were important. After 1933, occasions for Japanese delegations to participate in multinational gatherings diminished significantly. IPR conferences provided a rare opportunity for the 'correct Japanese perspective' to be presented to the 'world'. A few years before its absorption into the JIA (1935), however, government intervention in the JCIPR was still moderate.

There are far fewer official documents on the IPR of this period in the Ministry's archives than those of the 1920s. Foreign Ministers changed, and after the Inukai cabinet took over at the end of 1931, Shidehara did not resume the ministership. A former ambassador to the League, Yoshizawa Kenkichi became Foreign Minister in January 1932, succeeded by Saitō Makoto in May 1932, Uchida Yasuya in July 1932 and Hirota Kōki (September 1933 to April 1936). There were occasional requests for the proceedings of the previous IPR conferences, suggesting that they did not have much background knowledge. Were these post-Shidehara ministers and their governments hostile to the JCIPR? Certain groups within the authority definitely viewed it suspiciously. In the beginning of 1933, the Chief of the Metropolitan Police reported to the Foreign Minister and the Home Minister that the JCIPR provided information to foreigners, and that its activities should be closely monitored.[104] Preparation for the Banff conference was carried out under strict police surveillance.

This did not mean that the government had totally changed its views on the JCIPR or that it did not see 'positive' or 'useful' aspects of the JCIPR and IPR conferences. Despite change at the very top, the personnel within the Ministry did not change greatly; at least until mid-1933, and even after 1933, some continuity was evident. Furthermore, Matsuoka Yōsuke, who led the Japanese delegation in withdrawing from the League of Nations earlier in 1933, wrote a letter about the IPR conference to Foreign Minister (Uchida) and Director-General of the Bureau of Asian Affairs (Tani Masayuki). It was sent within a few months of the event. Matsuoka urged them to assist in sending 'excellent' (*yūryōnaru*) delegates to the coming IPR conference: 'Having discussed the matter with prominent people in London, New York, and Honolulu, I am convinced that Japan will need to take great interest in it and I hope that you will understand this.'[105] It is unclear whether Matsuoka was still a JCIPR member, but this note demonstrates some salient points. First, even for Matsuoka, withdrawal from the League did not mean the end of cooperative relationships with the powers. Second, JCIPR and IPR conferences were seen as important by prominent figures in diplomatic circles, both in Japan and other countries.

Official involvement in the Banff conference was similar to previous conferences, and nothing like the extent which was to be seen at the time of the next conference at Yosemite. There is little evidence that the government intervened to send 'important' delegates, as Matsuoka suggested. The fifteen Japanese delegates were mostly JCIPR members. New names included Mogi Soboi from Rōyama's Tokyo Institute of Political and Economic Research (TIPER), and Takahashi Kamekichi, an economist with socialist leanings, who was to be involved in *Showa kenkyūkai*. Preparation for the conference was also carried by JCIPR members in 1932–3, with no apparent government intervention. Although Foreign Minister Uchida was adamant about recognition of Manchuguo (founded in March 1932 and recognized by Japan in September), he did not agree with sending a Manchuguo delegation to the IPR conference. The issue was brought up by the Japanese 'ambassador' to Manchuguo in early 1933. Uchida had already read the report that said the Pacific Council was extremely reluctant to endorse Manchuguo representation. He also had heard that Nitobe held a similar view. Uchida notified the 'ambassador': 'while it is just in principle, ... realistically Manchuguo representation would be very difficult to realize in near future.'[106]

As at previous conferences, communication between the JCIPR and the Ministry of Foreign Affairs was close in 1933. The government contributed to its budget, and assisted in providing materials on the request of the JCIPR. Takaki also submitted a brief report on the conference to the Ministry.[107]

In April 1932, Nitobe, now seventy years old, sailed to the United States, and conducted almost a year-long lecture tour. A JCIPR booklet noted: 'At a time when public opinion in the United States was in uproar due to the Manchurian Incident and the Shanghai Incident', Nitobe, Chairperson of the JCIPR, sailed to North America for the first time since the passing of the anti-Japanese immigration law. The tour was to 'clarify the Japanese position'. The same booklet recorded that Tsurumi Yūsuke, another JCIPR member, also went to the United States and Europe from January 1932 for a year 'to talk about the Japanese position on the Manchurian Incident'.[108] Hoping to soften the opinion of public figures in Europe and the United States, the Ministry saw the JCIPR and its connections as useful, and backed their trips.[109] JCIPR members conducted activities which can be categorized as official propaganda. Yet their sense of mission, concern and enthusiasm made them believe that their actions were not subject to government pressure, but genuine and voluntary. Acting as international publicists was no novelty for JCIPR members. Tsurumi and Nitobe had conducted similar lecture tours in the 1920s, and other JCIPR members had played a similar role at previous IPR conferences. The effectiveness of their lectures on this occasion, however, was strongly questioned. Nitobe encountered much criticism on the grounds that he was a governmental propagandist in North America. IPR circles also regarded Tsurumi as a government spokesman.[110]

All the Japanese papers at the Banff conference were more or less a justification of Japanese economic activities or government policies. Participants presented these views voluntarily with a sense of mission, rather than under government pressure. One paper, entitled 'The control of industry in Japan', evaluated positively the concentration of capital, the state policy of rationalization of industry, and state control of industry and agriculture. This thorough paper was prepared by the staff of the TIPER, which Rōyama headed, and his influence was evident.[111] In 1932–3, the JCIPR's research committee allocated to him the study topic of the state and industry control, not the issue of Manchuria, another of his main interests. He argued for the state to take the lead in restructuring the economy by replacing capitalism with 'a socialistic and functional' system.[112] The Depression was serious in many countries, Roosevelt had begun New Deal policies and the Banff conference mainly concentrated on economic and trade problems. TIPER's paper which dealt with a statist solution to these problems was, therefore, not unfamiliar to representatives from other countries. At the same time, Tsurumi noted that some participants, such as Quincy Wright, professor of international law at the University of Chicago, or T.E. Gregory, professor of economics at the University of London, expressed great concern about the inward consolidation of economic activities within a nation-state and the formation of economic blocs.[113]

Takahashi, then heading his own research institute, also put a good case for Japanese economic activities in his paper 'On the standard of living'. Tsurumi recorded that Takahashi refuted the conventional belief that low wages and a low standard of living in Japan were a menace to the world market.[114] Takahashi pointed out that the assumptions behind this myth should be questioned. He stressed that the factors determining wages varied from one country to another, and so did standards of living: 'I leave it to the judgement of the fair-minded people of the world whether the so-called cheap labour of Japan is a menace to the so-called higher standard of living of the world, or whether the high tariffs of various countries are making it difficult for a nation like Japan to improve her labour conditions and increase the wages of her labourers.'[115]

The vision for the Pacific and the post-League order

There was one exception where the Japanese government exhibited great pressure – a paper entitled 'A security pact for the Pacific area'. Here, the government had a greater stake. The paper was drafted mainly by Yokota Kisaburō and Takaki Yasaka. As Yokota did not participate in the conference, it was presented by Takaki. Rōyama, who had been interested in the issue and was developing a theory of regional law, was not involved in the paper. Amō Eiji, the newly appointed Director-General of the Department of Information, sent comments (*ikensho*) on the paper to Nitobe in early August 1933. During the conference, Ishii, Consul in Vancouver, asked Foreign Minister Uchida for an official opinion on the paper and for instruction on the comment he should make.[116] Takaki later recorded that participants criticized the paper for its clear government involvement, indicating that this had indeed been the case.[117]

In this paper, Takaki and Yokota tried to present an alternative regional security framework to the League. They argued that the most important peace machinery in the Pacific would be periodical conferences of the Pacific powers like the Pan-American Conferences, and that their proposed security treaty was of secondary importance to these conferences.[118] Katagiri points out that the proposed treaty of 1933 was based on the Shotwell draft of 1927. The format and the content followed Shotwell's draft closely, with clauses on non-aggression, consultation and peaceful dispute settlement.[119]

How much official intervention shaped and changed the content of this paper is hard to assess. There is no indication that the government was closely involved in the preparation of the draft. Direct intervention only became evident in early August 1933, when Amō sent a memo about the paper to the JCIPR. Although the content of the note is not known, in April of the following year Amō was to declare what was called the Japanese Monroe Doctrine. It argued for a Japanese mission in East Asia to achieve peace and stability in cooperation with China, and criticized the other powers' intervention in China. It caused a sensation in the United States, China and Britain, stirring strong anti-Japanese sentiment. Amō made this declaration public without consulting Hirota, then Foreign Minister, or the heads of other bureaus. Hirota was very angry about this grandstanding. Yet Amō's declaration in fact reflected not only Hirota's view, but also the strong general concern in the Ministry about the development of consortiums between China and the powers. The development was already evident in mid-1933, and investment in China on the part of the powers increased again in 1934.[120] It is not unreasonable to assume that Amō already had held similar concerns in August 1933, and that these were reflected in his note on Yokota and Takaki's paper. This late stage of intervention, however, suggests that the draft was mainly shaped by Takaki and Yokota, and the note probably referred to the government's preferred manner of presentation and response at the conference.

The draft treaty of 1933 can best be understood not as part of the government's agenda, but as yet another attempt by Japanese post-League internationalists to reconcile the Japanese case within the international treaty framework. They now needed to devise a mechanism outside the League of Nations. On this point, American foreign policy was instructive. In the 1920s, the United States was outside the League and promoted its own multilateral frameworks of cooperation through the Washington Treaties in 1922, the Pact of Paris in 1928 and the Stimson Doctrine in 1932. Although the Manchurian crisis virtually made the United States a part of the League machinery (it joined the League's Council as an observer in October 1931), it prompted Japanese withdrawal. As a result, Japanese post-League internationalists began to see these American frameworks of the 1920s as models for Japan's new international frameworks.

The clause concerning consultation, Article 5, of the proposed draft treaty, states that:

[t]he Contracting Parties undertake not to recognize any situation, treaty, or agreement which may be brought about by means contrary to Article 1 and 2 [on non-aggression] of the present Treaty, pending the agreement which the parties concerned may ultimately enter into for the settlement of the dispute.

This positive evaluation of the Stimson Doctrine was not unusual among Japanese post-League internationalists. Rōyama regarded the doctrine highly, not because he was critical of Japanese action in North China; rather he thought Japan was not ready for a confrontation with the powers. For him, the doctrine, which utilized the Pact of Paris, provided Japan with a new framework for security outside the League machinery. His concerns were whether Stimson's view was dominant in the United States; and how the British would respond to the framework. If it were to become a dominant new framework among the great powers, Japan should pursue its imperial interests within it. Rōyama thought that Manchuguo should not be recognized without the approval of the other powers, as it would challenge this new order, and would lead inevitably to war.[121]

At Banff, a year after Rōyama's assessment on the Stimson Doctrine and the Japanese recognition of Manchuguo (without the approval of the other powers), and a few months after Japanese withdrawal from the League, Takaki and Yokota saw the doctrine as a new framework for international conduct. They argued that it held positive implications for a peaceful solution to the Manchurian problem:

[o]f course, the doctrine will not always have a great effect, because it is a sanction of a purely negative nature. But in general, it will be powerful enough to keep a state from attempting to violate the treaty. ... [I]t will also be difficult for other states to maintain a policy of non-recognition for ever. ... In consequence, both parties will be induced ultimately to be more conciliatory. ... [T]he essential meaning of the doctrine would be that an international dispute is always to be solved by international agreement...[122]

As long as the Japanese government could convince the powers of Manchuguo's legitimacy, the Stimson Doctrine, which condemned Japanese actions in Manchuria, could be interpreted as a conciliatory device for avoiding war. The proposed treaty was, therefore, cooperative to the powers and the League. The problem was not because previous international agreements or principles did not work. Rather what was needed was to 'develop' them in a more 'organically combined' form.[123]

By proposing a new framework, they were critical of the League and the post-League order:

[I]t would be well to consider once more the paramount importance of machinery for the peaceful readjustment of existing economic inequalities and political injustice in the world, especially in the Pacific area. It has been fully brought to light ... that the machinery for the mere maintenance of the status quo is, therefore, not enough to keep the peace effectively; and that it is absolutely necessary to devise some procedure to modify peacefully the status quo ... [121]

Criticism of the status quo echoed Konoe's thesis of 1918, which he restated in *Kingu*, a popular Japanese magazine, in February 1933. Takaki and Yokota's paper used it as a justification of Japanese action in Manchuria.

Did Yokota and Takaki need to 'bend' their principles in presenting this draft security treaty? Yokota's critical attitude to Japanese action in Manchuria had certainly caused concern in the government in 1931. Shidehara pressured Yokota to modify his critical stance, at least on the international stage, which he did. For a domestic audience, only a month before the Banff conference of 1933, however, Yokota demonstrated that he maintained a universalist approach. He criticized the Asian Monroe Doctrine, Japan's special interests and rights in East Asia. Instead he argued that promoting and strengthening existing international treaties and agreements would better serve the interests of the countries in Asia.[125] He maintained his faith in international treaties in January 1934. In an article in *Chūō kōron*, titled 'The decline of the League of Nations?', he argued that with or without the League Japan needed to pursue the peaceful solution of international disputes and disarmament, or a second world war would result.[126]

Yokota expressed views and sentiments that were common among post-League internationalists in North America and Europe. As his counterparts did not deny their colonial claims, Yokota did not dismiss Japanese colonial interests in China. He argued that it had the exactly same interests as other colonial powers, and that these interests could be protected by existing international treaties. The difference between these international treaties and the proposed treaty was slight. If Yokota needed to 'bend' his beliefs, that was his critical view of a special Japanese role in Asia. There was a definite emphasis on the 'special circumstances of the Pacific area' in the paper, although it also stressed the importance of the 'fundamental principles' of the machinery of peace. On the other hand, Yokota's argument was flawed when it argued that existing treaties would best serve the countries of Asia. The treaties prevented the powers from expanding their territories in Asia, but they largely glossed over the exploitative relations between colonies and colonial powers.

Yokota was critical of Japanese actions, taking a universalist approach and advocating faith in international treaties, but without being critical of the regional colonial status quo before the Mukden Incident. Yanaihara Tadao (1893–1961), professor of colonial policy at Tokyo Imperial University and JCIPR member, demonstrated a similar view. He criticized Japanese policies in Manchuria. He argued the importance of Chinese nationalism, and the need to assist it. He argued for Japanese trade with Manchuria, not colonial relations.[127] Because of this critical views, especially of the Sino-Japanese War, he was forced to resign his post in 1937. Yet Yanaihara was not against Japanese colonial holdings if the rule was 'appropriate'. In 1932 the JCIPR asked him to conduct research on Japanese management of the Pacific Islands mandates. After extensive research in 1933 and 1934, partially funded by the IPR, he published the results in Japanese in June 1935. His research was probably used by the Japanese government, which was claiming the continuation of Japanese control of the mandate even after its withdrawal from the League. In early January 1935, the League approved this claim. Adding a further analysis of the South Sea Colonial Company (*Nanyō takushoku kabushiki gaisha*, established in 1936), his work was published in English as *Pacific Islands Under Japanese Mandate* by the IPR in 1940. It was a justification of Japanese colonial administration.[128] His stance on colonial holdings, therefore, depended on the particular colony, and his view was clearly supported by the League.

The framework of 'liberal' internationalists against the 'reactionary' state leads to the interpretation that liberal internationalists were oppressed and isolated in the 1930s.[129] JCIPR members, as well as other IPR members, were, however, not exactly anti-state, or anti-empire. In 1931–3, Takaki maintained a position consistent with his views in the 1920s. His role was promoter of peace and advocate of the 'Japanese perspective' to the world. According to Takaki, the fault of Japanese 'liberals' like himself was not failure to condemn military aggression or government actions in Manchuria. They should have made a greater effort to make Japanese people understand the concept and mechanisms of international peace, and to explain the aspirations of the Japanese people to foreign countries. Takaki felt that this was the case especially at the conclusion of the Pact of Paris: 'We did not make enough effort to mould public opinion which would demand the need for the reservation on [Japanese interests in] Manchuria and Mongolia, and to make the powers understand the Japanese position.'[130] While some may see this as in conflict with liberal principles, it is a logical consequences of their post-League internationalism.

What sort of regional or international order did the proposed pact of Takaki and Yokota present, and how did other IPR members react? As noted, the pact can be interpreted as an attempt by Japanese post-League internationalists to shape the peace machinery of the post-Manchuguo era within the existing framework of international treaties. Although it was clearly designed to establish an alternative mechanism, it did not challenge the League. It was definitely cooperative towards the powers. At the same time, its regional focus was clear. It was designed specifically for the Pacific, not for the world. The members of this Japanese regional peace machinery were the United States, China, France, Britain, Japan and the USSR, the powers in the region or with regional colonial interests. After discussion at the conference, Canada, Australia, New Zealand and the Netherlands were included.[131]

Carter's introduction to the proceedings of the Banff conference was highly critical of the proposal. He conceded that it had valid points, such as a plan to hold a regular conference of the Pacific countries, and the need for adjustment of inequality among 'the community of nations'. He, however, voiced the 'greatest objection' to the proposal:

> ... peace is a world problem, and ... any proposal like this which tended to decentralize the peace machinery of the world and further prejudice the authority of the League of Nations, was to be discouraged.[132]

This reflected Carter's view of the post-League international order. The entity of the Pacific region was seen as a challenge to the order. Carter needed to redefine the order, because for him its centre was located on the East coast of the United States, not in Europe. It is, therefore, rather ironic that he took a position critical to the proposed draft security pact in 1933, as it envisaged a new, yet cooperative peace machinery, modelled after American initiatives of the 1920s. While the JCIPR was strengthening its regional focus, the ISIPR and various IPR operations were to reflect Carter's view, further straining the relationship between the JCIPR and the ISIPR. This became evident, particularly after the outbreak of the Sino-Japanese War in 1937.

8 The IPR and the Sino-Japanese War, 1936–9

The Yosemite conference in 1936

The Yosemite conference of 1936 was the last major IPR event before the outbreak of the Sino-Japanese War – the war, which had an immense impact on regional politics, and affected IPR operations. The conference was the last to follow the established format, the last to be open to the public and the press, and the last to be held on the Pacific coast. It was also the last that the Japanese group attended before 1954. It was the first to take place fully under the leadership of Carter who was consolidating his base in New York. Like Banff, Yosemite was a scenic attraction, and the conference was held at the Ahwahnee Hotel in Yosemite National Park between 15 and 29 August 1936. Participants stayed at a camping village, almost four kilometres from the hotel. Ushiba Tomohiko (1902–93), Secretary of the JCIPR, recorded that whereas major participants stayed in wood cabins, young secretaries camped in tents, which they soon began to call 'slums'. He noted that the only service was bed-making. Even former Japanese Foreign Minister Yoshizawa and former French Prime Minister Sarraut (and former Governor-General of Indo-China) had to carry their own washing to the laundry.[1] Although these participants enjoyed the experience as an American style of hospitality, Ushiba's note illuminated the undeniable 'class' of the IPR.

Colonialism

One of the major developments in the Pacific since the previous IPR conference was the American government's 1935 proclamation setting the date for Philippine independence. Although this might have been seen as an American precedent for the independence of colonies throughout the Pacific region, it did not seem to have affected the consciousness and discussion of IPR members in quite that way. Perhaps because the announcement had long been expected, it did not change anything much. The Philippine group's request for autonomous status had already been granted by the ACIPR and was approved by the Pacific Council in 1931, and the Philippines had been represented at the Pacific Council since 1933. In principle, this was done within the colonial framework – the Philippines was an ethnic or local group within the territory of the United States. When the Philippines became a member of the Pacific Council, so did the Netherlands East Indies (colonial authority), France (colonial power) and the USSR. Although the Philippine groups consisted of local members after 1929, IPR members from the Netherlands East Indies and France were mainly former or current colonial officers. The acceptance of the Philippines group hardly constituted a challenge to the colonial status quo in IPR operations.

The 1935 development did not change this framework. American IPR members did not see it as a reflection of American commitment to anti-colonialism. They saw the main causes as domestic and economic. Concerned industry leaders and organized labour wanted to reduce competition from the Philippines, particularly its sugar, cotton-seed oil, cordage and dairy products. Ending the colonial relationship meant the end of special tariff arrangements. Conference discussion mainly addressed economic issues: how the Philippines and the United States would adjust to a new trade arrangement; and how local industries in the Philippines should be restructured.[2] American paternalism was strongly evident in the discussions on security issues. Whereas the Philippine group argued for self-defence capacity, American IPR members stressed the continued importance of US naval bases as the key to Philippine defence.[3] New attitudes towards decolonization were yet to emerge in IPR operations.

The state and the IPR conference

The most significant development at Yosemite was a closer relationship between IPR operations and the state. The trend had existed earlier, but at Yosemite it was more obvious. Although Carter's ambition for the IPR's greater political influence was a major factor, the process was furthered by the actions of governments. They recognized the IPR's significance or even felt the need to make use of the IPR. It was a time of intensifying conflict in Europe and Asia. In 1935 Italy invaded Ethiopia, and in 1936 Germany moved into the Rhineland. Fascism was gaining force, and the Spanish Civil War broke out in 1936. In the United States, Roosevelt's New Deal measures were transforming political, economic and social structures. Trade competition among the powers was intensifying, and this was accentuated by rapid increases in Japan's exports. Trade disputes between Japan and other powers intensified, and tariff blocs were being formed.

The JCIPR and the Ministry of Foreign Affairs

In 1936, Japan was also in the midst of political crisis and confusion. Another major military coup was attempted in February 1936. In the succeeding Hirota cabinet, the military influence was undoubtedly strong. As state control of the population, especially of socialists and communists, increased during this period, scholars often assume that the military-dominated state repressed non-official, 'liberal' and internationalist organizations such as the JCIPR. The relationship between the state and these organizations was, however, not necessarily oppositional. First, the military was influential in successive governments and advocated Japanese leadership in East Asia. Yet, it still largely argued for the maintenance of cooperative relationships with the powers.[4] Second, various political forces, including the military, were far from coherent. As the Manchurian crisis developed, political parties declined, leaving other forces competing for the dominance. Bureaucrats at the Ministry of Foreign Affairs, particularly the statist reformist faction (*kakushinha*), also jockeyed for influence in foreign policy.

In this context, the JCIPR was useful to the Ministry. Especially after Japanese withdrawal from the League in 1933, the Ministry made greater efforts to co-opt post-League internationalists as international publicists. Its intervention in the JIA (formerly the LNA) and the JCIPR became more systematic. The process reached a new stage in May 1935, when the decision was made to absorb the JCIPR into the JIA. This was completed at the end of 1935. Iwanaga Yūkichi, JCIPR member, journalist and newspaper proprietor, reportedly initiated this move because he felt the need to consolidate the 'weakening' forces of 'liberal' internationalists.[5]

Iwanaga's post-League internationalism, however, sheds another light on this event. Iwanaga shared Konoe's idea that international public opinion and 'national' control of overseas news was extremely significant in modern international affairs. He developed the idea of a national news agency when he was working at the South Manchurian Railway in 1911–17. His conviction strengthened after observing the way foreign agencies reported Japanese policies and anti-Japanese movements in the United States.[6] In his view, the dominance of foreigners in reporting foreign events to Japan, and Japanese events overseas was harmful to the Japanese state/empire. Iwanaga established his own news agency in 1920. He was concerned with the monopoly of overseas news by British Reuters. As proprietor, he worried not only about 'foreign bias' in news on Japan, but also the substantial fees he had to pay Reuters. With other news agencies, such as the American Associated Press (AP), he fought for a more equal deal.

Iwanaga's idea of a national news agency was not so much an expression of freedom and diversity of the press. It was more to do with his sense of duty to the state/empire as a member of the national elite and a post-League internationalist. His duty was to present a 'correct' picture of 'Japan' and ensure that the 'Japanese view' was understood 'correctly' in the world. The success story of wartime propaganda by Reuters during World War I inspired Iwanaga. He learned that the more credible a news agency was in peacetime, as Reuters was, the more effective its wartime propaganda would be.[7] In the 1920s and 1930s, Iwanaga enthusiastically lobbied politicians to form a national news agency. The first one, *Rengō*, was founded in 1926. It was the association of Japanese newspapers, and further absorbed various local newspapers in 1928.

As the Manchurian Incident unfolded, Iwanaga felt the need to expand the function of *Rengō*. He lobbied the government in 1931–5, arguing that a 'national policy news agency' (*kokusaku tsūshinsha*) was urgently needed. As a result, in 1936, the government granted the establishment of *Dōmei tsūshin*, a consolidated body of newspapers and news agencies. The government of the time shared Iwanaga's agenda. The newly founded Cabinet Information Committee (founded in July 1936) initiated this move and partially funded it.[8] State co-option was already evident at the *Rengō*'s Shanghai bureau before it became *Dōmei tsūshin*. The bureau was headed by JCIPR member and later Konoe's think-tank member, Matsumoto Shigeharu. In 1932 Iwanaga recruited Matsumoto as Shanghai bureau chief. He was impressed by Matsumoto's language, research and social skills as one of the secretarial staff of the JCIPR at the Kyoto conference in 1929. Other JCIPR members, such as Maeda Tamon, also recommended Matsumoto to Iwanaga. Matsumoto's job was not only reporting news. Iwanaga wanted him to lead the Press Union in Shanghai. It was initiated by the Japanese Ministry of Foreign Affairs and the Navy during the Shanghai Incident in 1932 to 'improve public opinion on Japan'.[9] Shanghai *Rengō* was expected to cooperate with the Japanese embassy, particularly its information department. Matsumoto stayed in Shanghai in 1932–8, a crucial period in the development of Sino-Japanese relations.

JCIPR members tailored their activities to the new agenda of the Ministry without official pressure, and its consequences were not small. Iwanaga's push for a consolidated national news agency ultimately contributed to state control of the mass media. As Kazsa notes, *Dōmei tsūshin* 'eventually became the exclusive source of foreign news' both in the press and radio broadcasting of the NHK (*Nihon hōsō kyōkai* or Japan Broadcasting Cooperation). It limited diversity and freedom of the press.[10] For Iwanaga and his colleagues at *Rengō* this did not seem to have been a major concern. He recorded his 'surprise' when he encountered strong opposition from local newspapers against consolidation in 1927.[11] What explains Iwanaga's commitment was clearly not profit, for he lost substantial sums establishing the news agency. For him, his duty as part of the national elite was paramount in the empire's hour of need. To Matsumoto, who was leaving for Shanghai, Iwanaga stressed the 'honour' of Japan as a priority in his work in Shanghai.[12]

Matsumoto was probably more aware of the tension in his roles. He was a non-official and a journalist in an organization commonly regarded as part of the government propaganda machinery. He was in Shanghai in the middle of intense conflicts and war. On his way to his new post in Shanghai, one of his Chinese friends asked him accusingly 'why he would work for an organization like *Rengō*'. Then he fully understood the basis for her accusation.[13] There is no question that Matsumoto opposed military aggression. In his memoir, he was critical of military aggression during the Sino-Japanese War, and his description of the Nanjing massacre is critical, if not condemnatory.[14] He was also involved in the peace negotiation with China.

As Mitani points out, there were the limited choices available to intellectuals and journalists in this period,[15] and this is by no means unusual in any country engaging at war. When Matsumoto's staff reported to him that many soldiers cried for their mother, not the Emperor, as they were dying in the field, he did not run the story. Did he have a choice, or was it self-censorship? If it was the latter, did he do this because he knew it would be censored in Tokyo anyway, or because of his sense of duty as head of a 'national agency'?

In the postscript to his memoir, he tries to reconcile the dilemma of post-League internationalists in the war context. He defines himself as an 'old liberal' because he adhered to 'liberal principles', such as individuality, tolerance, freedom of speech and peace. In his view, acceptance of the Meiji Constitution and the absoluteness of the Emperor compromised these principles. But it was justified because he was a patriot. He loved his country, and worried about it.[16] Patriotism was not incompatible with his 'liberal' principles. He tried to act in accordance with his principles and the needs of his state/empire. He communicated and cooperated with officials closely and voluntarily out of this sense of mission. When Matsumoto and his Shanghai staff heard the news that *Rengō* at last had become *Dōmei tsūshin*, it was an exciting, rather than a sad, moment. They reaffirmed their sense of mission.[17]

The Japanese nation-state, which was an empire, was the regime of truth for post-League internationalists. The state was morally right. Despite his claim in the post-war period, he was more New Liberal than *laissez-faire* liberal in the 1920s and 1930s. He was not a Marxist, and probably anti-socialist. He was definitely left-leaning, concerned with social issues from a 'humanitarian' perspective. He read socialist literature extensively. In the United States in the mid-1920s, he was interested in industrial relations in Japan, and wrote articles on the issue for American journals. After his return, and before he was involved with the IPR at the Kyoto conference, he was a member of *Shakai shisōsha*, along with Rōyama Masamichi and other social democratic members of *Shinjinkai*. For them, the state was crucial for the social welfare and reforms. Its nationals should be dedicated to it at all costs. This sense of mission was inevitably stronger in times of war, and among those who saw themselves as a part of the national elite. The state did not need to coerce these post-League internationalists.

The JCIPR's absorption into the JIA is best understood not as the desperate last resort of declining liberal internationalists. It was more likely a positive move by the JCIPR and the JIA to be co-opted into the state apparatus. Post-League internationalists tried to respond to new official agendas and fulfil their duty. Konoe was very supportive of the new initiative of the Ministry of Foreign Affairs – 'cultural diplomacy' and the state's co-option of non-governmental organizations. A leader of the *kakushin* group, Shiratori, who was very close to Konoe, pushed this move.[18] Konoe or someone like Shiratori at the Ministry might have suggested the absorption of the JCIPR into the JIA. Iwanaga, concurrently working with the government for the formation of *Dōmei tsūshin*, probably shared the view and pursued it. The consolidated

JIA made it much easier for the Ministry to supervise and control activities of post-League internationalists. The Yosemite conference was the first IPR conference under this new structure. Unsurprisingly, intervention by the Ministry was far more extensive than before.

The Yosemite conference was held during the term of the Hirota Kōki cabinet (March 1936 to February 1937) with Arita Hachirō as Foreign Minister (after April). Although a *kakushin* group pushed the new initiative of 'cultural diplomacy', it was a minority within the Ministry, and needed mainstream support. Incidentally, the top of the Ministry, Hirota and Arita, seem to have agreed on the view. In January 1934, Hirota, then Foreign Minister, for example, made a speech at the Diet, emphasizing the role of 'culture' in diplomatic relations. This was the first recognition of the significance of 'culture' in diplomacy by a Japanese foreign minister.[19] Arita also had led the original *kakushin* group in the 1920s, and he initiated the formation of the Department of Information within the Ministry in 1921. Although he was seen as part of the mainstream by the mid-1930s, he continued to share certain agendas with younger *kakushinha*. As the Manchurian crisis continued, he became concerned with retrieving the leadership in foreign policy-making from the military and restoring it to the Ministry. Consequently, he advocated the Ministry's restructure in 1936.[20] Hirota and Arita were keen on the new initiatives of 'cultural diplomacy', co-option of post-League internationalists and the 'recovery' of Ministry influence in foreign policy-making.

This led to greater state intervention in JCIPR activities in 1936. As a result of the disruption caused by the restructuring of the JCIPR at the end of 1935, preparation for the conference only began in January 1936. Exchanges between the JCIPR, now a section within the JIA called *Taiheiyō mondai chōsabu*, and the Ministry were frequent in the lead up to the conference. The JCIPR requested material on China from Amō, Director-General of the Department of Information, and on trade from Kurusu Saburō, Director-General of the Bureau of Trade Affairs.[21] Official intervention was not new. The Ministry had funded participants' travel, and provided materials on topics requested by the JCIPR. While there had been subtle pressure on a few occasions, however, preparation of research projects and selection of the delegates were mainly left to the JCIPR. Neither had official instruction been given to IPR conference delegates. This was not the case for the Yosemite conference.

The JCIPR initially invited official intervention in 1936, and the Ministry pressured the JCIPR to take up certain topics which it thought important.[22] Further intervention was evident in the selection of delegates. The JCIPR's main channel at the Ministry had been the Department of Information in the 1920s. In 1936, because a major conference topic was trade disputes, the Bureau of Trade Affairs was closely involved. The Bureau was keen to send a strong delegate from a relevant business group. It contacted prominent figures in the textile industry in the Kansai area, and finally decided on Hamano Kyōhei at Nihon menka gaisha (Japan Cotton Trading Company).[23] Two JCIPR members, Tsurumi Yūsuke and Saionji Kinkazu (1906–93), also participated with the status of Ministry employee (casual or temporary) (*Gaimushō shokutaku*). Tsurumi had been a founding member of the JCIPR and had participated in all IPR conferences to date. He was then a member of the House of Representatives, and was also working for the Ministry, probably in an advisory capacity. Saionji, aristocrat and grandson of the influential senior politician, Saionji Kinmochi, was also working at the Ministry and was sent as one of the secretarial staff of the JCIPR.[24] The Japanese Consul in Seattle also tried to send its own employee as a researcher to the conference. The Ministry in Tokyo, however, did not think this appropriate. It was well aware of the IPR's non-official 'principle'.[25] Sending a local embassy employee was perhaps a little too obvious.

Another significant intervention by the Ministry was seen in an exchange between Amō and the chairperson of the Japanese delegation, Yamakawa Tadao (1873–1962). Yamakawa, Vice-Chairperson of the JCIPR, was a leading post-League internationalist, and was a founding member of the LNA. In 1936, he was known as an expert on international law, and was a member of the House of Peers. He knew Ministry mechanisms very well as he was a former senior diplomat who had accompanied the Japanese delegates at the Paris Conference in 1919 and the London Naval Conference (for disarmament) in 1930. Just before departing for the conference, Yamakawa sent a letter to Amō. It noted that the JCIPR would like to present a paper on the Japanese government's attitude to the China issue at the beginning of the conference in order to deflect controversy. In this way, the conference would, Yamakawa argued, discuss official principles rather than the concrete details. Amō disagreed with Yamakawa, noting that it would guarantee controversy, and that the paper was not appropriate for circulation to 'outsiders'.[26]

More significantly, Amō sent Yamakawa a note of instructions for the Yosemite delegation the day before their departure. It made the following points: first, if anyone raises the issue of the stability of East Asia and Japan's 'living rights' (*seizonken*), try to discredit them, even if this leads to the withdrawal of the JCIPR from the IPR; second, try to emphasize the positive aspects of Japanese foreign policies rather than being defensive; third, try to enlighten American public opinion on the Japanese point of view; and fourth, Sino-Japanese relations should be discussed by China and Japan, and if possible, a permanent organization for this dialogue should be established.[27] Amō regarded the JCIPR as almost part of the state apparatus, and as valuable as long as it served the state's purposes.

The performance of the Japanese delegation at the conference suggests that they largely complied with Amō's instructions. In particular, Yamakawa emphasized the third point, the international publicist role. His efforts were devoted to 'enlighten' not only participants at Yosemite, but also concerned groups within Japan. He wrote articles on the conference in Japanese journals, such as *Gaikō jihō* and *Kokusai chishiki*, and tried to convey to domestic readers how badly Japan was understood, what the misunderstandings were, and how he and the Japanese delegates had contributed to 'correcting' them. Other Japanese participants also reported hostility towards Japan at the conference.[28]

Yamakawa explained these 'misunderstandings' were about Japan's trade expansion and actions in North China. He emphasized that the conference was 'the best opportunity to clarify the Japanese position'.[29] Katagiri suggests that Japanese participants took the line not only because of official pressure. They were convinced that Japanese policies were right. What was needed was a change of attitude by the powers towards Japan.[30] Yamakawa's emphasis on the 'private' nature of the IPR may also have been due to his genuine belief in the principle. He was, however, well aware of the heavy official intervention. It is more likely that he needed to make the point in order to refute the accusation made at the conference – the Japanese group represented official views.[31] An emphasis on 'non-governmentality' was important for the actions of the Japanese group to look genuine, and to be effective.

Politicization of IPR conferences

Increased state intervention in JCIPR activities in this period corresponded to a trend within IPR operations. Carter recognized the increased interest of various states in IPR operations, and encouraged the state orientation of IPR operations. He promoted its role as a think-tank, and made its research projects and conference discussions relevant to foreign policy-making. Many national groups sent prominent former and current politicians and cabinet ministers as their heads, and Carter welcomed them. Newton Baker (Democrat) headed for the United States, Newton Rowell for Canada, Albert Sarraut for France, A.V. Alexander (Labour) for Britain and Yoshizawa Kenkichi for Japan. Although emphasizing the 'non-governmentality' of the IPR, Yamakawa himself noted that the discussion at Yosemite was political, not academic. He regarded this politicization as being due to the ISIPR's choice of many political topics; the press conferences that were held after each Round Table discussion, increasing the element of 'official' propaganda; and the fact that there were more politicians at the conference than before.[32] He was one of many to point out this trend. A journalist from Honolulu also noted stronger governmental influence than at previous conferences, and that the discussions at the conference had been mainly on diplomacy.[33]

As many participants and observers pointed out, the conference was used as an unofficial diplomatic stage, and this met little opposition. The element had been present at previous conferences. Participants had criticized the policies of other governments and defended their own since the first conference. Although one of the most controversial issues, Manchuguo, was ruled out as a topic; the British argued that Japanese economic expansion was based on its imperial ambitions and the exploitation of Japanese workers. The Japanese refuted the claims. The Americans and the Chinese criticized

Japanese policies towards China. They argued that, in particular, the declaration of Amō in 1934 (often regarded as the Japanese Monroe Doctrine in East Asia) presented the biggest obstacle to the achievement of national unity in China, and of peace and security in the region. In reply, Japanese participants emphasized Japan's duty in the region and maintained that the issue should be solved between Japan and China. Although the first and only participation of the USSR group was well noted, Takayanagi thought that it had not altered the atmosphere of the conference. Their merit was to present their government's views.[34]

The 'unofficial diplomatic' component in 1936 differed from previous conferences. First, the Japanese government, or more precisely the Ministry of Foreign Affairs, used the Japanese group to create an environment favourable to their policy decisions. Second, British delegates initiated 'informal' discussions on diplomatic issues that entailed heavy government involvement. By spring 1936, more than a year before the outbreak of the Sino-Japanese War and a few months before the Yosemite conference, the Japanese Ministry of Foreign Affairs assessed the Washington Treaties which would expire that year. They concluded that the Nine Power Treaty (on China) should be seen virtually abrogated for two reasons: the treaty's open-door principle and equal opportunity policy (for the powers) were used by Britain and the United States to secure the Chinese market; and the treaty treated China as a 'semi-colonial special' market, not a 'completely independent' country. Yet the Ministry decided not to declare this view publicly. The sensation caused by Amō's statement was fresh in their memory, and a public announcement would once more provoke a hardline reaction and retaliation, particularly from the United States.[35] The Yosemite conference was the Ministry's best opportunity to make its view known among foreign policy experts in the United States and Britain.

There were indications that some members received 'informal' instructions on this point. Yoshizawa Kenkichi was one of them. He was a member of the House of Peers, a former Minister in China, a Japanese representative at the League Assembly in the early stages of the Manchurian Incident and Foreign Minister in January–May 1932. Yoshizawa advocated the Ministry line on the Nine Power Treaty at Yosemite. In the Japanese version of the conference proceedings, edited by the JCIPR, he noted that he argued that the treaty should be altered or abolished in reply to Canadian Newton Rowell. An unidentified Japanese newspaper of 1 September 1936, which was filed with the official document, also reported that Yoshizawa made this point clear at the conference, and shortly afterwards at the Commonwealth Club in San Francisco.[36]

Yamakawa recorded that the Japanese group at Yosemite argued the same line on the Nine Power Treaty. In a Japanese journal, he maintained that because of the recent great changes, the Nine Power Treaty needed amendment at the very least.[37] Utilizing the Stimson Doctrine, Tamura Kōsaku from the Japanese Institute for Foreign Affairs also argued that the treaty had become hard to maintain, not because of Japanese policies, but because of Chinese and Russian actions.[38] Yamakawa claimed that a majority at Yosemite agreed on the ineffectiveness of the treaty and the need for amendment.

It is hard to know whether this was actually the case. The ISIPR's version of the proceedings of the Yosemite conference suggests that Japanese members did not convey this point clearly. The only relevant paper in the conference was that of Quincy Wright, professor of international law, University of Chicago. It was entitled 'The working of diplomatic machinery in the Pacific'. Acknowledging the problem of the Nine Power Treaty, he stressed that what was needed was not a new treaty or a new arrangement, but a more rigorous reinforcement of existing arrangements.[39] Yoshizawa and Yamakawa may have been overly optimistic about the support of other participants for the Japanese government view.

By far the most important topic at Yosemite was trade disputes, and it was here that 'unofficial' diplomacy and the intervention of various governments, particularly Britain, was evident. Hamano from the Japan Cotton Trading Company, who was selected by the Bureau of Trade Affairs, recorded that an initiative to hold informal meetings came from the British, Australians and the Netherlands East Indies. Barnard Ellinger, British economist and retired merchant, attended the conference to represent the interests of the cotton industry in Britain. According to Hamano, Ellinger initiated trade discussions. Hamano, Ōshima Kenzō, Director of Sumitomo Bank, and Ueda Teijirō, professor of economics at Tokyo Imperial University, participated in these 'informal' discussions. Despite the substantial intervention of the Japanese Ministry of Foreign Affairs, Hamano was critical of Japan's poor economic diplomacy at Yosemite. He conceded that Japanese business leaders generally lacked the vigour and initiative needed for negotiations. Yet, a far greater problem was the lack of understanding and action of Japanese officials who led trade negotiations. In contrast, he was impressed by the much closer relationship between business and government in Britain.[40] The Japanese Consul-General's reports on these meetings suggest that these British delegates had government instructions. They were at Yosemite in order to negotiate a deal concerning British recognition of Manchuguo in exchange for a Japanese compromise on British interests in North China.[41] This is very significant as it suggests that the British government not only saw the merit of IPR operations, but also utilized its conference more aggressively and positively than the Japanese government. Yamakawa also noted a trend in most of the national groups. They discussed issues and reached a 'national' consensus before conference discussions.[42] An exception was the American group, which, as the host country, was the largest.

Participants from Honolulu, Australia, New Zealand and the Pacific coast of America had objected to Carter's removal of the ISIPR from the Pacific, and his more obvious state orientation. Until this point, the JCIPR had not expressed strong opinions about this trend. Now in 1936, a few long-time

JCIPR members noticed the politicization of IPR operations. Nasu Shiroshi (1886–1982), Tsurumi and Takayanagi were all founding JCIPR members. Nasu, professor of agricultural policy at Tokyo Imperial University, had contributed to the IPR's research project on land utilization. Except for his absence at the first conference, these three had attended all the IPR conferences so far.

Although they noted the strong 'political' atmosphere at Yosemite, their reactions differed. Nasu shared common views with Honolulu, Australia and New Zealand members of the late 1920s. He felt that the IPR's principle of a 'scientific' and 'objective' search for 'facts' had been eroded. In his view, it was a principle compatible with 'true patriotism', and it was the basis of international cooperation. Because of the Anglo-Saxon emphasis on 'practical' effects and contemporary political changes, the IPR had begun to meddle with 'real politics' (*jissai seiji*). 'Should we be happy to see it as a sign of healthy growth that the IPR has put an end to the YMCA atmosphere and "professorial" ideals, and increased its activities as a political organization?' He thought that the IPR would become a government branch office, conducting 'private' diplomacy, propagating, defending and condemning official policies. He felt sad to see the 'initial' principle declining, although he remained hopeful that the IPR could still play a role as an educator of people.[43]

In contrast, Tsurumi was positive about the further politicization of the IPR. For Nasu, politicization sacrificed the principles of 'scientific rigour', 'objectivity' and academic integrity. For Tsurumi, it meant the professionalization of the IPR. In his view, research outcomes and data papers were of a better quality, and better prepared in 1936 than before. The expert knowledge of the participants was impressive and the conference organization had been perfected. The 'status' of participants was higher, making discussions at the conference more influential. Tsurumi did not dismiss the danger of IPR conferences becoming 'unofficial' diplomatic machinery, and noted that many suspected the Japanese government of using them for that very purpose. Nevertheless, he was content with the result, and thought that the conference would influence the opinions of prominent figures in Europe and America.[44] Similarly, Takayanagi saw politicization as a good sign. He thought it did not mean compromising the quality of research, but that the political significance was enhanced.[45]

Takayanagi and Nasu both saw an increase in the political aspects of IPR operations as signifying a transition from 'idealism' (*Risō shugi*) to 'neo-realism' (*Shin genjitsu shugi*) in the philosophical paradigm of international politics. This perception was dominant then, and only a few years later E.H. Carr published *The Twenty Years' Crisis*, reinforcing this framework. Nasu saw it negatively, feeling that founders of the IPR and supporters of the League of Nations were martyrs struggling against the odds. Yet these 'liberals' were no less free from politics than the 'realists' they criticized. Nasu was closely involved in agricultural policy-making back home. Although Tsurumi pointed to the danger of the IPR becoming a quasi-diplomatic organization, he himself attended the conference on an official passport as an employee of the Ministry of Foreign Affairs. Having proudly asserted that the IPR represented 'liberal' factors in the Pacific in 1931, Takayanagi now saw the rise of realism positively.

Such comments on increased politicization and the rise of realism reflected the enhanced state orientation of IPR operations. Although the nation-state had been always the foundation of IPR operations, initially the IPR emphasized 'individuals', and aimed to educate society/the public so as to be relevant to state policies. Clearly the emphasis was shifting to the latter in the 1930s. For a newcomer to the IPR like Ushiba Tomohiko, JCIPR Secretary from around 1934 and a first-time participant in an IPR conference in 1936, this state emphasis was a given. He noted that the National Council of the IPR was not a branch, but a completely autonomous body of national members. 'The relationship is like the League of Nations and member states.'[46] To some JCIPR members, such as Tsurumi and Takayanagi, this state orientation and increased politicization meant that the IPR had greater influence. Tsurumi congratulated the ISIPR for achieving this goal.[47]

To most Japanese participants at Yosemite, however, this move was damaging for Japan. They felt that the ISIPR and the ACIPR, and in particular younger officers such as William Holland, Research Secretary at the ISIPR, and Frederick V. Field, Secretary of the ACIPR, were hostile to Japanese policies. A Japanese participant described Holland's speech at the beginning of the conference as especially critical of Japanese policies. Although the speech was not included in the IPR's conference proceedings (edited by Holland and other ISIPR staff), Ushiba's article in the JCIPR version of the conference proceedings included a translated excerpt.[48]

Holland's critical view of Japanese politics, economy, society and policies towards China had much in common with those of North American IPR members who specialized in Japan, such as Thomas A. Bisson and E. Herbert Norman (1909–57). Later, both contributed to the IPR's Inquiry project – Bisson *America's Far Eastern Policy* and Norman *Japan's Emergence as a Modern State*. Norman's influence in Holland at this stage, however, is unlikely. Norman began publishing articles on Japan or China to journals such as *Amerasia* and *Pacific Affairs* in 1937 and 1938. If Holland shared some views with him, it may have been because they both studied at Cambridge in the mid-1930s – Holland in 1932–3 and Norman in 1933–5. There socialist and communist ideas were dominant. Although the extent and nature of this influence differed greatly, no doubt this intellectual context inspired these young minds with a strong sense of social justice.

Bisson's influence on Holland is reasonable to assume. Although Yosemite was the first IPR conference Bisson attended, he was already known as a 'Far Eastern' specialist at the Foreign Policy Association (based in New York). Holland was Research Secretary of the ISIPR as well as a scholar of the Japanese economy. He lived in Tokyo in 1934–5, and had articles published on the Japanese economy, including 'Silk control in Japan' (1935) and 'The plight of Japanese agriculture' (1936). The fact that Bisson was soon asked to contribute to the Inquiry project indicates a high regard for his work among the ISIPR staff, including Holland.

There were two major points in Holland's interpretation of Japanese policies in 1936. First, he saw current Japanese politics, economy and society as based on the exploitation of workers and peasants. Despite the prosperity of certain industries, the rural and agricultural sectors were severely depressed. The workers did not receive a fair share of the profits. Second, he regarded the Japanese Monroe Doctrine as the basis of the policy towards China. It aimed to achieve rule not only over Manchuria, but also in Inner Mongolia and North China, and to gain the powers' acceptance of these claims. He warned that even though the Nanjing government was reforming its infrastructure and currency system, if it did not take measures to improve the people's lives it would lose popular support. If this happened, China would fall into colonial status. The argument echoed North American Japanese experts' views, and those of contemporary Japanese Marxists. 'Japan was in a *distorted* and constrained condition because of immense economic and political *contradictions*', and 'the organization of parliamentary politics was *still* based on a social system dominated by *feudalistic* notions of loyalty'.[19]

Did this evaluation of Japan indicate the much-suspected New Deal ideology of Holland and the ISIPR (and the ACIPR) in general? It is not easy to give a clear answer. First, it is unclear what was meant by New Dealers in an international context, as the term was coined in the context of American domestic politics. Second, recent evaluations of New Dealers suggest that their ideological backgrounds were much more ambiguous than McCarthyist hysteria had portrayed.[50] Holland recorded that when he was asked about his politics in 1932 by Field, an aristocratic socialist soon to become a Communist Party member, he earned Field's scorn by replying that he considered himself a 'liberal, somewhat of the Manchester variety'. In his memoir, he emphasized moral, non-ideological factors that dominated his and Carter's views. They were not Marxist, and not interested in American domestic politics, although both supported Roosevelt's New Deal policies, like many concerned contemporary Americans. Holland also recorded that he was not ignorant of communism, but that he was uninformed about the activities of communist IPR members.[51] Such memories need to be filtered through the knowledge that from the 1950s Holland had to refute the label of 'communist sympathizer' for the IPR. For him it was important to stress non-ideological and non-political aspects of their guiding philosophy. In the 1930s, he was concerned with social and economic issues, lived in Cambridge and breathed the air of the New Deal. It would have been impossible for him to totally avoid the influence of Marxist thinking. He and Carter also must at least have suspected Field and other ACIPR staff of having communist leanings, and probably turned a blind eye to their activities. They had a common concern, Japanese aggression against 'free China'.

Holland's paper displayed socialist rhetoric – the dominance of the ruling class, the flaws of capitalism, exploitation of workers and imperialism as a result of domestic capitalism. Such views were not only popular, but they made good sense. Concerned people felt the need to seek alternatives to capitalism, which had resulted in the disaster of the Depression. A Marxist framework and perspective, although promoting the power of a specific country, appealed to many even if their ideological and political commitment might not have been as strong as others'. These 'progressives' of the 1930s probably *looked like* communists in the late 1940s and early 1950s to Americans like Joseph McCarthy. Positive assessment of Chinese communists in this period can be understood as an expression of a strong 'moral' sense of social injustice, not ideological commitment. Or in the light of future developments, it was simply an insightful analysis. To E.H. Carr in 1939, the fault of these 'morally-concerned' 'liberals' such as Carter or Holland was not their 'left-leaning' ideology. It was their uncritical evaluation of the post-League order which they saw as 'morally right'.

The post-League international order and the Pacific

How did the Yosemite conference handle the issue of the regional order, and how were the views of Carter and the ISIPR reflected? This was illuminated in the debate on 'peaceful adjustment', which Eggleston, leader of the Australian group in 1936, proposed. Eggleston argued what was needed now was not the preservation of the international status quo, but peaceful change and adjustment. Other key IPR figures, such as Newton Baker, Chairperson of the ACIPR and the Pacific Council, and long-time advocate for American entry to the League, had not yet lost faith in the League's collective security system in 1936. This support for the League, as Eggleston argued, should not be confused with the preservation of the status quo of the powerful. He pointed out that very rapid changes were occurring in the Pacific and the world, and adjustment, albeit difficult, was crucial.

Earlier at IPR forums, Eggleston had been known for his regionalist view on disarmament. In 1936, he maintained a regionalist criticism towards Britain, especially on the British imposition of imperial trade preferences on the Dominions in the Pacific.[52] As Takaki and Yokota argued in 1933, Eggleston stressed that reducing inequity among nations was the key to peaceful change. Now, however, he emphasized the significance of worldwide collective security:

> A collective system in which the problems of the world are viewed as a whole and their meaning recognized, and the responsibility of making the changes necessary for peace is placed on the leading members without compulsion, is still a feasible system.[53]

Japanese participants responded to Eggleston's 'peaceful adjustment' very positively. For them, it justified the 'changes' in East Asia – the foundation of Manchuguo and the virtual end of the Nine Power Treaty. By arguing 'peaceful adjustment', they were telling other powers to accept this new situation peacefully. The same line was often used by those who advocated appeasement policies towards Japan and Germany, particularly in Britain. Colonel House, who was foreign policy adviser to Woodrow Wilson at the Paris Peace Conference in 1919, also argued for the need for a 'New Deal' in the international order in 1935.[54] This sentiment was evident at the IPR conference in 1933. The introduction of the proceedings concluded that '[a]s long as there is a class of "have nots" in the community of nations, mere maintenance of the status quo will never be a workable principle for diplomatic machinery'.[55] This general tone, however, seems to have been lost in 1936.

Even a strong regionalist like Eggleston shifted his emphasis from the region to the 'world' in 1936. Interestingly, one British participant argued for the establishment of regional League. Aware of British interests in China, this Briton was sympathetic to the Japanese proposal to solve Sino-Japanese conflicts between China and Japan. Most participants, however, disagreed. They argued that it would be technically very difficult to establish a 'regional' League in the Pacific, mainly because European powers needed to be included. Instead, they urged that 'a universal agreement was essential' in order to preserve peace.[56] Similarly, in a paper on the diplomatic machinery in the Pacific, Quincy Wright, an expert on international law, examined the settlement of international disputes in the Pacific since World War I, and found that:

> ... in the Far East the tendency has been for the influence of general diplomatic machinery to increase at the expense of regional machinery. ... It is difficult to visualize [a regional] organization [in the Pacific] which would really be effective to maintain peace and stability unless founded on a balance of power. At the moment such a balance can hardly be made unless Powers whose major interest is not really in the region are brought in, and if that is done, the organization ceases to be regional. The Washington Conference was not in any genuine sense a regional organization of the Far Eastern Powers, and the Powers have subsequently preferred to utilize genuine world machinery such as the Pact [of Paris] or the Covenant [of the League]. ... It is possible that regional organization has inherent deficiencies for the maintenance of peace.

Unlike Croly in 1927, Wright saw the significance of a balance of power and 'world' machinery. The emphasis on the world was important for another reason. Wright regarded 'moral public opinion' as important, but it needed to be coherent and universal to be effective in solving international disputes:

> if action is divided between regional organizations and world organizations, public opinion will be confused and will lack the definiteness and unanimity which is necessary to bring results.[57]

Wright suggested the need for a single, unified moral code in international politics.

In contrast, the JCIPR maintained the regional focus. This was already evident at the JCIPR when it was absorbed into the JIA at the end of 1935. JCIPR members still did not dismiss the concept of the Pacific or the importance of US–Japan cooperation at this stage. In 1935, Ishii Kikujirō, Chairperson of the JIA, former diplomat and Japanese representative at the Assembly of the League of Nations in 1920–7, stressed the importance of the Pacific region in international politics.[58] Similarly, at Yosemite, Yoshizawa argued that the Pacific would become the centre of international politics and economy, because many countries in the region, such as China, India, Australia, New Zealand, Latin America and Canada, would increase in power. The involvement of European powers in regional politics would decline as they became preoccupied with European affairs. The crucial relationship would be the US–Japan relationship. Although Yoshizawa argued it was 'right' for the Japanese Navy to build up its capacity, he felt it wiser to avoid the confrontation, and to have good economic relations with the United States.[59] Except for a favourable attitude towards naval armament, his point did not differ much from the views of JCIPR members in the 1920s or what was termed Shidehara diplomacy.

On Japanese policies towards China, however, Japanese delegates were more inclined to argue for bilateral consultation between Japan and China, not a regional multilateral framework. This reflected instructions from Amō or the policy of the Ministry of Foreign Affairs in general. This was also a strong basis for dismissing the merit of IPR conferences. In a letter of 31 August 1936 to Ishii, Chairperson of the JIA, Amō included a note, titled 'Better to hold a Sino-Japanese conference: on the IPR conference'. It urged the JCIPR to withdraw from the IPR as Japan had from the League. It argued that the IPR believed in white supremacy, and suppressed the interests of latecomer nations, such as Japan. It would be more fruitful to hold a non-governmental Sino-Japanese conference.[60] The note was clearly written by officials who observed the conference at first hand. As Amō's instructions also showed, these officials thought JCIPR's withdrawal from the IPR's international operations was a serious option well before the actual withdrawal in 1939.

Konoe, the JCIPR and 'cultural diplomacy'

Not all bureaucrats or influential political figures dismissed the value of IPR operations. Konoe Fumimaro rated the IPR highly. The IPR first came to his attention during his trip to the United States in May to June 1934. At that time, Konoe was regarded as a likely contender for the next premiership. Not feeling ready, he wanted to remove himself from the public eye. The trip was reported to be 'private', so that he could attend his son's graduation ceremony from an American high school. It was, however, clear that Konoe had 'official' business as a 'non-official'. The trip was coordinated by the Saitō government, and Konoe held close discussions especially with Foreign Minister Hirota. The mission was in line with the objectives of the International Culture Promotion Association or ICPA, established earlier in the year. It was a 'non-official' organization to promote 'Japanese culture' overseas and central to the new initiative of 'cultural diplomacy'. Foreign Minister Hirota appointed Konoe as its chairperson. Konoe's trip coincided with a sharp decline in American public opinion about Japan in the wake of Amō's statement. Konoe was expected to play a role in smoothing out rough patches in US–Japanese relations. The trip was partially funded by the ICPA. Konoe took gifts with him, courtesy of ICPA, including photograph albums of Japanese gardens collected by Shiga Naoya. Two JCIPR members, Rōyama and Ushiba, were selected to accompany Konoe on this trip. Iwanaga, who was also concerned with the international image of Japan and who was close to Konoe, recommended these two to accompany Konoe.[61] This was recognition of the merit of the JCIPR as 'specialists' on American affairs in official circles in mid-1934.

Konoe and his staff travelled extensively, to Honolulu, San Francisco, New York, Washington, DC, Philadelphia, Boston, New Haven and Chicago. Meetings with prominent American figures, including Roosevelt, were lined up for Konoe. For Konoe, the meeting with Roosevelt was only a matter of protocol. He suggested that Roosevelt visit Japan on his next trip to Hawai'i, an offer Roosevelt politely declined. Konoe noted the most fruitful outcome of this trip was discussions with 'Far Eastern' specialists in the United States. As a result, he reaffirmed the significance of good publicity. Konoe met prominent figures, many of whom had connections with the IPR, such as Wilbur, Jerome Greene and Carter, and discussed Japanese and American foreign policies. Carter criticized Japanese policies in China at a luncheon at the Century Club. Through these discussions Konoe realized the need to present a 'new' image of Japan. An emphasis on its 'civilization' and 'culture' was critical, because he thought this would help to legitimize its rule in Manchuria. He stressed that an institution which would provide information on Japan was needed in key cities in the United States, such as New York, Washington, DC, and Chicago. He suggested that the JCIPR could operate more 'organically' for that purpose.[62] By 'organically', he meant that the state could more systematically coordinate and integrate its activities. Konoe particularly stressed its merit in promoting research on Japan overseas.[63]

Despite a rather negative assessment of the Yosemite conference by diplomats and observers of the Ministry of Foreign Affairs, there are reasons to assume that the IPR continued to be seen as useful in Japanese official circles in the late 1930s. First, Konoe's concern with the need to promote an image of 'civilized' Japan and 'correct knowledge' about Japan overseas did not abate after 1934. After the Sino-Japanese War broke out in July 1937, he was even more convinced. Second, having been the subject of speculation as a Prime Ministerial contender since the early 1930s, Konoe finally moved to political centre stage in 1937. He formed the government in June 1937 to January 1939, July 1940 to July 1941 and again in July 1941 to October 1941. Third, Konoe's close circle included JCIPR members, such as Ushiba, Rōyama, Iwanaga, Matsumoto and Saionji. Konoe's trip to the United States in 1934, and the Yosemite conference were both very important in further defining this circle. By 1934 Rōyama had already been involved in a predecessor of Konoe's think-tank, *Showa kenkyūkai*, and was to be regarded as one of Konoe's most influential advisers.[64] The trip was important for Rōyama as well as for Konoe. His experience helped to form his concept of the New Order in East Asia. As a result of this trip, Ushiba also became close to Konoe. He was soon to be appointed as Konoe's private secretary when he took up the premiership in 1937. Ushiba recruited Saionji Kinkazu and Ozaki Hotsumi (1901–44) into Konoe's circle as well as JCIPR circles.

Yosemite was the link connecting them. It was the first IPR conference for Ushiba as Secretary of the JCIPR. He knew Saionji as they had studied at Oxford together, and asked him to help with secretarial work at Yosemite. Ushiba had also been a classmate of Ozaki at *Ichikō*, and he knew Ozaki's reputation as a rising China specialist at the *Tokyo asahi* newspaper. He asked Ozaki to join the Japanese group and present a paper on China. These three younger members of the Japanese group became very close. Later they all would work for Konoe's first cabinet as secretary or adviser, and all were to become members of *Showa kenkyūkai*. For Ozaki, who is now better remembered for his espionage charge in relation to the Sorge Incident, this connection with Ushiba and Saionji was not planned, but fortuitous for his information collection. As a correspondent in Shanghai in 1928–32, he escaped a big police round-up of communists in Japan in 1929. His communist identity was unknown, and as an adviser to Konoe in his first cabinet he was closer to decision-making than any of his communist comrades. His arrest in October 1941 greatly shocked Ushiba, Saionji, and especially Konoe. Takahashi Kamekichi also attended the Yosemite conference (his second), and he was to be involved in *Showa kenkyūkai*. Konoe's future brains trust, therefore, consisted of a good proportion of the Japanese group of twenty-three (including eight secretarial staff) at Yosemite.

The IPR and the public

Carter wanted to make the IPR an important think-tank, and this inevitably emphasized its political dimension. On the other hand, he was also keen on education of the public about international and regional issues, and he promoted an educational scheme in the United States. Public attention increased at Yosemite. The conference was broadcast through the American NBC network. Although round table sessions were closed to the public and press, a press conference was held after each session.[65] Major news agencies, such as UP and AP, and newspapers from the United States, Japan and China gave extensive coverage to the conference.[66]

Ozaki, a journalist and first-time participant, considered that as a political element increased, press interest in the IPR would inevitably grow in the United States. In contrast, he felt that the Japanese press did not pay much attention to the IPR. He thought this was due to the JCIPR's elitism. It did little to appeal to the press or the public, and IPR conferences were understood as a social club for those who enjoyed speaking English. Convinced of the importance of IPR conferences, he argued that it should appeal to the public.[67] Despite this seeming 'openness' to the press in the United States, however, on another level, there was a more closed atmosphere. A journalist from Honolulu observed that most of the internal politicking of the ISIPR and the Pacific Council occurred in closed sessions.[68] As a result of the politicization of IPR operations and the outbreak of the Sino-Japanese War, the Yosemite conference was the last one open to the press before the end of World War II.

The ISIPR and the international order

On the surface, Manchuguo was almost a settled issue. Although Japan was the only great power which recognized it, the other powers did not question its legitimacy strongly. There was no full-scale military confrontation between China and Japan. Under the surface, however, numerous conflicts simmered. There were also many unsolved issues over China between Japan and the other powers. Competition for the market in China among Japan, the United States and Britain was intensifying, with the Japanese government seeking to establish exclusive rights. The Guomindang government undertook currency reform, aided by the British government. This stirred concerns in Japan and Japanese smuggling increased in North China, creating further conflicts with China and the other powers, particularly Britain.

Potential for full confrontation between Japan and China was building from late 1936 to early 1937. In Japan, the new Hayashi cabinet was formed in February 1937. After the previous Hirota cabinet had tried and failed in negotiations with China, a new and stronger policy towards China was expected. Meanwhile, a united front in China was gradually forming. Until the end of 1936, confrontation between the Guomindang and the Chinese Communist Party (CCP) made a united front against Japanese aggression impossible, despite Japan's increasingly clear intention to extend its rule south of the Great Wall. There was an attempt to make North China autonomous, largely manipulated by the Japanese military. The civil war between the Guomindang and the CCP continued. There were factions within the Guomindang which were strongly against communism, and favoured close cooperation with Japan. After the Xi'an Incident in December 1936, the first step was taken towards a united front between the Guomindang and the CCP, and negotiations continued. This meant not only unity against Japan, but also greater cooperation with the United States and Britain. By the time the Japanese army attacked the Marco Polo Bridge in July 1937, there was the basis for a 'national' front to combat aggression. Efforts to contain the conflict within the area were made by both sides, but soon full-scale confrontation began. It was the beginning of the long Sino-Japanese War.

The Inquiry project and Japanese withdrawal, 1937–9

The Sino-Japanese War strengthened the state orientation of IPR operations. This did not mean the decline of post-League internationalism or a loss of faith in the post-League order at the ISIPR (and the ACIPR), as is often assumed. Rather they became more committed to the order because of intensified Japanese aggression in China. They saw Japanese aggression as a challenge to the order, and the role of the ISIPR as 'defending' it. The Sino-Japanese War also hastened the centralization of IPR operations on the East coast. Regionalist initiatives, which had been evident in the activities of Holland and Lattimore earlier in Carter's administration, disappeared. It was difficult to continue working in wartime China and Japan. Lattimore returned from China to the United States in 1938, and took a post at Johns Hopkins University. He continued to be the editor of *Pacific Affairs* until 1941. Then he was sent by the American government as an adviser to Jiang Jieshi, who headed the Guomindang government. Holland also came back from Shanghai in 1937 and made New York his base, except for a year in Berkeley in 1940/1.

The 'Inquiry' project on the Sino-Japanese War was a clear indication that the IPR aimed to be a think-tank for the state on 'Far Eastern' policies. Works that came out of the project were well received. Their findings were, however, not available until later, and their content is best examined in relation to the IPR conferences of 1942 and 1945 in the Chapter 9. Here, I concentrate on a few issues relevant to the ISIPR's directions and visions for the region: how the project was initiated and how it proceeded; how it resulted in the withdrawal of the JCIPR from the project in 1939; and what were the implications of this development.

Carter initiated the Inquiry soon after the outbreak of the Sino-Japanese War. Initial negotiations proceeded without consulting the JCIPR, which was notified only in early 1938. The JCIPR sought to revise a few crucial points of the proposed project, and negotiations with the ISIPR began. In August 1938, Takayanagi attended a meeting at Lee, Carter's farm house in Massachusetts. In December 1938 – January 1939 Takaki also participated in a meeting at Princeton. Although compromises were made, in July 1939 Takayanagi notified Philip Jessup, professor of international law at Columbia and then Chairperson of the Pacific Council: while the JCIPR would continue to cooperate with the IPR, it would not participate in the Inquiry project, and would conduct an independent study.[69]

This decision did not mean a complete break between the ISIPR and the JCIPR, nor the end of the activities of the JCIPR. Rather the JCIPR considered that this was the only way to continue its affiliation with the IPR.[70] Its withdrawal from other international activities, such as IPR conferences, was not considered inevitable at this stage, either. The JCIPR did not attend the IPR conference or what was termed a study meeting at the end of 1939, for its topic was the Inquiry project. There is no evidence of a decision not to attend later IPR conferences at this stage. JCIPR members probably thought that they would resume conference participation after the end of the Sino-Japanese War, which they hoped would come very soon. Even after 1939, the JCIPR continued to communicate with the ISIPR. They exchanged letters, visitors and staff, including Carter's visit to Tokyo. In early 1941, one JCIPR staff member, Matsuo Matsuhei, was still working as an ISIPR staffer in New York. JCIPR's contributions to IPR's publications also continued. Its independent research project on the Sino-Japanese War was published by the IPR as the Far Eastern Conflict series. Other research by JCIPR members, such as the work on the Japanese mandate in the South Pacific by Yanaihara Tadao was published by the IPR after 1939.

The Japanese government was concerned about the JCIPR's involvement in IPR operations in general, and it watched developments in the Inquiry project closely. As well as contributing to the annual budget of the JCIPR, the Ministry of Foreign Affairs funded Takaki's trip to the United States in December 1939. It also paid the JCIPR's quota for the ISIPR budget in 1938. During the negotiation, correspondence from JCIPR members in the United States came through diplomatic channels.[71] The Ministry, however, left the matter with the JCIPR.

The negotiation took place largely during the first Konoe cabinet, June 1937 to January 1939. Konoe was known for his positive attitudes to the JCIPR and the IPR, and Hirota and Arita, both of whom were supportive of 'cultural diplomacy', held the post of Foreign Minister. Ushiba and Saionji, two main figures in the JCIPR secretariat, also worked for Konoe. This may explain the lack of strong official pressure on the JCIPR to withdraw from IPR operations altogether. Throughout the negotiations, the JCIPR did not see the withdrawal from the project as desirable, and emphasized the merit of maintaining the connection with the IPR. It hoped for a compromise. In the context of the war and Japan's withdrawal from the League, the JCIPR and Konoe, Hirota and Arita might have regarded the IPR as the only organization that provided the occasion for dialogue with the other powers, and possibly China. Withdrawal was not mentioned until December 1938. Even then the JCIPR still considered IPR operations valuable, and instructed Takaki to make the utmost effort to maintain a smooth relationship.[72] When Takayanagi later conveyed the decision to withdraw from the Inquiry, he promised to continue the affiliation and cooperation with the IPR.

In Carter's mind, the Sino-Japanese War had great implications for the IPR. In autumn 1937, only a few months after the war began, he quickly proposed an investigative study on the war, the Inquiry. It was a research project aimed at preparing for a future peace conference. No doubt what Carter had in his mind was Colonel House's 'Inquiry' group at the time of the Paris Peace Conference. The objectives of Carter's Inquiry read:

The purpose of this Inquiry is to relate unofficial scholarship to the problems arising from the present situation in the Far East. Its purpose is to provide members of the Institute in all countries and the members of IPR Conference with an impartial and constructive analysis of the situation in the Far East with a view to indicating the major issues which must be considered in any future adjustment of international relations in that area. To this end, the analysis will include an account of the economic and political conditions which produced the situation existing in July 1937, with respect to China, to Japan, and to the other foreign Powers concerned; an evaluation of developments during the war period ...; and ... an estimate of the principal political, economic, and social conditions which may be expected in a post-war period, the possible forms of adjustment...[73]

This paragraph, which was in the preface to every publication of the Inquiry series, indicates that it was to contribute to policy formulation not only during the war, but also in the postwar reconstruction period. For Carter, the war provided the best opportunity to advance the significance of the IPR.

What was the major reason for the Japanese withdrawal? Was it due to the 'anti-Japanese' bias of Carter and the ISIPR, as some suspected?[74] There were grounds for this judgement, although sentiment against Japanese aggression in China can hardly be viewed as personal prejudice. It represented an attitude common among IPR members and the concerned general public in the United States. Already in 1933, reports of Japanese aggression were changing the views even of those previously regarded as pro-Japan. In January 1933, George Wickersham, who led a movement against anti-Japanese immigrants in the mid-1920s, sent a letter to Carter saying that Japan had 'thrown away the goodwill which she built up among our people'.[75] Wickersham was not a member of the ACIPR, but his view was probably representative of many so-called pro-Japan Americans, who made up a good portion of founding members of the ACIPR. Reports of the Nanjing Massacre in 1937 were the last straw for those, such as Thomas Lamont and Jerome Greene.[76]

As well as pro-Japan Americans, the IPR also included missionary members whose attachment to China was strong. Compassion for China in the United States had existed among certain elite circles especially after 1911, as they saw the new Chinese republic as America's 'sister republic'. This favourable sentiment was strengthened as Japanese aggression progressed. Some ACIPR members had been classmates of the Chinese who were now leading the new, 'young' China. Roger Greene, younger brother of Jerome Greene, and a founding member of the IPR, also became close to many Chinese notables connected with the Guomindang and the IPR, such as Hu Shuxi. Greene worked as director of the China Medical Board funded by the Rockefeller Foundation, and as medical administrator at the Beijing Union Medical College in 1914–35. After returning to the United States in 1935, he began active lobbying for American intervention in China against Japanese aggression, and became one of the founders of the American Committee for Non-Participation in Japanese Aggression (ACNJA) in 1938. Carter and Field joined it. Carter had no missionary experience in China, but had assisted with a mass education movement in China from 1928.[77]

If there was a 'personal' element that contributed to the decision of the JCIPR in 1939, it was the manner in which Carter pursued the 'Inquiry' project. Carter conceived the idea for the Inquiry project in August 1937.[78] He began negotiations with other National Councils, but the JCIPR was not notified until early 1938. In April 1938, Saionji Kinkazu, then Secretary of the JCIPR, complained to Carter that so far there had been no formal consultation with the JCIPR.[79] When, on Carter's instructions, Holland travelled to Japan to inform people there about the project in late 1937, he had a very difficult task. Carter told Holland to suggest the project, but in such a way not to 'alarm them or give too many details'.[80] As a result, JCIPR members had no idea about the main purpose of Holland's visit, let alone the proposed project. This created great mistrust on the part of the JCIPR. To make JCIPR members even more suspicious, in the meeting with Chatham House (RIIA) members in London in August 1938, Takayanagi discovered that Carter had told them that he had already received a favourable response from the JCIPR. It was Carter's way of persuading the very reluctant Chatham House.[81] Having attended further negotiations with the ISIPR and representatives of other National Councils at Princeton at the end of 1938, Takaki complained about Carter's lack of honesty in negotiations.[82]

Although this ill-feeling among JCIPR members must have been a critical factor in their final decision, the conflict between the JCIPR and the ISIPR over the Inquiry had wider implications. The ISIPR regarded Japanese aggression in China as a threat not only to China, but also to the post-League international order. From the time China lodged an appeal at the League of Nations after the Mukden Incident, opposing Japanese aggression meant protecting the League and the post-League order. Stanley Hornbeck, a founding member of the IPR and head of the Far Eastern section (1928–37) and political adviser (1937–44) at the State Department, had been a strong advocate of tough measures against Japan from the very early stages of the Manchurian crisis. His position did not gain strong support at IPR conferences. Nor did the Roosevelt administration take up the position. But the ISIPR was moving closer to it, and individual ACIPR members lobbied for stronger American intervention through other organizations. Newton Baker, Chairperson of the Pacific Council and the ACIPR, for example, was involved in the American Committee on the Far Eastern Crisis. Carter and Field were members of the ACNJA. They saw not only Japan, but also Germany as a 'menace' to the post-League order, and China and Britain as its fortress.[83].

The JCIPR was probably not aware of these developments among key figures at the ISIPR and the ACIPR. They interpreted it as growing 'anti-Japan' sentiment. Yet this was not reason enough for the JCIPR's withdrawal.

Strong criticism of Japanese policies had been evident since 1929. Even when withdrawal of the JCIPR from IPR operations was recommended soon after the Yosemite conference, the JCIPR did not take this step. The ISIPR's anti-Japanese stance may have made the JCIPR more convinced of the importance of its contribution to the Inquiry.

The crux of the negotiations between the JCIPR and the ISIPR was the control of the National Council in the proposed Inquiry. As Lattimore had articulated in the mid-1930s, the basis of a 'national research body' presented problems for 'international' research projects and *Pacific Affairs*. It was even more the case for an 'international' research project on a particular war (the Sino-Japanese War). The biggest objection of the JCIPR to the Inquiry project was what they saw as a lack of control by the National Council (the JCIPR) over the selection of researchers, the content of research and the independence from the 'international' body – the ISIPR.[84] The JCIPR interpreted international research as a federation of 'national' research, not a collection of research free from what Lattimore described as the censorship of National Councils. There was no doubt that the JCIPR considered studies on the Sino-Japanese War important, but they felt that their 'sovereign' right should not have been violated. For JCIPR members, this appeared to be a reasonable post-League internationalists' claim. Only certain Japanese, not even Japanese scholars resident in the United States, could 'explain the Japanese position' adequately. Significantly, the British group, Chatham House members, took a similar view on this issue, and opposed the Inquiry project.[85]

It would be misleading to conclude that Carter pushed a 'transnational' type of research project. While the ISIPR recruited scholars, mainly Americans, to conduct research on various countries, that was not the case for other National Councils. They mainly conducted research on their own government's policies. Eager to preserve the right to control how 'Japanese perspectives and facts' were formed and distributed in an international arena, the JCIPR probably overemphasized the 'transnational' nature of the ISIPR. In fact, National Councils held great, if not absolute, control over the selection of researchers and the content of research on its country.

The JCIPR argued that the Inquiry project betrayed the 'traditions' of IPR research. These 'traditions' referred to three main practices: unofficial studies for IPR conferences; allocation of individual country studies to the relevant National Council; and control of the Pacific Council over the project.[86] For the JCIPR the practice that each National Council took charge of research on its country was well established. It criticized the Inquiry for being an 'official' study in preparation for a governmental conference, and held that the ISIPR, an administrative body dominated by Americans, was assuming policy-making power, instead of the Pacific Council, the executive body of national representatives.

The JCIPR had a point. One of the most significant implications of the proposed Inquiry project was an expansion of the power of the ISIPR, which was virtually synonymous with the ACIPR at this stage. In the IPR's constitution and earlier IPR operations, the ISIPR was defined as an administrative body with no policy-making function. During the negotiations over the details of the Inquiry, the ISIPR emerged as a strong policy-making body. Although the Chairperson of the Pacific Council, first J.W. Dafoe in 1938, then Jessup in 1939–40, had the final say, a formal meeting of the Pacific Council with representatives of National Councils was not held during the negotiation. This was probably deliberate, so that the Japanese representative could not exercise the right of veto. The convention on the veto was changed after the 1939 IPR conference precisely to avoid such an occurrence. Given the fact that the Inquiry was to occupy a significant position in IPR operations in the coming years, ISIPR control of the project meant its greater influence in policy-making not only in administrative matters, but in research projects and conference programming.

Another JCIPR claim was also valid. JCIPR members suspected that the project was Carter's stunt to obtain funding and to salvage ISIPR finances. Previously, as Jerome Greene had clarified, the IPR's budget had been divided between the ISIPR and international research projects. While the latter was well funded due to grants from foundations, particularly the Rockefeller Foundation, the former had constant problems balancing its budget. By making the ISIPR more involved in the Inquiry, Carter made it possible to utilize its funds for administrative purposes. A massive extra grant of around US$90,000 for the Inquiry was reportedly won from the Rockefeller Foundation.[87] The proceedings of 1939 recorded:

> The IPR Inquiry ... was initiated early in 1938 under the direction of the International Secretariat with the aid of a grant from the Rockefeller Foundation.[88]

Although emphasizing the importance of the private capacity of the study, Carter argued that it was useful to the government too. Demonstrating the think-tank nature of the Inquiry, the ISIPR planned the IPR conference of 1939 (on the Inquiry) to be closed to the public and press, and attended by a very small number of specialists.[89] Colonel House had instructions from President Wilson when he formed the first think-tank on foreign policy in the United States. Now Carter took the initiative to promote the IPR to a similar status for a future peace conference, but without any official instructions.

The conference (study meeting) at Virginia Beach in 1939

The 1939 conference (study meeting), which focused on the Inquiry project, defined the future development of IPR conferences as think-tank forums. It discussed mainly security issues, war strategies and postwar reconstruction, and it was not open to the public. It was attended by fewer participants than usual, mainly from the United States, Canada and China, and only a few, almost token, members from Australia, New Zealand and the Philippines. It is best described as a meeting of the inner group of the IPR. Here, the leadership of the ISIPR was clear, demonstrating that the Inquiry project and the Sino-Japanese War advanced the power of the ISIPR within IPR operations.

The JCIPR and Chatham House did not participate. The JCIPR's reason was simple. The meeting planned to focus on the Inquiry project, the format of which it did not agree on. As the JCIPR could veto the Pacific Council decisions under the constitution, it was decided that no formal conference should take place in 1939, hence it was termed a study meeting. Chatham House's non-participation may also have been due to their unhappiness with the general direction of the Inquiry project, but it was more likely because of their urgent concern with the war in Europe. Earlier, in September, Hitler had attacked Poland, marking the beginning of World War II. Although one European group, France, sent two observers, they were based in New York. European members probably felt it impossible to send members.

The meeting largely focused on war strategies (for the Sino-Japanese War) and postwar reconstruction. According to the structure of the Inquiry projects, the discussion was divided into four sections: background to the 'Far Eastern' conflict; the positions of Japan and China; third parties in the 'Far Eastern' conflict; and possibilities for adjustment in the 'Far East'. They laid out various scenarios, depending on which side would win, and spent a great deal of time discussing American policies towards the region. Holland remembered that great attention was also paid to recent developments in Europe.[90]

'Far Eastern' specialists at this meeting regarded Konoe Fumimaro as the key to leading Japan into conflict with the United States and Britain. Konoe formed the first cabinet (June 1937 to January 1939) only a month before the outbreak of the Sino-Japanese War, and declared the New Order in East Asia in late 1938. They saw him as a leader of a political party with fascist tendencies, and his first cabinet as containing much stronger military and other 'extreme nationalist' groups than previous cabinets. In their view, the cabinet would 'pursue an aggressive foreign policy in line with the wishes of the Armed Services'. It would also further the 'Asiatic Monroe Doctrine', 'demanding the elimination of all Western influence from Eastern Asia and the South Seas', and 'bringing all countries in this area under the political and military domination of Japan'. They even predicted Japanese expansion into Southeast Asia and alliance with the Axis powers. There was 'every evidence Japan [would] henceforth adopt a much more aggressive attitude towards Britain and the United States unless these countries [were] willing to acquiesce in her "New Order"'. Konoe and his 'New Order' were, therefore, a challenge to their post-League order, and under Konoe's leadership, confrontation between Japan and the United States and Britain was predicted to be likely.[91]

The JCIPR and the New Order in East Asia

Konoe as a post-League internationalist

Their predictions were right. The policies of Konoe, who formed another two cabinets in the crucial period between June 1940 and October 1941, smoothed the path for wartime mobilization. Japan went to war with the United States in December 1941. In 1945, Konoe was charged with being a war criminal at the Tokyo War Tribunal, and he committed suicide the night before his arrest. Did he really lead the opposition to the post-League order, and did his 'New Order in East Asia' challenge the order, as it was understood in 1939 and 1945? His close connection with the JCIPR, or more precisely with some key JCIPR members in 1938–41, sheds new light on this enigmatic politician.

The previous chapters have demonstrated that it was possible to see Konoe as a post-League internationalist. Despite his strong criticism of the League of Nations in 1918, he was closely involved with post-League internationalist organizations. He became a council member of the Japanese LNA, and he was close to the JCIPR, especially in the 1930s. He shared many ideas with post-League internationalists in Japan and elsewhere. Acutely aware of new democratic trends, he stressed the significance of public opinion in foreign policy-making, and the need for readjustment of the diplomatic machinery. Like Colonel House and members of the IPW, Chatham House, the CFR and the IPR, he felt the need for a think-tank specializing in policy analysis, and recruited non-official 'experts' from the military, universities, business and the press as members of his brains trust.

Konoe had strong faith in the Japanese national polity and the imperial system, and believed in Japan's mission in East Asia. For him, the United States was a privileged power, and one which should understand the needs of the less privileged. Nevertheless, he also regarded the United States as a great power to admire and emulate. He was well attuned to intellectual and political trends in the United States. He sent his son to an American high school and university. His entourage of JCIPR members had close connections with Americans, and were regarded as US 'experts' or 'pro-America'. The America which inspired him was also a changing America. He had been fascinated by New Deal schemes when he visited the United States in 1934.[92] One can easily see a Fascist influence in his policies of giving greater power to the cabinet office and of utilizing non-official 'experts' in policy-making. Yet these moves could also be interpreted as Konoe's attempts to pursue a new political style: the American model from the New Deal era.

Konoe was critical of the dominant interpretation of Japanese politics among 'Far Eastern' specialists whom he met in the United States in 1934 – the pendulum theory that power swung between 'reactionary' nationalists and militarists and 'liberal' internationalists. The reality was far more complex. Soon after the outbreak of the Sino-Japanese War, he set out the policy of his first cabinet. He noted that war was inevitable. Although some Japanese military actions could not be justified, Japan had no choice. If the military had not taken the course they did from 1931, Japan would have lost overseas markets and raw material supplies because of the development of trade blocs, and the foundations of its national economy would have collapsed:

> Of course if one looks at it superficially, the main force in Japanese diplomacy since the Manchurian Incident was the military, and it is true that one can criticize military actions on many accounts. It is understandable that Americans thought that as long as they could suppress the despotic military, Japanese diplomacy would return to its orthodoxy [the cooperative diplomacy], and that they could count on liberal politicians. This is, however, a very superficial view.[93]

In Konoe's view, suppressing the military, as many American experts suggested, would not solve the problem because military actions were expressions of the nation, not the military roping in an unwilling populace. They indicated profound problems in domestic and international politics. Politicians needed to understand and solve these problems. Accordingly, he co-opted and promoted military agendas, but often looked for alternatives to achieve the same outcomes. During his first cabinet, Konoe contributed to the foundation of the Japan Institute in 1938; declared the New Order in East Asia in 1938; and engaged in peace negotiations with China. During his second and third cabinet, he continued negotiations with China, initiated the New Order Movement in Japan and engaged in the last-ditch peace negotiations with the United States, particularly in August–September 1941. In each of these projects, JCIPR members were involved. What follows focuses on his first cabinet and these JCIPR members' involvement.

Konoe and the Japan Institute: international publicist

Konoe had been well aware of the significance of JCIPR members as international publicists or propagandists. In his view, the Sino-Japanese War increased, not decreased, their significance. In the inter-war period, propaganda was seen as important not only for 'fascists' or 'evil nationalists', but by many post-League internationalists. The LNA, which had worldwide membership, adopted propaganda as a legitimate tool to increase support for their agenda, world peace. Recognizing the growing significance of public opinion in international politics, Konoe backed Iwanaga's plea to establish a 'national news agency' and the establishment of the International Culture Promotion Association (ICPA) in 1934, in which he was appointed Chairperson. Despite the facade of ICPA's non-official status, Konoe remained its Chairperson during his premiership.

The prolonged Sino-Japanese War made Konoe and many other like-minded officials and non-officials concerned with Japan's international image. They felt the new need to expand 'cultural' activities, especially in the United States. More than a year after the outbreak of the war, Konoe was keen on justifying and explaining the Japanese position in the war, particularly to influential policy-makers in the United States. With this in mind, but probably with broader motivations to address American 'public opinion', the Japan Institute (*Nihon bunka kaikan*) was founded at the Rockefeller Center in New York in November 1938. Maeda Tamon, one of Nitobe's disciples, key JCIPR member, and commentator at *Asahi* newspaper, was appointed Director. According to Shibasaki, the Konoe government financed the institute. The budget of 400,000 yen came from the Ministry of Foreign Affairs.[94] Almost 10,000 books and materials were brought from Japan, as well as 16-mm films introducing 'Japan'. Demand for these materials in the United States was great. Between ten and thirty requests were recorded daily. The institute continued its activities, and Maeda remained in New York until he was detained on Ellis Island after the Pacific War broke out.

The activities of the Japan Institute were in line with post-League internationalism since the 1920s. Although Maeda noted in his memoirs that the aim was to provide material for serious Japanese studies, not propaganda, he also realized that it was imperative for the Japanese government to improve public opinion about Japan in the United States.[95] These activities were not particular to Japanese post-League internationalists or the Japanese government. Maeda recorded that the model for this institute was the British Council.[96] Its establishment was a response to fierce propaganda competition among the organizations of other countries in New York. There were, thus, 'successful' predecessors before the Japan Institute. It is not hard to imagine that post-League internationalists in various countries, with their ability, experience and connections, were involved in these activities. Certainly, the Japan Institute utilized the JCIPR connection in the United States.[97] It was probably no coincidence that the Institute was housed at the Rockefeller Center. John Rockefeller III, who had attended the IPR conference in Kyoto in 1929, was supportive of the IPR and was involved in the Japan Society in New York. His presence at the opening of the institute indicated his support and perhaps some special office arrangements.

The New Order in East Asia: Konoe's first cabinet and his think-tank

The international and domestic crises enhanced the role of non-officials in policy-making. Roosevelt's brains trust groups for the New Deal schemes demonstrated the point. As Edward Carter had argued, the war enhanced the IPR's significance. While the ISIPR tried to make the IPR a think-tank through the Inquiry project, a parallel was evident at the JCIPR. The often assumed tension between the state and intellectuals was largely absent for both the ISIPR and the JCIPR. The 'Far Eastern Conflict' series was the JCIPR's independent research project on the Sino-Japanese War, and it was published in English by the IPR. The volumes of this series included Rōyama Masamichi's *Foreign Policy of Japan, 1914–1939*, Sassa Hiroshi and Ryū Shintarō's

Recent Political and Economic Developments in Japan, Ozaki Hotsumi's *Sino-Japanese Relations in the Twentieth Century*, Miki Kiyoshi and Hosokawa Karoku's *Introductory Studies on the Sino-Japanese Conflict*. They were all members of Konoe's think-tank, *Showa kenkyūkai*, and Rōyama, Miki and Ozaki were regarded as the three key architects of the concept of the East Asia Cooperative Body (*Tōa kyōdōtai*), an intellectual base of the New Order in East Asia.

Konoe's first cabinet proposed this New Order in East Asia in late 1938. JCIPR members were involved as think-tank members, and also as non-official negotiators of peace with China within this regional vision. Was this New Order in East Asia a challenge to the post-League international order, as understood at the IPR conference in 1939? How were JCIPR members utilized, and did their vision present a critical alternative to colonialism and military aggression? What was their relationship with the state?

Konoe, the JCIPR and Showa kenkyūkai

The nature of Konoe's think-tank group and its relationship with the JCIPR and Konoe need to be clarified first. Rōyama, Ozaki, Miki (1897–1945), Ushiba Tomohiko, Sanonji Kinkazu and Matsumoto Shigeharu were all members of *Showa kenkyūkai*. While they were involved in the JCIPR, the nature and extent of their involvement in the JCIPR varied greatly. Rōyama was a founding member of the JCIPR. Although he attended only two conferences, in 1927 and 1929, and his main activity base was not the JCIPR, he remained as a JCIPR member. He also made valuable contributions to JCIPR's research projects. Ushiba's connection with the JCIPR began after the Banff conference (1933). By 1936, he was Secretary of the JCIPR section within the JIA. Like Ushiba, Saionji's main contribution to the JCIPR was in administration. He joined the JCIPR at the time of the Yosemite conference, and he was Secretary of the JCIPR in 1937–8. Although Matsumoto's involvement in the JCIPR dated from 1929, and he participated in the IPR conference in 1931, he had known key IPR figures, such as Takaki, Maeda and Tsurumi since the mid-1920s. He also knew Rōyama well when they set up the TIPER (Tokyo Institute of Political and Economic Research) in 1930. Because he was in Shanghai in 1932–8, his involvement in the JCIPR and *Showa kenkyūkai* became active only after 1939. Ozaki's and Miki's involvement in the JCIPR was mainly through their research and *Showa kenkyūkai*. Although Ozaki attended the 1936 Yosemite conference and became very close to Ushiba and Saionji, whether he was actually a JCIPR member is unclear. The JCIPR recognized Ozaki and Miki's expertise on China, and they asked them to contribute to the Far Eastern Conflict series.

Although they belonged to the closely knit elite expert groups based in Tokyo, it is still not possible to see them as a coherent group with a coherent view and ideology. They were left-leaning, and except Ozaki, they were counter- or anti-Marxist. Many would have been called *kakushinha* (statist reformists) a group Konoe was seen as being close to until 1940. The nature of their ideology, however, varied so greatly that it makes the label 'leftist' meaningless. What connected them were the high social status of their families, their elite education and/or elite position as professionals. The Saionji and Konoe families, both aristocratic, knew each other well. Matsumoto came from the family of a notable Meiji politician, and Ushiba from an affluent family. Ushiba and Saionji studied together at Oxford, and Matsumoto and Ushiba were classmates of Ozaki at *Ichikō*. Rōyama was also a graduate of *Ichikō* and the Tokyo Imperial University where he taught. Miki had a slightly different background as he was a graduate of Kyoto Imperial University. He taught at Hōsei University briefly before he was arrested in 1930 for his alleged donations to the Japanese Communist Party. As he was banned from the public office after this, his writing career took place outside academic institutions. His works on philosophy were highly regarded among intellectual elites as original and ground-breaking.

Konoe was the magnet which connected them. Ushiba was private secretary to Konoe during all his prime ministerial terms. Ozaki was a cabinet adviser to Konoe in July 1938 to January 1939. Saionji was seconded as *shokutaku* to the Ministry of Foreign Affairs for two years from November 1934 and in August 1940 to November 1941 (during Konoe's second and third cabinets). He also worked at the cabinet office as *shokutaku* in August–October 1941, with particular responsibility for peace negotiations with the United States.[98] Matsumoto was involved with the peace negotiations with China while he was in Shanghai in 1937–8. During Konoe's second cabinet, he became close to Konoe in his capacity as an expert on the United States. Rōyama, who was a core member in *Showa kenkyūkai* since its inception, was regarded as an influential adviser to Konoe. Although Miki had been a member of *Showa kenkyūkai* since 1937, the talk he gave in July 1938, 'The meaning of the China Incident [Sino-Japanese War] in world history' (Shina jihen no sekaishiteki igi), greatly influenced views about the Sino-Japanese War among the members, and he began to be regarded as an ideologue of *Showa kenkyūkai*.[99]

With the exception of Miki, they were all members of the Breakfast Society (*Asameshikai*), Konoe's entourage (*sokkin*). It started in November 1937 during the first Konoe cabinet, and its object was to discuss policy issues and to advise Konoe. Konoe himself occasionally joined the meetings. They took place at the Prime Minister's official residence while he was Prime Minister, and after Ozaki became a cabinet adviser in mid-1938 they were held fortnightly. They continued even during the break between the first and second Konoe cabinets, and lasted until Ozaki was arrested on an espionage charge in October 1941.[100]

The closeness between Konoe and these *Showa kenkyūkai* members did not mean that they had a disproportionate influence in Konoe's policies. He cultivated specialists from diverse fields, and listened to a range of views of many groups and individuals. *Showa kenkyūkai* members were important, but the group was one of many. Konoe was a young politician with ideals and vision. His mind and power inspired, excited and attracted people from all walks of life with diverse motivations, ideologies and political inclinations.[101] The fact that these Konoe's retinue included key JCIPR figures did not mean great political influence for the JCIPR either. It simply meant that the ability, aptitude and background required to be a JCIPR member were more likely to be found in this elite male circle than in other parts of society. Konoe was close to them and had enough insight to utilize them.

Despite his position close to the Emperor, his charisma and the fact that he served as Prime Minister three times in 1937–41, whether Konoe had ultimate policy-making power is also doubtful. Like military officers and bureaucrats, Konoe wanted to fill a power vacuum created by the decline of political parties. He expanded the power of Prime Minister and that of the cabinet office by restructuring and enlarging their functions. To strengthen its policy-making capability, he created the *Kikakuin* (Cabinet Planning Board) in October 1937, which combined the Resource Bureau and the Planning Agency.[102] He used non-bureaucrats extensively, including private secretaries and cabinet advisers, and allowed non-official 'experts' to influence policy more than before. Yet he, his cabinet office and his 'experts' were but one force competing for influence in policy-making. Other forces, such as various factions within the military and the bureaucracy – the true 'experts' according to E.H. Carr – remained formidable. They often blocked policies proposed by Konoe's think-tank members, and these members felt Konoe was too weak to push their policies.

The nature of the New Order in East Asia

Eighteen months had passed since the outbreak of the Sino-Japanese War when the first Konoe cabinet issued the declaration of the New Order in East Asia on 3 November 1938. This was further elaborated in another declaration of 22 December. The latter was more detailed with specific policies, and further clarified the nature of the New Order. It is significant that Konoe's vision of the New Order only came into being in the process of serious re-evaluation of the Japanese policy towards China to break the deadlock of the Sino-Japanese War. Although there were attempts by Konoe to contain the war in its initial stage, Usui argues that he and then Foreign Minister Hirota positively backed military actions in China in the latter half of 1937. These military actions extended the Japanese occupation and advanced its exclusive economic rights in China.[103] Further reducing the prospects of peace negotiations, in January 1938, Konoe declared that the Japanese government would not negotiate with the Jiang Jieshi government. Soon, however, Konoe realized the war was not proceeding the way he expected, and he needed to revise the China policy. In May, Konoe reshuffled the cabinet, and appointed Ugaki Kazushige as Foreign Minister. Ugaki, military general and former Minister of the Military, had supported disarmament in 1930, and was known as pro-Anglo-American and close to big business. Konoe consulted his think-tank members on formulating a new policy towards China, and proceeded with the peace negotiations with pro-Japan and anti-communist factions of the Guomindang.

Ozaki, Miki, Rōyama, Ushiba, Saionji and Matsumoto welcomed this new development. While Ushiba, Saionji and Matsumoto were involved in peace negotiations with China, Ozaki, Miki and Rōyama now had a great opportunity to influence new policy. They vigorously presented their vision for East Asia both as think-tank members and in public forums. They were members of *Showa kenkyūkai*, and close to the policy-making process. Rōyama was a key adviser to Konoe. The November and December declarations were the result of this re-evaluation process and written in relation to the ongoing peace negotiation, the details of which, especially the nature of JCIPR members' involvement, will be assessed in Chapter 9. The November declaration read:

> Now under the authority of the Emperor, our Imperial Army and Navy … took control of major parts of China. … As long as the Nationalist government persists in an anti-Japanese policy, and cooperates with communists, the Japanese empire will fight with China to the death. What the Japanese empire desires is the construction of the new order which would secure eternal stability in East Asia. This is the ultimate goal of this war. The core of this new order is the establishment of mutual relationships between Japan, Manchuria and China in political, economic, cultural and other domains. On this basis, it plans to establish *international justice*, to mount a joint defence against communism, and to realize the creation of a new cultural and economic unity. The Japanese empire wishes China to take part in this project. It hopes that the Chinese people will understand our true intentions and cooperate with us. If the Nationalist government abandons its previous policies and reorganizes its personnel effectively and cooperates, the Japanese empire will not reject it. The empire also does not doubt that the other powers will understand its intentions and that they will adjust to the new situation in East Asia. It deeply appreciates the goodwill which the powers have shown towards us in the past. [emphasis added][104]

What potential did this New Order have? As 'Far Eastern' specialists assessed at an IPR meeting in 1939, Miwa Kimitada regards it as the first official statement of Asianist thinking in Japanese foreign policy[105] – a view accepted by many scholars. They see it as an assertion of the Japanese Asian Monroe Doctrine and a challenge to the other powers. Iriye, however, points out that Konoe's New Order in East Asia had a universalist aspect, and contained Wilsonian ideas. This is a theme he furthers in an analysis of Japanese and American policies in 1943–5.[106]

Konoe inherited his father's Asianism. He valued and nurtured *Tōa dōbun kai*, the East Asia Common Culture Association, which his father, Atsumaro, founded in 1898. Konoe was Chairperson from 1922 until just before its dissolution in 1945.[107] Ozaki saw a revival of the idealistic element of Atsumaro's Asianism in the November declaration.[108] *Tōa dōbun kai* established an educational institution, *Tōa dōbun shoin* or the East Asia Common Culture Academy in China in 1901. Its students (Japanese) were schooled in Atsumaro's style of Asianism, and upon graduation they were recruited into a wide range of organizations connected to China, including officialdom in Manchuguo and at the Japanese Ministry of Foreign Affairs. Konoe reportedly chose the draft of Nakayama Yū (1895–1973), a 1918 graduate of *Tōa dōbun shoin*, for the December declaration,[109] despite the fact he had also asked Ushiba, Matsumoto and Ozaki to prepare a draft.[110] Miwa argues that Konoe made this choice because he thought Nakayama's nativist and Asianist tone would have an emotional appeal.[111]

The government, however, did not accept all Asianist thinking. Like socialist and communist organizations, the 'subversive' elements of Asianist organizations were severely checked by the authority.[112] The acceptable Asianism of *Tōa dōbunkai* had to blend in with the policy outlines discussed at the Imperial Conference (*Gozen kaigi*) on 30 November 1938.[113] The visions of *Showa kenkyūkai*, which influenced a theoretical framework of the New Order in East Asia, overlapped substantially with that of *Tōa dōbunkai*. This meant not only the strength of Asianist thinking at *Showa kenkyūkai*, but also the dominance of post-League internationalist thinking among so-called Asianists at *Tōa dōbunkai*. The above November declaration reflected this, especially in the attitudes towards the great powers. The December declaration also did not restrict the interests of third powers in China. Although often understood as a challenge to the post-League order, the New Order in East Asia in 1938 was not necessarily confrontational to the great powers.

The New Order declaration can be understood as not so much as a challenge to the powers as a way of winning their approval. As JCIPR members had been attempting to do since the 1920s, Konoe tried to explain the Japanese case in a post-League internationalist framework. When Konoe visited the United States in 1934, he recognized that new and clear principles in East Asia needed to be established. This would clarify the wrongs of the American approach (the Washington Treaties and other international conventions). Some Americans he met suggested to him that without these principles negotiations between Japan and the United States would be difficult.[114] These principles needed to be written in a language and framework which American foreign policy specialists could understand. It is reasonable to assume that his declaration was an attempt to clarify these new principles to the other powers, especially to the United States, as well as to China. Tobe argues that Japanese diplomacy in this period emphasized the moral aspect to appease American foreign policy-makers, because Japanese officials thought 'humanitarian moral principles' drove American foreign policy.[115] This suggests that the moral and nativist tone of the New Order declaration was not exactly an adaptation of 'traditional' Asianist thinking. Rather it was a deliberate and tactical reinvention of 'Japanese' or 'Asian' morality in an American style.

Was Konoe's New Order in East Asia merely the rhetoric of aggression and exploitation, or did it present any positive potential? The more elaborated December declaration proposed to China friendly relations; cooperative defence against communism; economic cooperation; no request for compensation of land or money; respect for Chinese sovereignty; and no restriction on the interests of third powers in China. As Matsumoto recorded, it did not include the withdrawal of Japanese troops – the most important condition for the Chinese, who wanted an early peace. Nevertheless, it challenged the dominant view and conduct of international politics in one respect: it made a gesture towards achieving a more equal relationship with China. It was the first proposal for the abolition of extraterritorial rights among the powers – a point China had been arguing for some time. Although this policy won support among certain military factions in Japan, hardliners severely attacked it as a great 'compromise' of Japanese interests.

Was this proposal for a more equal relationship with China based on Konoe's genuine concern with the principles of international justice? The November declaration certainly noted that the New Order in East Asia was based on this sense of international justice. Konoe had expressed this concern first in 1918, and restated it in 1933. Despite a greater emphasis on East Asia in 1938, an article which was probably originally written in the summer of 1937 demonstrates that this notion of 'international justice' still preoccupied him. The mission of his current cabinet (the first cabinet) was to reconcile the conflicts between opposing forces. One of the most serious conflicts was that between the 'haves' and the 'have nots'. 'The guiding ideology of political leaders should be to achieve justice in international and domestic politics.'[116]

On the other hand, Konoe did not propose the New Order until 1938. If the Japanese military had scored decisive victories before then, he might not have needed it. In 1918, he was concerned with international justice for Japan, not for China or colonies in Asia. In 1938, despite the 'concessions' he made to China, Japan's superior status to China and its regional leadership was not questioned. The Japanese invasion of North China and the puppet regime, Manchuguo, were *faits accomplis*, and Chinese resistance movements were largely dismissed. Konoe's New Order, therefore, can be understood as a combination of his post-League internationalism and shrewd war strategy. The issues of an equal relationship with China and the abolition of extraterritorial rights of the powers in China soon would become crucial during the Pacific War. Towards the end of 1942, a moral emphasis resurfaces in the Japanese war ideology, the Greater East Asian Co-prosperity Sphere. Like Konoe's New Order, Japanese political leaders probably were concerned not so much with justice for China as with the fact that Japan was losing the war. It was imperative to gain its support.

Theorizing the New Order in East Asia: Rōyama and Miki

Rōyama, Miki and Ozaki were regarded as the three key architects of the East Asia Cooperative Body, and the intellectual base of the New Order in East Asia. They adopted Euro-American scholarly frameworks, formulated Japanese policies and presented them to the other powers. It is significant that the JCIPR chose their works to be published in the IPR's Far Eastern Conflict series. Their work and actions illuminated both the potential and the danger of 'non-official' experts on international affairs and public intellectuals in a war context.

Baba argues that *Showa kenkyūkai* did not formulate policy alternatives. Rather they rationalised and justified established policies and 'facts'.[117] This is a significant point, as the loss of a critical capability could easily happen to any think-tank, including all National Councils of the IPR in this period. Rōyama, Miki and even communist Ozaki demonstrated this danger. Their works were not merely academic explorations of new concepts. They were profoundly conscious of their role as Konoe's think-tank and 'public' intellectuals. Soon after the November declaration of the New Order, Rōyama and Ozaki noted that it was their role to *give meaning* to the policies and the events of the day. Miki shared this sense of purpose.[118]

Miki is better known as a martyr of freedom. His academic career suffered due to his support for the Japanese Communist Party. He defended his socialist friends and died in prison soon after the end of the Pacific War. Miki's activities at *Showa kenkyūkai* illuminate another aspect of his work and actions. Shimizu sees this positively: 'In a time when silence was the only means of resistance against the war', Miki was 'contemptuous of those who kept silent'.[119] Takaki, a long-time JCIPR member, who maintained his silence during the war, suggested later that this difference was due to ideology. He was not actively involved with *Showa kenkyūkai* (he was a member) because of his dislike of its statist reformist orientation.[120] What should be stressed here, however, is the lack of tension between the state and intellectuals or experts whose sense of a mission for the state/empire was strong and whose aspirations for political influence was great. This inclination had been apparent even at the height of the cooperative policy in the 1920s. In the 1930s, these intellectuals clustered around the JCIPR or *Showa kenkyūkai*, in which Miki and Rōyama played a prominent role.

As Baba noted, involvement of these experts in state policy formulation meant the danger, not just of accepting *faits accomplis*, but of *justifying* them. The object of Miki's work, 'The meaning of the China Incident in world history', was precisely that. The most significant point Miki achieved in this article was that he consciously *gave* a positive meaning to the seemingly futile war. He argued that this war was meaningful because it was an inevitable and significant process of developing a new ideology. The new ideology would break the impasse of the current system and ideologies, such as capitalism, liberalism, communism and fascism. Japan had a mission to create this ideology, and this would become the basis of the unified East/Orient (*Tōyō*).[121]

Miki further developed and extended the main points in 'Shin Nihon no shisō genri' (Ideological principle of new Japan). To achieve this Japanese mission, a new Japan, based on the new order, was needed, and it would be the basis of the unified *Tōyō*.[122] The core of the new ideology for this new Japan and the newly unified *Tōyō* would be the ideal of the cooperative body (*kyōdōtai rinen*).[123] This was regarded as a leading tenet of *Showa kenkyūkai*, and became the basis for the concept of the East Asia Cooperative Body. Here, as with New Liberalism, the emphasis was on the public interest of the community as a whole.[124]

There was some potential for their concept of the East Asia Cooperative Body to challenge dominant ideologies of the time. For example, Miki questioned the Eurocentricity of the concept of *sekai*, the world. Furthermore, Miki reversed the view, which had been dominant among intellectual elites since Meiji, the 'Western' superiority over the 'East', and Japanese identification with the 'West', not the 'East'. The view was common among JCIPR members, especially in the 1920s. In contrast, Miki identified Japan with the 'East', and argued the case of 'Eastern' superiority to the 'West'.[125]

Rōyama followed a similar line of argument in 'The theory of the East Asia Cooperative Body', published in September 1938. Miki's influence was apparent. Rōyama saw the Sino-Japanese War as the awakening of the 'East' (*Tōyō*), as well as recognition of the 'East' by the 'world' or the 'West': 'It is impossible to [acknowledge the existence of the East] if one thinks that Europe is the world, and that European culture is the world culture.' He further argued that the League of Nations was an embodiment of this dominant ideology of the 'West'. It was this domination by the 'Western' powers that had diminished the potential of the League and caused the current war among the nations in the 'East'.[126]

In this critical exercise, they redefined Asia, the Orient, the East and Japan with strong political agendas. Although extensively utilizing the work of European scholars, they were conscious of their action in creating a new concept of Asia and Japan. For them, the 'East' *did not exist* as a coherent entity, and its unifying factors *needed to be invented and created*. Miki stated that he *gave a new meaning* to the concepts of the Orient, Japanism (*Nihon shugi*) and cooperative body. If contemporary intellectuals had not supplied new meanings, the 'old' words would have lost their relevance in the current context.[127] Rōyama also argued that 'the new ideal of the East is not out there as the basis of the new order, but it will be created as the process of the rationalization of the current war'.[128] Unlike Miki, however, Rōyama emphasized 'scientific' and 'logical' factors to unite the region. He argued that culture and nature were not enough. The consciousness of regional destiny (*raumsschicksal*) – the recognition of the common destiny of the region, a prominent concept of the German school of geopolitics – was needed to achieve a regional community.[129] He did not use 'race' or 'culture' in his argument because of his experience in the United States in 1934. Then he realized these concepts were inadequate in justifying Japanese actions in China to the American specialists he met.[130]

Despite their critical stance towards European dominance, including European colonialism in the region, however, the new concepts of Asia/Orient/East, Japan or the East Asia Cooperative Body were designed to justify Japanese colonialism in the region. They worked hard to differentiate Japanese actions from those of 'Western' imperialism. Rōyama argued that the East Asia Cooperative Body should be a federal system with a degree of autonomy. Under the system, mutuality in decision-making would be achieved, national and cultural difference would be respected and living standards would be improved.[131] Miki also argued that the East Asia Cooperative Body could be achieved only by the realization of commonality of Japanese and Chinese culture, and Japan should not obstruct the Chinese movement from uniting China.[132]

Miki and Rōyama did not doubt the leading position of Japan in Asia. Miki stated that Japan had a special mission to lead the order.[133] For Rōyama too, there was no question about leadership.[134] It must have been obvious to them that the Chinese people were fighting not only for the unity of China, but against this Japanese 'leadership'. Furthermore, although the cooperative body emphasized individuality and mutuality, the unity of the whole and the interests of the whole were more highly valued. According to this logic, nationalism in each nation should be restricted to achieve the greater good of the whole.[135]

Communist vision for East Asia: Ozaki

Ozaki joined *Showa kenkyūkai* in 1937, and was asked to become a cabinet adviser (*Naikaku shokutaku*) to the first Konoe cabinet in July 1938. It was the time when Konoe was exploring the possibilities of extricating itself from the Sino-Japanese War. By then, Ozaki, a journalist with the newspaper *Tokyo asahi*, was a well-known China specialist. He had established a close relationship with Konoe's private secretary, Ushiba, and another of Konoe's circle, Saionji, through the IPR conference at Yosemite in 1936. As a leading expert, Ozaki regularly discussed current issues with Miki, Rōyama, Ushiba and Saionji. Despite his communist background, they had much in common. Ozaki belonged to the national elite. A graduate of *Ichikō* and Tokyo Imperial University, he had a successful career with a top newspaper. Like Miki and Rōyama, Ozaki recognized his mission as one of the national elite and as a public intellectual. The New Order of Konoe was an expression of a basic direction for a new policy towards China, but it was his *duty* and that of other intellectuals to formulate its concrete policies.[136] Like Miki and Rōyama, Ozaki accepted as *faits accomplis* the establishment of Manchuguo and the outcome of the Sino-Japanese War to date. He was also clear about Japanese leadership in the East Asia Cooperative Body. He emphasized the 'semi-feudal' and semi-colonial aspects of China,[137] displaying his own hierarchical view towards China.

Although he sounded hopeful that the East Asia Cooperative Body would provide an alternative to Japanese colonial rule in China,[138] whether he genuinely believed this is doubtful. Rather than simply accepting government policies, he presented rare criticism. How did he escape the danger of the co-option? First, as a correspondent in China in 1928–32, he had an unusually extensive exposure to the situation in China, and he understood the nature of nationalism in China. He argued that even if Japan won this war, the issue of nationhood (*minzoku*) would remain a great problem for Japanese rulers. Protracted war experience should have taught the Japanese that military force alone would not conquer Chinese nationalism. Effective management of the East Asia Cooperative Body would require recognition of and active cooperation with the Chinese people.[139] This was a convincing argument against military aggression and a colonial relationship.

Second, Ozaki's critical analysis was based on specifics, which led him to scrutinize the highly ideological rhetoric of 'culture' and 'race'. He argued that the East Asia Cooperative Body should not be too ideological but should be more concrete.[140] Its purpose should be increased production in East Asia, a contribution to the liberation and the welfare of the nations currently under semi-colonial rule.[141] Third, Ozaki's argument was based on a Marxist critique of capitalism and imperialism. While Rōyama also emphasized non-culture and non-race elements as the base of the cooperative body, he deployed geopolitical theory, the 'scientific' camouflage of Nazi ideology. Ozaki used Marxist analysis, although he modified the Marxist framework in order to make sense of his observations and experience. Lastly, in contrast to many left-leaning, yet counter-socialist think-tank members whose goal was reform and ultimately the preservation of the national polity, Ozaki wanted a region-wide communist revolution. Baba argues that this clear goal prevented him from rationalizing current events and policies. His New Order was a regional communist federation, which communist Japan would lead.[142] His wish was partially realized after the end of the Pacific War, although its leader was not Japan. In the early 1940s, however, Ozaki was an isolated case,[143] and he was executed in 1944.

Did those who regarded themselves as 'liberal', elite, non-official experts on international affairs have the alternative of becoming an effective critical force against military aggression and the state/empire in the war context? Were their choices constrained by the threat of coercion or death?[144] Was the only alternative communist revolution in Japan and the region? How viable were these options? To what extent can later generations accuse those who did not take up these options, if indeed they were available? It is easy for later scholars to condemn, but this right should probably be reserved for those who took a stand in the face of significant risks in the context of wartime mobilization. What one can do now, however, is to scrutinize the process in which many, including so-called 'liberals', were virtually willingly to be co-opted into state/imperial agendas and its apparatus.

What emerges from an examination of the JCIPR and *Showa kenkyūkai* is that the assumed oppositional position between 'liberals' or even 'socialists' and the state misses a crucial point. It is true that *Showa kenkyūkai* displayed left-leaning inclinations. Its members included many former socialists, and its economic measures were often described as 'red' by the business sector. Yet this leftist element did not challenge the state,[145] but rather enhanced its power. Although Konoe and his think-tank members referred to social justice for the underprivileged, their priority was the preservation of the imperial system and the national polity.[146]

'Non-official' think-tank members of *Showa kenkyūkai* did not need to be coerced or pressured to conform to the statist/imperial discourse. A crisis, such as war, provided them with all the opportunity they wanted, and they utilized the opportunity as much as Konoe used them. Was this action peculiar to Japanese post-League internationalists? We move now to an analysis of the ISIPR and IPR conferences during the Pacific War and World War II, and the answer seems to be a clear no.

9 Redefining the international order

The Pacific War and the IPR, 1940–5

The IPR was at the height of its political influence during the Pacific War. The war strengthened existing trends within its operations – state orientation and world focus. The JCIPR did not attend the conferences in 1942 and 1945, and as a result they became a think-tank forum for the Allied countries. Discussion was addressed to policy-makers, covered mainly security issues and the press was shut out. As in Japan, the Allied states co-opted IPR activities. In most cases, coercion was not necessary. IPR members took up service for the state with enthusiasm, excitement and a sense of mission, or they willingly worked closely with their governments. Their regional expertise was vital, not only in the task of winning the war, but also in postwar reconstruction.

World War II heightened enthusiasm for Wilsonian ideas.[1] The Atlantic Charter of August 1941 was almost a restatement of Wilsonian principles – self-determination, the Open Door policy, disarmament and economic cooperation. It was, however, a reworking of Wilsonian principles. It reflected the mentality of the New Deal era, as shown by its enhanced concern with social security.[2] It was also a very effective wartime ideology. It portrayed a black and white picture of the 'good, democratic, and internationalist West' (which obviously did not include Italy and Germany) and the 'bad, totalitarian, and nationalistic' Japanese, Italian and German fascists and imperialists. Roosevelt might have seen these restated Wilsonian ideals as an expression of the American ideals of freedom and democracy, and the United States resuming global leadership in the redefined international order. The ISIPR fully endorsed the Charter and tried to apply it to the postwar order in the Pacific region.

Konoe and the JCIPR, 1940–1

Like the ISIPR and other National Councils, the JCIPR further strengthened its state orientation and its role as a think-tank in this period. This had been evident during Konoe's first cabinet (June 1937 to January 1939), which overlapped with the Sino-Japanese War. Konoe continued to utilize JCIPR members in his later cabinets, the second in July 1940 to July 1941 and the third in July 1941 to October 1941. In this critical period leading to the Pacific

War, Konoe remained central in Japanese politics, closely connected to the government even between his first and second cabinet. Hiranuma Kiichirō, Abe Nobuyuki and Yonai Mitsumasa, prime ministers from January 1939 to July 1940, largely implemented policies Konoe had initiated. National mobilization for the war effort was furthered, Japanese occupation in China extended and the southward advance began. What were the roles of JCIPR members during Konoe's second and third cabinets?

New Order Movement in Japan (Shin taisei undō) in 1940

Konoe attempted to restructure the government machinery. *Showa kenkyūkai* members, including some JCIPR members, saw it as a great opportunity to increase their influence, and were actively involved in policy formulation. This advanced the co-option of non-official experts into the state apparatus. As the Sino-Japanese War developed, Konoe and his think-tank members felt the need to expand the power of the prime minister and the cabinet office. The cabinet office would have a number of brains trust bureaus (general affairs, planning and information) directly under it, where think-tank members would be utilized. Existing ministerial departments would be restructured under these bureaus.[3] Accordingly, *Kikakuin* (The Cabinet Planning Board) was established in October 1937. Its core members were from *Showa kenkyūkai*. The Cabinet Information Committee (*Naikaku jōhō iinkai*) became the Department of Information (*Naikaku jōhōbu*) (within the cabinet office) in September 1937, and then was elevated to the Bureau of Information (*Naikaku jōhōkyoku*) in December 1940. The bureau consolidated information gathering and propaganda activities which had so far been carried out independently by various ministries. It eventually became the central organ to control the press, and to suppress freedom of thought during the Pacific War. It was part of the state apparatus to which JCIPR members and other post-League internationalists were co-opted.

Konoe recruited members of *Showa kenkyūkai* and the JCIPR to his cabinet office during his terms. Since 1919, he had believed that non-official experts should be utilized in officialdom. Ushiba became Konoe's private secretary, and Ozaki and Saionji were recruited as *shokutaku* for the cabinet office. This *shokutaku* system, which had existed as a means to employ non-bureaucrats, was used to inject non-official 'experts'. It was open to non-bureaucrats whose expertise was seen as useful, and connections must have been a great advantage. Konoe's attempts met strong opposition from the bureaucracy and the military. When Saionji was employed as a *shokutaku* for the cabinet office in August 1941, the army and the Ministry of Foreign Affairs expressed great discontent. Konoe had to argue against Tōjō Hideki, then Army Minister, that unlike other ministers, the Prime Minister did not have staff to assist him, and it was natural that he would use trusted friends in this role.[1]

Konoe advanced domestic reforms after the declaration of the New Order in East Asia in late 1938. The November declaration clearly stated that domestic reforms were the basis of this regional order:

The Japanese empire will pursue various necessary domestic reforms, strengthen national power and achieve this goal [of the New Order in East Asia] against all odds.[5]

This was also the point which Miki, Rōyama and Ozaki all argued for their conception of the East Asia Cooperative Body. The New Order Movement (*Shin taisei undō*) of 1940 was initiated with this objective. In June 1940, Konoe resigned from the chair of the Privy Council to instigate the movement. Members of *Showa kenkyūkai*, such as Rōyama and Ozaki, were asked to formulate the structure of the movement. The Breakfast Society mediated between these planners and Konoe. Although those who sent their plans to Konoe naturally felt that their ideas defined the policy, it is not clear how influential each plan was and who was most influential. There were simply many 'think-tanks'. Nevertheless, they more or less agreed that the New Order Movement aimed to establish a national organization (*kokumin soshiki*) which would consolidate the power of the people. Konoe, its leader, needed to be a layperson as it was meant to be a people's movement. Less than a month later, however, he was pressured to form a cabinet, and he became Prime Minister. Despite this, the New Order Movement continued, with Konoe's leadership intact. In October 1940, it achieved its ultimate goal, the formation of the 'people's association', the Imperial Rule Assistance Association or the IRAA (*Taisei yokusankai*), and Konoe became its president. *Showa kenkyūkai* was dissolved around the same period.

What was the nature of this domestic reform which Konoe and *Showa kenkyūkai* members envisaged as the basis for the New Order in East Asia? How did they see their role as 'non-official' experts? For them, the IRAA had merits not only for the state, but also for the population. The state would be able to implement 'bold' policies with greater popular support which the IRAA could consolidate. Given the decline of political parties, this consolidated popular will might, they hoped, counterbalance the power of the military.[6] On the other hand, the IRAA would provide a channel for the population to influence policy-making. Those who were envisaged as the IRAA's major components were not politicians, but middle-ranking members of guilds and unions, members of youth associations and non-political organizations, and reformist (*kakushin*) parties. With Prime Minister Konoe as its head, it quickly became a most powerful political organization. Major political parties, *Seiyūkai* and *Minseitō*, as well as the non-propertied parties, quickly dissolved themselves, and joined the IRAA. Furthermore, because it aimed to be a 'grass roots' organization, its control was extended into people's lives. As a result, it prompted greater national mobilization, by consolidating diverse forces for the war effort. Many members of *Showa kenkyūkai* who were involved in the New Order Movement stressed that this was not their initial intention, but the result of military pressure.[7] Yet Rōyama himself admitted not only that the military was far more influential than *Showa kenkyūkai*, but also that even the initial agendas of *Showa kenkyūkai* were not in opposition to those of the military.[8]

These 'non-official' think-tank members shared a vision of radical statist reforms with some military officers.[9] This was a reason for critics to see 'red' elements in *Showa kenkyūkai* and its policies. They attacked that the IRAA challenged the Emperor's power, and therefore, was unconstitutional.[10] *Showa kenkyūkai*'s economic policies also promoted a state-controlled economy, and stressed the 'public responsibility' of private companies at an expense of 'private profit'.[11] Big business attacked these policies as 'red'. These 'left' inclinations among Konoe's think-tank members began to be severely checked by the strengthened national security law in 1941. Six bureaucrats were arrested on an espionage charge in the Cabinet Planning Board Incident in March 1941, and five were former *Showa kenkyūkai* members.[12] The arrest of Ozaki as a communist spy in relation to the Sorge Incident in October 1941 further shocked Konoe. Ozaki was a member of *Showa kenkyūkai* and had been his cabinet adviser. Konoe himself was interrogated by the police, and his cabinet resigned the day after Ozaki's arrest. Konoe became increasingly sceptical about *kakushinha* or statist reformists, and more and more concerned with a communist threat to the national polity.[13]

Showa kenkyūkai members were influenced not only by Marxism, but by fascist thinking.[14] Nazi Germany was revered, and it was Japan's ally. It is, however, worth noting that, like Thomas Green, these statist reformists or *kakushin* groups felt that the state needed to play a central role in the crisis period. Its power needed to be centralized and strengthened. Just as they did not problematize their service to the state, neither did they see greater state intervention as problematic. The effect was double-edged. On the one hand, organizations such as the IRAA enhanced state control of society, and people's freedom was severely restricted. At the same time, social welfare was a significant issue for the wartime state. The Ministry of Welfare was established, and various social welfare schemes for national insurance, and protection of maternity and workers' rights were promoted.

JCIPR members and non-official diplomacy

Konoe also used JCIPR members in two major peace negotiations during his terms of office: negotiations with China in 1937–41 and with the United States in late August in 1941. After briefly describing the processes of these negotiations, I will examine the role of these JCIPR members. Here, the main objective is not to stress their significance, but to scrutinize the nature and implications of non-official involvement in diplomatic negotiations.

Peace negotiation with China in 1937–41

JCIPR members Matsumoto, Saionji, Ushiba and Iwanaga were involved in the peace negotiation. It corresponded to the revised China policy of Konoe's first cabinet, which aimed to end the Sino-Japanese War. The New Order in East Asia corresponded to this new policy. Matsumoto was first the Shanghai bureau chief of *Dōmei tsūshin*, and then became head of its central and south

China bureau. Ushiba was private secretary to Konoe, and Saionji ran a current affair journal called *Gurafikku* (1936–40) and an international affairs year book, *Sekai nenkan* (1939–). The first initiative in the peace negotiation came from the Japanese officials, and they were negotiating with Jiang. Soon after the Marco Polo Incident, Konoe, Ishihara Kanji, Deputy Chief of Staff for Military Operations (*Rikugun sanbō honbu sakusen buchō*) at the military headquarters, and Kazami Akira, Secretary of the Konoe cabinet, tried to arrange a meeting between Konoe and Jiang for an early solution. Konoe sent Miyazaki Ryūsuke to Shanghai to prepare this meeting. Miyazaki was chosen because Konoe heard he had a good reputation among Guomindang members. Matsumoto and Saionji were to assist the process. Miyazaki, however, was arrested by Japanese military police upon boarding.[15] Despite this, Saionji thought that the negotiation almost succeeded as Jiang agreed even with the condition of *de facto* recognition of Manchuguo. Its eventual failure was, he recollected later, due to Konoe's lack of will.[16]

Around March 1938, another peace negotiation was taking shape among 'unofficial' Japanese, such as Matsumoto and Nishi Yoshiaki, head of Nanjing branch of the South Manchurian Railway, and pro-Japan, anti-communist factions within the Guomindang.[17] Jiang was not involved with this, although he secretly continued to seek a peace mediation through a third power. Konoe's cabinet, exploring ways to end the war, saw good prospects in this negotiation.[18] Matsumoto, now head of *Dōmei tsūshin*'s bureau for central and south China, was a key coordinator on the Japanese side. The reshuffle of the Konoe cabinet in May 1938 encouraged this 'unofficial' group. In June, Gao Zongwu (Kao Tsung-wu), one of the initiators of this peace negotiation, visited Tokyo to advance the process. Matsumoto, who followed him to Tokyo, and Iwanaga, proprietor of *Dōmei tsūshin*, assisted Gao to meet Konoe, Itagaki Military Minister and other key pro-peace figures (including the top brass in the Military and the Navy).[19] It was done secretly, as they did not want to provoke reactions from hardliners. Their 'unofficial status was an advantage.

The negotiation continued, so did preparation for the terms of peace in Japan. The November declaration of the New Order in East Asia corresponded to this process. While urging Jiang to consider the possibility of peace with Japan, the pro-Japan faction, headed by Wang Zhaoyao (Wang Chao-yao), escaped from Chongqing (Chungking), the capital of the Jiang government, to Hanoi on 19 December 1938. Konoe waited for news of Wang's safe escape, and issued another declaration on 22 December detailing policies on the New Order in East Asia. With Major Kagesa Sadaaki, another member of Konoe's entourage, Inukai Ken (member of the House of Representatives), assisted Wang to move to Shanghai. In March 1940, Wang established the Reorganized National Government of the Republic of China in Nanjing, and it concluded the basic treaty with Japan in November. Matsumoto and Saionji continued to be involved in smoothing the relationship between the Wang government and Japan. They argued that major conditions for the agreement between Wang and Japan should include Japanese military withdrawal, respect for Chinese sovereignty, abolition of extraterritoriality and no demand for compensation. Indeed the December declaration of 1938 and the following treaty between Japan and the Wang government included many of these points.

As noted, however, the December declaration did not include the withdrawal of the Japanese army. The Wang government was a puppet regime. This makes various clauses mentioned above a facade for virtual Japanese control. No doubt, Matsumoto and Saionji wanted military confrontation to end. It is hard to imagine that they saw the Wang government simply as a tool for Japanese control of China. Did they really believe that their plan would bring about more equal relationship between China and Japan? Perhaps it was their only way to rationalize and reconcile their 'consciousness' and their loyalty to the Japanese state/empire. They were aware of the nature of the Wang government, and they knew that Wang was regarded as a betrayer of the Chinese nationalists.[20]

Peace negotiation with the United States in 1941

Konoe also utilized Matsumoto, Saionji and Ushiba for a last-ditch peace negotiation between Japan and the United States in late August 1941. Although the whole process has been rigorously examined,[21] I will first briefly sketch the process and the involvement of JCIPR members. In August 1941, Ushiba was still Konoe's private secretary, and Saionji was recruited as *shokutaku* to the cabinet office to work on the negotiations. Matsumoto had returned from Shanghai, and Konoe regarded him as an adviser on the US–Japan relationship.

Non-official negotiations had begun in November 1940. They had been initiated by two American Catholic priests, and the above JCIPR members were not involved at this stage. By this time, new agreements on trade and navigation needed to be negotiated between the US and Japanese governments. In January 1940, the US–Japan Commerce and Navigation Treaty (1911) was annulled after the US announcement of this intention six months earlier. It was part of the American sanctions against Japanese aggression in China. In Autumn 1940, both governments still had not figured out where and how to open the negotiations. US–Japan diplomatic relations were at an all-time low, but they worsened when Matsuoka Yōsuke, Foreign Minister in Konoe's second cabinet, concluded the Tripartite Pact with Germany and Italy in September 1940. The situation deteriorated further with the conclusion of the Non-Aggression Pact between Japan and the USSR in April 1941, again on the initiative of Matsuoka. Matsuoka went to high school and university in the United States and claimed to understand Americans. For him the backing of Germany, Italy and the USSR was critical to strengthen Japan's position in negotiating new agreements with the United States. The American government, however, became alarmed and hardened its attitude towards Japan.

In late 1940 and early 1941, an unofficial initiative provided an opportunity for negotiations to begin. The above mentioned Americans and two Japanese who had contacts with them (they were called John Doe associates) together wrote a draft of an agreement in the United States. This was brought to the attention of their Japanese ambassador to the United States, Nomura Kichijirō, JCIPR member at least in the 1920s, and Secretary of State, Cordel Hull. In April 1941, Nomura sent this draft to the Japanese government, to which Hull's note was attached. According to Sudō, there was a serious misunderstanding between the US and Japanese governments in this exchange. The Japanese government interpreted this as an official US proposal which had the full endorsement of the State Department. In fact it was mainly drafted by Japanese non-officials, and Hull only expressed an opinion that this draft understanding could be a basis for future negotiation.[22]

This draft covered three main points: the European war, China and Southwestern Pacific (American vocabulary for Southeast Asia). First, the draft intended to water down the Tripartite Pact, aiming to reduce the possibility of the US–Japan confrontation through German actions. Second, it suggested an American mediation of peace between Japan and the Jiang (not the Wang) government. The conditions were that Japan would accept Chinese independence; withdraw its military from China; not seek annexation or repatriation; and follow the Open Door policy. It noted that the United States would even recognize Manchuguo. Third, it emphasized Japan's peaceful means of accessing resources in the Southwestern Pacific. Konoe, assuming wrongly that this was an American official agreement, thought this too good an opportunity to miss. He could achieve an agreement with the United States and peace with China. The Army and Navy Minister agreed. Matsuoka, who came back from Europe and the USSR in late April, however, was greatly offended because it bypassed him as Foreign Minister, and undermined his plans for negotiations with the United States. After further discussion, the Japanese government sent its draft back to the United States. It insisted on observance of the Tripartite Pact and contained no reference to Japanese withdrawal from China.

The American government replied with its draft in June. It asked Japan not to apply the Tripartite Pact to the European war. There was no mention of American mediation between Japan and Jiang. It warned against Japan's military actions in the Southwestern Pacific. Hull's oral statement was attached to it, which strongly criticized Matsuoka as a promoter of Nazi Germany. This offended Matsuoka enormously. When this June draft was sent to Japan, the war between the USSR and Germany broke out, destroying Matsuoka's plans for negotiations. He was seen as an obstacle not only in the United States, but also in Japan. The change from Konoe's second to third cabinet in July was understood as a device to reappoint the Foreign Minister. Despite this, Konoe continued to send confusing messages to the United States. At this very critical stage, he supported Japanese military advancement to southern French Indochina. The Imperial Conference (*Gozen kaigi*) of 2 July decided this southward advancement, and the action was taken later that month. If Konoe and others thought that this would have no significant impact on the negotiations,[23] they were grossly mistaken. The action was understood as a threat to US national security as well as to the British and Dutch empires. The consequence was immediate and dire. The United States, the British Commonwealth and the Netherlands East Indies froze Japanese capital in their territories, and the United States placed an oil embargo on Japan. Churchill urged the cooperation of the United States in the war effort, and met with Roosevelt in August. Together, they declared the Atlantic Charter. The United States sent a message to the Japanese government warning against Japanese southward advancement.

At this stage, Konoe proposed a top-level meeting between him and Roosevelt. The State Department opposed the idea as a second Munich, but Roosevelt appeared to be keen. Nomura, ambassador in Washington, DC, reported this keen interest to Konoe. It was at this stage that Ushiba, Saionji and Matsumoto were brought into the negotiation. On the last weekend in August 1941, they met Konoe at the Fujiya Hotel in Hakone, a place of retreat that Konoe often used, and prepared a draft agreement for this proposed meeting. According to them, they wrote the draft based on the June American draft. It was called the cabinet draft, or the Prime Minister's draft.[24] Saionji showed this copy to Ozaki in late September, over which Saionji was subsequently charged in relation to the Sorge Incident.

Konoe distributed the draft to the Army, Navy and Ministry of Foreign Affairs, and intended to bring it to the Imperial Conference with the heads of these ministries on 6 September. Saionji recorded that it was not even brought into the conference because of very strong opposition from these ministries.[25] Sudō, however, argues that the reason for this dismissal, especially by the Ministry of Foreign Affairs, was its 'bad' quality. In his view, this cabinet draft was 'carelessly compiled'. It was obviously a hurried job. Japanese withdrawal from China and the Tripartite Pact were not even mentioned, and it proposed the withdrawal from southern French Indochina only after the end of the Sino-Japanese War.[26] Instead, the Ministry of Foreign Affairs sent its own draft agreement to the United States for the proposed top-level meeting. Despite this continued diplomatic effort, however, the same Imperial Conference of 6 September also set a time limit. It decided to aim to complete preparations for war with the United States, Britain and the Netherlands by the end of October. The State Department opposed the top-level meeting in any case, and it was increasingly clear that an agreement between the two countries was extremely unlikely. Unable to break the diplomatic deadlock, and shaken by the Sorge Incident, Konoe's third cabinet resigned in mid-October 1941. The diplomatic negotiations continued without success, and less than two months later, Japan attacked Pearl Harbour.

Non-official diplomacy

What were the implications of JCIPR members' involvement in this non-official diplomacy? Many contemporaries and later scholars regarded 'unofficial' involvement as one of major reasons for the failure of the US–Japan negotiations in 1940–1.[27] Nevertheless, it reflected an unusual style of diplomacy during Konoe's premiership. First, China and Japan were at war, and the peace negotiations needed to be secretive if they were not to impede the war efforts. Although the United States and Japan were not at war until the very end of 1941, concern with the impact on public morale and on the perception of other countries might have influenced the negotiations. Initial sounding out of the other side's intent would be inconspicuous and effective if it were carried out by non-officials. Second, the partner in the negotiation with China was not the internationally acknowledged government, but a faction that had defected from the government. 'Official' diplomatic channels, therefore, did not exist in 1938 to early 1940. Third, in Japan, since the Manchurian Incident, normal policy-making and diplomatic mechanisms were largely in abeyance. This meant that there was greater scope for 'non-officials' to play a more influential role than in peace time.

Fourth, and probably most important, was Konoe's personal style. As noted, Konoe wanted to expand the power of the cabinet office and Prime Minister, and used his circle of JCIPR members as his cabinet staff. Matsumoto and Saionji suggest that the strong objection from the military or the Ministry of Foreign Affairs was because Konoe and his group were trying to curtail Japanese military aggression. It could have been simply because these 'officials' saw their actions as an invasion of their domains. It is hard to see Konoe as a martyr to the cause of peace. He was not against the military agenda. He did not oppose the military advance in southern French Indochina and after September the peace negotiations went hand in hand with preparations for war. The peace terms which the JCIPR members formulated with the United States were not particularly opposed to military aggression either. Officers and bureaucrats displayed a very strong hostility towards the non-officials that Konoe utilized, whether they were think-tank members or peace negotiators. Konoe's failure to push through their plan was, therefore, not due to the 'liberal' nature of their peace terms. Rather, it failed because the Prime Minister was weak against other forces. JCIPR members also lacked a strong base. Other than coming from good families or their elite school backgrounds, their power resided with their expertise on China and the United States and their connections with Konoe. They had no backing from other political forces, nor did they have any popular support or mandate. They depended solely on Konoe and his relationship with the Emperor.

On the other hand, despite strong 'official' opposition, the above two negotiation processes indicate that the line between officials and non-officials was largely blurred in this period. Many who did not have governmental positions but were close to the government played a 'semi-official' role. Saionji recorded that in 1938 Matsuoka Yōsuke, then at the South Manchurian

Railway, initiated peace negotiations with China. A company employee, Nishi, was involved in the process throughout. Matsumoto also suggested that Iwanaga and his partner Furuno Inosuke at the Tokyo headquarters of *Dōmei tsūshin* had various missions in close cooperation with military officers and diplomats.[28] 'Officials' themselves were deeply divided. While Matsumoto communicated to Konoe developments in the negotiation with China,[29] he received only fragmentary instructions, mainly from pro-peace groups within the military. Divisions within the military were sharp, making the line between the military and 'liberal'/'moderate' camps unclear.

JCIPR members, often regarded as 'liberal internationalists', had not only contributed to the improvement of the US–Japan relationship in this period. They had a close connection with those who were to be charged as war criminals in 1945, Konoe, Matsuoka and Hirota. The connection with Hirota was indirect. Hirota enthusiastically promoted 'cultural diplomacy' in which JCIPR members were utilized. As well as Konoe, however, Matsuoka had very close relations with JCIPR members. Matsuoka, a JCIPR member in the late 1920s and early 1930s, was close to Matsumoto and Saionji. He maintained good contact with them during the peace negotiations with China. Matsuoka wanted to appoint Matsumoto as an ambassador to the United States when he became Foreign Minister in 1940. The plan did not materialize partly because Matsumoto declined the offer. Saionji was private secretary to Matsuoka when he was Foreign Minister in this period, and he accompanied Matsuoka to Europe and the USSR in March–April 1941, which resulted in damaging the US–Japan relations further. The line between the military and 'liberal' camps was not as clear as was assumed later.

The Pacific War and the IPR: think-tanks and propaganda

The IPR and the state: Allied agendas and think-tanks

In 1942, the ISIPR clearly sided with the Allied powers. It was committed to the Atlantic Charter. The charter was the restatement of Wilsonian principles in 1941, and it was the wartime ideology for the Allied forces:

> The noble if somewhat nebulous words of the Atlantic Charter had expressed some of the nations' needs for a statement of basic war aims. … The Declaration of the United Nations in January 1942 and indeed the whole concept of the United Nations, though still far from denoting an effective executive entity, was a great achievement.[30]

The 'United Nations' here referred to the policy-making organization for the Allied forces during World War II, although its role for the postwar world was also indicated. The ISIPR and the ACIPR tried to contribute to the institutionalization of this 'united nations'. Already in late 1940, Carter had asked Percy E. Corbett, Canadian expert of international law, to work on possible forms of a new international organization (this was subsequently published as *Post-war World* in 1942 as a part of the Inquiry series).[31] The move corresponded to that of Hull, Secretary of State, who initiated a preparatory study on postwar organizations within the State Department soon after the outbreak of the European war. This led to the formation of the Advisory Committee on Problems of Foreign Relations in January 1940. Sumner Welles, Under-Secretary of State and soon to be involved in the ACIPR, was its chairperson and Stanley Hornbeck, a founding member of the IPR and political adviser at the Department, was also involved. In order to strengthen the research capacity, the Division of Special Research was also established in February 1941 (within the Department). Until the establishment of the Advisory Committee on Post-War Foreign Policy in December 1941 (soon after the Japanese attack on Pearl Harbour), however, these policy agencies were rather inactive and understaffed. Their research was also mainly concerned with Europe, and other than the CFR, they tried not to rely on non-governmental organizations.[32] This indicated very little possibility of cooperation with the ISIPR and the ACIPR at least, until late 1941.

Whereas the Sino-Japanese War accelerated the co-option of the JCIPR into the state apparatus, the war and the following Pacific War affected the ISIPR and other National Councils in a similar way. For Carter, the development in September 1940 proved his point, the significance of the Pacific region (and the IPR) in the global politics. Carter, then acting Secretary of the ACIPR as well as Secretary General of the IPR, wrote to his long-time friend at the Rockefeller Foundation, Raymond Fosdick:

> The news flash on September 27, 1940, of the Berlin Pact (the Tokyo–Berlin–Rome Axis) did more perhaps to bring home to the American people one of the Institute's main theses than fifteen years of patient, scholarly effort of the American Council. In almost the twinkling of an eye, millions of Americans awoke to the tragic fact that what was happening in the Pacific was as much the concern of every American as events in Europe. ... Within the last few months it has become plain that [the wars in Europe and Asia] are inextricably linked. ... For the United States and for the British Pacific Dominions, as well as *for the orphaned French and Dutch colonies in the Far East and the Pacific, the new situation has brought new and critical dangers.*[33] [emphasis added]

Here, Carter did not challenge the European colonial status quo in the region, but warned of the great danger to it. At the same time, he was critical of the dominant Eurocentricity. Recent developments made one realize 'the neglect of the Far East and the Pacific in the schools, universities, the press and research institutions'. In his view, the neglect was due to 'the tradition of looking at Far Eastern problems through European glasses'.

In Carter's view, the wars prompted an emerging sense of a community in the Pacific – 'the rapidly increasing consciousness of the community of interests between [the United States, the British Empire, the USSR and the Orient]'. Unlike the Pacific Community Herbert Croly envisaged in 1927, this community did not include Japan. The sense of community arose out of a shared concern over Japanese aggression in the region. The USSR remained a member. Although it did not participate in the IPR conferences in 1942 and 1945, IPR members still regarded the USSR as a 'natural' and important member of the regional and world community they envisaged.

In Carter's view, the wars also stimulated the IPR's work both in Europe and Asia:

> In France and Holland the activity has been curtailed but not completely wiped out. In Japan it has become more cautious but is nevertheless proceeding. The national office of [the IPR] in China has had to move five times but manages, through the use of the air mails, to service its widely scattered members in the out-of-the-way cities of Free China. ... In spite of the violent and continued air attacks on England, the studies and discussions of our English colleagues in [Chatham House] constitute and are in fact greater in volume and more fundamental in character than in pre-war days. Under these circumstances the Institute's work seems more essential to the American public today than ever before. The American Council's close affiliation with a group of national councils ... constitutes an added obligation to press forward with its essential task.[34]

Carter had a strong backer. Sydnor Walker at the Rockefeller Foundation regarded the IPR's work very highly, and even felt that the foundation had a certain responsibility for the IPR. In 1940, she noted that 'a good case should be made for the Institute's carrying on expanded research [the Inquiry] on problems of the Pacific'.[35]

National interests held priority over other causes not only at the JCIPR, but also in other National Councils. War furthered this tendency. In 1938, Field, then Secretary of the ACIPR, stressed American interests and responsibility in East Asia. The ACIPR, he argued, had a vital role in keeping American leaders well informed with current events (the Sino-Japanese War) in 'an area which American people have a particular interest and responsibility'.[36] Immediately after the Japanese attack on Pearl Harbour, Ray Wilbur, then Chairperson of the American Council, also announced:

> [T]he American Councils of the Institute of Pacific Relations must define the course ... in the emergency. ... [T]he war situation, far from negating the purpose of the Council, lends new and crucial importance to its program of study and widespread discussion of the issues at stake. ... The immediate job of the American people is the prosecution of war

against the military imperialism of Japan and the other Axis powers. ...
In support of this aim the American Council pledges its full resources. It
is making available to all agencies, public and private, its libraries, its
publications, and the service of its staff in meeting the unprecedented
need for reliable information and analysis.[37]

Their emphasis on the American national interest did not contradict their
internationalism or the interests of the international community. This could
explain the fact that there was no serious opposition towards the virtual
integration of the ISIPR and ACIPR and greater Americanization of IPR
operations in this period. Soon after being appointed ACIPR Secretary in
November 1941, William W. Lockwood sent a note to Carter, stressing the
need for the ISIPR to take the initiative independently from other National
Councils, except the ACIPR. This indicated greater discretion to the ISIPR
on policy matters and its closer relationship with the ACIPR, the trend which
he noted had begun in 1939. It was the year when the Inquiry project fully
took over.[38] Carter hastened the move in 1940–1, when he took up the position
of acting Secretary of the ACIPR while remaining Secretary General of the
ISIPR. This was accidental, rather than strategic. He filled the position that
Frederick Field had quit in mid-1940, and served until Lockwood was
appointed. Nevertheless, Carter did not regard this double appointment
problematic, nor was there much opposition to the move. As a result, Carter
and the ISIPR became closely involved with forums on 'American policies in
the Far East', which were organized by various branches of the American
Council. These forums played a role as a preliminary discussion for IPR
conferences. Non-Americans participated at times and various countries'
policies were discussed, but American policies occupied centre stage.

The wars boosted the status and significance of the ACIPR in the United
States. Policy-makers recognized its usefulness, and this furthered the co-
option of ACIPR members into the state apparatus. The process corresponded
to the restructuring of the state apparatus to wartime needs, and the New
Deal projects which expanded the power of the state probably provided a
good base for this restructuring. As in Japan, the state utilized IPR members
in two major areas, publicity or wartime propaganda, and policy analysis and
formulation. Furthermore, as in Japan, most IPR members cooperated with
the state willingly and enthusiastically, with excitement and a sense of mission.
These trends were also evident in other 'non-governmental' organizations,
such as the Foreign Policy Association and the CFR.

In the United States, many ACIPR (and Canadian) members were
recruited to new wartime organizations. By mid-1941 the European war or
World War II was well under way, and in July 1941, the Office of the
Coordinator of Information (COI) was established. It consisted of two
sections: overseas information and research. Almost six months after the
outbreak of the Pacific War, in June 1942 the former section became the
Office of War Information (OWI) and the latter, the Office of Strategic

Services (OSS). The OSS included the functions of research, analysis and intelligence. IPR members, such as Holland and Lattimore, were recruited by the OWI. Lattimore returned from China in 1942, and took charge of the OWI's San Francisco branch. It mainly produced propaganda directed at Japan.[39] This move was reflected in the IPR's research projects and conference topics. The IPR conducted a research series on wartime propaganda and press in the region, and the IPR conference in 1942 discussed effective propaganda tactics by the Allied countries.[40]

The OSS also recruited IPR members. In August 1942, Blakeslee at Clark University, a founding member of the IPR, became head of the Far Eastern section. Hugh Borton, a young scholar of Japanese history at Columbia University and an IPR member, also joined the section. The ISIPR encouraged this co-option to the state apparatus. Carter wrote a strong recommendation for Borton's appointment. Similarly, Lockwood resigned from his position as Secretary of the ACIPR to join the Far Eastern section of the OSS in 1943. The section had been absorbed into the State Department in January of that year. This meant IPR members contributed to the Department's policy formation related to Japan and the 'Far East' during and after the Pacific War.[11] Iriye suggests that the views of Borton and Blakeslee on policies towards Japan were influential in 1943.[42] This was, however, not always the case. Strongly conflicting views existed among policy-makers within the US government. If, along with American ambassador in Tokyo, Joseph Grew, Borton and Blakeslee tended to argue for a 'moderate' policy towards Japan, Stanley Hornbeck had been urging 'tough' measures since 1931. Hornbeck was also a founding member of the IPR, and participated in the IPR conference in 1925, 1927 and 1942. Sudō argues that he was most influential on the views of Roosevelt, Hull, Secretary of State, and Sumner Welles, Under-Secretary of State, in the crucial period leading up to the Pacific War in 1941.[13] These conflicting views reflected opinions among 'Far Eastern' specialists at the IPR. The Allied policy towards Japan would emerge as one of the divisive issues among conference participants in 1942 and 1945.

Not only individual ACIPR members, but also the ACIPR as an organization corresponded to state needs. Although some members resisted moving the entire office from New York to Washington, DC,[11] a branch office was founded there in the early 1940s. It was explained as a response to 'heavy demands from Washington for advice and assistance', and to maintain 'close liaison with government agencies'.[15] After September 1943, Welles, former Under-Secretary of State, became the branch head. Under Hull, Secretary of State, Welles had been central in the Advisory Committee on Post-War Foreign Policy in the previous few years, discussing the postwar order and organizations with experts both within and outside the Department.[16] It is, therefore, likely that Welles, who was now organizing regular ACIPR's seminars and meetings in Washington, DC, for specialists and policy-makers on East Asia,[17] could feed some ideas of ACIPR members to the Department.

This state co-option was evident in other countries, and nowhere was strong resistance to this development evident. It was war, and they had useful skills. For IPR members, this co-option meant a ticket to tremendous political influence. In Britain, the headquarters of the RIIA was moved to Oxford for intelligence work with other government departments, and a government grant was provided for RIIA activities.[48] Members of the Australian Institute of International Affairs (AIIA), the amalgamated national body of the Australian branches of the RIIA and the IPR, worked in intelligence agencies for the government during the war.[49]

In Japan, this process, which was strongly promoted during Konoe's three cabinets in 1937–41, went into a new stage after the outbreak of the Pacific War. The JIA (formerly the LNA), into which the JCIPR was absorbed, was restructured and renamed *Nihon gaisei kyōkai* (Japan Foreign Policy Association) in 1942. The change was explained as necessary to pursue JIA's mission in the current critical international context. Its main function was the publication of two major journals, *Gaikō hyōron* and *Sekai to warera*. The former was addressed to specialists, and changes were made:

> The beginning of each issue will explain imperial foreign policies on significant issues. ... There will be less focus on commentary in favour of articles which contribute to foreign policy formulation. ... To compensate for the lack of sources due to the suspension of activities of international news agencies, it will collect the latest information with the help of the Ministry of Foreign Affairs, and make it widely available.

Sekai to warera was addressed to a wider public, and its propaganda function became more explicit:

> This journal's objective is the enlightenment of the masses. Because of its great demand at this moment, it will renew the format in general, and it will make it possible for our readers to have a bird's eye view of the current world situation based on solid and authoritative sources.[50]

The Ministry of Foreign Affairs completed the co-option of the JIA. Its activities had increased in significance and demand during the war. When the JCIPR was dissolved in the spring of 1943, reportedly it was due to its pro-American outlook. The incident can also be seen as the completion of the state co-option of the JCIPR. Ushiba Tomohiko, Secretary of the JCIPR, negotiated the terms with the Ministry. The JCIPR's library and materials were absorbed into the Department of Research within the Ministry.[51]

Was the ACIPR, whose members were becoming influential in US policy-making towards the Pacific region in this period, important in bringing the United States into the war? Probably their contribution was less direct than lobby groups, such as the American Committee for Non-Participation in Japanese Aggression (ACNJA). One of the major promoters of the ACNJA was Roger Greene, an ACIPR member, [52] and Carter and Field were active members. The ACNJA lobbied for economic sanctions against Japan. This, combined with pressures from the Congress and State Department support, especially from Hornbeck, resulted in the US government's notification of the annulment of the US–Japan Commerce and Navigation Treaty in July 1939 (annulled in January 1940).[53] The action could be seen as a major cause for the eventual clash between the two countries.

The IPR and the public: propaganda and knowledge of the region

Rather than lobbying Congress, the ISIPR and the ACIPR continued to advocate American commitment to 'the defence of the post-League order' by educating national leaders and concerned members of the public. While Carter was keen to promote the IPR as a think-tank, he also had a firm belief that more and better knowledge of Asia was needed among the American public. The education scheme was one of his main initiatives when he took up the position of Secretary General in 1933,[54] but this concern went further back. In 1928–9, as Secretary of the ACIPR, he conducted a survey of Chinese and Japanese studies at 546 higher institutions in the United States. The results suggested that these studies were sorely neglected. In 1933, Carter asked Takaki Yasaka to conduct a study on the state of Japanese studies in American universities. The study, published in 1935, urged the improvement of Japanese language teachers' qualifications, the elevation of Japanese studies as an accepted academic field, the publication of a good dictionary, and securing positions for young academics specializing in Japanese studies.[55] Accordingly, Carter worked with Field and the ACIPR for the promotion of a programme to educate teachers at tertiary and secondary levels, and to disseminate the results of IPR research to the wider public.[56] In conjunction with the American Council of Learned Societies (ACLS), they also tried to foster specialists with proper academic training who could teach the subject at higher institutions. They set up positions on these subjects at prestigious universities.

The ACIPR's concerns arose not so much out of genuine academic fascination with the region, as the concern with American national interests in the region. This became more explicit as Japanese aggression intensified in China – the period which coincided with Carter's term as Secretary General. Soon after the Mukden Incident, Carter had argued that the IPR's education schemes needed to be concrete and organized on a national footing.[57] In his view, the economic and strategic interests of a particular nation should define what 'knowledge' would be significant in the nation. He was further convinced after he saw American interests in the 'Far East' grow during the Sino-Japanese War. More Americans were beginning to see that America's economic and strategic position was at stake in East Asia, or perhaps the publicity of the event simply drew people's attention to the region. In the

1935 report, Takaki pointed out that the growing American interest in Japan and international relations in the 'Far East' was a result of the Manchurian Incident.[58]

The crisis in the region also changed the views of the academic establishment. Prestigious universities, such as Harvard, Columbia and the University of California, began summer seminars on 'Far Eastern' problems. Carter also got the IPR involved in setting up intensive summer language courses (Russian at Harvard from 1933, Chinese and Japanese from 1937).[59] The Manchurian crisis marked a turning point for the Rockefeller Foundation, which had been reluctant to give scholarships in the area of 'Far Eastern' studies. In 1933, for the first time, it decided to provide fellowships for pre-doctoral researchers in this area. Borton noted the influence of the Yenching Institute and Evarts B. Greene, brother of Jerome and Roger Greene and professor of history at Columbia University, in this decision.[60] The timing, however, indicates that the Manchurian crisis was another important factor. As a result, by the end of the 1930s, Japanese studies had established its position in American academia.

While Evarts Greene at Columbia gave priority to research on humanities in East Asian studies, Carter and the ACIPR promoted a study of current affairs in the region. As Borton notes, the language courses, in which the ACIPR was involved, were addressed not at prospective academics, but towards professionals who were already dealing with these countries, and needed knowledge of the language for practical reasons.[61] It was a prototype of the area studies which flourished after World War II in the United States. It emphasized practical language skills and analysis of current affairs, using the methodologies of the new disciplines of social sciences. Harvard shared this view, and took the lead. The Rockefeller Foundation was crucial in promoting this type of study.

In November 1940, Carter stressed the importance of IPR works in providing 'knowledge' of the region:

> [A] great deal has to be done today to make available to the public of as many as possible of the Pacific countries some of the vital developments which have been taking place in China and Southeast Asia.[62]

In Carter's view, 'public understanding' needed to be improved in the United States, 'the British Empire, the USSR and the Orient' alike. He advocated this not only to fulfil an academic objective, but more to urge American involvement in the war effort. It was an indirect method. Rather than lobbying Congress, he tried to 'educate' the concerned public about the significance of the region and the need for American leadership.

Once the United States was at war with Japan, much of the ACIPR's work became a voluntary support for the US (and Allied) war efforts. Early in the Pacific War, the Army and Navy established schools at notable universities, such as Harvard, Columbia, Virginia, and trained officers in languages and other subjects. Holland taught at a school of navy strategy which was set up at Columbia University, and Thomas Bisson and other IPR members lectured at these institutions.[63] Officers who studied Japanese at these institutions were later sent to Japan as staff of the Occupation forces.

The Pacific War increased demands for ACIPR work substantially. The Rockefeller Foundation recorded at the end of 1942: 'The events of today re-emphasize the value of the IPR.' Sales of ACIPR publications increased 140 per cent in 1942, and the IPR was seen the sole 'competent agency' to provide 'information and a comprehensive analysis of the problems of the Pacific'.[64] The ACIPR provided many booklets on countries in the region. They were read by members of military forces and at schools. As many as 200,000 wartime pamphlets were distributed to the army.[65] It is easy to assume that there was some link between this activity and the OWI. As well as 'informing' people about enemies and allies in Asia, the ACIPR also tried to foster a closer relationship with more familiar yet still little known allies in the region: Australia and New Zealand. It published pamphlets, such as *Meet the ANZAC* for that purpose. This was important. As Carter noted in late 1940, clichés like kangaroos, Ford and Hollywood obstructed better understanding, while there was an urgent recognition for the need for the 'direct diplomatic relations' and 'possible cooperative defence agreement'.[66]

The ACIPR's educational schemes addressed the general public, and they complemented the activities of IPR conferences which were aimed at the state and policy-makers. These educational schemes were no doubt important in widening general knowledge of the Asia–Pacific region, and in the future development of area studies in the United States. Despite the high-quality works produced by the IPR in this period, however, knowledge of the region was inevitably shaped, presented and promoted by American strategic concerns. These schemes can be seen as a tool to mobilize the population for the war effort.

Visions for the new world order: the conferences in 1942 and 1945

Think-tank for the Allies

The outbreak of the Pacific War in December 1941 marked a new stage of international politics in the region. Many trends were, however, already apparent in IPR operations in 1939. First, the conference locations moved from the Pacific to the Atlantic coast. They were held at Virginia Beach, Virginia on 18 November to 2 December, 1939, Mont Tremblant, Quebec on 4–14 December, 1942, and Hot Springs, Virginia on 6–17 January 1945. Second, the conferences discussed mainly security issues, and proposed policy directions. While the conference proceedings of 1939 retained the title 'Problems of the Pacific', which had been used since 1927, it was about policies of reconstruction after the Sino-Japanese War. The titles of the last two conferences were *War and Peace in the Pacific* (1942) and *Security in the Pacific* (1945).

IPR conferences in 1942 and 1945 were directed to the state. The veto power of the JCIPR was eliminated at the conference in 1942.[67] As a result of this decision and the absence of Japan, the conferences during the Pacific War became Allied policy forums. They were attended by a great many current office holders (diplomats, advisers, army and navy officers, senior bureaucrats and parliamentary members). The percentage of officials from each national group differed, but almost half were officials in 1942 and the figure was slightly lower in 1945. This was very different from previous conferences.[68] It was wartime and, as Holland points out, many IPR members became advisers or diplomats. The IPR still emphasized the private capacity of these officials. Yet to achieve such a high level of official representation, it is reasonable to assume that there was a deliberate push to encourage and attract official participation, and that the state regarded IPR forums as important. In 1943 Alan Watt, Counsellor at Australian Legation in Washington, DC, who himself was to attend the 1945 conference, noted 'the increasingly official character' of the IPR and the significance of its works and networks:

> By far the greatest value of these meetings ... is in the contacts I make. The IPR in this country is now in close contact with all relevant Embassies and Legations, which regard the IPR's work of sufficient importance to make it desirable that some official representative should attend its meetings.[69]

These conferences were influential in policy-making among the Allies, and governments took careful note of the discussions. Conference agendas were discussed within the US government, and detailed reports were sent back. The involvement of the British government in Chatham House was extensive during this period. The government provided funds to send delegates to both conferences, and in return it was involved in the selection of delegates. It also shared reports of the proceedings of the 1942 conference with the governments of Australia and the Netherlands.[70] This close relationship with the state was largely not problematized. In 1943, the New South Wales branch of the AIIA, for example, noted:

> [I]t sees no reason to stress unduly the need for complete independence from reasonable government assistance in the case of future delegations. All the other delegations at the conference were frankly sponsored by the governments.[71]

The secrecy of the conferences increased as the topics were relevant to Allied policies. The press had been shut out since 1939. From 1942, conference documents were confidential, mainly prepared for government use, and generally not available to the public.[72]

Although they aimed at coherent policies among the Allied countries, and envisaged a new postwar world order, the IPR conferences of 1942 and 1945 exposed more disunity than unity. Just as their Japanese counterparts felt that East Asian unity needed to be 'created', in 1942 the ISIPR argued that the 'united nations' existed only as a framework. There was sharp disagreement especially on policies towards postwar reconstruction in Japan and colonialism in the region. The situation was no better in 1945. Carter was particularly concerned with divisions between the United States and Britain. He warned that 'in the Far East, more than anywhere else, there lay a grave threat to understanding between the two countries'.[73] Division was also strong among American participants. It was seen as damaging to a successful war effort and postwar reconstruction. By discussing these issues, IPR members were negotiating and redefining the international order for the postwar period.

Conflicting visions for postwar Japan in 1942 and 1945

In the late 1930s and during the Pacific War, there were conflicting views on policies towards Japan within the US government. IPR members, such as Borton, Blakeslee and Hornbeck, were in a position to influence top policy-makers. Their divided opinions reflected those of 'Far Eastern' specialists at the IPR. This was the case not only within the United States, but in IPR operations at large. It was evident especially in 1945. One of the critical factors which defined these experts' views was their understanding of Japanese modern history, its politics, economy and society. In 1945, Canadian E. Herbert Norman represented a group who argued for a thorough and democratic reform for postwar Japan. How did Norman understand 'Japan', and how did this understanding influence his views towards Japanese postwar reconstruction? How dominant was his view at the IPR conferences in 1942 and 1945?

E.H. Norman between scholar and practitioner

E.H. Norman's understanding of modern Japanese history was best illuminated in his first book on Japan, *Japan's Emergence as a Modern State*. It was his PhD thesis, which he completed, and for which he received a degree from Harvard in 1939.[74] It was also published as a part of the Inquiry series by the IPR in 1939. As the year of publication indicates, Norman wrote it in the middle of the Sino-Japanese War, and completed it before the outbreak of the Pacific War. *Emergence* and Norman himself aroused great controversy. Japanese Marxist scholars debated *Emergence*'s interpretation of Meiji Japan. Norman was charged with espionage (not proven) in Canada and the United Sates at the height of McCarthyism, and he committed suicide in Cairo in 1957. John Dower's reappraisal of *Emergence* in the mid-1970s opened a debate in North America which Gary Allinson described as harsh, biting and spiteful even in the mid-1980s.[75] Although it is now clear that these controversies do not diminish the merit of Norman's scholarship,[76] Norman's close connection with the IPR sheds a different light on the circumstances.

A key to understanding Norman's works and life is his role both as a theorist (scholar) and as a practitioner (think-tank member and diplomat), as well as his sense of duty to history. The fact that his *Emergence* was included in the IPR's Inquiry series is significant. His main concern was why Japan began the Sino-Japanese War, otherwise it would not have been in the Inquiry series. On the surface, Norman's scholarship and career choices had parallels with JCIPR members who were Konoe's think-tank members and who contributed to the IPR's Far Eastern Conflict series. Like his Japanese counterparts and many academics who joined the IPR, Norman was interested in influencing policy. The IPR that Norman joined was also the IPR which Carter was promoting as a think-tank. His life and career choices demonstrate his inclination towards 'practitioner'. Norman was the son of a Canadian missionary family, born and brought up in Japan until 1926. His knowledge of and interest in Japan were natural. He was a genuine intellectual with a profound knowledge of Greek and Roman classics and European literature and history. Academia was the first career he set himself, which he could easily have pursued. Yet he wanted something different. He sought a diplomatic position at the Canadian embassy in Tokyo. When he found out this was not possible, in October 1936 he took up a Rockefeller fellowship, and began an MA on East Asian history at the Yenching Institute at Harvard.

The research he wanted to pursue matched what Carter thought the IPR should engage in and what was needed in the United States then. Ōkubo Genji (1915–86) indicates Carter may have recommended Norman for the fellowship.[77] Norman's writings on Japan and China began to appear in journals. He finished his MA in 1937, and proceeded to work on his PhD thesis in early 1938. Around then, he was asked to contribute to the Inquiry project.[78] In summer 1938, Norman visited Tokyo for research. At the JCIPR office, he met the young Ōkubo Genji, who had just begun work at the JCIPR secretariat in February 1938. The connection was crucial to Norman's work.[79] Ōkubo introduced Norman to Japanese scholars and their works. His respect for Norman and his works was profound. Even in the difficult times of the immediate postwar period, he worked hard to translate Norman's works for a Japanese audience, who replied to this effort with enormous appreciation.[80] Ōkubo's sense of purpose was strengthened when he learned of Norman's suicide in Cairo in 1957.

Norman continued his research and publication after he joined the Canadian diplomatic corps. In 1940 he began his work at the Canadian embassy in Tokyo. He was never short of offers of academic posts, but he remained a diplomat. The governments appreciated and utilized his expertise and talent during the Pacific War, the Occupation period in Japan and during the San Francisco Peace Treaty talks and the Suez crisis. His career and life illuminate his strong inclination for policy-making as an 'expert', not merely as an observer and analyst. In retrospect, this probably cost his life.

What drove him from academia to diplomacy and positioned him close to the IPR and the state apparatus? Was it his alleged espionage activity? Or was it his patriotism or his desire for power? His works, his life, his writings and memories of him among people who knew him and later scholars' assessment of his works all suggest that he was driven by his compassion for the underprivileged, his strong social consciousness and 'idealism, a basic humanism and the classic ethics of liberalism' to use Dower's words.[81] This commitment to his principles and idealism did not draw him away from politics, but made him more determined to be involved in it, and to change the course of history. His IPR-related works were written not only for students and academics, but for policy-makers. It was an area bound to attract controversy.

In *Emergence* Norman saw the causes of the Sino-Japanese War in the nature of the Meiji state. Eschewing a strict application of Marxism, Norman argued what characterized Japanese modern politics was not the domination of the coherent ruling class, but complex relationships of various political forces, such as the bureaucracy, the financial houses, the armed forces and the political parties. He noted that this complexity was reflected in 'the bewildering variety and sharp contrasts ... in the history of Japan in recent times'.[82] Although Norman stressed the feudal element in the agrarian sector and its exploitative nature, the role of the imperial system is largely absent in *Emergence*. Was it because he saw it holding little significance for politics in the Meiji era or in the late 1930s? This is a curious omission, especially considering his strong criticism of the imperial system in his later works.

Emergence is revealing on the subject of the postwar (the Sino-Japanese War) reconstruction of Japan – especially its analysis of 'civilians' and 'liberalism'. He stressed the futility of distinguishing between 'civilians' and 'militarists':

> The neat division of the Japanese governing circles into military and civil despite its conveniences is an over simplified if not unreal manner of speaking. These two categories were misleading, as the role of the bureaucracy lies not in opposing the military from some abstract 'civilian' viewpoint, but in the steadying influence they exert upon the whole administrative machine.

Here Norman was concerned almost exclusively with 'civilians' within the government, namely bureaucrats. No line was drawn between official and non-official 'civilians'. Although he did not use the term 'liberals' here, he referred to 'liberals' and 'civilians' interchangeably. Norman's examination of Japanese 'liberals' in late Meiji led him to conclude that they largely supported imperial expansion. He noted: 'it has became axiomatic that liberalism is inimical to a policy of expansion'. In Norman's view, this was in no way a historical phenomenon peculiar to Japan. As the cases of Lloyd George and Theodore Roosevelt demonstrated, those who pursued reformist domestic policies advocated aggressive foreign policies.[83]

The role of 'civilians' or the bureaucracy in Japanese politics, however, was complex. Norman argued that while they acted hand in glove with the military and obstructed the progress of democracy, they also prevented Japan from becoming a fascist regime in 1938:

> [T]hey act as mediators who reconcile the conflicts between the military and financial or industrial groups, shifting their weight ... to prevent the complete domination of the military clique and to check big business from controlling politics in its exclusive interests. ... [T]his almost anonymous but experienced bureaucracy has gradually snuffed out all signs of genuine democratic activity, but on the other hand it has blocked the victory of outright fascist forces. ... [I]t lacks the distinctive full-blown features of a fascist dictatorship.[84]

Norman's view of 'civilians'/'liberals' was quite different from his contemporaries, such as Joseph Grew, the American ambassador to Japan in this period. Grew saw Japanese politics in a pendulum theory framework, moving between two distinct opposing forces of militarists and liberals. As a result, Grew argued the need to encourage the 'liberal' elements to take charge, and suppress the militarists.[85] The US policy towards Japan, therefore, should be moderate, not condemning. Other IPR members, such as Borton and Blakeslee, who would become influential in the Far Eastern section of the State Department in late 1943, shared Grew's view. Ironically, the view was even evident among those who opposed this moderate policy, such as Hornbeck. Hornbeck differed only in that he believed the militarists were too strong to be suppressed other than by a tough external pressure. In mid-1937, Konoe found this black and white picture 'superficial', albeit dominant in the United States as well as among Japanese 'liberals' themselves.[86] From Konoe's point of view, Norman had rare insight. It was, however, this insight that led Norman to argue for the inclusion of 'civilians', such as Konoe and Hirota, as war criminals at the Tokyo Tribunal.

Norman's views on 'civilians' and 'liberals' were relevant to the reconstruction of Japan after the end of the Pacific War. In order for expansionism not to recommence, who should lead postwar Japan? What should be the structure to support these leaders, and what should be the policies of the Allied countries, especially the United States? These were significant questions as the Allies prepared a policy on Japan, and proved to be a dividing point at IPR conferences especially in 1945.

Policies towards postwar reconstruction

Norman did not participate in the 1939 conference. He was in Ottawa preparing for his future post at the Canadian embassy in Tokyo. He did, however, submit a data paper, entitled 'The establishment of a modern state in Japan'. This was ninety pages shorter than the published *Emergence*, and it was most likely an excerpt from the book. The paper was considered very valuable among participants.[87] It was clear that his view did influence some IPR members. In November 1940, Carter noted: '... a transformed Japan does not automatically become the same as a totalitarian Germany or Italy'.[88] Despite this and despite Norman's participation, however, the next IPR conference of 1942 did not demonstrate that it had been much influenced by the argument in *Emergence*. The conference mainly focused on war strategies rather than postwar policies, and discussion on Japan was sketchy and rather simplistic. The dominant view of Japan saw a clear distinction between liberals and militarists. The conference argued the need for recognizing and strengthening liberal elements in Japan. It acknowledged that 'so-called liberals had always retreated under pressure' and 'a reactionary chauvinism' had taken over.[89]

The next conference took place in January 1945. The Allied victory was in sight. The terms of Japan's surrender and the Allied postwar reconstruction policy were among the most significant topics. Participants largely agreed on Japanese relinquishment of colonial possessions, prosecution of Japanese war criminals and the abolition of 'evil' organizations and institutions, such as 'the secret police, the gendarmerie, the secret societies, and the super patriotic societies'. It was also agreed to utilize Japanese infrastructure and institutions to the full. On other crucial issues, however, opinions differed greatly, and no consensus was achieved. These issues were the degree of change to the Meiji Constitution; the role of the Emperor; the nature of political leaders in postwar Japan; the existence of the military; the power of *Zaibatsu*; and the duration of the occupation.

Norman, who participated in the conference as a Canadian diplomat in the Far Eastern Division of the Department of External Affairs, represented a group which argued for a thorough democratic reform from the bottom up. By then, Norman had developed a much more critical stance towards the imperial system and the residual feudalism in the Japanese political system than he presented in *Emergence*. This was clear in *Soldier and Peasant* (1943) and *Feudal Background of Japanese Politics* (1944). The latter was prepared as a data paper for the IPR conference of 1945. In *Feudal*, he argued that the Emperor and ultra-nationalistic organizations were major causes of militarism – opinions shared by Japanese Marxist scholars. He probably had developed a clear political agenda for postwar Japan, and saw himself as closely involved with its reconstruction. His mistrust of 'liberals', however, remained intact. For thorough democratic reform to be achieved, new leaders of grassroots movements should lead Japanese politics, not the old 'liberal' elite.

Thomas Bisson, Another Canadian, advocated a similar view in 1945. Bisson attended as an ISIPR staffer. His *America's Far Eastern Policy* was published in 1944 as part of the Inquiry series. The book is not about Japanese politics, and he did not refer to Japanese materials. His interpretation was probably less sophisticated than *Emergence*, but it was close to Norman's works of this period. According to Bisson, Japanese aggression was a result of the joint *Zaibatsu*–landlord economic monopoly under which peasants and workers were exploited. The 'God–Emperor' played a crucial ideological role in reinforcing the structure. Democratic moves were crushed in the name of the Emperor in order to maintain harmony with the 'national polity peculiar to Japan'. He noted that 'the hard inner core of the Imperial ideology [was] absolutist, aggressive, and essentially inimical to democratic concepts'. The abolition of the system, however, should be carried out by the Japanese people. Bisson and Norman shared the view that *Zaibatsu* was a threat to the development of democracy in Japan, and agreed on the need for its dissolution and land reforms. Like Norman, Bisson was also sceptical about so-called 'liberals' or 'moderates', and thought that postwar leadership should come from organized grassroots movements. While Bisson noted that armament expenditure should be reduced, he did not argue for the complete demolition of the Japanese military. Furthermore, he emphasized that Japan should have access to markets and raw materials.[90]

Others argued for more moderate reform from the top down. The main advocate for this line was the British. The conflict of opinions was already evident in a preparatory meeting which the ACIPR held in Atlantic City in January 1944. Chatham House, the British group, sent their report to this meeting, which argued for minimal reform by 'old liberals' and leaving the imperial system intact. This was understandable, considering Britain's constitutional monarchy and colonial holdings. Yui points out the view was very similar to that of George Sansom, British historian of Japan and then adviser on Far Eastern Affairs at the British embassy in Washington, DC.[91] Quite a few American IPR members supported this moderate policy, and they were influential among policy-makers. Borton, who was working at the State Department, for example, took this position in late 1943, and Iriye argues that this was a dominant view within the Department.[92] Borton and Blakeslee, another IPR member within the Department, continued to hold this view, and Grew, who became Under-Secretary of State in October 1944, pursued this line of policy until the end of the Pacific War. Opposition to this line was not negligible and increasing in other sections of the State Department. The conflict between the two groups became fierce in July–August 1945.[93] This divergence of opinion remained and would soon become a harbinger of conflicts within the Occupation forces in Japan after the war.

In 1945, the 'moderate' group argued that the imperial system should be preserved as long as the Emperor was willing to support democratic reforms. *Zaibatsu* would be useful to the Occupation, and the 'old liberals' should resume political leadership. On the issue of military capability, one British participant argued that for internal order and scientific research purposes, some forces should be left. Those who argued for thorough reform were inclined to insist on its abolition, although Bisson's case suggests there were differences among this group. The proceedings noted that because it would take a long time for democracy to be established in Japan, 'it would be undesirable' for the Allied countries to attempt too much by way of supporting democratic reforms within Japan. The primary object was to maintain internal stability in Japan in the immediate postwar period.[94]

Clearly, at the IPR conference in 1945 a 'thoroughly democratic Japan' was not an agreed agenda. The initial reforms of the Occupation forces were more 'radical' than envisaged then. Norman, his works and his line of thinking were influential in the initial Occupation period. Early reforms included release of political prisoners, encouragement of labour union movements, women's franchise, abolition of the military and the destruction of armament industries and aviation facilities, banning of statist, *Shintō* or Asianist organizations, drafting the new constitution and insertion of the peace article in it, land reforms, the dissolution of *Zaibatsu*, anti-trust law and reform of education and local government. Occupation officers often had little knowledge of Japan. Colonel Charles Kades, a member of the Government Section of the Supreme Commander of the Allied Powers (SCAP), and a major drafter of the new Japanese constitution, for example, recalled that his understanding of Japan derived largely from his reading of works by Norman.[95] As an expert, Norman was influential in the Occupational forces. Borton and other staff at the State Department regarded Konoe as an 'old liberal' or moderate in 1941 and during the Pacific War.[96] In contrast, Norman did not believe there was a clear line between 'liberal civilians' and 'militarists', and strongly condemned 'civilian' ministers, especially Konoe, as being responsible for leading Japan into the war. His opinion was a critical factor in the Occupation force's decision to regard Konoe as a war criminal.[97]

As Cold War preoccupations became dominant in the US government, the priority of the Occupation shifted to economic recovery and remilitarization. Norman and others were suppressed and even persecuted.[98] Yet opposition to 'thorough democratic reforms' did not emerge suddenly when the Cold War concern began to dominate the US government. It existed much earlier. Even in the initial Occupation period, SCAP was sending contradictory messages. The 'Reverse Course' meant a shift of emphasis, rather than a complete change in Occupation policies.

Colonialism, collective security and the United Nations

Another contentious issue at the IPR conferences during the Pacific War was colonialism. Anti-colonialism was a new development and it was a significant challenge to the post-League international order. Although Japanese aggression had been strongly condemned since 1931, this criticism did not encompass all colonialism in the region. During the Pacific War, the criticism was extended to other colonial powers. As colonial rule had been assumed to be the foundation for regional security, the possibility of decolonization meant the need to reassess the whole structure of collective security in the region and the world. In this discussion, clearer visions for the new world order and the United Nations began to emerge.

Independence and equality: ideals or war strategy?

The categorical challenge to colonialism marked a major departure from the framework of previous IPR operations, and suggested that the IPR's postwar focus would be on independence and nationalism in Asia. The American founders of the IPR advocated a more equal relationship with the 'Orient'. By the Orient they mainly meant the powers in East Asia, Japan and China. In particular, they saw a good relationship between Japan and the United States as essential. Even for those, such as Croly, who saw radical implications for the IPR, a Pacific Community was a community of colonial powers. Accordingly, the proposal for independent Korean participation was rejected in 1931, and the Japanese, American and European colonial status quo was assumed and accepted in the 1920s. Although the Philippine group was accepted as an autonomous body, this did not mean a rejection of the colonial framework of IPR operations. Britain joined the IPR in 1927, and France and the Netherlands began full participation in IPR conferences from 1933 on the grounds that they had colonial interests in the region. Those who attended IPR conferences from France, the Netherlands and to a lesser extent Britain were mainly former or current colonial office holders. The IPR's constitution, which allowed the participation of European powers with colonies in the region, was not amended.

Anti-colonialism developed not so much from the high ideals of post-League internationalism. It was a result of shrewd wartime negotiation. Certain colonies bargained and negotiated equal status with the colonial powers, which in turn desperately needed the full commitment of these colonies to win the war against Japan. The Atlantic Charter of August 1941 was their reference point. The charter's first five articles dealt with the principles of freedom to pursue life, liberty and happiness, and the other three pledged the signatory powers to effective participation in the maintenance of 'external security'. In this first part, one article proposed self-determination. This was interpreted as a challenge to colonial rule and indicated a new system of governance. Because the Atlantic Charter was regarded as the war ideology for the Allied countries, China as well as colonies in the region used it as a strong reference point to argue for equal status with, or independence from, colonial powers.

China had been arguing for equal relations with the powers for a while – the abolition of extraterritoriality and tariff rights of the powers in China, and the abolition of discriminatory treatment of Chinese immigrants. IPR conferences had been one significant venue for Chinese members to advocate their causes since 1925. Their focus was on the powers' actions in China.

They first addressed their criticism towards the British in China, and then the Japanese after 1929. For China, the war provided an opportunity to relinquish 'colonial' privilege in China.

'Equality' was a significant strategic matter for the Allied forces and Japan, for both needed the cooperation of China and other colonies. Already in 1938, in order to break the deadlock of the Sino-Japanese War and legitimize Japanese war goals, Konoe had to argue for a more equal relationship between China and Japan. He emphasized respect for Chinese sovereignty, and included Japanese repudiation of extraterritoriality in China in his proposal for the New Order in East Asia. This became a significant point of negotiation between Japan and the pro-Japan Wang government in Nanjing. It was even more important after the outbreak of the Pacific War. The Japanese empire defined its war ideology, the Greater East Asian Co-Prosperity Sphere, which proposed equality and independence of colonies from European powers. In January 1943, the Wang government issued a joint communiqué with Japan, and declared war against the United States and Britain. As a reward, the Japanese government promised to return its settlement, and to relinquish its extraterritorial rights.[99] Given the nature of the Wang government, a puppet regime largely manipulated by the Japanese military, the pledge was little more than a facade and a war tactic against the Allied forces.

The Japanese rhetoric of equality and anti-European colonialism aimed to promote Japanese rule in the region. Nevertheless, it was a powerful tool to consolidate regional leaders who were discontent with European colonialism and racial discrimination in the Allied countries. When the likelihood of Japanese defeat became more apparent, this was propagated more strongly and in more ideological terms. In November 1943, the Japanese government held the Greater East Asia Congress (*Daitōa kaigi*) in Tokyo, which was attended by pro-Japan independent leaders from the Philippines, Burma and India, and pro-Japan leaders from China and Thailand. Their joint declaration of war goals against the Allied countries stressed liberation from European powers and racial equality for the population in Asia.

Colonialism and the concept of security: Mont Tremblant, Quebec, 1942

As for the Japanese empire, the support of these countries was crucial for Allied victory, and the Allies needed to provide equivalent assurances. Extraterritoriality, discriminatory immigration laws and colonialism were key issues. It was a sore point among the Allies, chipping away at their much-needed unity. The United States took the lead. In May 1942, Sumner Welles, Under-Secretary of State, reflecting American public opinion, declared willingness to support decolonization. Iriye suggests that Roosevelt concurred.[100] Churchill, however, made it clear that the self-determination in the Atlantic Charter did not apply to British colonies.[101] Frustrated with this British attitude, the Indian independence movement intensified in this period, resulting in the arrests of Gandhi and Nehru in mid-1942.[102] A clash of opinion at the coming IPR conferences (December 1942 to January 1943) was inevitable, and the issue was central to defining not only the war ideology, but the nature of the postwar world order.

Reflecting the mood and trends of the time, anti-colonialism in Asia began to gain momentum in 1942. One official forum organized by the IPR – the Princeton conference which took place from 28 February to 1 March 1942 – was attended by fifty-eight government officials from (non-pro-Japan) China, India, the Netherlands East Indies and the Philippines. They strongly voiced the importance of abolishing white supremacy in Asia,[103] and opposed European colonial rule in the region – an issue which had not been seriously questioned by post-League internationalists until then. Some at the ISIPR and the ACIPR adopted this strong anti-colonial stance. Admiral Harry Yarnell, Chairperson of the ACIPR, for example, developed the idea of a Pacific Charter, under which a gradual path for independence of colonies was proposed.

Fierce debates took place between those for and against colonialism at Mont Tremblant. Those against colonialism were from North America, Australia, China and India, and the European groups defended it. The issue was discussed in relation to the implications of the Atlantic Charter for Asia and the Pacific – the document that opened the debate on decolonization. For the first time, India and Thailand (non-pro-Japan groups) participated in an IPR conference, and the Korean group (with observer status) attended for the first time since the 1929 conference. These participants from Asia demanded justice and equality with the powers. They argued for equal treatment in trade, immigration and war policy-making, stressing that they were a significant part of the Allies' war effort against Japan, and that their performance was a decisive factor in the outcome of the war.[104] These demands required the fundamental reassessment of domestic and external policies of the many Allied countries – policies towards decolonization, immigration, race relations and citizenship.

Taking an anti-colonial stance, some North Americans and Australians joined in the attack on European colonial powers.[105] The colonial powers did not want to give up their colonies or colonial rights in China. They argued the non-applicability of the Atlantic Charter to certain regions in the world, such as Asia. The British group, therefore, strictly followed Churchill's statements. They used the familiar rhetoric of 'native incapacity': 'there cannot be a divorce of power from responsibility', and colonial powers were responsible for the welfare and 'the security of the people'. This met with considerable criticism.[106] Rather than trying to reach a compromise, the British group attacked racial discrimination and the concentration camps for the Japanese in North America. While the White Australia Policy was not brought up here, this counterargument exposed the double standard of the accusers.

Soon after the 1942 conference, the US government announced some major policy changes on these controversial points. Although war developments probably explained this change, it is possible that discussions at the IPR conference may have had some impact on policy-makers. In January 1943, the US government signed a treaty with China promising to relinquish US extraterritoriality in China. At the end of the year, it abolished discrimination against Chinese immigrants to the United States, which had been practiced since the end of the nineteenth century. It also decided to grant citizenship to first-generation Chinese immigrants. On the issue of Allied unity, the British and US governments tried to reach some agreement on colonial issues in January 1943. British concessions to the colonies, however, remained minimal at this stage.[107] The Allied countries were yet to become the 'united nations'.

The proceedings of 1942 noted that two main themes (supporting liberation and guaranteeing collective security in the region) 'were destined to run through the conference as a sort of continuing counterpoint'.[108] Decolonization forced participants to reassess the structure of collective security of the region, where nation-states were yet to achieve independence. An international organization called the International Authority (IA) was proposed as a mediating body between colonial powers and local governments. It was to include not only the current (or former) colonial powers, but also the United States, China and the USSR. It was also noted that:

> [P]rovision should be made, where necessary, for the special ad hoc representation of colonial peoples when matters affecting them are under discussion.[109]

This was a significant step forward from the Fourteen Points of 1918. Colonial powers, however, demanded more power, and the discussion concluded to leave colonial powers with larger responsibility than initially proposed. Nevertheless, the IA would have significant rights: to investigate grievances presented by indigenous groups against a colonial power; to suggest general lines of policy for the development of self-governing institutions and the improvement of the well-being of the colonial people; and to demand and publish progress reports toward complete self-government of colonial people in the region.[110] Despite strong paternalism even among North Americans, the aim of the IA was clearly to secure smooth transition towards self-government of the colonies.

In 1942 'security' of Southeast Asia, where the major decolonization process was expected, meant security of the population in the region, not security of the individual state. This was a consequence of the absence of independent states, not a conscious decision to put priority on the security of the population over that of the state. Nevertheless, as a result, the notion of security encompassed social and economic spheres, and was not confined to the domain of defence.

> [P]roblems of a political, a strategic and a social or cultural nature cannot

in practice be separated. Political freedom – even where it already exists, as in Thailand and the Philippines – would soon collapse if a nation found itself barred from economic opportunity. Full protection against outside aggressors requires more than a military and naval preparedness guaranteed or undertaken by a combination of great powers...[111]

Terms such as 'social security' and 'economic security' were often used. 'Improved labor standards, economic adjustment and social security' were critical for the security of the region.[112] The IA was envisaged as a regional organization with considerable autonomy from the central body.[113] The role of the United States, however, was clear:

> ... the United States as possibly the strongest nation likely to emerge from the war ... would have to pledge its share in the maintenance of that international law and order without which all hopes of reforms in that area might prove illusory.[114]

The United Nations and the New World Order: Hot Springs, Virginia, 1945

Decolonization in the Pacific was the most divisive topic among participants in 1945. In 1942, the issue was discussed largely in terms of the Atlantic Charter. The ninth IPR conference was held at Hot Springs, Virginia, in January 1945. A few months earlier, in August 1944, the United States, Britain, the USSR and China met at the Dumbarton Oaks, an eighteenth-century mansion near by Washington, DC, and produced a document called 'Proposals for the establishment of a general international organization'. Later in 1945, the document would become the base for the charter of the envisaged new international organization, the United Nations. The draft charter was discussed, modified and signed by member countries at the San Francisco conference in June 1945, and the United Nations was formally established in October. This 1944 draft charter (or the Dumbarton Oaks plan) was largely based on a draft prepared by the American Group (originally called the Agenda Group, and largely overlapping with the Advisory Committee on Post-War Foreign Policy), in which Welles and Hornbeck were involved. 'Various experts, never many', were involved in this group's discussion on the postwar international organization.[115] At Hot Springs, this draft charter was a reference point for the discussion on decolonization and its implication for collective security both in the region and the world. The nature of the United Nations and the new world order they envisaged was becoming clear.

The great powers of the Allies had already agreed that this 1944 draft charter would be the foundation of a new international security system. Participants at Hot Springs accepted this. They wanted no radical changes, but 'clarification of meaning and substantial improvement'.[116] According to the draft, the United Nations' purposes were to maintain peace and security, to promote closer relations among nations, and to assist in achieving common ends among nations. It was 'based on the principle of the sovereign equality of all peace-loving states'. Its principal organs were: a General Assembly of all member states; a Security Council of the great powers (the United States, Britain, the USSR and China and 'in due course' France); an international court of justice; and a Secretariat. Unlike the League of Nations, the use of force was thought crucial for international security. Chapter 8, Section B, detailed the role and procedures of its military operations.

Like the League of Nations, the United Nations was envisaged as not supranational, but inter-national, firmly based on the sovereignty of each state. While each state, small, middle or great powers, had equally one vote, the role of the great powers was critical. Three 'great' powers in the Security Council, the United States, the USSR and China, indicated a dramatic change from the League days. The first two were outside the League, which many thought crippled its function. The choice of China probably reflected American strategic thinking more than a consensus among other powers, given the state of its internal conflict and devastated economy. Japan, one of the great powers in the League mechanism until 1933, was an enemy. It was assumed that China would take up the position.

The central role of the United State in the new world order was taken for granted, rather than asserted by American members. Its role in postwar Japan was considered a key factor, and its economic assistance towards the Pacific region vital. Andrew McFadyean, leader of the British group, maintained:

> ... the world's future depended to a very special degree on the policy of the United States – the world's greatest industrial power, the world's sole creditor – during the next few years. On this policy, which would substantially determine the prospects of world economic expansion, the issue of war and peace in the future might well depend. ... This was true of the Pacific, as it was of Europe.[117]

When they discussed 'public opinion' in support of collective security and the United Nations, despite the acknowledgment of its significance in each country, participants almost exclusively discussed American public opinion. Its optimistic, enthusiastic and positive support, not a disillusioned, cynical and critical view, was vital. Participants seem to have forgotten America's close ties with the Pacific earlier in the century. They were glad to know that American public opinion 'began to recognize the increasing importance of Asia and the part which the United States was bound to play in the Pacific'.[118]

Decolonization continued to be the most divisive topic among participants in 1945. Along with Chinese and Indian members, many North American members attacked European colonialism. This shocked and angered members from Britain, France and the Netherlands. Since the last conference, Chatham House had been contemplating withdrawal from the IPR for that reason. The discussion in 1945 made British and other European groups consider this option anew.[119] European groups were not ready to commit to the self-determination of colonies or to give up their colonial rights. They continued to argue native incapacity and 'white man's burden'. The concluding statement of a member from the Netherlands read: [Colonial powers] 'brought civilization' to their colonies, knew the best way to develop them, and had 'the special responsibility'.[120] Chinese and Indians pointed out that Japanese, German and Italian imperialists used the same rhetoric to justify their colonial possessions. Significantly, although Chinese members argued for equal treatment with the other powers, in the discussion of Korea's decolonization, they sided with the British and doubted the Korean people's capacity for self-rule.[121]

Discussion of decolonization led to debates on racial discrimination. In response to strong criticism of colonialism, British members questioned the double standard of American treatment of 'coloured' people. On this issue of racial equality opinions were unanimous, marking another significant difference from the Paris Peace Conference of 1919. Participants noted that this was a revisiting of the initial IPR agenda. It was, however, not a simple revisit, as the initial agenda did not largely encompass colonies. Furthermore, although participants of 1945 used a rather Orientalist framework of the dichotomy between East and West, discussion included complex ethnic conflicts within Asia and Europe. The session called 'cultural and race relations' produced unanimous endorsement of the universal principle of non-discrimination on the basis of race. Not only a strong sense of social justice, but also a concern with a pragmatic war tactics was responsible for this statement.

> [I]t would be difficult if not impossible to counter [Japanese propaganda of interracial grievances] effectively with words alone. ... the United Nations should as soon as possible issue a joint declaration of policy repudiating every kind of racial discrimination. ... Although nothing more than a declaration of principle, such a statement, it was thought, might go far to reassure Asiatics of the intentions of the Allied Powers.[122]

Throughout the Pacific War, a concern with equality and human rights had been expressed by the Allies. But in Hot Springs, the IPR went further to draft a preliminary statement on human rights. It 'proclaimed the fundamental equality of all peoples and pledged the United Nations to increasing efforts to enable all peoples to enjoy the benefits of that equality'. It also announced 'the principle of universal international accountability' for 'colonial and dependent peoples' as well as minority groups within a nation.[123] In 1948, a few years after the end of World War II, the United Nations proclaimed the Universal Declaration of Human Rights. The Nazi holocaust was probably the main catalyst. The statement written at Hot Springs in 1945 may or may not have had a connection to this monumental declaration. Nevertheless, it suggests a strong contribution from Asia to a concept which is now regarded as 'Western'. It also indicated that the war and decolonization process in the Pacific region prompted significant self-reflection among the Allies, and their reassessment of what had been seen as dominant notions of international politics.

The concept of 'security' was more narrowly defined in 1945 than in 1942. This grew from not the dismissal of, but the recognition of the importance of social and economic factors in international politics. Humanitarian, social and economic factors were discussed extensively in the 1944 draft charter and at Hot Springs. Participants emphasized the significance of public opinion and educational measures, and argued for strengthening the IPR's research projects on intellectual relations. Social and economic issues, such as 'the improvement of labour standards, health and nutrition', were regarded as critical especially in 'dependent territories'. Reflecting the mood, the 1944 draft charter proposed the establishment of an Economic and Social Council, with regional agencies. The move clarified the domain of the Economic and Social Council, clearly distinguishing it from that of the Security Council.[124] Now with the proposal of the military function in the United Nations, the Security Council dealt with the 'real' security issue, defence.

Less emphasis on regional autonomy and more on the world centre was clear in discussions on security at Hot Springs. The 1944 draft charter had a provision for regional arrangements or agencies, although it was noted that it should be consistent with a wider framework. Participants discussed whether a regional security organization should be established for the Pacific. Although this autonomous regional organization was supported enthusiastically at Mont Tremblant in 1942, this was not the case in 1945. The dominant opinion was that 'security was a world problem'. It was because 'in the last resort effective measures of enforcement' must depend on an accord among the great powers, they should be 'associated from the start in every decision to be taken'. '[S]ecurity should not and cannot be segmented'.[125] This centrality of the great powers was criticized especially by Australia and New Zealand members, who promoted a more regional, and more middle power based organization, especially in the South Pacific.

In 1942 Corbett, an author of *Post-War World* (the Inquiry series), also had envisaged an international organization in which an assembly of nation-states had the executive power, and regretted the tendency of the centrality of the great powers. At Hot Springs, however, he emphasized the pragmatism in order to realize the ideals:

> ... imperfect as it is, the [Dumbarton Oaks] plan is much better than nothing, and we can, by getting into the organization and working the proposed institutions, stimulate that education process that is essential condition of further progress. ... Bearing the essential limitations, we can, I believe, make useful proposals whereby the principles of the general organization may be carried out in the Pacific area which is our domain. ... What I urge is *not* a sacrifice of our ideals. ... With skill and patience

let us seek the places where advance is possible now, keeping well in hand the reserves that we shall need for the long pull towards an ultimate world commonwealth.[126] (emphasis in original)

This was a statement of a post-League internationalist, an expert working in close connection with the state and inter-state organizations. For him, the ideals are far from having been realised, but one needs to start somewhere and keep making efforts.

Postscript

The course the IPR took in 1925–45 reflected visions for the Pacific region and the world among American post-League internationalists. It also demonstrated how their counterparts in other countries, especially in Japan, reacted to their envisaged order. In the 1920s, American founders of the IPR advocated the concept of the Pacific Community, an embodiment of an American regional order. They promoted a Pacific-centred perspective and a relatively equal relationship with the new powers in Asia, Japan and China. They emphasized a mission of educating the public/society. By the mid-1930s, however, the emphasis had clearly shifted. The region-centred perspective and enthusiasm had been lost. Key IPR figures, particularly Carter, wanted IPR operations to be more world-oriented, and for the focus to be on the state rather than society. The region was a sub-unit of the world, rather than the area on which the world was centred. For Carter, the centre of world politics was the Atlantic side of the United States. The United States should play an expanded role in the region and in the world, and its involvement should not only be economic, but also in the security domain.

The IPR's shift was underscored by two major wars in the region. The Sino-Japanese War (1937–45) strengthened Carter's conviction about the significance of the region in global politics, the IPR's need for addressing policy matters and the US global mission. Carter envisaged an IPR that was more relevant to, useful for and influential in foreign policy formulation. He saw China as a fortress of the post-League international order against Japanese aggression, and felt vindicated when the two wars in Europe and East Asia were connected through the Tripartite Pact of Japan, Germany and Italy of 1940. This global perspective and the state orientation of IPR operations were accentuated during the Pacific War. With Japan absent (from 1939), IPR conferences became high-level policy forums for the Allies after 1941. The ISIPR endorsed the war ideology of the Allied forces, and redefined post-League internationalism accordingly.

The 'shift' of emphasis within IPR operations in the 1930s should not be viewed as a departure from the 'unrealistic' or 'idealistic' visions of IPR members in the 1920s. It is best understood as a manifestation of certain factors in the IPR's initial vision. Because American post-League internationalism largely shaped this vision, it meant that these increasingly dominant factors were inherent in this American internationalism. The parameters of the American global order, which became more evident in IPR operations during the Pacific War, therefore, originated in the 1920s. Carter did not change the course of the IPR, but only accentuated factors which were already present and were growing stronger. Most IPR members believed that the post-League order was morally right, they reified the nation and identified it with the state. Their positive view of the role of the state and their cordial relations with it were furthered in a war context.

The trends were largely paralleled in Japan and other countries, despite the difference in their regional and global visions, and domestic political and intellectual contexts. Post-League internationalists at various National Councils were experts on regional affairs and foreign policies dealing with the region. While they were committed to international organizations and agreements, they were equally concerned with the 'national interests' of their nation-states. They played a role as international publicists and think-tank members for their state, and their activities were increasingly co-opted to the state apparatus as the wars developed.

At the end of the war, it seemed that Carter's vision of the world order had triumphed. The United States had emerged as a global superpower. American involvement in European politics increased, and the Pax Americana reigned globally. Some even began to call the twentieth century the American Century. The United Nations took over from the League of Nations. Symbolically, its headquarters moved to New York, on the Atlantic coast of the United States. American dominance of the United Nations has been evident from its inception. Post-League internationalism, which was redefined during the Pacific War, also seems to have been advanced. It was a 1945 interpretation, that defined the Charter of the United Nations. The basic structures and personnel of the League of Nations were largely inherited by its successor. The United States championed liberal democracy, which was regarded as the core ideology of American global hegemony. It had a mission to preach this ideal and its successes to the world. It had the resources for the task.

Ironically, at this precise moment that Carter and IPR members in North America felt that their vision had been realized, the fall of the IPR began. On this point, it is important to draw a comparison between 1919 and 1945. Wilson's vision was a bulwark against Bolshevism as well as the Axis powers. Similarly, the American ideal of 'liberal democracy', which appeared to have triumphed by defeating the totalitarian and fascist regimes of Germany, Japan and Italy, was double-edged. As the Cold War mentality became dominant, it quickly became the rhetoric against the communist bloc. Domestic and international politics were at the crossroads. In the late 1940s, soon after the war, Carter was the target of severe criticism of the ISIPR's handling of China during the war. This may have been the result of personal animosity against Carter, or a manifestation of jealousy over the influence the ISIPR and the

ACIPR had enjoyed during the war. Regardless, their supposed communist sympathies were the target of attack.

When McCarthyism swept American life in the early 1950s, it attacked the IPR specifically for its sympathetic attitude towards communism in China, and accused it of responsibility for the 'loss' of China from the 'liberal democratic' camp to the communist camp. It is ironic that a domestic expression of a particular interpretation of the American ideal contributed greatly to the denigration of the moral and intellectual integrity of American society. It is symbolic that the hearing committee was named the House of Un-American Activities Committee. It furthered ideological intolerance towards communists or those who were suspected of being communists inside and outside the United States. There were many casualties not only among Asia specialists in North America, including Lattimore and Norman, but also among North American UN officers and prominent post-League internationalists, mainly from the East coast establishment. They labelled these Asia specialists or post-League internationalists as disloyal to the United States, while in reality their faith in American ideals was probably even stronger than their accusers'.

A 'left-wing' tendency was growing in IPR operations in the postwar period. The IPR made a conscious adjustment to various postwar developments. The IPR conferences after 1945, particularly the one held in Lachnow in India in 1950, focused on nationalism in Asia, and the IPR published works on nationalism and independence movements. The roles of India and countries in Southeast Asia became much more dominant, indicating strong IPR support for the Asia–Africa conference. The IPR survived continued attacks and the damage that resulted until 1961. Around that time, however, as Thomas suggests, the fields and agendas which the IPR initiated were taken up by other institutions, marking the end of the historical mission of the IPR.

North American post-League internationalists suffered greatly under the banner of anti-communism in which the rhetoric of American ideals and 'liberal democracy' played a critical role. There were parallels in Japan and other countries. Konoe and Matsuoka, who were closely connected with younger JCIPR members in the late 1930s and early 1940s, were convicted as war criminals and died before the Tokyo Tribunal ended. Like their counterparts in the Allied countries, Maeda, Rōyama, Matsumoto and other key JCIPR members 'collaborated' with the state in the war effort. As a consequence, they were purged in 1946, and this was not lifted until 1950. Soon after they were rehabilitated, however, most of them resumed 'internationalist' activities.[1] They may have been 'tainted' or stigmatized, but they were also highly sought after in the new 'democratic' and 'internationalist' Japan. These new slogans were to flourish under the long conservative reign of the 'Liberal Democratic' Party. Rōyama, Maeda, Matsumoto and others worked for the ILO, UNESCO and the United Nations. Matsumoto and Takaki contributed to the development of the American studies in postwar Japan. Both were founding members of the American

Studies Association in Japan (*Amerika gakkai*) (founded in 1947), in which Takaki became the first President. Both also promoted Japanese–American relations, and Matsumoto contributed to the foundation of the International House (*Kokusai bunka kaikan*) in Tokyo in 1952 to foster international exchange. Rōyama advanced his prewar social democratic vision by becoming one of the founders of the Democratic Socialist Party (*Minshatō*) in 1960.

In his memoir, Matsumoto defined himself as an 'old liberal'. The term 'old liberal', however, tends to neglect the fact that they were quite ready to accept great state intervention and to cooperate with the state. Although many wished a complete break with the past, there were many pre-war legacies in postwar Japan. It was still a period of crisis. For the national elite, service to the state/nation remained critical not for wartime efforts, but for postwar reconstruction and economic recovery. There were 'new' efforts to make the Japanese nation-state respectable and 'democratic' enough to be part of the 'international community' (*kokusai shakai*). In this sense, 'post-League internationalism' became significant again in the era of the United Nations.

The world after World War II looked radically different from the world Carter and many IPR members knew. The Cold War and the bipolar politics of the superpowers dominated international relations. Nuclear weapons brought a very different dimension. The Pacific region was transformed, too. The Japanese empire had been dismantled, the United States ruled an occupied Japan and communist China emerged in 1949. The Cold War's influence in the region was apparent. The Korean War began in 1950, which ignited the first of the Japanese economic booms. The conclusion of the San Francisco Treaty of 1951 meant Japan's regained independence and re-entry to the international community, while the United States retained its military base in Japan. Many Japanese were, however, aware that this 'international community' they had joined was the anti-communist camp. Nationalism and independence movements were intensifying in former colonies in Asia, but neither were they free from the Cold War. Southeast Asia was structured into the Cold War security framework, and the Vietnam War began.

The ideas and actions of post-League internationalists at the IPR had been shaped and constricted by the inter-war framework, which now seemed dated. These IPR members' experiences and their domestic contexts varied greatly from one country to another. Yet, despite all these differences, the issues the IPR grappled with have surprisingly universal and relevant implications for contemporary debates in the post-Cold War period. First, despite the global dominance of the United States after World War II and its central position in the United States, as in the 1920s, the United States needed to cooperate with other important states. It needed to negotiate with them on the terms of agreements for its global order. Second, just as had been the case in the 1920s, whether this cooperation was based on an equal relationship was questionable. Dower, for example, defined the US–Japan relationship in the postwar period as Japanese subordination to the United States.[2] Even after Japan achieved the status of a great economic power, and began to be regarded as a superpower in the late 1980s, the equality of the relationship has remained contentious. The issue resurfaced more prominently in the recession of the late 1990s, while the debate over the revision of Article Nine of the Japanese Constitution and the US–Japan Security Treaty certainly are challenging the postwar status quo. One of the agendas of the Pacific Community, an equal relationship with the powers in East Asia, therefore, is yet to be realized as far as Japan is concerned.

Third, the relationship between former colonizers and colonized in Asia remains unequal long after the demise of colonialism. Colonialism (European, Japanese and American) in Asia left behind many problems. Much of the economic inequality between North and South originated in the colonial structure. Furthermore, the issue of an equal relationship is not confined to the domain of politics and the economy. It was only in 1978 that Edward Said problematized what many had seen as the 'reality' and 'fact' of life, the perception of the dichotomy between East and West and that of the superiority of the latter over the former. Remarkable economic growth in Japan, followed by the newly industrialized economies (NIEs), and other countries in the region provided the basis for a challenge to the dominant perception of this power relationship. Indeed, shortly before the 'Asian economic crisis' in the mid-1990s, there was a voluminous literature claiming the resurgence of a Pacific-centred perspective on the world and a more equal relationship between the 'West' and Asia.

Yet the demise of colonialism did not result in an equal partnership, and even recent economic achievement of Asia did not appear to be sufficient to realize this ultimate goal. The colonial legacy reverberates in popular assumptions and rhetoric which, consciously or unconsciously, reinforce the existing structure of dominance. This is most evident in the very popular and dominant notion of the 'West' (probably one of the most dominant ideologies in the twentieth century). The concept or ideology of the 'West' continues to reinforce the notion of the moral superiority of former Euro-American colonial powers. This sense of moral superiority is evident not only in Euro-American dealings with non-Euro-Americans in the region. It is also relevant to Japanese people dealing with the 'rest' of Asia, or dominant groups of Japanese dealing with what are regarded as minority groups in Japan. It also applies to almost all nations in Asia and the world. It seems that it is not easy to be free from forming hierarchical relations with neighbours or minority groups within one's own nation.

Fourth, the notion of 'culture', particularly 'national culture', held by IPR members retains dominant rhetorical power. It is much more subtle to assert one's power over other groups in the domain of culture than in economic and political domains. The claim is hard to validate and therefore not easy to refute. The rhetoric of 'culture' or 'national culture' has been used to dismiss the interests and rights of minority groups, and to eliminate external intervention in 'domestic' affairs.

Fifth, the IPR's case has relevance in contemporary debates on the role of

INGOs in the region and in the world. As was the case for the IPR before 1945, the nature of an INGO is still largely defined by its relationship with the state, and this is determined by its aims, not its self-proclaimed status as 'private', 'non-official' or 'non-governmental'. Recent developments among INGOs indicate that they are less confined by the nation-state framework than was the IPR. They are freer to imagine and voice views which could challenge state policies. Their issue-focused organization (political rights, indigenous rights, minority rights, environment, women's rights, economic cooperation), as distinct from country-focused organizations like the IPR, seems to more easily create a shared identity and interests beyond nation-state boundaries. This makes a transnational network and alliance among non-official experts easier to achieve, although there is another danger of domination by certain agendas and marginalization of others.

Despite some successes in creating alternative channels in international politics, as long as states hold the key policy-making power, their relations with the state remain a critical issue.[3] Contemporary INGOs experience a similar dilemma in their dual quest for influence and autonomy. Influence often comes at the expense of a critical stance and transnational perspective. As the IPR's case demonstrated, the relationship between the state and intellectuals, especially the intellectual establishment, was not oppositional. It was the case not only in Japan, but also in the United States and other so-called 'Western' countries. The relationship between 'liberal' intellectuals and the state during wartime in the Allied countries remains a rich area for future research.[4] What needs to be done is not so much the accusation of individuals' actions, but a rigorous scrutiny of the mechanism which makes this 'co-option' almost voluntary. This 'collaboration' can easily resurface especially in a time of external crisis. Sixth, although it is easy to condemn the national elite nature and status of IPR members before 1945, whether this has changed much is doubtful.[5] Members of INGOs still often come from high socio-economic groups with high educational levels. Their elite nature, their lack of public accountability, and their class interests in terms of shaping a new paradigm and of creating new hegemonic knowledge are often criticized. As the IPR case demonstrated, the key was not the fact that it was a 'non-state' agency, but what sort of knowledge was being created, for what purpose, and whose interests this knowledge served.

The notions 'liberalism' or 'liberal democracy' contain contradictory elements. The meaning depends on the people who believe in it, and the context the term is used both in international and domestic politics. *Laissez-faire* liberals generally oppose state intervention. They stress the political rights of citizens against state oppression, and the 'independence' of 'private' and 'civil' forces from state control. *Laissez-faire* liberalism also implies the survival of the fittest and minimal state intervention to 'correct' inequality, leading to the reinforcement of existing power relations. Welfare liberals, or what I call New Liberals, on the other hand, emphasize the social and economic rights of the people. Although this means the enhancement of equity and welfare for the needy, it strengthens state power, and furthers the cooperation between the intellectual establishment (still regarded as a part of civil society) and the state. This may result in the suppression of political rights of certain groups within a country.

Although I have offered a very critical approach to post-League liberals at the IPR, focusing on their limitations and strong state orientation, this is not to negate their positive impacts. A strong stance against colonialism and racial discrimination, although it became a dominant force at the IPR only during the Pacific War, was a very significant step. This also led IPR members to draft a statement of universal human rights in 1945. It was a concept which was furthered in the UN's Universal Declaration of Human Rights in 1948. The declaration counterposed a strong pole, the priority of the people or individuals, against the dominant pole, the priority of the state, in international and domestic politics. The significance of this action has reverberated, especially in the last few decades. The abstract principles post-League internationalists adhered to also remain significant. Historically, these principles were initiated by and thought applicable only to certain class, gender, racial, ethnic, cultural, regional or national groups, or those with certain ideologies, beliefs or religions. Yet their potential was clear when they were taken up by an ever wider group of people. It can be realized only when access to these principles is not denied in any way to current 'outsiders'. There are numerous historical occasions when 'liberalism' and 'liberal democracy', which have been seen as defining the international community, have been tools of 'exclusion' as much as of inclusion and tolerance. Class, gender and colonial 'outsiders' had to problematize the 'accepted' facts at certain historical periods. For this reason, one needs to constantly scrutinize what is regarded as the 'established fact', because once one starts to celebrate its 'liberal democratic' nature, it becomes a tool to justify the status quo.

The case of the IPR has demonstrated the significance of this constant examination of the structure of dominance. It is only through a critical assessment of the 'international community', into which the IPR was eager to integrate the Pacific region, that equity can be advanced in international and domestic politics. The time has come to take the experiment of this forgotten and stigmatized organization seriously.

Appendix 1: IPR conferences

The first conference
1925, 30 June to 14 July, Honolulu (US)
Main agenda
Immigration and inter-racial problems
Round Table discussions[1]
Immigration, Inter-racial relations, The role of religion and missionaries in inter-racial and international relations, Industrialization in the Far East, Custom, tariff and foreign loans, National economic policies throughout the Pacific, The government diplomatic organizations in the Pacific countries

The second conference
1927, 15–29 July, Honolulu (US)
Main agenda
China's foreign relations, Food and population
Round Table discussions
Tariff autonomy in China, Extra-territoriality in China, Foreign concessions and settlements in China, Foreign missions and Pacific relations, Population and food supply, Industrialization and foreign investment, Immigration and emigration in the Pacific, Diplomatic relations in the Pacific, International education and communication, The Pacific mandates, The future of the Institute

The third conference
1929, 23 October to 9 November, Kyoto (Japan)
Main agenda
China's foreign relations, the Manchurian issue
Round Table discussions
The machine age and traditional culture, Food and population in the Pacific, Industrialization in the Pacific countries, China's foreign relations, The financial reconstruction of China, The problems of Manchuria, Diplomatic relations in the Pacific

The fourth conference
1931, 21 October–2 November, Hangzhou and Shanghai (China)

Main agenda
Economic relations in the Pacific, China's economic development
Round Table discussions
Economic relations in the Pacific, China's economic development, Political relations in the Pacific, China's international relations, Cultural relations in the Pacific

The fifth conference
1933, 14–26 August, Banff (Canada)
Main agenda
Economic conflict and control in the Pacific
Round Table discussions
Economic conflict and control, Shipping in the Pacific, Instability of currency, Differences of standards of living, Differences in labour standards, Japanese expansion, the United States recovery programme, China's reconstruction programme, Ottawa: A cooperative attempt at recovery, Economic conflict and public opinion

The sixth conference
1936, 15–29 August, Yosemite (US)
Main agenda
Aims and results of social and economic policies in Pacific countries
Round Table discussions[2]
Trade and trade rivalry between the US and Japan, Factors affecting the recent industrial development of Japan, The resources and economic development of the Soviet Far East, The reconstruction movement in China, The working of diplomatic machinery in the Pacific

The seventh conference
1939, 18 November–2 December, Virginia Beach (US) (Study meeting for the proposed Inquiry series)
Main agenda
The Far Eastern conflict
Round Table discussions
The position of Japan and China, Third parties in the Far Eastern conflict, Possibilities of adjustment in the Far East

The eighth conference
1942, 4–14 December, Mont Tremblant (Canada)
Main agenda
Wartime and post-war cooperation of the United Nations in the Pacific and the Far East
Round Table discussions
United Nations Cooperation in the Pacific, Political military problems, Military-political problems, Economic problems, Social and demographic problems, (mainly focused on China, Japan, Southeast Asia, and India)

The ninth conference
1945, 6–17 January, Hot Springs (US)
Main agenda
Security in the Pacific
Round Table discussions
The future of Japan, Economic recovery and progress in Pacific countries, Cultural and race relations, The future of dependent areas, Collective security

The tenth conference
1947, 5–20 September, Stratford-upon-Avon (Britain)
Main agenda
Problems of economic reconstruction in the Far East
Round Table discussions
Japan and Korea, China, Southeast Asia and the Southwest Pacific, Agricultural improvement, Industrial development, International economic problems, Education and technology

The eleventh conference[3]
1950, 3–15 October, Lachnow (India)
Main agenda
Nationalism in the Far East

The twelfth conference
1954, 27 September–8 October, Kyoto (Japan)
Main agenda
Problems with the development of living standard in the Far East

The thirteenth conference
1958, 3–12 February, Lahol (Pakistan)
Main agenda
Problems of foreign relations in South Asia and East Asia

Appendix 2: participants at the IPR conferences, 1925–47[1]

1925/140[2]	Australia 6, Canada 7, China 14, Hawai'i 29, Japan 20, Korea 8, New Zealand 11, Philippine 3, US 39 (2 from YMCA in England and Geneva, and 1 from England)
1927/136	Australia 5, Britain 14, Canada 15, China 14, Hawai'i 15, Japan 18, Korea 3, New Zealand 5, Philippine 3, US 44
Observer	League of Nations (LN), International Labour Organization (ILO)
1929/212	Australia 11, Britain 17, Canada 34, China 31, Japan 56, New Zealand 7, Philippine 8, US 48
Observer	LN, ILO, France, the Netherlands, USSR, Mexico
1931/156	Australia 9, Britain 31, Canada 14, China 37, Japan 21, New Zealand 6, Philippine 6, US 32
Observer	LN, ILO, the Netherlands
1933/176	Australia 4, Britain 24, Canada 43, China 19, France 2, Japan 23, Netherlands-Netherlands Indies 4, New Zealand 6, Philippine 7, US 44
Observer	LN, ILO, International Studies Conference of LN
1936/177	Australia 9, Britain 22, Canada 27, China 21, France 5, Japan 22, Netherlands-Netherlands Indies 6, New Zealand 5, Philippine 3, US 54, USSR 3
Observer	LN, ILO, International Institute of Intellectual Cooperation
1939/48	Australia 4, Canada 11, China 13, New Zealand 1, Philippine 4, US 15
Observer	LN, ILO, Rockefeller Foundation, Geneva Research Centre, France, India
1942/131	Australia 4, Britain 20, Canada 18, China 18, (Fighting) France 4, India 10, Korea 1, Netherlands-Netherlands Indies 13, New Zealand 3, Philippines 4, Thailand 2, US 34
Observer	LN, ILO, Carnegie Corporation, Rockefeller Foundation

1945/157	Australia 7, Britain 22, Canada 15, China 25, France 13, India 5, Korea 3, Netherlands-Netherlands Indies 14, New Zealand 2, Philippines 4, Thailand 3, US 44
Observer	LN, ILO, Rockefeller Foundation, United Nations Relief and Rehabilitation Administration
1947/73	Australia 4, Britain 22, Canada 11, China 8, France 3, New Zealand 3, US 22
Observer	United Nations, Rockefeller Foundation, Burma, India, Korea, Netherlands-Netherlands Indies, Siam

Appendix 3: IPR office holders

The International Secretariat of the IPR (the ISIPR)[1]

1925
Executive Secretary   Merle Davis (US, H)[2]
     Charles Loomis (US, H)

1926–29
General Secretary   M. Davis (1926–30)
Associate General Secretary   C. Loomis (1926–29)
Research Secretary   John Condliffe (NZ) (1927–31)
Research Assistant   William Holland (NZ) (1928–31)

1930–33
Acting General Secretary   C. Loomis (1929–33)
Acting Research Secretary   William Holland (1931–33)
Editor, *Pacific Affairs*   Elizabeth Green (US, H) (1927–33)[3]

1933–46
Secretary General   Edward Carter (US, E)[4] (1933–46)
Research Secretary   W. Holland (1933–1943)
Editor of *Pacific Affairs*   Owen Lattimore(US, E) (1933–41)
Conference Secretary   C. Loomis (1933)
Assistant Treasurer   Hilda Austern (US, E)

1946–61
Secretary-General   W. Holland (1946–61)
Publication Secretary   Mary Healy

The Pacific Council[5]

1925–27
Chairperson   Ray Wilbur (US, W)[6]
Treasurer   Frank Atherton (US, H)
Other members   Inoue Junnosuke (Japan)
     David Yui (China)
     Mungo MacCallum (Australia)

Robert Borden (Canada)
James Allen (NZ)

1927–33
Chairperson   Jerome Greene (US, E) (until 1932)
Treasurer   F. Atherton
Other members   Nitobe Inazō (Japan)
                          Newton Rowell (Canada)
                          Frederic Eggleston (Australia)
                          Lionel Curtis (Britain)
                          D. Yui
                          J. Allen

1933–[1935][7]
Chairperson   Newton Baker (US) (from 1932)
Treasurer   F. Atherton
Members   F. Eggleston
                          Nitobe I. (until 1933)
                          J. Allen
                          N. Rowell
                          Hu Shuxi (China)
                          Archibold Rose (Britain)
                          L.P. Le C. De Bussy (Netherlands–
                            Netherlands Indies)
                          Manuel Camus (Philippines)
                          F.N. Petroff (USSR)

[1935]–1936
Chairperson   N. Baker
Other members   F. Eggleston
                          J.W. Dafoe (Canada)
                          H. Shuxi
                          A. Sarraut (France)
                          Takayanagi Kenzō (Japan)
                          H. Belshaw (NZ)
                          C. Benitez (Philippines)
                          A.V. Alexander (Britain)
                          V.E. Motylev (USSR)
                          G.A Dunlop (Netherlands-NI)
                          R.B. Anderson (Advisory Committee in
                            Honolulu)

[1937]–1939
Chairperson   J.W. Dafoe (Canada) (1936–38)
Treasurer   N. Baker (died in 1937)
Honorary Vice-Chairperson F. Atherton
Other members   F. Eggleston
                          N. Rowell (1939)

H. Shuxi
R.L. Wilbur
Ishii Kikujirō (Japan)

1939–42	
Chairperson	Philip Jessup (US, E)
Other members	Jack Shepherd (Australia)
	Edgar Tarr (Canada)
	W.W. Yen (China)
	J. Condliffe (NZ)
	C. Osias (Philippines)
	Frederick Field (US, E)

1942–45	
Chairperson	E. Tarr
Other members	unknown

1945–47	
Chairperson	Percy Corbett (Canada)
Vice-Chairperson	R.J.F. Boyer (Australia)
	Chiang Mon-lin (China)
	Paul Pelliot (France)
	Francis Visman (Netherlands-NI)
Other members	I. Clunies Ross (Australia)
	R.G. Gavell (Canada)
	Paul Emile Naggiar (France)
	Jaime Herhandez (Philippines)
	E. Zhukov (USSR)
	Andrew McFadyean (Britain)
	Robert Sproul (US)

Archival sources

Australia

Official documents in Australian Archives, Canberra (AA) (series number; item number)

The Institute of Pacific Relations (IPR):
A981; Org 93, Org 94, Org 95, M1942; 6

Pacific Branch:
A1; 1919/8756

Pan-Pacific Science Congress:
A981; Conf 256 and Conf 262

Pan-Pacific Women's Conference:
A981; Conf 232

Pan-Pacific Trade Union Conference:
A981; Conf 258

Institutional and private papers

Frederic Eggleston: MS 423, National Library of Australia, Canberra (NLA)

Hessel Duncan-Hall: MS 5547, NLA

John Latham: MS 1009, NLA

Harrison Moore: Harrison Moore Papers, Group 11, Archives of University of Melbourne (AUM)

Keith Officer: MS 2629, NLA

E. L. Piesse: MS 882, NLA

The Australian Institute of International Affairs (AIIA):
AIIA Papers (uncatalogued), the New South Wales Branch, The Glavor Cottage, Sydney (GC)
AIIA Papers, MS 2821, NLA

Britain

Lionel Curtis: MS Curtis, Bodleian Library, Oxford (BL)

Charles Kingsley Webster: Webster Papers, Library of London School of Economics and Politics, London (LSEP)

English Speaking Union: English Speaking Union Papers, Library of English Speaking Union, London (LESU)

The Round Table: MS Eng Hist, BL

The RIIA: The RIIA Papers, Library of Chatham House, London (LCH)

Japan

Official Documents at Gaikō shiryōkan (Archives of the Japanese Ministry of Foreign Affairs), Tokyo

Taiheiyō mondai chōsakai kankei ikken (TMCK) [Files related to the Japanese Council of the IPR], Vols 1–9, photocopied by Yamaoka Michio, and housed at the Research Institute of Pacific Studies at Waseda University

Institutional and Private Papers

Ōkubo Genji: Ōkubo Genji Collection (OG), Library of Hitotsubashi University, Kunitachi (LHU)

Takaki Yasaka: Takaki Yasaka Bunko (TYB), American Centre of Tokyo University at Komaba (ACTU)

The US

Edward Carter: Carter Papers, Butler Library of Columbia University, New York (BLCU)

Ray L. Wilbur: Wilbur Papers, Hoover Institute Archives, Palo Alto, Cal (HI)

Woodrow Wilson: Wilson Papers, Library of Congress, Washington, DC

The IPR:
IPR Papers, Archives of University of Hawai'i at Manoa, Honolulu (AUH)
Pacific Relations Collection (PRC), BLCU

Laura Spelman Rockefeller Memorial (LSRM)/54/582–584, Rockefeller Archives, North Tarrytown, NY (RA)
Rockefeller Family Archives/III-2-Q/9/62–63, and 10/68, RA
Rockefeller Foundation Archive/1.1/200/351/4171–4180, RA

The Institute of Politics:
Papers of Institute of Politics, Series III, vols 1–31, Library of Williams College, Williamstown, MA

New Inquiry:
LSRM/III-2-N/47/376, RA

YMCA:
LSRM/III-4/55/588–589, RA

Notes

Introduction

1 Various other discourses were also significant. For example, on the impact of the concept of international law, see Christian Reus-Smit, *The Moral Purpose of the State: Culture, Social Identity, and Institutional Rationality in International Relations*, Princeton, NJ: Princeton University Press, 1999, Chapter 6.
2 Akira Iriye, *After Imperialism: The Search for a New Order in the Far East, 1921–1931*, Cambridge, MA: Harvard University Press, 1965, p. 4.
3 John Dower, *Empire and Aftermath: Yoshida Shigeru and the Japanese Experience, 1878–1954*, Cambridge, MA: Harvard University Press, 1979, p. 47.
4 Frank Atherton, 'The purpose of the Institute of Pacific Relations', in IPR, ed., *Institute of Pacific Relations, 1925*, Honolulu: IPR, 1925, p. 59.
5 Steigerwald, for example, defines Wilsonian internationalists in the United States as a group of moderate liberals who attempted to sustain faith in reason, and who were committed to international organizations. David Steigerwald, *Wilsonian Idealism in America*, Ithaca: Cornell University Press, 1994, pp. x–xi.
6 John Fairbank, 'William L. Holland and the IPR in historical perspective', *Pacific Affairs*, vol. 52, no. 4, winter, 1979–1980, p. 587.
7 Lyman C. White, *The Structure of Private International Organizations*, Philadelphia, PA: George S. Ferguson Company, 1933, pp. 130–1. The IPR's headquarters would move to New York in the mid-1930s.
8 White defines 'private' in terms of membership rather than the way an organization was established. Ibid., pp. 13–14. The term INGO was first defined by the Economic and Social Council of the United Nations in 1948 as 'any international organization which is not established by intergovernmental agreement'. 'Arrangements of the Economic and Social Council of the United Nations for Consultation with Non-Governmental Organizations, Guide for Consultations', 30 April 1948. In 1951 White uses the term INGO. Lyman C. White, *International Non-Governmental Organizations: Their Purpose, Methods, and Accomplishments*, New Brunswick, NJ: Rutgers University Press, 1951, p. ix.
9 This was especially the case in the 1930s and during the Pacific War. Robert Newman, *Owen Lattimore and the "Loss" of China*, Berkeley: University of California Press, 1992, p. 22. Charmers Johnson, *An Instance of Treason: Ozaki Hotsumi and the Sorge Spy Ring*, Stanford, CA: Stanford University Press, 1990, expanded edition, first published in 1964, p. 111; and Fairbank, 'William Holland', p. 589.
10 William Holland, 'Source materials on the Institute of Pacific Relations: bibliographical note', *Pacific Affairs*, vol. 58, no. 1, spring, 1985, p. 92.
11 The Japanese name of the JCIPR was *Taiheiyō mondai chōsakai*, and the IPR was translated in Japanese as *Taiheiyō kaigi*. Nakami and Wilson use the term the Japan Council of the IPR, not the Japanese Council of the IPR. Nakami Mari,

'Taiheiyō mondai chōsakai to Nihon no chishikijin', *Shisō*, no. 728, February 1985; and Sandra Wilson, 'The Manchurian Crisis and moderate Japanese intellectuals: the Japan Council of the Institute of Pacific Relations', *Modern Asian Studies*, vol. 26, no. 3, 1992. Both terms appear in the documents. Because the latter appeared more frequently, and because it corresponds to the names of other National Councils, I use the term the Japanese Council of the IPR.

12 See Appendix 1.

13 The documents on the IPR collected in this period were (US) Congress, Senate, Committee on the Judiciary, Report on the Institute of Pacific Relations, Report No. 2050, 82nd Cong., 2nd sess., 1952 (McCarran Report); and (US) Congress, Senate, Committee on Foreign Relations, Subcommittee Pursuant to S. Resolution 23, Hearings on the State Department Employee Loyalty Investigation, 3 vols, 81st Cong., 2nd sess., 1950 (Tydings Hearings).

14 I thank Diane Stone and Greg Noble for this point. On class and philanthropic foundations, see Edward H. Berman, *The Ideology of Philanthropy: The Influence of the Carnegie, Ford, and Rockefeller Foundations on American Foreign Policy*, Albany: State University of New York Press, 1983, p. 40.

15 Shiozaki Hiroaki, *Kokusai shinchitsujo o motomete: RIIA, CFR, IPR no keifu to ryōtaisenkan no renkei kankei*, Fukuoka: Kyushu daigaku shuppankai, 1998, pp. 3–4; and Carroll Quigley, *The Anglo-American Establishment: From Rhodes to Cliveden*, New York: Books in Focus, 1981, pp. 227–310.

16 See also T. Akami, 'The rise and fall of a "Pacific sense": the experiment of the Institute of Pacific Relations, 1925–1930', *Sibusawa kenkyū*, vol. 7, October 1994, pp. 2–37; and 'Synthesis and dilemma of a political identity: the "Pacific" and pro-American foreign experts in Japan in the 1920s', presented at a conference on '1998, From Far and Near: The Genesis of the Balance of Power in the Asia–Pacific Region', Canberra, 19 May 1998.

17 See, for example, Hamashita Takeshi and Kawakatsu Heita, eds, *Ajia kōekiken to Nihon kōgyōka, 1500–1900*, Riburopōto, 1991.

18 Arif Dirlik, 'The Asia–Pacific idea: reality and representation in the invention of a regional structure', *Journal of World History*, vol. 3, no. 1, spring, 1992, pp. 64–6.

19 See, for example, Frank Gibney, *The Pacific Century: America and Asia in a Changing World*, Sydney: Maxwell Macmillan International, 1992. For the meaning of the term the Asia–Pacific region and the role of the US see Peter J. Katzenstein, 'Introduction: Asian regionalism in comparative perspective', in P.J. Katzenstein and Takashi Shiraishi, eds, *Network Power: Japan and Asia*, Ithaca: Cornell University Press, 1997, pp. 15, 27, 40–1; and Mark Selden, 'China, Japan and the regional political economy of East Asia, 1945–1995', in ibid., pp. 313, 319–20; T. Akami, 'Synthesis and dilemma'; and T. Akami, '1920 nendai niokeru ōsutoraria no Taiheiyō ishiki to Taiheiyō mondai chōsakai', *Ōsutoraria kenkyū*, vol. 5, December 1994, p. 58.

20 Katzenstein, 'Introduction', pp. 16–18. See also Richard Higgott, Andrew Cooper and Jennell Bonner, *Cooperation-Building in the Asia–Pacific Region: APEC and the New Institutionalism* (Pacific Economic Papers, no. 199), Canberra: Australia–Japan Research Centre, 1991.

21 Recent studies on the IPR examining its role as an INGO in the regional integration include Lawrence Woods, *Asia–Pacific Diplomacy: Nongovernmental Organizations and International Relations*, Vancouver: University of British Columbia Press, 1993; Yamaoka Michio, *Ajia Taiheiyō jidai ni mukete: Sono zenshi to shite no Taiheiyō mondai chōsakai to Taiheiyō kaigi*, Hokuju shuppan, 1991; and Pekka Korhonen, 'The Pacific Age in World History', *Journal of World History*, vol. 7, no. 1, Spring 1996, pp. 41–70.

22 Critical works on dominant assumptions of international politics tend to focus on the sixteenth century, not the inter-war period. Michael Banks, 'The evolution of international relations theory', in Michael Banks, ed., *Conflict in World Society: A New Perspective on International Relations*, Brighton: Wheatsheaf Books, 1984, p. 8; Jim George, *Discourses of Global Politics: A Critical (Re)Introduction to International Relations*, Boulder, CO: Lynne Rienner Publishers, 1994, pp. 74–83; and Robert Walker, 'The Prince and "The Pauper": tradition, modernity and practice in the theory of international relations', in J. Der Derian and M.J. Shapiro, eds, *International/Intertextual Relations: Postmodern Readings of World Politics*, London: Lexington Books, 1989, p. 29.

23 The trend is evident in the Asia–Pacific region, as the recent debate over 'Asian values' demonstrated. See, for example, Gavan McCormack, *The Emptiness of Japanese Affluence*, Armonk, NY: M.E. Sharpe, 1996, Chapter 4; and Pete Van Ness, ed., *Debating Human Rights: Critical Essays from the United States and Asia*, London: Routledge, 1999.

24 Arthur Schlesinger Jr, 'A living thing is born: Woodrow Wilson's fight for the federation of the world', *Times Literary Supplement*, 21 May 1993, p. 3.

25 To name a few of these works: Akira Iriye, *The Cambridge History of American Foreign Relations*, vol. III, Cambridge: Cambridge University Press, 1993; Thomas J. Knock, *To End All Wars: Woodrow Wilson and the Quest for a New World Order*, New York: Oxford University Press, 1993; Frank Ninkovich, *Modernity and Power: A History of the Domino Theory in the Twentieth Century*, Chicago: University of Chicago Press, 1994; Tony Smith, *America's Mission: The United States and the Worldwide Struggle for Democracy in the Twentieth Century*, Princeton, NJ: Princeton University Press, 1994; and Steigerwald, *Wilsonian Idealism*.

26 T. Akami, 'Post-League Wilsonian internationalism and the Institute of Pacific Relations, 1925–1945', *Shibusawa kenkyū*, no. 11, October 1998, p. 4.

27 'The diplomatic machinery of the Pacific', in Bruno Lasker and William Holland, eds, *Problems of the Pacific 1931*, Chicago: The University of Chicago Press, 1932, p. 230.

28 On the complexity of defining liberalism in domestic and international politics, see James L. Richardson, 'Contending liberalism: past and present', *European Journal of International Relations*, vol. 3, no. 1, March 1997, p. 14.

29 For a critical assessment of the gender bias of inter-war liberal internationalists, see Christine Sylvester, *Feminist Theory and International Relations in a Postmodern Era*, Cambridge: Cambridge University Press, 1994.

30 I thank Akira Iriye and Mark Selden for furthering my thoughts on this issue.

31 E.H. Carr, *The Twenty Years' Crisis, 1919–1939: An Introduction to the Study of International Relations*, London: Papermac, 1993, first published in 1939, second edition in 1946, p. 94.

32 Knock, *To End All Wars*, p. 275.

33 Michel Foucault, *The History of Sexuality*, vol. 1, New York: Vintage Books, 1980, pp. 100–2. I thank Lewis Mayo for furthering my thought on this point. On the discourse and policy making, see Diane Stone, *Capturing the Political Imagination: Think Tanks and the Policy Process*, London: Frank Cass, 1996, p. 94; and Frank Fisher and John Forester, eds, *The Argumentative Turn in Policy Analysis and Planning*, London: UCL Press, 1993.

34 W.A. Williams, *The Tragedy of American Diplomacy*, New York: Dell Publishing Co., 1972, first published in 1959, pp. 52 and 84.

35 Paul Hirst and Graham Thompson, *Globalization in Question: The International Economy and the Possibilities of Governance*, Cambridge: Polity Press, 1996, pp. 16–19.

36 Joseph S. Nye Jr and Robert O. Keohane 'Transnational relations and world politics: an introduction', in Robert O. Keohane and Joseph S. Nye Jr, eds,

Transnational Relations and World Politics, Cambridge, MA: Harvard University Press, 1972, pp. ix–x. Robert O. Keohane and Joseph S. Nye, 'Transgovernmental relations and international organizations', in Richard Little and Michael Smith, eds, *Perspectives on World Politics*, New York: Routledge, 1991, second edition, p. 232.

37 Samuel P. Huntington, 'Transnational organizations in world politics', in Little and Smith, eds, *Perspectives on World Politics*, pp. 214–15.

38 Carr, *Twenty Years*, p. 27.

39 Ernest Barker, *Political Thought in England, 1848 to 1914*, London: Thornton Butterworth, 1932, first published in 1915, p. 11.

40 Walter Lippmann, *The Method of Freedom*, London: George Allen and Unwin, 1934, pp. 24–8 and 33–6.

41 Ian Nish, *Japan's Struggle with Internationalism: Japan, China and the League of Nations, 1931–1933*, London: Kegan Paul International, 1993, p. 243.

42 Yabe Teiji, *Konoe Ayamaro* (Fumimaro), vol. 1, Kōbundō, 1952, pp. 89–90. Although Yabe reads Konoe's given name as Ayamaro, I use the more generally accepted Fumimaro. Carr, *Twenty Years*, pp. 80–2. International Military Tribunal for the Far East, Judgement, vols. 157–8, pp. 732–4, cited in Christopher Thorne, *The Limits of Foreign Policy: The West, the League and the Far Eastern Crisis of 1931–33*, New York: Capricorn Books, 1973, p. 418.

43 John Dower, *Empire and Aftermath: Yoshida Shigeru and the Japanese Experience, 1878–1954*, pp. 3–6.

44 Gavan McCormack, 'The Japanese movement to "correct" history', in Laura Hein and Mark Selden, eds, *Censoring History: Citizenship and Memory in Japan, Germany and the United States*, Armonk, NY: M.E. Sharpe, 2000, pp. 56–9.

45 Herbert Croly, 'The human potential in Pacific politics', in John B. Condliffe, ed., *Problems of the Pacific: Proceedings of the Second Conference of the Institute of Pacific Relations, Honolulu, Hawaii, July 15 to 29, 1927*, Chicago: University of Chicago Press, 1928, p. 578.

46 These books include John Thomas, *The Institute of Pacific Relations: Asian Scholars and American Politics*, Seattle: University of Washington Press, 1974; Roger Bowen, *Innocence is not Enough: The Life and Death of Herbert Norman*, Vancouver: Douglas & McIntyre, 1986; and Newman, *Lattimore*. Unpublished other works include G.H. Davis, 'The Dissolution of the Institute of Pacific Relations, 1944–1961', PhD thesis, University of Chicago, 1966; T.E. Carpenter III, 'The Institute of Pacific Relations and American Foreign Policy', PhD thesis, Fletcher School of Law and Diplomacy, 1968; and B.L. Martin, 'Interpretations of United States Policy toward the Chinese Communists, 1944–1968', PhD thesis, Fletcher School of Law and Diplomacy, 1968.

47 Edward Said, *Orientalism: Western Conceptions of the Orient*, London: Penguin Books, 1991, first published in 1978, p. 3. Stuart Hall and Bram Gieben, eds, *Formations of Modernity*, Cambridge: Polity Press, 1992, pp. 291 and 293.

48 Stefan Tanaka, *Japan's Orient: Rendering Pasts into History*, Berkeley: University of California Press, 1993, p. 18. On the complex implication of Orientalism in Japanese colonial and post-colonial contexts, see, for example, Kan Sanjun and Murai Osamu, 'Ranhansha suru Orientarizumu', *Gendai shisō*, vol. 21, no. 5, May 1993, p. 186.

49 Margaret E. Keck and Kathryn Sikkink, *Activists Beyond Borders: Advocacy Networks in International Politics*, Ithaca: Cornell University Press, 1998.

50 J. Merle Davis, 'Foreword,' in Condliffe, ed., *Problems of the Pacific, 1927*, p. vi.

51 I follow Ceadel's definition: pacifism considers war to be wrong under all circumstances. Martin Ceadel, *Pacifism in Britain, 1914–1945: The Defining of a Faith*, Oxford: Clarendon Press, 1980, p. 3.

52 Although I use the term, 'think-tank', for the inter-war period, it is a post World War II construct. D. Stone, *Political Imagination*, p. 9. In the inter-war period, the usual term was expert organization.
53 Alfred Zimmern, 'Democracy and the expert', *Political Quarterly*, vol. 1, 1930, pp. 13–15.
54 White, *Private International Organizations*, p. 12.
55 Ibid., pp. 90–3 and 121–3. The contributions of Japan and China were already substantial in this period.
56 Norman Stone, 'Grim eminence', *London Review of Books*, 20 January to 3 February 1983, p. 3 and Carr, *Twenty Years*, pp. 1 and 16.
57 White, *INGOs*, p. 228.
58 IPR members included many who were regarded as pioneers in this field. Zimmern, for example, was professor of international relations at Aberystwyth in 1919–20 and at Oxford in 1930–44.
59 In countries outside the United States, IPR members were also founders of American studies. See Chapter 4.
60 See Thomas, *Institute of Pacific Relations*; Hugh Borton, Saitō Makoto, trans., 'Nihon kenkyū no kaitakushatachi', in Hosoya Chihiro and Saitō Makoto, eds, *Washinton taisei to Nichibei kankei*, Tokyo daigaku shuppankai, 1978; Nicholas Brown, 'Australian intellectuals and the image of Asia, 1920–1960', *Australian Cultural History*, no. 9, 1990; and Hara Kakuten, *Gendai Ajia kenkyū seiritsushiron*, Keisō shobō, 1984. The IPR promoted regional studies on the Asia–Pacific region not only in English-speaking countries, but also in France and the Netherlands.
61 Fairbank, 'William Holland', p. 589.
62 John Dower, 'Ōkubo Genji: the unfinished agenda', in Ōkubo Genji tsuitōshū kankōkai, ed., *Tsuisō Ōkubo Genji* [Editor] 1987, p. 165.
63 In the 1950s the IPR was damaged and various key members were publically attacked. However, it survived until 1961, after which the organization was disbanded. Holland, the last General Secretary of the IPR, took up a position at the University of British Columbia, and from there the journal of the IPR, *Pacific Affairs*, continued to be published.

1 The Paris Peace Conference and post-League internationalism

1 James T. Shotwell, *At the Paris Peace Conference*, New York: Macmillan, 1937, p. 86.
2 'The final draft of the Fourteen Points', in Arthur S. Link, ed., *The Papers of Woodrow Wilson (PWW)* vol. 45, Princeton, NJ: Princeton University Press, 1984, pp. 519–31.
3 N. Gordon Levin Jr, *Woodrow Wilson and World Politics: America's Response to War and Revolution*, New York: Oxford University Press, 1968, pp. 7–8.
4 Charles DeBenedetti, *Origins of the Modern American Peace Movement, 1915–1929*, New York: KTO Press, 1978, pp. 17 and 27; and House to Governor, 20 April 1919, in Link, ed., *PWW*, vol. 57, Princeton, NJ: Princeton University Press, 1987, p. 528.
5 DeBenedetti, *Origins*, pp. 17 and 19.
6 Yabe, *Konoe*, vol. 1, pp. 89–90.
7 Dower, *Empire*, pp. 46–7.
8 James T. Shotwell, *The Origins of the International Labour Organization*, vol. 2, New York: Columbia University Press, 1934, pp. 387–409.
9 Woodrow Wilson, *The New Freedom*, London: J.M. Dent and Sons, 1916, pp. 8 and 272–3. Knock, *To End All Wars*, pp. 17, 195–7 and 236–7.
10 'Final draft of the Fourteen Points', p. 531.

11 Ibid., p. 525.
12 'President Wilson explains American goals on the eve of the Paris Conference, December 28, 1918', in Arthur S. Link and William M. Leary Jr, eds, *The Diplomacy of World Power: The United States, 1889–1920*, Edinburgh: Edward Arnold, 1970, p. 157.
13 'Appendix: draft resolutions in reference to mandatories, 29 January 1919', Link, ed., *PWW*, vol. 54, Princeton, NJ: Princeton University Press, 1986, p. 361.
14 Thorne, *Limits*, p. 419.
15 Donald S. Birn, *The League of Nations Union, 1918–1945*, Oxford: Clarendon Press, 1981, p. 228.
16 The denial of this proposal is often considered to be significant, because it was later seen as a major reason for Japan's entry into the Pacific War. 'Confession of the Japanese Emperor', cited in note 3 in Asada Sadao, *Ryōtaisen kan no Nichibei kankei: Kaigun to seisaku kettei katei*, Tokyo daigaku shuppankai, 1993, p. 318. Piesse to Latham, 7 May 1919, MS 882/5/25, NLA.
17 Konoe Fumimaro, 'Eibei hon'i no heiwa shugi o haisu', cited in Itō Takeshi, ed., *Konoekō seidan roku*, Chikuma shobō, 1937, pp. 231–41.
18 'Jinshuteki sabetsu taigū teppai mondai ni kansuru Makino zenken no enzetsu', 28 April 1919, in Inoki Masamichi ed., *Nihon seiji gaikōshi shiryōsen*, Yūshindō, 1973, pp. 44–5.
19 'Minutes of a meeting of the League of Nations Commission, 11 April 1919', *PWW*, vol. 57, pp. 262–4.
20 Nagaoka Harukazu, 'Tsuikairoku', in Gaimushō, ed., *Nihon gaikō monjo: Nihon gaikō tsuikairoku, 1900–1935*, Gaimushō, 1983, pp. 498–501.
21 Diary of Colonel House, 12 April 1919, *PWW*, vol. 57, p. 285.
22 Diary of Colonel House, 13 February 1919, *PWW*, vol. 55, p. 155.
23 Nagaoka, 'Tsuikairoku', p. 499.
24 Kazumata Masao, 'Nichibei imin mondai to kokunai mondai: kokusaihō ni okeru kokunai mondai riron shutsugen no tancho', in Ueda Toshio, ed., *Kindai Nihon gaikōshi no kenkyū*, Yūhikaku, 1956, p. 425.
25 'Minutes of a meeting of the League of Nations Commission, 11 April 1919', *PWW*, vol. 57, p. 261.
26 Robert Garran, 'League of Nations: proposed Japanese amendment', n.d., cited in Peter Spartalis, *The Diplomatic Battles of Billy Hughes*, Sydney: Hale and Iremonger, 1983, p. 181. Hughes was convinced that the Japanese government would challenge the White Australia Policy. L.F. Fitzhardinge, 'Australia, Japan and Great Britain, 1914–1918', *Historical Studies*, vol. 14, no. 54, April 1970, pp. 250–9.
27 Diary of Dr Grayson, 11 April 1919, *PWW*, vol. 57, pp. 239–40.
28 Borden to White, 15 April 1919, ibid., p. 373.
29 Carr, *Twenty Years*, pp. 165 and 227.
30 Alfred Zimmern, *The Prospects of Democracy and Other Essays*, London: Chatto and Windus, 1929, p. 191.
31 Kazumata, 'Nichibei imin', pp. 234–5.
32 The British League of Nations Union *The Covenant of the League of Nations and the Geneva Protocol*, London: [The British] League of Nations Union, n.d., p. 20.
33 R. Lansing, *The Peace Negotiations: A Personal Narrative*, 1921, p. 243, cited in Kobayashi Tatsuo, 'Pari heiwa kaigi to Nihon no gaikō', in Ueda, ed., *Kindai Nihon gaikōshi*, p. 420.
34 'Kōwa no sandai hōshin' and 'Uiruson Beidaitōryō no jūyonkajō kōryō ni taisuru iken oyobi Chintao shobun ni kansuru hōshin', in Kajima Morinosuke, ed., *Nihon gaikōshi*, vol. 12, Kajima kenkyūsho shuppankai, 1971, p. 63.
35 'Minutes of a meeting of the League of Nations Commission, 11 April 1919', *PWW*, vol. 57, p. 260; and Yoshida Shigeru, *Kaisō jūnen*, vol. 4, Shinchōsha, 1958, pp. 97–8.

36 The Japanese regulation of 1899 was particularly aimed at banning the immigration of Chinese labourers. Hōmushō nyūkoku kanrikyoku, ed., *Shutsunyūkoku kanri to sono jittai*, Ōkurashō insatsu kyoku, 1964, pp. 7–8. I thank Tessa Morris-Suzuki for this reference. On criticism, see, E.L. Piesse, 'Australia's position in the Pacific', [IPR] *News Bulletin*, March 1927, p. 3. Ishibashi Tanzan, 'Dai Nihonshugi no gensō', *Tōyō keizai shimpō*, vol. 13, 1921, reprinted in Ishibashi Tanzan, *Ishibashi Tanzan hyōron senshū, 1884–1973*, Tōyō keizai shimpōsha, 1990, p. 215.

37 'Jinshuteki sabetsu taigū teppai mondai,' in Inoki, ed., *Nihon seiji gaikōshi shiryōsen*, p. 44.

38 'Minutes of a meeting of the League of Nations Commission, 11 April 1919', *PWW*, vol. 57, p. 259.

39 Nagaoka, 'Tsuikairoku', pp. 465–77 and Imaizumi Yumiko, 'Nanyō guntō inin tōchi seisaku no keisei', in Ōe Shinobu *et al.*, eds, *Kindai Nihon to shokuminchi*, vol. 4, Iwanami shoten, 1993, p. 58. On the issue of labour conditions, the Japanese delegates needed to take another position, and argue their relatively 'undeveloped' state. Although this was an embarrassment, the government did not seem to have found it as humiliating as racial inequality. Usui Katsumi, *Chūgoku o meguru kindai Nihon no gaikō*, Chikuma shobō, 1983, pp. 30–2.

40 Ronald Steel, *Walter Lippmann and the American Century*, New York: Vintage Books, 1981, pp. 128–34.

41 Knock, *To End All Wars*, p. 140.

42 Robert Schulzinger, *American Diplomacy in the Twentieth Century*, New York: Oxford University Press, 1994, p. 88.

43 Shotwell, *Peace Conference*, pp. 5 and 12–13.

44 Ibid., pp. 12 and 17.

45 John Kendle, *The Round Table Movement and Imperial Union*, Toronto: University of Toronto Press, 1975, Chapters 1–4.

46 Henry R. Winkler, *The League of Nations Movement in Great Britain, 1914–1919*, New Brunswick, NJ: Rutgers Press, 1952, p. 156. Milner was then Secretary of State for War and for the Colonies, and Kerr was Private Secretary to Lloyd George.

47 Shigemitsu Mamoru, *Shigemitsu Mamoru gaikō kaisōroku*, Mainichi shimbunsha, 1953, p. 44.

48 It was first called the British Institute of International Affairs (BIIA), and was chartered in 1926 (then renamed the RIIA). I use the term RIIA even for the period 1920–6. Chatham House was the name of the RIIA's headquarters in London. S. King-Hall, *Chatham House: A Brief Account of the Origins, Purposes, and Method of the Royal Institute of International Affairs*, London: Oxford University Press, 1937, pp. 18–20.

49 They included Dominion members. 'Minutes on the establishment of the Royal Institute of International Affairs', Webster Paper, 3/12, LLSEP.

50 'Minutes of a meeting at the Hotel Majestic on Friday, 30 May 1919', Webster Paper, 3/12, LLSEP.

51 Ibid.

52 For example, see also Walter Lippmann, *The Phantom Public*, New Brunswick, NJ: Transaction Publishers, 1993, first published in 1927, pp. 28–9.

53 Kendle, *Round Table*, pp. 18, 172 and 182. Carroll Quigley, *Tragedy and Hope: A History of the World in Our Time*, New York: Macmillan, 1966, p. 132.

54 Wilson, *New Freedom*, p. 23.

55 Niels A. Thorsen, *The Political Thought of Woodrow Wilson, 1875–1910*, Princeton, NJ: Princeton University Press, 1988, pp. 220 and 230.

56 Zimmern, *Prospects*, pp. 79, 166 and 214.

57 Tessa Morris-Suzuki, 'The invention and reinvention of "Japanese culture"', *Journal of Asian Studies*, vol. 54, no. 3, August 1995, p. 761. Mark H. Haller, *Eugenics: Hereditarian Attitudes in American Thought*, New Brunswick, NJ: Rutgers University

Press, 1963, pp. 155–9; and Jonas Frykman, 'Becoming the perfect Swede', Paper presented at a work-in-progress seminar at the Humanities Research Centre, Australian National University, 11 August 1992.

58   Inter-war economic crises, for example, reinforced the belief in a self-contained 'national' economy. Eric Hobsbawm, *Nations and Nationalism since 1780: Programme, Myth, Reality*, Cambridge: Cambridge University Press, 1990, p. 132.

59   For example, the works of a prominent sociologist of the time, Emile Durkheim, were concerned with the unity of society. *De la division du travail social* [The social division of labour] was first published in Paris in 1926 and an English translation appeared in 1933. For 'society' as an imaginary construction, see Cornelius Catoriadis and K. Blamey trans., *The Imaginary Institution of Society*, Cambridge: Polity Press, 1987, first published in 1975, Chapter 7.

60   David Cannadine, 'The context, performance and meaning of ritual: the British monarchy and the "invention of tradition", *c*. 1820–1977', in Eric Hobsbawm and Terrence Ranger, eds, *Invention of Tradition*, Cambridge: Cambridge University Press, 1983, pp. 139–50.

61   Carr, *Twenty Years*, p. 44.

62   Zimmern, *Prospects*, pp. 175 and 181.

63   Kendle, *Round Table*, pp. 302 and 303.

64   Shiozaki, *Kokusai shinchitsujo*, p. 32.

65   Quigley, *Tragedy*, p. 130.

66   T. Akami, 'The Liberal Dilemma: Internationalism and the Institute of Pacific Relations in Japan, Australia and the USA, 1919–1942', PhD thesis, Australian National University, 1996, pp. 116–18.

2   The Pacific Community: an American vision of the regional order

1   Ruhl F. Bartlett, *The League to Enforce Peace*, Chapel Hill, NC: University of North Carolina Press, 1944, p. 3.

2   Wilson, *New Freedom*, pp. 261 and 278.

3   Elihu Root, 'Speech at a meeting under the direction of the national Republican Club, in the presidential election of 1920, New York, 19 October, 1920', in Robert Bacon and James B. Scott, eds, *Men and Policies: Addresses by Elihu Root*, Cambridge, MA, Harvard University Press, 1924, pp. 278–9.

4   R.F. Smith, 'American foreign relations 1920–1942', cited in DeBenedetti, *Origins*, p. xi.

5   E. Root, 'A request for the success of popular democracy', *Foreign Affairs*, no. 1, 15 September 1922, reprinted in Bacon and Scott, eds, *Men and Policies*, p. 483.

6   DeBenedetti, *Origins*, Chapter 4 and p. 235.

7   Steigerwald, *Wilsonian Idealism*, 1994, pp. x–xi.

8   Levin, *Woodrow Wilson*, p. 254.

9   Theodore Roosevelt, Republican, founded the Progressive Party in 1912, and this split resulted in the Democrat rule of 1913–21 under Wilson. Schulzinger, *American Diplomacy*, p. 44.

10   E. Root, 'Speech in the Committee on Foreign Relations and National Defense of the National Civic Federation, Washington, 17 January 1923', reprinted in Bacon and Scott, eds, *Men and Policies*, pp. 486 and 488.

11   'Senator Lodge opposes the Treaty, 12 August 1919', reprinted in Link and Leary, eds, *Diplomacy*, p. 163.

12   Schulzinger, *American Diplomacy*, pp. 16–25 and 31.

13   Yale University took the lead among college missionary groups. E. T. Bachmann, 'Kenneth Scott Latourette: historian and friend', in Wilbur C. Harr, ed., *Frontiers*

of the Christian World Mission since 1938: Essays in Honour of K.S. Latourette, New York: Harper and Brother, 1962, p. 237; and Reuben Holden, *Yale in China: The Mainland 1901–1951*, New Haven: The Yale in China Association, 1964, pp. 5 and 72.

14 In the 1910s, American tourists to the Pacific amounted to 2,000 to 5,000 annually. In 1929, 8,500 were recorded, and in 1920s, a relatively peaceful period between wars, a total of 55,368 visitors was recorded. Asada, *Ryōtaisen*, p. 333.

15 On the formation of the knowledge of East Asia, see Daniel B. Ramsdell, 'Asia askew: U.S. best-sellers on Asia, 1931–1980', *Bulletin of Concerned Asian Scholars*, vol. 15, no. 4, 1983, p. 8. This 'knowledge' often justified the advancement of American power by portraying the people of the region as backward and needing guidance. See, for example, Katherine Mayo, *The Isles of Fear: The Truth about the Philippines*, London: Faber and Gwyer, 1925.

16 American anthropologists were also increasingly interested in the Pacific, especially the islands. The Bishop Museum in Honolulu became a centre of anthropological research. Herbert Gregory of Yale University, who became Director of the Bernice P. Bishop Museum in 1919, was also a founder of the Pacific Science Association. Philip F. Rehbock, 'Organizing Pacific science: local and international origins of the Pacific Science Association', in Roy MacLeod and Philip F. Rehbock, eds, *Nature in its Greatest Extent: Western Science in the Pacific*, Honolulu: University of Hawaii Press, 1988, p. 206; and A.P. Elkin, *Pacific Science Association: Its History and Role in International Cooperation*, Honolulu: Bishop Museum Press, 1961, pp. 9 and 19.

17 Alexander H. Ford, *Genesis: Part 1*, p. 269, cited in Paul F. Hooper, *Elusive Destiny: The Internationalist Movement in Modern Hawaii*, Honolulu: University of Hawaii Press, 1980, p. 76.

18 Anonymous, 'The Pan-Pacific Union is doing for the Pacific what the Pan-American Union has done for Latin America', *The Pan-Pacific Union Bulletin* [1923], p. 11, and P. F. Hooper, 'Alexander Ford: shaping Hawaii's image', *Honolulu*, xiv, no. 5, November 1979, p. 172. The Pan-American Union was originally formed in 1889 and named the Pan-American Union in 1910.

19 These conferences included the Pan-Pacific Science Congress (1920–); the Pan-Pacific Educational, Press and Commercial Conference, 1921; the Pan-Pacific Surgical Conference, 1928; and the Pan-Pacific Food Conservation Conference, 1924.

20 Hooper, *Elusive Destiny*, pp. 179–81.

21 Ko Sakatani shishaku kinen jigyōkai, ed., *Sakatani Yoshirō den*, Ko Sakatani shishaku kinen jigyōkai, 1951, pp. 601–2; and anonymous, 'The Pan-Pacific Club in Tokyo', *The Mid-Pacific Magazine*, May 1924, pp. 17, 19, 21 and 29. Kawai to Shibusawa, 16 July 1924, in Shibusawa Eiichi denki shiryō kankōkai, ed., *Shibusawa Eiichi denki shiryō (SEDS)*, vol. 37, Shibusawa Eiichi denki shiryō kankōkai, 1961, p. 452.

22 For example, the Pan-Pacific Rotary Conference was held in Tokyo in 1928.

23 Tilley to Lord Cushendun, 18 October 1928, A 981; Org 93, AA.

24 Ueda Toshio, 'Nichiro sensō to Rūzuberuto', in Ueda, ed., *Kindai Nihon gaikōshi*, pp. 112–25.

25 Asada, *Ryōtaisen*, pp. 1–50.

26 Anonymous, 'Canadian affairs', *The Round Table*, vol. 1, November 1910 to August 1911, p. 494.

27 These included the Root–Takahira (1908) and Ishii–Lansing (1917) agreements.

28 S. Gulick, 'Nichibei mondai ni tsuite', statement presented at the Tokyo Bank Club on 5 June 1923, translated into Japanese for the publication, *Ryūmon zasshi*, July 1923, reprinted in *SEDS*, vol. 34, Shibusawa Eiichi denki shiryō kankōkai, 1960, p. 26.

29 Shibusawa Masahide, *Taiheiyō ni kakeru hashi: Shibusawa Eiichi no shōgai*, Yomiuri shimbunsha, 1970, p. 229.
30 Jack London, 'Yellow Peril', in Jack London, *Revolution and Other Essays*, London: Mills and Boon, 1910, pp. 220–37. It was originally written in Manchuria in 1904. Homer Lea's *Valor of Ignorance* (published in 1909 and translated into Japanese in 1911) sold 40,000 copies. Shibusawa M., *Taiheiyō*, p. 239; and Asada, *Ryōtaisen*, pp. 231 and 291.
31 Asada Sadao, 'Washinton kaigi to Nihon no taiō: "kyū gaikō" to "shin gaikō" no hazama', in Iriye Akira and Aruga Tadashi, eds, *Senkanki no Nihon gaikō*, Tokyo daigaku shuppankai, 1984, pp. 21–2 and 54. Iriye, *After Imperialism*, pp. 13–22 and 301, and R. Dingman, *Power in the Pacific: The Origins of Naval Arms Limitation, 1914–1922*, Chicago: The University of Chicago Press, 1976, pp. 215–16. Iriye argues that this Washington system collapsed in 1925–6. Iriye, *After Imperialism*, pp. 87–8.
32 T. Akami, 'The "new" discourse of international politics and a new generation of foreign experts in Australia in 1919–1929', in Chūkyō daigaku shakai kagaku kenkyūsho Ōsutoraria kenkyūbu, ed., *Nichi Gō no shakai to bunka, Part II*, Seibundō, 1999, p. 164.
33 Asada, 'Washinton kaigi to Nihon', pp. 42 and 46.
34 Croly, 'The human potential in Pacific politics', in Condliffe, ed., *Problems of the Pacific, 1927*, pp. 580–1.
35 Ibid., pp. 582–3.
36 Tilley to Lord Cushendun, 18 October 1928, A 981; Org 93, AA.
37 Hosoya Chihiro, 'Washinton taisei no tokushitsu to henyō', in Hosoya Chihiro and Saitō Makoto, eds, *Washinton taisei to Nichibei kankei*, Tokyo daigaku shuppankai, 1978, p. 34. Usui, *Chūgoku*, pp. 91–2.
38 Shibusawa M., *Taiheiyō*, p. 417; and Asada, *Ryōtaisen*, pp. 338–40.
39 Asada, *Ryōtaisen*, pp. 275 and 312.
40 Ron Chernow, *The House of Morgan: An American Banking Dynasty and the Rise of Modern Finance*, New York: Touchstone, 1990, p. 236.
41 Shibusawa M., *Taiheiyō*, pp. 331 and 339. Yamaoka Michio, 'Taiheiyō mondai kenkyūkai ni okeru Nichibei kankei iinkai no katsudō', *Shakai kagaku tōkyū*, no. 105, December 1990, p. 99.
42 Avner Offer, *The First World War: An Agrarian Interpretation*, Melbourne: Clarendon Press, 1989, chapters 12–14. I thank Donald Denoon for this reference.
43 Shibusawa M., *Taiheiyō*, p. 384.
44 Haller, *Eugenics* pp. 53–4, 154 and 157–9.
45 Cited in Gulick to McClatchy, 17 November 1924, *SEDS*, vol. 34, p. 404.
46 The YMCA International Immigration Service, based in New York, dealt with problems of mainly European immigrants. LSRM/III-4/55/588, RA. A German Jewish anthropologist, Franz Boas, fought against the trend around the time of World War I. C.W. Stocking, *Race, Culture and Evolution: Essays in the History of Anthropology*, New York: The Free Press, 1968, p. 287.
47 DeBenedetti, *Origins*, pp. 75 and 112–13.
48 Gulick was the author of *The Growth of the Kingdom of God, Evolution of the Japanese, The White Peril in the Far East*, and *Towards Understanding Japan*. Gulick to McClatchy, 17 November 1924, reprinted in *SEDS*, vol. 34, pp. 404–5.
49 Letters of Wickersham in protest against this legislation, reprinted in ibid., pp. 157–9.
50 Shibusawa M., *Taiheiyō*, p. 350.
51 'Minute of a meeting at the Hotel Majestic on Friday, 30 May 1919', Webster Paper, 3/12, LLSEP. Note from Curtis to the secretaries of the Round Table in the Dominions, 29 November 1919, MS 1009/19, NLA.

52 E. Wrench, 'The English-Speaking Union: the story of its founding', (unpublished manuscript) pp. 7–9, LESU. The scholarship was set up by the Rhodes Foundation, established by Cecil Rhodes, a mining millionaire in South Africa, to promote the solidarity of Anglo-Saxons (the British empire, Germany and the US). It also funded Round Table activities.

53 Shotwell, *Peace Conference*, p. 111.

54 Latham to a secretary of the League of Nations in Paris, 23 February 1920, MS 1009/23, NLA. Hazel King, *At Mid-Century: A Short History of the New South Wales Branch of the Australian Institute of International Affairs, 1924–1980*, Sydney: the AIIA, 1982, p. 1.

55 W.R. Shepardson to BIIA, 19 July 1921, cited in Robert Schulzinger, *Wise Men of Foreign Affairs: The History of the Council on Foreign Relations*, New York: Columbia University Press, 1984, pp. 5–6.

56 Quigley, *Anglo-American*, pp. 227–310. Laurence H. Shoup and William Minter, *Imperial Brain Trust: The Council on Foreign Relations and United States Foreign Policy*, New York: Monthly Review Press, 1977, p. 5. Shiozaki, *Kokusai shinchitsujo*, pp. 6–8.

57 Carr, *Twenty Years*, p. 233; and Diary of Colonel House, 12 April 1919, *PWW*, vol. 57, p. 285.

58 Debora Lavin, 'Lionel Curtis and the idea of Commonwealth', in F. Madden and D.K. Fieldhouse, eds, *Oxford and the Idea of Commonwealth*, London: Croom Helm, 1982, p. 113. Curtis to Shepardson, 30 March 1923, Curtis to Shepardson, 25 February 1925, Shepardson to Curtis, 21 July 1925, and Shepardson to Professor Corelius, 29 July 1925, MS Eng Hist 872, BL.

59 Except for those from the US, very few were from non-European countries (Japan, China, Turkey, Brazil and Russia). The Institute of Politics, *Its First Decade*, Williamstown, MA: The Institute of Politics, 1931, pp. 47–8.

60 These newspaper cuttings of 1921–1931 were housed in the Library of Williams College, Papers of Institute of Politics, Series III, vols 1–31, Library of Williams College. Numerous newspaper articles on the Institute appeared in 1921–31. On 31 July 1921, for example, the *Boston Sunday Herald* had a long article titled 'Viscount Bryce gets warm welcome at Williamstown'. Series III, vol. 3, Library of Williams College.

61 Institute of Politics, *First Decade*, pp. 7–8.

62 Kendle, *Round Table*, pp. 238 and 304–5. Schulzinger, *Wise Men*, pp. 247, 249 and 253.

63 Kendle, *Round Table*, p. 290.

64 Ibid., pp. 281–3 and 293–300.

65 Carr, *Twenty Years*, p. 232.

66 Shepardson to Brandeis, 26 September 1925, MS Eng Hist 872, BL.

67 Iriye, *After Imperialism*, pp. 302–3.

68 Alan P. Grimes, *American Political Thought*, New York: Holt, Rinehart and Winston, 1964, p. 387.

3 From vision to influence: founding the Institute of Pacific Relations

1 Letter of invitation, 5 February 1925, A1/2, AUH.

2 Davis to Atherton, 26 December 1924, A1/1, AUH.

3 'History and organization', in IPR, ed., *Institute of Pacific Relations, 1925*, pp. 7–13.

4 Report of J.O. Miller, 4 May 1921, A981; Org 93, AA.

5 Gwenfread E. Allen, *Bridge Builders: The Story of Theodore and Mary Atherton Richards*, Honolulu, publisher unknown, 1970, p. 195.

6   Gwenfread E. Allen, *The YMCA in Hawaii, 1869–1969*, Honolulu, Honolulu YMCA, 1969, p. 99.

7   B. Hyams and E.C. Cluff, *Centennial Memories of the Pacific Club in Honolulu, 1851–1951*, Honolulu, the Pacific Club, 1951, p. 92.

8   'History and organization', in IPR, ed., *Institute of Pacific Relations, 1925*, p. 8.

9   Ibid., p. 9. The title of the conference at Portschach is as listed in the document.

10 The Rockefeller Foundation was called the Laura Spelman Rockefeller Memorial until 1929. I use the term the Rockefeller Foundation even before 1929.

11 Atherton to General Education Board, 24 April 1924, A1/1, AUH.

12 Memorandum of J.A. Urice, 30 April 1924, A1/1, AUH.

13 Urice to Looms, 2 May 1924, A1/1, AUH.

14 Atherton to General Education Board, 24 April 1924, A1/1, AUH.

15 Paul F. Hooper, ed., *Remembering the Institute of Pacific Relations: The Memoirs of William L. Holland*, Ryūkei shōsha, 1995, p. 203. Carter to Rockefeller, 26 August 1926, LSRM/III-2-N/47/376, RA.

16 Fosdick to Rockefeller, 22 January 1924, LSRM/III-2-N/47/376, RA.

17 John B. Condliffe, *Reminiscences of the Institute of Pacific Relations*, Vancouver, BC: Institute of Asian Research, University of British Columbia, 1981, p. 2. I thank Dr Holland for this copy. It is now reprinted in Hooper, ed., *Remembering*.

18 Edgar E. Robinson and Paul C. Edwards, eds, *The Memoirs of Ray Lyman Wilbur, 1875–1949*, Stanford: Stanford University Press, 1960, p. 315.

19 Davis to Atherton, 30 December 1924, A1/1, AUH.

20 Draft letter from Davis to J.D. Rockefeller Jr, 19 December 1924, A1/1, AUH.

21 Davis to Atherton, 30 December 1924, A1/1, AUH.

22 Davis to Atherton, 12 December 1924, A1/1, AUH.

23 Robinson and Edwards, eds, *Memoirs*, pp. 316 and 317.

24 Davis to Atherton, 30 December 1924, A1/1, AUH.

25 Robinson and Edwards, eds, *Memoirs*, p. 318.

26 Davis to Atherton, 26 December 1924, A1/1, AUH.

27 Interview with John MacMurray, Assistant Secretary of State, 22 January 1925, A1/2, AUH.

28 Davis to Atherton, 27 January 1925, A1/2, AUH.

29 An official at the State Department suggested excluding South America: '… the Latin countries would be liable to stand solidly with the United States against the Oriental nations'. Representatives of the Pan-American Union also did not show much interest in the project: '… the Latin American countries were not specially interested in racial matters'. Interview with MacMurray, 22 January 1925, A1/2, AUH.

30 The following discussion at the Yale Club is based on 'The minutes of the Yale Club meeting', 22 February 1925, A981; Org 93, AA.

31 'Davis's record of the Yale Club meeting', n.d., A1/2, AUH.

32 The minutes of the meeting state that: 'forty-one men came', but the report sent to Honolulu on 6 March attached a list of forty-six attendants. The list of attendants in the proceedings of the first conference shows only thirty-eight. This last list included five names which were not on the report of 6 March. The table combines these two lists and analyzes the background of all fifty-one.

33 Davis to Atherton, 12 December 1924, A1/1, AUH.

34 Thomas Lamont was Republican League supporter. He called himself 'a poor Republican … who has faith in our present Democratic [Wilson] administration'. Chernow, *House of Morgan*, pp. 206–7. Wilbur was another pro-League Republican. Robinson and Edwards, eds, *Memoirs*, p. 370.

35 Wickersham to Field, 21 November 1934, PRC, Box 145/Wickersham, BLCU.

36 Davis's record of the Yale Club meeting, n.d., A1/1, AUH.

37 Taft's speech at the Bankers' Club, New York, 15 July 1920, cited in Shibusawa M., *Taiheiyō*, p. 351.

38 Katagiri Nobuo, 'Taiheiyō mondai chōsakai to Chōsen daihyōken mondai: Chōsen gurūpu no dattai, 1925–1931', *Hōgaku kenkyū*, vol. 59, no. 4, April 1986, p. 49.
39 Condliffe, *Reminiscences*, p. 4. Davis' record of the Yale Club meeting, n.d., A1/1, AUH. M. Davis, 'An inside story of the Institute' [written after the first conference], p. 14, Wilbur Papers, 40/5, HI.

4 The Japanese Council of the IPR in the 1920s

1 Hosoya Chihiro, 'Nihon no Eibeikan to senkanki no Higashi Ajia', in Hosoya Chihiro, ed., *Nichiei kankei shi 1917–1949*, Tokyo daigaku shuppankai, 1982, pp. 4, 8 and 10. On the opposition in the Navy, see Asada, *Ryōtaisen*, pp. 22–3 and 38–41.
2 'Kōwa no sandai hōshin' and 'Uiruson Beidaitōryō no jūyonkajō kōryō ni taisuru iken oyobi Chintao shobun ni kansuru hōshin', in Kajima, ed., *Nihon gaikōshi*, vol. 12, pp. 53–63.
3 Hosoya, 'Nihon no Eibeikan', p. 1; and Dower, *Empire*, pp. 38 and 46–7.
4 Nish, *Japan's Struggle*, p. 14.
5 Asada Sadao, 'Washinton kaigi o meguru Nichibei no seisaku kettei katei no hikaku: hito to kikō', in Hosoya Chihiro and Watanuki Jōji, eds, *Taigai seisaku kettei katei no Nichibei hikaku*, Tokyo daigaku shuppankai, 1977, pp. 440–1.
6 Usui, *Chūgoku*, pp. 91–2.
7 N.M. Bamba, 'Japanese Diplomacy in Dilemma: A Comparative Analysis of Shidehara Kijūrō's and Tanaka Giichi's Politics toward China, 1924–9', PhD thesis, University of California, Berkeley, 1970.
8 Hosoya, 'Nihon no Eibeikan', p. 10.
9 Ōhata Tokushirō, 'Fusen jōyaku to Nihon', *Kokusai seiji*, vol. 28, no. 2, 1964, p. 83.
10 Mitani Taichirō, '"Tenkanki" (1918–1921) no gaikō shidō', in Shinohara Hajime and Mitani Taichirō, eds, *Kindai Nihon no seiji shidō: Seijika kenkyū II*, Tokyo daigaku shuppankai, 1965, p. 332; and Mitani Taichirō, 'Shohyō: John Dower,Ōkubo Genji, trans., *Yoshida Shigeru to sono jidai*', in Kindai Nihon kenkyūkai, ed., *Taiheiyō sensō: Kaisen kara kōwa made*, Yamakawa shuppansha, 1982, p. 488.
11 Mitani, '"Tenkanki"', pp. 333–40.
12 Fujisawa Chikao, 'Kokusai shugi no kiso kannen', *Kokusai chishiki*, vol. 8, no. 9, 1928, p. 32.
13 Extract from a statement of *Minseitō* cabinet in July 1929, translated and reprinted in R. Tsunoda and W.T. de Bary, eds, *Sources of Japanese Tradition*, vol. 2, New York: Columbia University, 1958, p. 756.
14 Yabe, *Konoe*, vol. 1, pp. 28–9 and Tsurumi Shunsuke, *Tenkō kenkyū*, Chikuma shobō, 1976, p. 157.
15 Donald Roden, *Schooldays in Imperial Japan: A Study in the Culture of a Student Elite*, Berkeley: University of California Press, 1980, Chapter 2 and pp. 31–41. Nakayama Shigeru, *Teikoku daigaku no tanjō: Kokusai hikaku no nakadeno Tōdai*, Chūō kōronsha, 1978, Chapters 3 and 4.
16 The journal was sympathetic to the Modernism movement. Akutagawa Ryūnosuke and Kikuchi Hiroshi were representative figures.
17 Fujiwara Akira, *Tennōsei to guntai*, Aoki shoten, 1978, p. 204. Henry D. Smith II, *Japan's First Student Radicals*, Cambridge, MA: Harvard University Press, 1972, Chapter 2.
18 Itō Takeshi, ed., *Konoekō seidan roku*, Chikuma shobō, 1937, pp. 231–41, cited in Miwa Kimitada, *Matsuoka Yōsuke: Sono ningen to gaikō*, Chūō kōronsha, 1971, pp. 60–1.
19 Yabe, *Konoe*, vol. 1, pp. 89–90.
20 Ibid., pp. 111–13.
21 Ibid., pp. 90–1.

22 Miwa Kimitada, '"Tōa shin chitsujo" sengen to "Daitōa kyōeiken" kōsō no dansō', in Miwa Kimitada, ed., *Saikō Taiheiyō sensō zenya: Nihon no 1930 nendai ron toshite*, Sōseiki, 1981, pp. 196–7.

23 Kōyūkai, ed., *Tōa dōbun shoin daigakushi*, Kōyūkai, 1955, pp. 10–11, 28 and 31.

24 Yabe, *Konoe*, vol. 1, p. 83.

25 Carr, *Twenty Years*, pp. 82–3.

26 Akami, '"New" discourse', pp. 165–6.

27 Kanzaki Kiichi, 'Taiheiyō mondai to Kokusai renmei: Renmei wa Ōshū renmei taru bekarazu', *Kokusai chishiki*, vol. 6, no. 6, June 1926, pp. 51–7; and Inoue's speech and the response in *Kokusai chishiki*, March 1926, reprinted in *SEDS*, vol. 37, p. 13.

28 Shibusawa E., 'Rajio bukku: heiwa kinembi ni tsuite', broadcast on 11 November 1926, ibid., p. 113. In the English translation of this speech, the part referring to the Pacific was cut. Ibid., pp. 114–16.

29 Saitō Sōichi, 'Taiheiyō jidai no tōrai to sono shomondai', *Bōeki*, vol. 28, no. 7, July, 1928, pp. 18 and 19.

30 Sawayanagi Masatarō, 'The general features of Pacific relations as viewed by Japan', in Condliffe, ed., *Problems of the Pacific, 1927*, p. 30.

31 Zumoto Motosada, 'Japan and the Pan-Asiatic movement', *News Bulletin [of the IPR]*, January 1927, p. 15.

32 Anonymous, 'Naval policy and the Pacific ocean', *The Round Table*, vol. 4, December 1913 to September 1914, p. 432; and Inoki Masamichi, *Yoshida Shigeru*, Jiji tūshinsha, 1986, pp. 43–5.

33 Nagatomi Morinosuke, 'Gendai no chōkokkateki rengō undō no ichi shimyaku to shite no Pan-Ajia undō', *Kokusai chishiki*, vol. 6, no. 10, October 1926, p. 3.

34 T. Akami, 'International Justice or Justification of Expansion?: Asianism and the New Order in East Asia', pp. 7–8, presented at the conference on 'East Asian Perspectives in the World Order' at the State University of New York, Buffalo, NY, February 1998.

35 Ko Sakatani shishaku kinen jigyōkai, ed., *Sakatani*, pp. 587–91.

36 Ozawa Yūsaku, 'Sawayanagi Masatarō no shokuminchi kyōikukan', in Sawayanagi Masatarō, *Sawayanagi Masatarō zenshū*, Bekkan, Kokudosha, 1979, pp. 205–12.

37 Ko Sakatani shishaku kinen jigyōkai, ed., *Sakatani*, pp. 587–91.

38 Zumoto, 'Pan-Asiatic movement', p. 15.

39 Davis to Wilbur, 11 May 1926, E-12b/29, AUH.

40 Sabey argues that it declined in influence and popularity through most of the 1920s. J.W. Sabey, 'The Gen'yōsha, the Kokuryūkai and Japanese Expansionism', PhD Thesis, The University of Michigan, 1972, pp. 275 and 277–96. In contrast, Norman indicates its growing significance in politics. E.H. Norman, Ōkubo Genji trans., 'Nihon niokeru kageki kokka shugi dantai no gaiyō', [Feudal Background of Japanese Politics, ISIPR data paper, No. 9 at the Ninth IPR conference of 1945] compiled in Herbert Norman, Ōkubo Genji, trans. and ed., *Herbert Norman zenshū*, vol. 2, Iwanami shoten, 1978, pp. 288–9.

41 Nagatomi, 'Chōkokkateki rengo', pp. 9 and 10.

42 Mitani Taichirō, *Taisho demokurashiron: Yoshino Sakuzō to sono jidai*, Chūō kōronsha, 1974, pp. 128–9.

43 Saitō Makoto, 'Sōseiki Amerika kenkyū no mokuteki ishiki: Nitobe Inazō to "Beikoku kenkyū"', in Hosoya and Saitō M., eds, *Washinton taisei*, p. 577.

44 Although some scholars use the name Takagi, I use Takaki. Igarashi Takeshi at Shibusawa Museum confirms that it was Takaki, and IPR documents also use Takaki.

45 Saitō M., 'Sōseiki', pp. 582–3; and Saitō Makoto *et al.*, eds, *Amerika seishin o motomete: Takaki Yasaka no shōgai*, Tokyo daigaku shuppankai, 1985, p. 133.

46 Davis to Wilbur, 26 May 1926, E-12b/29, AUH.

47 Ibid.
48 Sakatani Yoshirō, 'Shiryoaru Beikokujin ni uttau', *Kokusai chishiki*, vol. 4, no. 4, 1923, reprinted in *SEDS*, vol. 34, Shibusawa Eiichi denki shiryō kankōkai, 1960, pp. 221–4; and Yamada Sanzō, 'Beikoku iminhōan ni tsuite', *Ryūmon zasshi*, vol. 429, 1923, reprinted in *SEDS*, vol. 34, pp. 224–5.
49 Shibusawa to the members of the JARC, 21 April 1924, in ibid., p. 192; George Ōshiro, *Nitobe Inazō: Kokusai shugi no kaitakusha*, Chūō daigaku shuppansha, 1992, p. 183; and Ogata Sadako, 'Kokusai shugi dantai no yakuwari', in Hosoya Chihiro *et al.*, eds, *Nichibei kankeishi: Kaisen ni itaru jūnen*, vol. 3, Tokyo daigaku shuppankai, 1971, pp. 320–1.
50 Takaki Yasaka, 'Taiheiyō kankei chōsakai no seiritsu nituite', *Gaikō jihō*, vol. 42, no. 501, October, 1925, p. 67.
51 Davis to Wilbur, 26 May 1926, E-12b/29, AUH.
52 Saitō Makoto, 'Nihon ni okeru kokusaigaku no senkusha I: Takaki Yasaka', *Kokusaigaku kenkyū*, no. 1, 1987, no. 19, pp. 29–30.
53 Davis to Wilbur, 11 May 1926, E-12b/29, AUH.
54 'Taiheiyō mondai chōsakai kaiin meibo, November 1927', TYB, 19/3/9, ACTU.
55 Akami, 'Liberal Dilemma', pp. 138 and 156.
56 Horikiri Zenjirō, rep. ed., *Maeda Tamon: Sono bun sono hito*, Maeda Tamon kankōkai, 1963, pp. 37–8.
57 Roden, *Schooldays*, pp. 51–2.
58 'Tomiyama Setsuzō danwa hikki', 1 May 1936, in *SEDS*, vol. 35, Shibusawa Eiichi denki shiryō kankōkai, 1961, pp. 497–8. In March, Shibusawa contributed 500 yen to the association.
59 Kimura Masato, *Shibusawa Eiichi: Minkan keizai gaikō no sōshisha*, Chūō kōronsha, 1991, pp. 17–19 and 20–2.
60 Shibusawa Eiichi, 'Jitsugyōkai yori mitaru heiwa', *Ryūmon zasshi*, reprinted in *SEDS*, vol. 35, pp. 501–6.
61 Ogata, however, points out the reluctance of Japanese Christian societies to deal with social issues, such as peace and disarmament in the initial stages. Ogata, 'Kokusai shugi', p. 314.
62 'Daiheiwa kyōkai ichiran, February 1912', *SEDS*, vol. 35, p. 496.
63 Shibusawa E., 'Kokusai renmei gakusei shibu hakkai shiki ni', *Katei shūhō*, vol. 859, reprinted in *SEDS*, vol. 37, p. 146.
64 Ogata, 'Kokusai shugi', p. 312.
65 Kishimoto Hideo and Kaigo Muneomi, eds, *Nichibei bunka kōshōshi*, vol. 3, Yōyōsha, 1956, pp. 131–6.
66 Sheldon Garon, 'Women's groups and the Japanese state: contending approaches to political integration, 1890–1945', *The Journal of Japanese Studies*, vol. 19, no. 1, winter, 1993, pp. 24–8 and 37–9; Suzuki Yūko, *Feminizumu to sensō: Fujin undōka no sensō kyōryoku*, Marujusha, 1997; and Ogata, 'Kokusai shugi', pp. 325, 333 and 344.
67 Chihō senden kakuchō iinkai, 26 March 1924, *SEDS*, vol. 36, Shibusawa Eiichi denki shiryō kankōkai, 1961, p. 564.
68 Zenkoku shibuchō kaigi giji yōroku, 8 May 1926 (minutes of the national meeting of the branch heads of the LNA); and Shibusawa E., 'Heiwa kinembi', *SEDS*, vol. 37, pp. 76 and 113. Sawada Setsuzō, 'Nihon ni okeru heiwa shisō no hatten', *Kokusai chishiki*, vol. 5, no. 11, November 1925, pp. 19–20.
69 Kaisoku, *SEDS*, vol. 37, p. 531.
70 Nakami, 'Taiheiyō', p. 117.
71 Zimmern, 'Democracy and the expert', pp. 13 and 24–5.
72 Sawada, 'Nihon ni okeru heiwa', pp. 15–17.
73 Ibid., p. 20.
74 Shibusawa E., 'Heiwa kinembi', p. 111.

75 'The diplomatic machinery of the Pacific', in Lasker and Holland, eds, *Problems of the Pacific, 1931*, p. 230.

76 See, for example, Tetsuo Najita, *Hara Kei in the Politics of Compromise 1905–1915*, Cambridge, MA: Harvard University Press, 1967.

77 Michael Lewis, *Rioters and Citizens: Mass Protest in Imperial Japan*, Berkeley: University of California Press, 1990, p. 114.

78 Dorothy Robins-Mowry, *The Hidden Sun: Women of Modern Japan*, Boulder, CO: Westview, 1983, p. 49; and Buraku mondai kenkyūsho, ed., *Buraku no rekishi to kaihō undō*, Kyoto: Buraku mondai kenkyūsho, 1954, p. 219. I thank Yasuko Shin for this reference.

79 Andrew Gordon, *Labor and Imperial Democracy in Prewar Japan*, Berkeley: University of California Press, 1991, pp. 5–9.

80 See, for example, Masuda Hiroshi, *Ishibashi Tanzan kenkyū: "Shō Nihon shugisha" no kokusai ninshiki*, Tōyō keizai shimpōsha, 1990, pp. 3, 6 and 254, Sharon Nolte, *Liberalism in Modern Japan: Ishibashi Tanzan and His Teachers, 1905–1960*, Berkeley: University of California Press, 1987, pp. 6 and 340; and Naga Yukio, 'Nihon shihon shugi ni okeru riberarizumu no saihyōka: Ishibashi Tanzan ron', *Shisō*, no. 437, 1960, pp. 20–1.

81 Matsuzawa Hiroaki, 'Jiyū shugi ron', *Iwanami kōza, Nihon tsūshi*, vol. 18, Iwanami shoten, 1994, pp. 241 and 268–70.

82 Hoston notes that Japanese liberalism was similar to British New Liberalism. Yet still the framework of collectivity vs. individuality, and Japan vs. the West seems to be assumed. Germaine Hoston, 'The state, modernity, and the fate of liberalism in prewar Japan', *The Journal of Asian Studies*, vol. 51, no. 2, 1992, p. 289.

83 Nakami, 'Taiheiyō', p. 117; Ogata 'Kokusai shugi', p. 346; Wilson, 'Manchurian Crisis', pp. 522–8 and 537; and Kitaoka Shin'ichi, 'Nitobe Inazō ni okeru teikoku shugi to kokusai shugi', *Kindai Nihon to shokuminchi*, vol. 4, Iwanami shoten, 1993, p. 199.

84 On Wilsonianism and Americanisation, see Mitani, *Taisho*, pp. 138–41.

85 Warren Cohen, Hirai Atsuko, trans., 'Ajia mondai to Amerika minkan dantai', in Hosoya *et al.*, eds, *Nichibei kankeishi*, pp. 418–19.

86 Sheldon Garon, *The State and Labor in Modern Japan*, Berkeley: University of California Press, 1987, especially Chapter 6.

87 Itō Takashi, *Showa shoki seijishi kenkyū: Rondon kaigun gunshuku mondai o meguru shoseiji dantai no taikō to teikei*, Tokyo daigaku shuppankai, 1991, first published in 1969, pp. 8–9. Itō Takashi, 'Nihon kakushinha no seiritsu', *Chūō kōron, Rekishi to jimbutsu*, December 1972, pp. 28–53; and 'Showa seijishi kenkyū eno ichi shikaku', *Shisō*, vol. 624, June 1976, pp. 222–7. Spaulding uses the term renovationists, as he argues that it is more politically neutral than the term 'reformists'. Robert M. Spaulding, 'Japan's new bureaucrats, 1932–45', in George M. Wilson, ed., *Crisis Politics in Prewar Japan: Institutional and Ideological Problems of the 1930s*, Sophia University, 1970, p. 59.

88 Matsuo Shōichi, 'Taikai hōkoku ni yosete: gendai handōteki rekishikan no ichi tenkei – Itō Takashi', *Rekishi hyōron*, August 1977, p. 5; and Gavan McCormack, 'Fashizumu to Nihon shakai', in Sugimoto Yoshio and Ross Mouer, eds, *Nihonjin ron ni kansuru jūnishō: Tsūsetsu ni igiari*, Gakuyō shobō, 1982, pp. 144–5.

89 Kita Ikki, 'Nihon kaizō hōan taikō', published in 1926 (first published in 1919), reprinted in Takahashi Masae, ed., *Gendaishi shiryō*, vol. 5, Misuzu shobō, 1964, p. 11.

90 Matsuzawa, 'Jiyū shugi ron', pp. 276–9.

91 Nakami, 'Taiheiyō', p. 111; Ogata, 'Kokusai shugi', pp. 316–17; and Yoshida Toshihiko, *Rekidai Nihon ginkō sōsai ron*, Mainichi shimbunsha, 1976, pp. 147–8.

Debuchi to Inoue, 2 February 1927, 21 July 1927, 16 April 1928 and 30 May 1928, TMCK, vols 1–2, GS.

92 'Kondankai, 17 June 1926', *SEDS*, vol. 37, pp. 95–6.

93 Fujisawa, 'Kokusai shugi', p. 24, Yamamoto Miono, 'Kokumin shugi oyobi kokusai shugi no saiginmi', *Gaikō jihō*, vol. 76, no. 740, 1 October 1935, p. 126; and Yasutomi Masazō, 'Taiheiyō kaigi nyōze gakan', *Gaikō jihō*, vol. 52, no. 601, 15 December 1929, p. 57.

94 Nakami, 'Taiheiyō', p. 106.

95 'Kaisoku', *SEDS*, vol. 37, p. 531.

96 'No title, 31 March 1925', ibid., p. 478.

97 J.A.M. Elder to PM (Australia), 12 May 1925, A981; Org 93, AA.

98 Condliffe, *Reminiscences*, p. 19.

99 Atherton to Hanihara and Atherton to Shibusawa, both dated 24 July 1924, *SEDS*, vol. 37, pp. 458–60.

100 Note of Walter Henderson, 24 October, 1924, A981; Org 93, AA and see also Chapter 3 on the attitude of the US State Department.

101 'Masuda Meiroku nisshi, 12 May 1925', *SEDS*, vol. 37, p. 485.

102 'Rijikai, 20 February 1921', 'Kaikei hōkoku, April to September 1923' and 'Yosan [1924]', *SEDS*, vol. 36, pp. 419, 522 and 565; and Ogata S., 'Kokusai shugi', p. 312.

103 Tanaka to Kokusai renmei kyōkai, 2 May 1927 and 24 May 1928; and Kaimu hōkoku [1931], *SEDS*, vol. 37, pp. 132–3, 212–13 and 356.

104 Kimura, *Shibusawa*, p. 95.

105 'Kaimu hōkoku, no. 29, 1925', *SEDS*, vol. 36, p. 652.

106 Sunada Minoru, ed., *Nikka gakkai nijūnen shi*, 1939, reprinted in *SEDS*, vol. 36, p. 117.

107 Mitani, '"Tenkanki"', pp. 314–6; and Iriye Akira, *Beichū kankei no imeji*, Nihon kokusai mondai kenkyūsho, 1965, pp. 42, 47 and 52.

108 Sunada, ed., *Nikka gakkai nijūnen shi*, pp. 99–102.

109 Ko Sakatani shishaku kinen jigyōkai, ed., *Sakatani*, p. 585.

110 Shibasaki Atsushi, *Kindai Nihon to kokusai bunka kōryū: Kokusai bunka shinkōkai no sōsetsu to tenkai*, Yūshindō kōbunsha, 1999, p. 41.

111 Nakami, 'Taiheiyō', p. 106.

112 Nitobe to Chase, 12 August 1919, cited in Ōshiro, *Nitobe*, p. 173. Thomas Burgman, 'Nitobe Inazō as Under-Secretary General of the League of Nations, 1920–1926', *The Journal of International Studies*, Institute of International Relations, Sophia University, Tokyo, no. 14, January 1985, p. 82.

113 Yanaihara Tadao, *Yo no sonkeisuru jimbutsu*, Iwanami shoten, 1940, pp. 199 and 219; and Roden, *Schooldays*, p. 207.

114 Ibid., pp. 206–7.

115 Horikiri, rep. ed., *Maeda*, p. 15.

116 Nitobe Inazō, 'Kaishiki no ji', in Nitobe Inazō, ed., *Taiheiyō mondai: 1929 nen Kyoto kaigi*, Taiheiyō mondai chōsakai, 1930, p. 85.

117 Nitobe Inazō, *Jikei roku: Kokoro no mochikata*, Kōdansha, 1982, Chapter 17.

118 Ishii Kikujirō, *Gaikō yoroku*, Iwanami shoten, 1930, pp. 22 and 25.

119 Ibuka Kajinosuke to sono jidai kankō iinkai, ed., *Ibuka Kajinosuke to sono jidai*, vol. 2, Sangodō, 1970, pp. 393–8; and Ishii Mitsuru, *Nagao Hampei den*, Kyōbunkan, 1937, Chapter 16.

120 Ōshiro, *Nitobe*, pp. 143–4.

121 Nitobe began to lecture at Tokyo Imperial University a few times a week when he was still Principal of *Ichikō*. He resigned from *Ichikō* in 1913 and became a professor at the university.

122 Tsurumi Yūsuke, *Gotō Shimpei*, vol. 1, Gotō Shimpei denki hensankai, 1937, pp. 359–66.

123 Ishii M., *Nagao Hampei*, p. 210. Gotō also became an admirer of John Mott, the leader of the YMCA internationalist movement and one of the founders of the IPR. Tsurumi Y., *Gotō Shimpei*, vol. 3, Gotō Shimpei denki hensankai, 1937, pp. 357–62.
124 Nakami, 'Taiheiyō', p. 118. Also on the anti-colonial potential among contemporary Japanese, see Mitani, *Taisho*, pp. 191–7; Tsurumi S., *Tenkō*, pp. 191–3; Iokibe Makoto, 'Tōa renmei no kihonteki seikaku', *Ajia kenkyū*, vol. 22, no. 1, April 1975, pp. 22–58.
125 Saitō M. *et al.*, eds., *Amerika seishin*, pp. 25 and 80.
126 Horikiri, rep. ed., *Maeda*, p. 14
127 Tsurumi Yūsuke, 'Shin jiyū shugi no tachiba yori', *Kaizō*, vol. 10, no. 5, May 1928, p. 26.
128 Tsurumi Yūsuke, *Chūdō o ayumu kokoro*, Shinshakai, 1927, pp. 86–7.
129 Ibid., p. 105.
130 Ibid., p. 277.
131 Ibid., p. 279.
132 Tsurumi Yūsuke, 'Joshi kōminken fuyo ni tsuite', *Toshi mondai*, vol. 7, no. 3, September 1928, pp. 13–4.
133 Tsurumi Y., *Chūdō*, p. 89.
134 Ibid., p 329.
135 Tsurumi Yūsuke, 'Kokusai heiwa to kokumin seigi', *Tōyō keizai shimpō*, no. 1553, June 1933, p. 21.
136 'Nenpyō', in Toshino Inosuke, ed., *Iwanaga Yūkichi kun*, Iwanaga Yūkichi kun denki hensan iinkai, 1941, pp. 1–6.

5 The Pacific Community and the experiment of the IPR in 1925–7

1 See, for example, Andrew Cooper, Richard Higgott and Kim Nossal, *Relocating Middle Powers: Australia and Canada in a Changing World Order*, Vancouver, BC: University of British Columbia Press, 1993.
2 Croly, 'Human potential', in Condliffe, ed., *Problems of the Pacific, 1927*, p. 581.
3 Ibid., pp. 582–3.
4 In Australia, for example, a separate Department of External Affairs was not established until 1934. Except for one High Commissioner in London, Australia had no independent diplomats until 1940. From 1937 to 1940 there was an Australian Counsellor at the British Embassy in Washington, DC.
5 Duncan-Hall to Amery, 3 August 1925, A981; Org 93, AA; and Condliffe, 'New Zealand's outlook', in IPR, ed., *Institute of Pacific Relations, 1925*, p. 91.
6 Report of Wilson Harris, 24 May 1926, PRC, Box 108/Curtis 3, BLCU. Note of Joseph Flavett, 18 May 1926, MS 2629/6, NLA.
7 Davis, 'Report of committee on permanent organization', in Condliffe, ed., *Problems of the Pacific, 1927*, p. 591.
8 Nelson to Cathorne-Hardy, 12 March 1926, PRC, Box 108/Curtis 3, BLCU.
9 Beasley to Secretary of CH, 30 March 1926, MS 2821/1, NLA, IPR: Report Letter, no. iv by J.M. Davis, 14 August 1926, A981; Org 93, AA and memo of conversation with Major Keith Officer, M.E. Cleeve, 10 August 1928, MS 2821/1, NLA. On this readiness, see Shiozaki Hiroaki, 'Nichibei kaisen to Eiteikokuken', in Hosoya Chihiro *et al.*, eds, *Taiheiyō sensō*, Tokyo daigaku shuppankai, 1993, pp. 283–4.
10 Frederick Whyte, 'Opening statement for the British group', in Condliffe, ed., *Problems of the Pacific, 1927*, p. 23.
11 MS Eng Hist 778 and 798, BL; and Warren Osmond, *Frederic Eggleston: An Intellectual in Australian Politics*, Sydney: Allen and Unwin, 1985, p. 61.

12 Eggleston, Diary, 1927, MS 423/2, NLA.
13 F. Eggleston, 'Australia and the Pacific', [Melbourne] *Herald*, 23 December 1929. I thank Dr W. Osmond for the copies of newspaper articles written by Eggleston in 1929–30.
14 Condliffe, 'New Zealand's outlook', p. 91. Frederic Eggleston, 'The viewpoint of Australia on Pacific affairs', in Condliffe, ed., *Problems of the Pacific, 1927*, p. 4.
15 Croly, 'Human potential' in Condliffe, ed., *Problems of the Pacific, 1927*, p. 583.
16 Ibid., p. 586.
17 Frank Atherton, 'The purpose of the Institute of Pacific Relations', in IPR, ed., *Institute of Pacific Relations, 1925*, p. 55.
18 Ibid.
19 Duncan-Hall to Amery, 3 August 1925, A981; Org 93, AA.
20 Hoshino Aiko, 'Taiheiyō mondai chōsakai ni shusseki shite', *Fusen*, October, 1927, p. 6.
21 J.M. Davis, 'An inside story of the Institute', Wilbur Papers, 40/5, HI.
22 Allen, *Bridge Builders*, pp. 130 and 144–5. Harada Ken, ed., *Harada Tasuku*, Ahoku insatsu, 1971, pp. 498–9.
23 Harada Tasuku, 'Taiheiyō kaigi no seishitsu', *Osaka ginkō tsūshinroku*, no. 386, October 1929, pp. 28–9.
24 Eggleston, Diary, 1927, MS 423/2, NLA.
25 'History and organization', in IPR, ed., *Institute of Pacific Relations, 1925*, p. 12.
26 S. Carpenter, 'Honolulu Institute of Pacific Relations', *The Pan-Pacific Worker*, 1 May 1928, p. 8; S. Carpenter, 'Honolulu Institute of Pacific Relations', *The Pan-Pacific Worker*, 15 May 1928, pp. 6–8; and Watabiki Misao, 'Taiheiyō kaigi yori dattai seyo', *Nihon oyobi Nihonjin*, no. 226, June 1931, pp. 28–9.
27 Davis to Atherton, 14 October 1927, E-13/6, AUH.
28 Jerome Greene, 'The role of the banker in international relations', in Condliffe, ed., *Problems of the Pacific, 1927*, p. 450.
29 Carter wrote: 'capital and labor, East and West, North and South, Jew and Gentile, Catholic and Protestant, Universities, large national organizations interested in international affairs, together with men and women who have expert knowledge with reference to cultural, trade, political and missionary interests in the different Pacific countries'. Carter to Curtis, 2 February 1927, PRC, Box 108/Curtis 3, BLCU.
30 Carter to Curtis, 11 May 1927, PRC Box 108/Curtis 3, BLCU.
31 Paul Scharrenberg, 'The interest of labor in the problems of the Pacific', in IPR, ed., *The Institute of Pacific Relations, 1925*, pp. 112–16.
32 Davis to Gilchrist, 26 April 1928, Paper of Huntington Gilchrist, Library of Congress. In 1928 Davis recorded that the Foreign Office of the USSR seemed favorable to the idea of Russian participation in the IPR.
33 They included Grace Abbott, Chief of the Children's Bureau of United States Department of Labor, Carrie C. Catt, Chairperson of Conference on the Cause and Cure of War, Ada Comsock, President of Radcliffe College, Mabel Cratty, General Secretary of the National Board of the YWCA, Mrs William G. Hibbard, Regional Director (Chicago) of National League of Women Voters, Marry E. Wooley, President of Mount Holyoke College.
34 Saitō Sōchi, 'Taiheiyō kaigi to fujin', *Fujin no tomo*, October 1927, pp. 6–9; and Tsurumi Y., 'Joshi kōminken fuyo ni tsuite', *Toshi mondai*, vol. 7, no. 3, September 1928, pp. 11–16.
35 J.M. Davis, 'The opportunities, limitations and problems of the international conference', in *Women of the Pacific*, Honolulu, 1928, pp. 24–5.
36 The importance of women's participation in international affairs was discussed in 1930. G. Sweet 'Women and international relations', in *Women of the Pacific, 1930*, Honolulu, 1930, pp. 335–42. P. Hooper 'Feminism in the Pacific: The Pan-

Pacific and Southeast Asia Women's Association', *The Pacific Historian*, vol. 20, no. 4, winter, 1976, pp. 367–77. Whether the PPWC demonstrated less a state-centred framework than the IPR, however, remains to be examined.

37 Eggleston, Diary, 1927, MS 423/2, NLA. H. Duncan-Hall, 'The changing East: Chinese nationalism and liberalism in Japan', in H. Duncan-Hall and J.B. Condliffe, *What of the Pacific?: A Searchlight on its Problems*, Honolulu, 1925, p. 7, A981; Org93, AA.

38 Miwa, *Matuoka Yōsuke*, pp. 56–7. Shibusawa M., *Taiheiyō*, p. 388.

39 Matsumoto Shigeharu, *Showashi no ichishōgen*, Mainichi shinbumsha, 1986, p. 24.

40 Tsurumi Y., *Chūdō*, pp. 497–9.

41 Komatsu to Davis, 31 August 1928, E-13/10, AUH.

42 'Diplomatic relations in the Pacific', in Condliffe, ed., *Problems of the Pacific, 1927*, p. 167.

43 Elkin, *Pacific Science Association*, p. 30. On a strong lobby by a Japanese to make English the official conference language, see James R. Bartholomew, *The Formation of Science in Japan*, London: Yale University Press, 1989, pp. 254–63.

44 Eggleston, 'Viewpoint of Australia', in Condliffe, ed., *Problems of the Pacific, 1927*, pp. 4 and 8.

45 L.T. Chen, 'Present day China', in IPR, ed., *Institute of Pacific Relations, 1925*, p. 110.

46 H. Cynn, 'A Korean view of Pacific relations', in ibid., pp. 80–1.

47 H.K. Kim, 'Pacific relations as viewed by Korea', in Condliffe, ed., *Problems of the Pacific, 1927*, pp. 34–7.

48 Kuwashima to Tanaka, 28 July 1927, TMCK, vol. 1, GS.

49 Lawrence Woods, 'Canada and the Institute of Pacific Relations: lessons from an earlier voyage', *Canadian Foreign Policy/La Politique Étrangère du Canada*, vol. 6, no. 2, winter, 1999, p. 122.

50 Katagiri, 'Chōsen daihyōken', p. 49.

51 'Appendix III: constitution of the IPR', in Condliffe, ed., *Problems of the Pacific, 1927*, p. 607.

52 Only a few, such as the Women's International League for Peace and Freedom, opened membership to colonies. White, *Private International Organizations*, p. 220.

53 Whyte, 'Opening statement', in Condliffe, ed., *Problems of the Pacific, 1927*, pp. 26–9.

54 Conrado Benitez, 'The viewpoint of the Philippines', in IPR, ed., *Institute of Pacific Relations, 1925*, p. 86.

55 Fred C. Fisher, 'Present-day problems of the Philippines', in Condliffe, ed., *Problems of the Pacific, 1927*, pp. 44–54.

56 Ray L. Wilbur, 'An interpretation of America in Pacific relations', in Condliffe, ed., *Problems of the Pacific, 1927*, pp. 58–9.

57 Ibid., p. 61.

58 Said, *Orientalism*, p. 3.

59 'Diplomatic relations in the Pacific', in Condliffe, ed., *Problems of the Pacific, 1927*, pp. 167–8.

60 Takaki Yasaka, 'Taiheiyō kankei chōsakai no seiritsu nituite', *Gaikō jihō*, vol. 42, no. 501, October 1925, p. 67.

61 Sawayanagi Masatarō, 'The general features of Pacific relations as viewed by Japan', in Condliffe, ed., *Problems of the Pacific, 1927*, p. 31.

62 Duncan-Hall to Amery, 3 August 1925, A981; Org 93, AA. Davis recorded a similar impression in Tokyo in 1926. Davis to Wilbur, 26 May 1926, E-12b/29, AUH.

63 Tanaka, *Japan's Orient*, p. 18.

64 Zumoto's note on incapability of Koreans and the need for Japanese guidance in 'Pacific Relations from the standpoint of the Pacific countries', in IPR, ed., *Institute of Pacific Relations, 1925*, p. 158; and Tsurumi Yūsuke, 'Japan's internal

problems and her relationships with China, Russia, America and the British Commonwealth', in Condliffe, ed., *Problems of the Pacific, 1927*, p. 498. On Nitobe's attitude, see Nakami, 'Taiheiyō', pp. 109–10.

65 Anezaki Masaharu, 'Eastern and Western civilizations', in IPR, ed., *Institute of Pacific Relations, 1925*, pp. 100–1 and 102.

66 Eggleston, Diary, 1927, MS 423/2, NLA.

67 F. Eggleston 'Canton's ideal of ten cents daily', [Melbourne] *Herald*, 25 January 1930.

68 Sawayanagi, 'General features of Pacific relations', in Condliffe, ed., *Problems of the Pacific, 1927*, p. 33.

69 Robinson and Edwards, eds, *Memoirs*, pp. 316–17.

70 Eggleston, 'Viewpoint of Australia', in Condliffe, ed., *Problems of the Pacific, 1927*, p. 7.

71 Tsurumi Y., *Chūdō*, p. 443.

72 C. Batchelder, 'The far reaching effects of industrialization', in IPR, ed., *Institute of Pacific Relations, 1925*, p. 123.

73 Ibid.

74 T. Akami, 'A Useful Culture: Rhetoric of Culture in International Politics and the Institute of Pacific Relations in the Inter-war Period', paper presented at the 13th International Conference of the New Zealand Asian Studies Society, 24–7 November 1999, pp. 3–4.

75 Sawayanagi Masatarō, 'A Japanese view of Pacific relations', in IPR, ed., *Institute of Pacific Relations, 1925*, p. 79.

76 Matsumoto S., *Showashi no ichishōgen*, p. 24.

77 Duncan-Hall, 'Changing East', Duncan-Hall and Condliffe, *What of the Pacific?*, p. 8.

78 Eggleston, Diary, 1927, MS 423/2, NLA.

79 Condliffe, *Reminiscences*, p. 19.

80 Wilbur, 'Interpretation of America', in Condliffe, ed., *Problems of the Pacific, 1927*, p. 58.

81 John Nelson, 'Canadian view of Pacific relations', in IPR, ed., *Institute of Pacific Relations, 1925*, pp. 66–7.

82 Arthur Currie, 'Canada and Pacific relations', in Condliffe, ed., *Problems of the Pacific, 1927*, p. 14.

83 Hooper, ed., *Remembering*, p. 5.

84 Woods, 'Canada', pp. 121–2.

85 Takaki, 'Taiheiyō kankei chōsakai', p. 62.

86 'Appendix III: constitution of the IPR', in Condliffe, ed., *Problems of the Pacific, 1927*, p. 607.

87 White, *Private International Organizations*, pp. 31 and 34–6. Exceptions included the Institute of International Law, Institute of the Olympic Committee, and the Universal Esperanto Association. Ibid., p. 235.

88 White, pp. 35–6.

89 'Membership', in IPR, ed., *Institute of Pacific Relations, 1925*, pp. 35–40.

90 Croly, 'Human potential', in Condliffe, ed., *Problems of the Pacific, 1927*, p. 588.

91 This report was titled 'For information from Commissioner for Australia in the USA', n.d. [in 1926], A981; Org 93, AA.

92 *San Francisco Chronicle*, 14 August 1927 and *New York Sun*, 10 June 1927.

93 Aoki Setsuichi, 'Taiheiyō mondai chōsakai: dainikai Honoruru taikai o miru', *Kokusai chishiki*, vol. 7, no. 9, September 1927; Saitō Sōichi, 'Taiheiyō jidai no tōrai to sono shomondai', *Bōeki*, vol. 28, no. 7, July 1928; Takaki Yasaka, ' "Institute of Pacific Relations" ni tsuite', *Kokka gakkai zasshi*, vol. 39, no. 12, December 1925; and Takaki Yasaka, 'Kokusai shugi ni taisuru ichikōken: Taiheiyō kankei chōsakai no kansō', *Chūō kōron*, no. 40, December 1925.

94 Duncan-Hall to Amery, 3 August 1925, A981; Org 93, AA.
95 Note of Walter Henderson, 24 October 1924, A981; Org 93, AA.
96 'History and organization', in IPR, ed., *Institute of Pacific Relations, 1925*, p. 14.
97 Katagiri Nobuo, 'Taiheiyō mondai chōsakai to imin mondai: daiikkai Hawai kaigi o chūshin toshite, part 2', *Hōgaku kenkyū*, vol. 58, no. 7, July 1985, p.29
98 Takayanagi Kenzō, 'A suggestion for more enlightened immigration and emigration policies', in IPR, ed., *Institute of Pacific Relations, 1925*, p. 111.
99 Tsurumi Y., *Chūdō*, p. 443.
100 Duncan-Hall to Amery, 3 August 1925, A 981; Org93, AA.
101 Akagi Hidemichi, 'Immin mondai', in Inoue Junnosuke, ed., *Taiheiyō mondai*, cited in Katagiri Nobuo, 'Taiheiyō mondai chōsakai to imin mondai: dainikai Hawai kaigi o chūshin toshite', *Hōgaku kenkyū*, vol. 65, no. 2, February 1992, p. 181.
102 Duncan-Hall to Amery, 3 August 1925, A 981; Org93, AA.
103 Duncan-Hall, 'The searchlight on immigration legislation', in Duncan-Hall and Condliffe, *What of the Pacific?*, p. 9.
104 Takayanagi, 'Suggestion', in IPR, ed., *Institute of Pacific Relations, 1925*, p. 111.
105 Katagiri, 'Imin mondai, part 2', p. 39.
106 Schulzinger, *American Diplomacy*, p. 137.
107 DeBenedetti, *Origins*, p. 235. See also S.J. Kneeshaw, *In Pursuit of Peace: The American Relation to Kellog–Briand Pact 1928–1929*, Garland Publishing, 1991.
108 James T. Shotwell and J.P. Chamberlain, 'Draft treaty of permanent peace between the United States of America and...', in Condliffe ed., *Problems of the Pacific, 1927*, p. 507.
109 Part II on arbitration and conciliation was 'taken almost literally' from American treaties with France. Part III was on ratification.
110 'The governmental organization of each of the Pacific countries with special reference to its machinery for handling international affairs', in IPR, ed., *Institute of Pacific Relations, 1925*, p. 204 and 'Co-operation among Pacific countries', in ibid., pp. 136–8.
111 'Diplomatic relations in the Pacific', in Condliffe, ed., *Problems of the Pacific, 1927*, pp. 171–2.
112 Note by E. Drummond, 6 April 1927, Paper of Huntington Gilchrist, Library of Congress. I am grateful to Mr Frank Moorhouse for bringing this document to my attention.
113 Katagiri Nobuo, 'Senkanki Taiheiyō jidai no anzen hoshō imegi', *Kokusai seiji*, no. 102, February 1993, p. 87.
114 Shotwell and Chamberlain, 'Draft treaty', in Condliffe, ed., *Problems of the Pacific, 1927*, p. 508.
115 Rōyama Masamichi, 'Fusen jōyaku to Nihon gaikō no shōrai', July 1928, compiled by Rōyama Masamichi, *Nihon seiji dōkōron*, Kōyō shoin, 1933, pp. 539, 541 and 546. Katagiri, 'Senkanki Taiheiyō jidai', pp. 91 and 93.
116 Rōyama, 'Fusen jōyaku', p. 545.
117 'Daijin kaiken roku (Minutes of a meeting of American Ambassador and Tanaka Foreign Minister), 14 April 1928', reprinted in Gaimu shō, ed., *Nihon gaikō monjo*, Showaki I, Part II, vol. 1, Gaimu shō, 1988, pp. 93–4.
118 Debuchi to Tanaka, 6 June 1929, reprinted in ibid., pp. 350–1.
119 Tsurumi Y., 'Shin jiyū shugi', p. 26; and Tsurumi Y., *Chūdō*, pp. 100 and 107.
120 Ketsugi, no. 7, submitted on 21 March 1929, reprinted in Gaimu shō, ed., *Nihon gaikō monjo*, Showaki I, Part II, vol. 1, pp. 320–1.
121 Davis, 'Inside story', Wilbur Papers, 40/5, HI.
122 See also Appendix A.
123 Curtis to Carter, 23 January 1928, PRC, Box 108/Curtis 2, BLCU.
124 Note of conversation with Eggleston (in 1927), MS 2629/6, NLA.
125 T. Akami, 'Setting agendas for modern middle classes: Christian institutions

and the colonial discourse in Japan in the early half of the twentieth century', in Vera Mackie *et al.*, eds, *Coloniality, Postcoloniality and Modernity in Japan*, Clayton: Monash Asia Institute, 2000, pp. 129–31.

126 The IPR conferences between 1925 to 1933 took place every two years. Between 1933 and 1945, they were held every three years.

127 Davis, 'Report of committee on permanent organization', in Condliffe, ed., *Problems of the Pacific, 1927*, p. 591.

128 'Statement showing the receipts and disbursements of the Institute of Pacific Relations for the years 1925–1935 and the first six months of 1936, compared with the budget for 1936', in IPR, *Report of the International Secretariat to the Pacific Council, 1933–1936*, New York: IPR, 1936, p. 173.

129 Davis, 'Foreword', in Condliffe, ed., *Problems of the Pacific, 1927*, p. vi.

130 Davis visited Japan, China, Australia and New Zealand in 1926, and Europe and the USSR in 1927. In mid-1928 he spent a few months in Tokyo and China to organize the conference. Davis to Wilbur, 11 and 26 May 1926, E-12b/29 and Davis to Atherton, 11 August 1926, E-12b/32, AUH.

131 Carter to Greene, 1 October 1928, PRC, Box 112/J. Greene, BLCU.

132 Pacific Council Minutes, 9 November 1929, A-1/PC 1929, AUH.

133 Carter to Greene, 15 December 1928, PRC, Box 112/J. Greene, BLCU.

134 Davis to Atherton, 24 October 1927, E-13/6, AUH.

135 Curtis to Blakeslee, 16 July 1926, PRC, Box 108/Curtis 3, BLCU.

136 Edmund Gay, Grafton Wilson and Blakeslee, as well as Carter and Loomis, were involved in this reorganization. Carter to Greene, 20 June 1926, PRC, Box 112/J. Greene, BLCU.

137 During this period, they discussed a gradualist approach for the future self-rule of India. Shiozaki, *Kokusai shinchitsujo*, pp. 37–8.

138 See also Chapter 3.

139 Carter to Rockefeller, 26 August 1926, LSRM/III-2-N/47/376, RA.

140 Curtis to Carter, 23 January 1928, PRC, Box 108/Curtis 2, BLCU.

141 Kuwashima to Tanaka, 28 July 1927, TMCK, vol. 1, GS. Tsurumi Yūsuke, 'Taiheiyō kaigi chōkakan', in Inoue Junnosuke, ed., *Taiheiyō mondai: 1927 nen Honoruru*, Nihon hyōronsha, 1927, pp. 43–4.

142 Tsurumi Y., *Chūdō*, pp. 44–5

143 Eggleston, Diary, 1927, MS 423/2, NLA.

144 Curtis to Babcock, 9 November 1925, PRC, Box 108/Curtis 2, BLCU.

145 'For information from Commissioner for Australia in the USA', n.d. [in 1926], A981; Org 93, AA.

146 Tsurumi Y., *Chūdō*, pp. 492–3.

147 Babb to Loomis, 19 November 1930, MS 423/14, NLA

6 From the Pacific to the Atlantic, 1928–32

1 Curtis to Carter, 23 January 1928, PRC, Box 108/Curtis 2, BLCU.

2 In the definition of being 'truly international', however, the lack of attention to the non-Euro-American world is noteworthy. White, *INGOs*, p. 4.

3 Curtis to Carter, 24 July 1928, PRC, Box 108/Curtis 2, BLCU.

4 Atherton to Davis, 9 August 1927, E-13/4, AUH.

5 Davis to Atherton, 16 September 1927, E-13/5, AUH.

6 Atherton to Davis, 5 October 1927, E-13/6, AUH.

7 Davis to Atherton, 24 October 1927, E-13/6, AUH.

8 In London, Curtis entertained Davis and his wife. Curtis now viewed Davis in a more favourable light, but still considered him to be inadequate as General Secretary. Curtis to Carter, 23 January 1928, PRC, Box 108/Curtis 2, BLCU.

9 Sawada to Shidehara, 2 June 1930, TMCK, vol. 4, GS.
10 Debuchi to Inoue, 21 February 1927, TMCK, vol. 2, GS.
11 Davis to Loomis, 18 August 1928, E-13/9, AUH.
12 Debuchi to Tanaka, 4 May 1928, Akamatsu to Tanaka, 28 March 1929, Yoshida to Inoue, 30 April 1929, TMCK, vol. 2, GS and Saitō to Davis, 15 April 1929, E-13/15, AUH.
13 Davis to Atherton, 12 March 1928, E-13/6, 12 October 1928 and 17 October 1928, E-13/11, AUH.
14 Davis to Greene, 18 July 1930, E-17/6, AUH.
15 Minutes of Pacific Council, 7 November 1929, A-1/PC 1929, AUH.
16 Greene to Carter, 12 December 1928 and Carter to Greene, 15 December 1928, PRC, Box 112/J. Greene, BLCU.
17 Greene to Curtis, 3 January 1929, PRC, Box 112/J. Greene, BLCU.
18 Curtis to Greene, 7–13 November 1928, A-1/PC 1929, AUH.
19 Davis to Wilbur, 15 February 1929, A-1/PC 1929, AUH.
20 Carter to Greene, 10 December 1928, PRC, Box 112/J. Greene, BLCU.
21 Greene to Curtis, 13 December 1928, PRC, Box 112/J. Greene, BLCU.
22 Greene to Curtis, 3 January 1929, PRC, Box 112/J. Greene, BLCU.
23 Laura Spelman Rockefeller Memorial became the Rockefeller Foundation in 1929.
24 Greene to Curtis, 3 January 1929, PRC, Box 112/J. Greene, BLCU.
25 Ibid.
26 Curtis to Babcock, 9 November 1925, PRC Box 108/Curtis 2, BLCU.
27 Ibid.
28 Condliffe, *Reminiscences*, p. 8.
29 Ibid., pp. 13 and 26.
30 Atherton to Davis, 16 August 1927, E-13/5, AUH.
31 Condliffe, *Reminiscences*, p. 12.
32 Resolution, 22 May 1931, RFnA/1.1/200/350/4171, RA.
33 Condliffe, *Reminiscences*, p. 39.
34 Davis, 'Foreword', in Condliffe, ed., *Problems of the Pacific, 1927*, p. vi.
35 Atherton to Davis, 5 October 1927, E-13/6, AUH.
36 Condliffe, *Reminiscences*, pp. 11 and 33.
37 Ibid., p. 15.
38 These economists were Franklin Ho, Li Choh-ming and H.D. Fong.
39 Condliffe, *Reminiscences*, p. 37.
40 Anonymous, 'The Kyoto conference', *The Round Table*, vol. 20, December 1929 to September 1930, p. 338.
41 Davis to Greene, 18 July 1930, E-17/6, AUH.
42 Eggleston to Greene, 18 September 1930, MS 423/14, NLA.
43 Greene to Curtis, 21 August 1930, MS Curtis 3, BL.
44 Curtis to Greene, 20 September 1930, MS Curtis 3, BL.
45 Davis to Cuthwaite, 2 December 1925 and Carter to Ruml, 11 June 1926, LSRM/54/582/IPR 1925–1926, RA.
46 Greene to Fosdick, 7 August 1929, LSRM/54/584/IPR 1929, RA.
47 Eggleston to Greene, 18 September 1930, MS 423/14, NLA.
48 Allen to Greene, 10 April 1930, PRC, Box 112/J. Greene, BLCU.
49 Eggleston to Greene, 18 September 1930, MS 423/14, NLA.
50 Davis to Eggleston, 30 July 1930, MS 423/14, NLA.
51 Eggleston, 'Australia and the Pacific', [Melbourne] *Herald*, 30 December 1929.
52 Akami, '"New" discourse', p. 166.
53 Iriye, *After Imperialism*, p. 18.
54 Sawada to Shidehara, 2 June 1930, TMCK, vol. 4, GS.
55 Eggleston, 'Australia and the Pacific'.

56 *Osaka asahi*, 29 October 1929.

57 Tilley to Lord Cushendun, 18 October 1928, A 981; Org 93, AA.

58 Anonymous, 'Kyoto conference', *The Round Table*, vol. 20, p. 337.

59 For an analysis of Eggleston's articles, see T. Akami, 'Frederic Eggleston and Oriental Power, 1925–1929', in Vera Mackie and Paul Johns, eds, *Relationships: Australia and Japan, 1850s to 1950s*. Melbourne: University of Melbourne History Monograph no. 28, 2001.

60 *Tokyo nichinichi, yūkan* [evening issue], 29 October 1929.

61 Minutes of Pacific Council, 25 October 1929, A-1/PC 1929, AUH.

62 Minutes of Pacific Council, 4 November 1929, A-1/PC 1929, AUH. 'Appendix IV: minutes of meetings of the Pacific Council, Institute of Pacific Relations', in J.B. Condliffe, ed., *Problems of the Pacific, 1929*, Chicago: The University of Chicago Press, 1930, p. 653.

63 Katagiri, 'Chōsen daihyōken', pp. 59–60.

64 Notes on a conversation between Stimson, Atherton, Davis and Loomis, 14 March 1929, Wilbur Papers, 40/5, HI.

65 T.H. Yun *et al.* to the members of the Pacific Council, 19 October 1929, A-1/PC 1929, AUH.

66 Minutes of the Pacific Council, 4 November 1929, A-1/PC 1929, AUH.

67 'Appendix IV: minutes of meetings of the Pacific Council', p. 650.

68 Katagiri, 'Chōsen daihyōken', p. 61.

69 Soejima Masaomi, 'Futatabi Taiheiyō kaigi ni tsuite', *Gaikō jihō*, vol. 52, no. 599, 15 November 1929, pp. 86–7; and Zumoto Motosada, 'Kyoto kaigi no atoshimatsu', *Gaikō jihō*, vol. 53, no. 602, 1 January 1930, pp. 293–6.

70 Zumoto, 'Kyoto kaigi', p. 296.

71 Ōkawa Shūmei, 'Hashigaki' and Soejima Masaomi, 'Mitabi Taiheiyō kaigi ni tsuite', in Tōa keizai chōsakyoku, ed., *Taiheiyō kaigi ni tsuite*, Tōa keizai chōsa kyoku, 1929, pp. 2 and 34–6; and Watabiki, 'Taiheiyō kaigi', pp. 23 and 27.

72 Rōyama Masamichi, 'Kyoto kaigi kansō (1)', *Manmō*, January 1930, p. 205.

73 Greene to Loomis, 7 July 1930, E-17/5, AUH.

74 Greene to Nitobe, 24 January 1931, E-17/17, AUH.

75 Greene to Carter, 20 November 1928, PRC, Box 112/J. Greene, BLCU.

76 Matsuoka Yōsuke, 'Taiheiyō chōsa kaigi no gyōseki', *Gaikō jihō*, vol. 53, no. 602, 1 January 1930, pp. 283–5.

77 Yasutomi Masazō, 'Taiheiyō kaigi nyōze gakan', *Gaikō jihō*, vol. 52, no. 601, 15 December 1929, pp. 58–9.

78 Nitobe Inazō, 'Opening address', attached in a report of Sagami to Adachi and Shidehara, 28 October 1929, reprinted in Gaimushō, ed., *Nihon gaikō monjo*, Showaki I, Part II, vol. 4, Gaimushō, 1991, pp. 450–1.

79 Ibid., p. 452.

80 Zimmern, 'Democracy and the expert', pp. 14–15.

81 Davis to Atherton, 21 November 1928, E-13/12, AUH.

82 Inoue to Yoshida, 8 May 1929, TMCK, vol. 2, GS.

83 Matsumoto Shigeharu, *Shanhai jidai*, vol. 1, Chūō kōronsha, 1974, pp. 33–4.

84 See, for example, 1922 Prime Minister's Department of External Affairs Secretary to Honorary Secretary of the Australian National Research Council, 19 September 1922, Governor General Official Secretary to Secretary of the Prime Minister's Department, A981; Conf 256, AA.

85 Kuwashima to Tanaka, 28 July 1927, TMCK, vol. 2, GS.

86 Condliffe, *Reminiscences*, pp. 18, 21 and 32–3.

87 Kuwashima to Tanaka, 2 April 1928, TMCK, vol. 2, GS.

88 'Taiheiyō mondai chōsakai kenkyūbu sōdankai', 24 January 1928; and Rōyama to Takaki, 4 March 1928, TYB/28/2 and 8, ACTU.

89 Yano to Tanaka, 4 June 1929, TMCK, vol. 2, GS.

90 Katagiri, 'Taiheiyō mondai chōsakai to Manshū mondai', *Hōgaku kenkyū*, vol. 52, no. 9, 1979, pp. 61–4.
91 Kawagoe to Shidehara, 17 July 1929, TMCK, vol. 2, GS.
92 'Dai jūnanakai rijikai', 8 February 1929, and 'Taiheiyō mondai chōsakai jimusho hō', 1 July 1929, TYB/28/36 and 48, ACTU.
93 Yano to Tanaka, 4 June 1929, TMCK, vol. 2, GS.
94 Takaki to Yoshida, 25 July 1929, TMCK, vol. 2, GS.
95 Rōyama's comment on the Kyoto conference in Nitobe Inazō, ed., *Taiheiyō mondai: 1929 Kyoto kaigi*, Taiheiyō mondai chōsakai, 1930, cited in note 5 of Katagiri, 'Manshū mondai', p. 71.
96 Debuchi to Yoshida, 7 May 1929, TMCK, vol. 2, GS.
97 Uchiyama to Tanaka, 19 June 1929, TMCK, vol. 2, GS.
98 For example, Inoue to Yoshida, 19 June 1929, Takaki to Yoshida, 25 July 1929, Nitobe to Gaimushō, 31 July 1929 and Yoshida to Nitobe, 15 August 1929, TMCK, vol. 2, GS.
99 Eggleston, 'Australia and the Pacific'.
100 Rōyama Masamichi, 'Japan's position in Manchuria', in Condliffe, ed., *Problems of the Pacific, 1929*, pp. 592–3.
101 Hayashi to Shidehara, 7 October 1929, TMCK, vol. 2, GS.
102 Condliffe, *Reminiscences*, p. 41.
103 Greene to Curtis, 4 February 1950, MS Curtis 60, BL.
104 Greene to Fosdick, 7 August 1929, LSRM/54/584/IPR 1929, RA.
105 Fosdick to Day, 10 August 1929, LSRM/54/584/IPR 1929, RA.
106 Resolution, 22 May 1931, RFnA/1.1/200/350/4171, RA.
107 Carter to Eggleston, 10 February 1931, PRC, Box 110/Eggleston, BLCU; and Saitō M. *et al.*, eds, *Amerika seishin*, p. 68.
108 Greene to Eggleston, 30 January 1930, MS 423/14, NLA.
109 Loomis to Eggleston, 6 December 1930, MS 423/14, NLA.
110 'Appendix VI: summary of revenues and expenditures, 1932–3', in B. Lasker and W. Holland, eds, *Problems of the Pacific, 1933*, London: Oxford University Press, 1934, p. 478.
111 Atherton to Carter, 12 January 1931, E-1b/33 and 4 December 1935, E-2/20, AUH.
112 Atherton to Eggleston, 14 January 1931, MS 423/14, NLA.
113 Greene to the members of the Pacific Council, 3 April 1930, MS 423/14, NLA.
114 Condliffe, *Reminiscences*, pp. 43 and 47.
115 Greene to the members of the Pacific Council, 3 April 1930, MS 423/14, NLA. Atherton to Eggleston, 31 January 1931, MS 423/14, NLA.
116 Hooper, ed., *Remembering*, pp. 1–2.
117 William Holland, 'Preface', in Condliffe, *Reminiscences*, pp. i–ii.
118 Carter to Mrs Carter, 10 August 1933, Carter Papers, Box 1, BLCU.
119 Carter to Rockefeller III, 1 September 1932, RFmA/III-2-Q/9/62, RA.
120 Greene to Curtis, 15 March 1932, MS Curtis 6, BL.
121 Eggleston to Brooks, 15 April 1930, MS 423/14, NLA.
122 Ibid. and Greene to Curtis, 2 September 1930, MS Curtis 3, BL.
123 Cohen, Hirai trans., 'Ajia mondai', p. 356. Paul Evans, *John Fairbank and the American Understanding of Modern China*, New York: Basil Blackwell, 1988, pp. 62–3.
124 Macadam to Rose, 6 January 1933, 4/Rose, LCH.
125 Shimada Toshihiko, 'Manshū jihen no tenkai, 1931–1932', in Nihon kokusai seiji gakkai Taiheiyō sensō geiin kenkyūbu, ed., *Taiheiyō sensō eno michi*, vol. 2, Asahi shimbunsha, 1962, pp. 102–3.
126 Thorne, *Limits*, pp. 400–1 and 418–19.

127 Saitō Takashi, 'Beiei kokusai renmei no dōkō, 1931–1933', in Nihon kokusai seiji gakkai Taiheiyō sensō geiin kenkyūbu, ed., *Taiheiyō sensō eno michi* vol. 2, p. 361; and NHK shuzaihan, ed., *Manshū jihen: Sekai no koji e*, Kadokawa shoten, 1995, pp. 65–6.
128 Mitani, *Taisho*, p. 236.
129 Wilson, 'Manchurian crisis', p. 531.
130 Mitani, *Taisho*, pp. 233–4.
131 These reports included the following: Yano to Shidehara, 28 January 1931, Yoneuchi to Shidehara, 18 June 1931, Morishima to Shidehara, 7 June 1931, Kamimura to Shidehara, 14 September 1931, Murai to Shidehara, 24 September 1931 and Ishii to Shidehara, 10 November 1931, TMCK, vols 6–7, GS.
132 The opening speech by Hu Shuxi, cited in 'Preface', in Lasker and Holland, eds, *Problems of the Pacific, 1931*, pp. v–vi.
133 Takayanagi Kenzō, 'The application of existing instruments of policy', in ibid., pp. 232–4.
134 Hu Shuhsi (Shuxi), 'The pending cases and their adjustment', in ibid., pp. 237–9.
135 Eggleston to Loomis, 26 March 1931, Carter to Loomis, 13 May 1931 and Loomis to Saitō and Takayanagi, 27 May 1931, TYB/46/7, 8 and 9, ACTU. Eggleston himself could not attend the conference in 1931.
136 'The diplomatic machinery of the Pacific,' in Lasker and Holland, eds, *Problems of the Pacific, 1931*, pp. 221–2.
137 Mitani, *Taisho*, pp. 234–6.
138 Shidehara to Murai, 22 October 1931, TMCK, vol. 7, GS.
139 'Round table I: diplomatic machinery in the Pacific, 28 October 1931', p. 4 and 'Round table I: diplomatic machinery in the Pacific, 28 October 1931', (the second minute is clearly about a different session) pp. 2–3, TYB/55/7, ACTU.
140 Yokota Kisaburō, 'Taiheiyō ni okeru heiwa kikan', in Nasu Shiroshi, ed., *Shanhai ni okeru Taiheiyō kaigi*, Taiheiyō mondai chōsakai, 1932, pp. 142–4 and 146–8.
141 Takayanagi, 'Application', in Lasker and Holland, eds, *Problems of the Pacific, 1931*, p. 236; and Hu Shuhsi (Shuxi), 'Pending cases', p. 236.
142 'Round table I: diplomatic machinery in the Pacific, 27 October 1931', p. 1, TYB, 55/8, ACTU.
143 'Diplomatic machinery of the Pacific', p. 248.
144 Sakai Saburō, 'Showa kenkyūkai no higeki', *Bungei shunjū*, October 1964, pp. 235.
145 Smith, *Student Radicals*, pp. 74 and 265. Rōyama, *Nihon seiji*, pp. 1–7; and W. Miles Fletcher III, *The Search for a New Order: Intellectuals and Fascism in Prewar Japan*, Chapel Hill: University of North Carolina Press, 1982, pp. 14–15, 18 and 23.
146 Matsumoto S., *Shanhai*, vol. 1, pp. 35 and 38.
147 Nish, *Japan's Struggle*, pp. 181–2.
148 Matsumoto S., *Showashi*, p. 35.
149 Matsumoto S., *Shanhai*, vol. 1, p. 36.
150 Mitani, *Taisho*, p. 241 and n. 51.
151 Taiheiyō mondai chōsakai, *Kanada Banfu ni oite kaisai sarubeki daigokai Taiheiyō kaigi no junbi ni tsuite*, (Taiheiyō mondai shiryō 4), Taiheiyō mondai chōsakai, March 1933, p. 21, TYB/62/48, ACTU.
152 Mitani, *Taisho*, pp. 241–2 and Matsumoto S., *Shanhai*, vol. 1, p. 36.
153 Nish, *Japan's Struggle*, pp. 175–9.
154 Matsumoto S., *Showashi*, p. 35.
155 Rōyama, *Nihon seiji*, pp. 550–4.
156 Ibid., pp. 6–7; and Rōyama Masamichi, 'Hatanseru kokusai kikō no saikentō', *Gaikō jihō*, no. 680, April 1933, pp. 26–8.

7 Carter's vision, 1933–5

1 Katherine Mayo, *"That Damn Y": A Record of Overseas Service*, New York: Houghton Mifflin, 1920. W.F. Kuehl, ed., *Biographical Dictionary of Internationalists*, London: Greenwood Press, 1983, pp. 139–40.
2 Gordon M. Berger, 'Politics and mobilization in Japan, 1931–1945', in P. Duus, ed., *The Cambridge History of Japan*, vol. 6, Cambridge: Cambridge University Press, 1991, pp. 107–18.
3 Joseph C. Grew, *Ten Years in Japan*, New York: Simon and Schuster, 1944, p. 70.
4 Curtis to Wilbur, 18 November 1932, MS Curtis 8 and Curtis to Greene, 18 May 1933, MS Curtis 9, BL.
5 He was brought up in expatriate societies in China in 1901–12, educated in England in 1914–19, and worked for a British trading company in Tianjin in the 1920s. Owen Lattimore and Isono Fujiko, *China Memoirs: Chiang Kai-shek and the War against Japan*, University of Tokyo Press, 1990, pp. 3–34; and Newman, *Lattimore*, pp. 3–21.
6 Lattimore and Isono, *China Memoirs*, p. 34.
7 Baker to Atherton, 4 April 1933, E-2/4, AUH.
8 Douglas Craig, *After Wilson: The Structure for the Democratic Party, 1920–1934*, Chapel Hill: University of North Carolina Press, 1992, p. 233.
9 Rose to Malcolm, 10 August 1933, Rose to Malcolm, 23 August 1933 and Macadam to Curtis, 4 September 1933, RIIA file, LCH.
10 E.F. Ranshofen-Wertheimer, *The International Secretariat: A Great Experiment in International Administration*, Washington, DC: Carnegie Endowment for International Peace, 1945, p. 295.
11 Carter to Mrs Carter, 10 August 1933, Carter Papers, Box 1, BLCU.
12 Power to Curtis, 4 September 1933, 4/Curt, LCH.
13 'Preface', in Lasker and Holland, eds, *Problems of the Pacific, 1933*, p. v.
14 E. Carter 'Institute note', *Pacific Affairs*, November–December 1933, p. 617.
15 Loomis to Atherton, 2 September 1928, Wilbur Papers, 40/5, HI.
16 Davis recorded that the Dutch showed great interest in the IPR, but not the French. Davis to Atherton, 7 February 1928, E-13/6, AUH.
17 Condliffe to Greene, 21 June 1930, E-17/4, AUH.
18 Condliffe, *Reminiscences*, pp. 44–6.
19 Lattimore and Isono, *China Memoirs*, p. 37.
20 Newman, *Lattimore*, pp. 27 and 28.
21 Carter to Curtis, 16 March 1928, PRC, Box 108/Curtis 2 and Carter to Greene, 4 April 1930, PRC, Box 112/J. Greene, BLCU.
22 J. Merle Davis, 'Report of committee on permanent organization', in Condliffe ed., *Problems of the Pacific, 1927*, p. 591.
23 Curtis to Greene, 18 May 1933, MS Curtis 9, BL. During Carter's visit in Tokyo, Japanese discussed the possibility of Tokyo. 'Carter's visit in Tokyo in 1934', OC, B-7, LHU.
24 Ernest Scott, 'General report on the conference of the Institute of Pacific Relations held at Banff, Canada, August, 7–29, 1933', p. 3, Harrison Moore Paper, 11/3, AUM. Minutes of the Pacific Council meetings, 29 July 1933, E-2/22, AUH.
25 Carter to Mrs Carter, 10 August 1933, Carter Papers, Box 1, BLCU.
26 E. Carter, 'Tentative note' (August 1933), Carter Papers, Box 1, BLCU.
27 Carter to Atherton, 18 October 1933, E-2/6 and Carter to Atherton, 7 February 1934, E-2/9, AUH.
28 Carter to Atherton, 10 May 1935, E-2/15, AUH.
29 Atherton to Baker, 27 January 1936, E-2/25, AUH.
30 Carter to Greene, 20 June 1926, PRC, Box 112/J. Greene, BLCU.
31 Wilbur to Greene, 30 January 1929, PRC, Box 108/Curtis 2, BLCU.

32 Robinson and Edwards, eds, *Memoirs*, p. 608.
33 Carter to Greene, 19 August 1927, PRC, Box 112/J. Greene, BLCU.
34 Davis to Atherton, 20 January 1930, E-1b/27, AUH.
35 Atherton to Baker, 6 May 1933, E-2/4, AUH.
36 Alexander to Atherton, 17 January 1936, E-2/24, AUH.
37 Atherton to Loomis, 1 June 1937, E-3a/20, AUH.
38 'Appendix VI: conference organization and administrative decisions', in William Holland *et al.*, eds, *Problems of the Pacific, 1936*, London: Oxford University Press, 1937, p. 459.
39 Atherton to Carter, 4 December 1935, E-2/20, AUH.
40 '[Report of Australian delegate of the] Institute of Pacific Relations, Sixth Conference at Yosemite, August 15th–29th, 1936', A981/1/Org 95.
41 'Appendix VI: summary of revenues and expenditures, 1932–3', in Lasker and Holland, eds, *Problems of the Pacific, 1933*, p. 479.
42 Baker to Atherton, 11 February 1936, E-2/26 and Tarr to Atherton, 2 May 1936, E-3a/4, AUH.
43 Field to Walker, 10 December 1935, RFnA/1.1/200/351/4174, RA.
44 Atherton to Carter, 10 January 1936, E-2/23, AUH.
45 IPR, *Report of the International Secretariat*, p. 157.
46 Ibid., p. 8.
47 Ibid., p. 30.
48 Field to Atherton, 15 November 1934, E-2/12, AUH.
49 Hooper, ed., *Remembering*, pp. 81–3.
50 E. Carter, 'Tentative note', [August, 1933] Carter Papers, Box 1, BLCU.
51 'Carter's visit to Japan, 1934', OC, B-7, LHU. These initial three were Takaki, Uramatsu Samitarō and Matsukata Saburō. Carter to Cleeve, 25 September 1940, PRC, Box 42/RIIA 1939, BLCU.
52 Shepherd to Carter, 11 March 1938, PRC, Box 11/Australian Council, BLCU.
53 Hooper, ed., *Remembering*, pp. 1 and 4.
54 Ibid., p. 49.
55 Lattimore and Isono, *China Memoirs*, p. 34.
56 IPR, *Report of the International Secretariat*, pp. 115–29.
57 Ibid., p. 27.
58 The editors (Lattimore *et al.*), 'Comments and opinion', *Pacific Affairs*, March, 1934, pp. 83–4.
59 Ibid., p. 84.
60 IPR, *Report of the International Secretariat*, p. 30; and Hooper, ed., *Remembering*, p. 18.
61 Fujinuma to Yamamoto and Yasuda, 11 January 1933, TMCK, vol. 8, GS.
62 The decision was made in May 1935. Katagiri Nobuo, 'Taiheiyō mondai chōsakai (IPR) to seijiteki seiryoku kinkō oyobi heiwateki chōsei mondai: dai rokkai Yosemite kaigi o chūshin toshite', *Shakai kagaku tōkyū*, no. 125, September 1997, p. 258.
63 Hooper, ed., *Remembering*, p. 20.
64 IPR, *Report of the International Secretariat*, pp. 80 and 81.
65 Ibid., p. 82.
66 Newman, *Lattimore*, pp. 27–8, 42 and 44–5.
67 Lattimore and Isono, *China Memoirs*, p. 36.
68 IPR, *Report of the International Secretariat*, p. 133.
69 Ibid., pp. 122 and 137.
70 F. Field 'Notice of proposed amendment to the constitution of the American Council', 17 November 1936, RFnA/1.1/200/351/4175, RA.
71 Atherton to Carter, 10 January 1936, E-2/23, AUH.
72 Eggleston to Carter, 15 July 1935, PRC, Box 120/Australian Council, BLCU.

73 See, for example, Minutes of the council meeting [of the NSW branch of the AIIA], 28 October and 10 November 1938, AIIA Papers, GC.
74 Condliffe, *Reminiscences*, p. 41; and Shiozaki, *Kokusai shinchitsujo*, p. 128.
75 William Carter, 'Memories of Edward C. Carter by W.D. Carter: Addendum 1', (unpublished manuscript) 8 May 1986, p. 3. I am grateful to Carter's grandson, Paul Carter, for access to this document and also to Professor Mark Elvin for making this contact possible.
76 Shiozaki, *Kokusai shinchitsujo*, p. 32.
77 William Carter, 'Some memories of Edward C. Carter by his son', (unpublished manuscript), 17 April 1986, p. 5.
78 W. Carter, 'Memories of Edward Carter', 8 May 1986, p. 3; Shotwell, *Peace Conference*, p. 159; and Shiozaki, *Kokusai shinchitsujo*, pp. 37–8.
79 Carter to Loomis, 14 April 1931, TYB, 46/10, ACTU.
80 See Chapter 6.
81 Hinder to Eggleston, 8 January 1931, MS 423/14, NLA.
82 Macadam memo, 28 February 1934, AIIA file, LCH.
83 Carter to Greene, 30 June 1927, PRC, Box 112/J. Greene, BLCU.
84 Carter to Greene, 9 July 1929, PRC, Box 112/J. Greene, BLCU.
85 Tsurumi Y., *Chūdō*, pp. 478–9.
86 Atherton to Baker, 6 May 1933, E-2/4, AUH.
87 Carter to Greene, 30 June 1927, PRC, Box 112/J. Greene, BLCU.
88 Quigley, *Anglo-American*, pp. 188–9.
89 Ibid., pp. 227–310.
90 Shepardson to Brandeis, 26 September 1925, MS Eng Hist 872, BL.
91 Carter to Greene, 31 January 1930, PRC, Box 112/J. Greene, BLCU.
92 Anderson to Atherton, 21 August 1936, E-3a/11, AUH.
93 Eggleston Diary, 1927, MS 423/2, NLA; and Eggleston, 'Australia and the Pacific'. Arnold Toynbee, ed., *British Commonwealth Relations: Proceedings of the First Unofficial Conference at Toronto, 11–12 September 1933*, London: Oxford University Press, 1934, pp. 5–6.
94 These countries included Australia, Canada, India, New Zealand, South Africa and Britain. Toynbee, ed., ibid., pp. 3–5.
95 Hooper, ed., *Remembering*, p. 15.
96 Anonymous, 'Honolulu', *The Round Table*, vol. 18, December 1927 to September 1928, pp. 90–104; Anonymous, 'The Kyoto conference', *The Round Table*, vol. 20, December 1929 to September 1930, especially pp. 345–7; and Anonymous, 'Canada', *The Round Table*, vol. 24, December to September 1934, pp. 183–202.
97 J.G. Crawford, 'Australia as a Pacific power', in W.G.K. Duncan, ed., *Australia's Foreign Policy*, Sydney: Angus and Robertson, 1938, pp. 69–90.
98 Momose Takashi, *Jiten Showa senzenki no Nihon: Seido to jittai*, Yoshikawa kōbunkan, 1990, p. 174.
99 Shibasaki, *Kindai Nihon*, pp. 63, 71 and 72–3.
100 Ibid., pp. 42, 74, 78, 126 and 161.
101 Usui, *Chūgoku*, pp. 137–9.
102 Tobe Ryōichi, 'Gaimushō "kakushinha" to gunbu', in Miyake Masaki, ed., *Showashi no gunbu to seiji*, *2*, Daiichi hōki shuppan, 1983, pp. 100–1.
103 Tobe notes that it was Shidehara who appointed him to this position in 1930. Ibid., p. 95.
104 Fujinuma to Yamamoto and Yasuda, 11 January 1933, TMCK, vol. 8, GS.
105 Matsuoka to Uchida and Tani, 16 May 1933, TMCK, vol. 8, GS.
106 Mutō to Uchida, 17 March 1933, Kawamura to Uchida 16 June and 28 June 1933 and Uchida to Mutō, 4 July 1933, TMCK, vol. 8, GS.
107 Amō to Nitobe, 2 August 1933, Uchida to Ishii, 8 August 1933, Ishii to Uchida, 17 August 1933 and Kawamura to Uchida, 5 September 1933, TMCK, vol. 8, GS.

108 Taiheiyō mondai chōsakai, *Kanada Banfu ni oite kaisai sarubeki daigokai Taiheiyō kaigi no junbi ni tsuite,* (Taiheiyō mondai shiryō 4), Taiheiyō mondai chōsakai, March 1933, pp. 20–1, TYB/62/48, ACTU.
109 Ōshiro, *Nitobe,* pp. 219–28.
110 Interview with William Holland, Amherst, MA, 19 March 1993.
111 TIPER, 'The control of industry in Japan', in Lasker and Holland, eds, *Problems of the Pacific, 1933,* pp. 254–70.
112 Fletcher, *Search,* p. 57.
113 Tsurumi Yūsuke, 'Taiheiyō kaigi no ronsen', *Chūō kōron,* November 1933, p. 56.
114 Ibid., p. 54.
115 'Differences in labour standards', in Lasker and Holland, eds, *Problems of the Pacific, 1933,* pp. 104–5.
116 Amō to Nitobe, 2 August 1933 and Ishii to Uchida, 17 August 1933, TMCK, vol. 8, GS.
117 Saitō M. *et al.,* eds, *Amerika seishin,* p. 71.
118 Takaki Yasaka and Yokota Kisaburō, 'A security pact for the Pacific area', in Lasker and Holland, eds, *Problems of the Pacific, 1933,* p. 442.
119 Katagiri Nobuo, 'Taiheiyō mondai chōsakai (IPR) to Taiheiyō no heiwa kikan mondai', *Kenkyū shirizu,* no. 35, August 1996, p. 124.
120 Shimada Toshihiko, 'Kahoku kōsaku to kokkō chōsei, 1934–1937', in Nihon kokusai seiji gakkai Taiheiyō sensō gen'in kenkyūbu, ed., *Taiheiyō sensō eno michi,* vol. 3, no. 1, Asahi shimbunsha, 1962, pp. 73–85.
121 Rōyama, *Nihon seiji,* pp. 550–4.
122 Takaki and Yokota, 'Security pact', in Lasker and Holland, eds, *Problems of the Pacific, 1933,* pp. 445–6.
123 Ibid., p. 441.
124 Ibid., p. 442.
125 Yokota Kisaburō, 'Ajia Monrō shugi hihan', *Chūō kōron,* vol. 8, no. 7, July 1933, cited in Katagiri, 'Taiheiyō no heiwa kikan', pp. 110–13.
126 Yokota Kisdaburō, 'Kokusai renmei no botsuraku?', *Chūō kōron,* vol. 9, no. 1, cited in ibid., pp. 113–15.
127 Mitani, *Taisho,* pp. 234–7.
128 Yanaihara Tadao, *Pacific Islands Under Japanese Mandate,* London: Oxford University Press, 1940, pp. v–vii and 303–5.
129 Katagiri, 'Taiheiyō no heiwa kikan', pp. 102, 107 and 129.
130 Takaki Yasaka, 'Manshū mondai to Beikoku bōchōshi no kaiko: jishu gaikō ni taisuru jiyū shugiteki kenkai', *Kaizō,* September 1932, cited in ibid., p. 119.
131 Takaki and Yokota, 'Security pact', in Lasker and Holland, eds, *Problems of the Pacific, 1933,* p. 442.
132 'Introduction: the Pacific scene, 1931–1933', in Lasker and Holland, eds, *Problems of the Pacific, 1933,* p. 13.

8 The IPR and the Sino-Japanese War, 1936–9

1 Ushiba Tomohiko, 'Yosemite kaigi to sono zengo', in Nihon kokusai kyōkai, ed., *Taiheiyō mondai: Dairokkai Taiheiyō kaigi hōkoku,* Nihon kokusai kyōkai, 1937, p. 195.
2 'The United States', in Holland *et al.,* eds, *Problems of the Pacific, 1936,* pp. 42–3; and W.W. Lockwood, 'Trade and trade rivalry between the United States and Japan' in ibid., pp. 219–20.
3 'The United States', in ibid. pp. 44–5.
4 Itō Takashi, '"Kyokoku icchi" naikakuki no seikai saihensei mondai: Showa 13 nen Konoe shintō mondai kenkyū no tameni', *Shakai kagaku kenkyū,* vol. 24, no. 1, 1972, p. 95.

5 Ogata, 'Kokusai shugi', p. 334.
6 Toshino, ed., *Iwanaga*, pp. 163–6 and 242.
7 Matsumoto Shigeharu, *Shanhai jidai*, vol. 2, Chūō kōronsha, 1974, p. 120.
8 Gregory J. Kasza, *The State and the Mass Media in Japan, 1918–1945*, Berkeley, University of California Press, 1988, pp. 157 and 288.
9 Matsumoto Shigeharu, *Shanhai jidai*, vol. 1, Chūō kōronsha, 1974, pp. 72 and 77.
10 Kasza, *Mass Media*, pp. 157 and 194.
11 Toshino, ed., *Iwanaga*, pp. 214–18.
12 Matsumoto S., *Shanhai*, vol. 1, p. 76.
13 Ibid., p. 30.
14 Matsumoto S., *Shanhai jidai*, vol. 3, Chūō kōronsha, 1975, pp. 245–53.
15 Mitani, *Taisho*, p. 232.
16 Matsumoto S., *Shanhai*, vol. 3, pp. 318–19.
17 Matsumoto S., *Shanhai*, vol. 2, p. 119.
18 Shibasaki, *Kindai Nihon*, p. 76; and Tobe, 'Gaimushō "kakushinha" to gunbu', pp. 96 and 99.
19 Shibasaki, *Kindai Nihon*, p. 78.
20 Tobe, 'Gaimushō "kakushinha" to gunbu', pp. 91–2, 106 and 110.
21 Ishii to Amō, 15 January 1936, Ueda to Kurusu, 8 February 1936, Amō to Ishii, 21 April 1936; and Ishii to Amō, 24 April 1936, Ishii to Arita, 8 May 1936, Yamakawa to Amō, 20 June 1936; and Amō to Yamakawa, 9 July 1936, TMCK, vol. 8, GS.
22 Tsurumi (Consul in Portland, Oregon) to Arita, 16 July 1936, TMCK, vol. 8, GS.
23 Horiuchi to Sasaki, 15 June 1936, Matsushima to Ōhara, 17 June 1936, Sasaki to Horiuchi, 26 June 1936, Matsushima to Tsukawaki, 3 July 1936, Matsushima to Nangō, 7 July 1936 and Tsukawaki to Matsushima, 8 July 1936, TMCK, vol. 8, GS.
24 Arita to Inoue, 15 July 1936 and Shōmeisho, 21 July 1936, TMCK, vol. 8, GS.
25 Okamoto to Arita, 10 April 1936, Arita to Okamoto, 6 July 1936 and Tashiro to Okamoto, 7 July 1936, TMCK, vol. 8, GS.
26 Yamakawa to Amō, 16 July 1936 and Amō to Yamakawa, 22 July 1936, TMCK, vol. 8, GS.
27 Amō to Yamakawa, 28 July 1936, TMCK, vol. 8, GS.
28 For example, see Nasu Shiroshi, 'Hi no bakufu no shita ni', in Nihon kokusai kyōkai, ed., *Taiheiyō mondai*, pp. 182–3.
29 Yamakawa Tadao, 'Dairokkai Taiheiyō kaigi ni tsukite', *Kokusai chishiki*, vol. 16, no. 11, November 1936, p. 26. Other Yamakawa articles in a similar vein include 'Jo', in Nihon kokusai kyōkai, ed., *Taiheiyō mondai*, 'Konkai no Taiheiyō kaigi ni tsuite', *Gaikō jihō*, vol. 79, no. 4, August 1936, pp. 81–7; 'Dairokkai Taiheiyō kaigi no hirakaruru ni saishite', *Kokusai chishiki*, vol. 16, no. 8, August 1936, pp. 100–3; and 'Yosemite kaigi no keika narabi ni kekka', *Gaikō jihō*, vol. 80, no. 3, November 1936, pp. 123–4.
30 Katagiri, 'Seijiteki seiryoku', pp. 266–9.
31 Yamakawa, 'Dairokkai Taiheiyō kaigi ni tsuite', p. 2
32 Ibid., pp. 4–6.
33 Allen to Atherton, 1 September 1936, E-3a/12, AUH.
34 Takayanagi Kenzō, 'Dairokkai Taiheiyō kaigi no inshō', in Nihon kokusai kyōkai, ed., *Taiheiyō mondai*, pp. 167–8.
35 Tobe Ryōichi, 'Gaimushō kakushinha no taibeisaku', *Gaikō jihō*, no. 1273, 1990, p. 68.
36 Yoshizawa Kenkichi, 'Kokusai kankei no genjō', in Nihon kokusai kyōkai, ed., *Taiheiyō mondai*, p. 4; and an unidentified newspaper article, 1 September 1936, TMKS vol. 8, GS.
37 Yamakawa, 'Dairokkai Taiheiyō kaigi ni tsukite', p. 22.

9
9

38 Tamura Kōsaku, 'Taiheiyō heiwa kikō mondai', in Nihon kokusai kyōkai, ed., pp. 20–2.
39 Quincy Wright, 'The working of diplomatic machinery in the Pacific', in Holland *et al.*, eds, *Problems of the Pacific, 1936*, pp. 431–2.
40 Hamano Kyōhei, 'Yosemite kaishō to Osaka', *Kokusai chishiki*, vol. 16, no. 7, November 1936, pp. 53–5.
41 Shiozaki to Arita, 25 August 1936, cited in Katagiri, 'Seijiteki seiryoku', pp. 277–8. Shiozaki to Arita, 31 August 1936, TMKS, vol. 9, GS.
42 Yamakawa, 'Dairokkai Taiheiyō kaigi ni tsuite', pp. 8–9.
43 Nasu, 'Hi no bakufu', in Nihon kokusai kyōkai, ed., *Taiheiyō mondai*, pp. 179–81.
44 Tsurumi Y., 'Yosemite kaigi no kachi', in Nihon kokusai kyōkai, ed., *Taiheiyō mondai*, pp. 157–61 and 164.
45 Takayanagi, 'Dairokkai Taiheiyō kaigi no inshō', pp. 167–8.
46 Ushiba, 'Yosemite kaigi to sono zengo', p. 189.
47 Tsurumi Y., 'Yosemite kaigi no kachi', p. 159.
48 Yamakawa, 'Dairokkai Taiheiyō kaigi ni tsuite', p. 7; and Ushiba, 'Yosemite kaigi to sono zengo', p. 196.
49 Ibid., pp. 196–8 [emphasis added].
50 See, for example, J.A. Schwarz, *The New Dealers: Power Politics in the Age of Roosevelt*, New York: Alfred A. Knopf, 1993.
51 Hooper, ed., *Remembering*, pp. 83, 320 and 326.
52 Osmond, *Frederic Eggleston*, p. 183. See also David Sissons, 'Manchester vs. Japan: The Imperial Background of the Australian Trade Diversion Dispute with Japan, 1936', *Australian Outlook*, vol. 30, no. 3, 1976. Those who argued the importance of a non-British Commonwealth country, such as Japan, included Eggleston's young colleague at the Melbourne group of the IPR, John Crawford (1910–84). They were well ahead of their time, and a trade treaty between Japan and Australia was not concluded until 1957. See Alan Rix, *Coming to Terms: The Politics of Australia's Trade with Japan, 1945–57*, Sydney: Allen and Unwin, 1986.
53 'The changing balance of political forces in the Pacific and the possibilities of peaceful adjustment', in Holland *et al.*, eds, *Problems of the Pacific, 1936*, p. 182.
54 E.M. House, 'The need for an international New Deal', *Liberty*, September 1935, discussed in Yabe, *Konoe*, vol. 1, pp. 312–13.
55 'Introduction', in Lasker and Holland eds, *Problems of the Pacific, 1933*, p. 13.
56 'Changing balance of political forces', pp. 188–90.
57 Wright, 'Working of diplomatic machinery', pp. 421 and 425–6.
58 Ishii Kikujirō, 'Taiheiyō mondai chōsakai tono gappei ni tsuite', *Kokusai chishiki*, vol. 15, no. 12, December 1935, p. 80.
59 Yoshizawa, 'Kokusai kankei no genjō', pp. 5–7.
60 'Mushiro Nisshi kaigi o hirake: konkai no Taiheiyō kaigi ni tsuite', attached to Amō to Ishii, 31 August 1936, TMKS, vol. 9, GS.
61 Ogata, 'Kokusai shugi', p. 399.
62 Konoe Fumimaro, 'Shin Nihon no sugata o shimese', *Bungei shunjū*, 9 September 1934, reprinted in Bungei shunjū, ed., *"Bungei shunjū" ni miru Showashi*, Bungei shunjūsha, 1988, p. 236.
63 Yabe, *Konoe*, vol. 1, p. 282.
64 Mitani, *Taisho*, p. 237; and Baba Shūichi, '1930 nendai niokeru Nihon chishikijin no dōkō: Showa kenkyūkai no shisō to kōdō', *Shakai kagaku kiyō, 1969*, June 1969, pp. 101–4.
65 'Appendix VI: conference organization and administrative decisions', in Holland *et al.*, eds, *Problems of the Pacific, 1936*, p. 458.
66 Loomis to Atherton, 21 August 1936, E-3a/12, AUH.
67 Ozaki Hotsumi, 'Taiheiyō kaigi to shimbun', *Kokusai chishiki*, vol. 16, no. 11, November 1936, pp. 59–60.

68 Allen to Atherton, 1 September 1936, E-3a/12, AUH.

69 Jessup to Carter, 24 August 1939, PRC, Box 151/Japanese Council 2, BLCU.

70 Ibid. and Ushiba to Carter, n.d. [late 1939], TYB/94/39, ACTU.

71 Jōhōbu daiikka shukan, 'Tokyo teidai Takaki kyōju tobei ryohi hojo ni kansuru ken', 5 December 1938, Arita to Shiozaki, 7 December 1938, Wakasugi to Arita, 22 December 1938 and Arita to Wakasugi, 23 December 1938, TMKS, vol. 9, GS.

72 'Kyōgikaiin kaigō kiroku', 16 February and 22 March 1938; 'Nihon kenkyū yōkō daian sakusei iinkai shingi jikō', 26 November 1938; 'Kinkyū kyōgiinkai shingi jikō', 28 November 1938, TYB/87/15, 92/6 and 93/45 and 47; ACTU and 'Takaki Yasaka shi tobei sōbetsu kyōgiinkai', 5 December 1938, cited in Yamaoka Michio, 'Senzenki Nihon Taiheiyō mondai chōsakai to kokusai jimukyoku tono tairitsu: "Inkuaiari" mondai o chūshin toshite', *Shakai kagaku tōkyū*, no. 121, March 1996, p. 498.

73 'Appendix X: organization of the study meeting, the Inquiry and the research programme', in K. Mitchell and W.L. Holland, eds, *Problems of the Pacific, 1939*, New York, the IPR, 1940, pp. 287–8.

74 Saionji to Carter, 5 April 1938, OC, A-4/Pacific Council, 1938–39, LHU and 'Takayanagi Yasuo ryōshi yorino Ri kaidan narabini sono torikime ni kansuru shōsai hōkoku', 23 August 1938, TYB/91/4, ACTU.

75 Wickersham to Carter, 16 January 1933, PRC, Box 145/Wickersham, BLCU.

76 Chernow, *House of Morgan*, pp. 343–5; and Kuehl, ed., *Biographical Dictionary*, p. 299.

77 Charles W. Hayford, *To the People: James Yen and Village China*, New York: Columbia University Press, 1990, pp. 78–9.

78 Carter to Ruth and Orrick, 16 August 1937, Carter Papers, Box 5, BLCU.

79 Saionji to Carter, 5 April 1938, OC, A-4/Pacific Council, 1938–39, LHU.

80 Hooper, ed., *Remembering*, p. 21. The above quote is from the semi-final draft of the book, Part One, pp. 36–7, which Professor Hooper allowed me to read before publication.

81 'Kata shi to Chatamu hausu no sesshō ni tsuite', 23 August 1938', TYB/91/2, ACTU.

82 Takaki to Carter, 2 February 1939, PRC, Box 33/Takaki, BLCU.

83 Cohen, Hirai trans., 'Ajia mondai', pp. 376 and 383–6.

84 'Takaki Yasaka shi tobei', cited in Yamaoka, 'Senzenki Nihon Taiheiyō mondai chōsakai', pp. 498–500.

85 'Kata shi to Chatamu hausu' and 'Takayanagi Kenzō kyōgiin yorino Ri kaidan ni kansuru hōkoku shoshin', 23 August 1938, TYN/92/2 and 5, ACTU.

86 Takaki Yasaka, 'Re the international secretariat Inquiry', December 1938, TYB/ 95-2/13, ACTU.

87 'Takayanagi Yasuo ryōshi,' 23 August 1938, TYB/91/4, ACTU.

88 'Appendix X: organization of the study meeting', in Mitchell and Holland, eds, *Problems of the Pacific, 1939*, p. 287.

89 Carter to Dulles, 6 December 1937, Carter Papers, Box 5, BLCU and 'Pacific Council meeting', 3 and 5 January 1939, TYB/95/4, ACTU.

90 Hooper, ed., *Remembering*, p. 24.

91 'Introduction', in Mitchell and Holland, eds, *Problems of the Pacific, 1939*, p. 4.

92 Konoe, 'Shin Nihon', pp. 232–3.

93 Konoe Fumimaro, 'Jūshin to yo', (published posthumously in *Kaizō* in 1949, but the original was written probably in summer of 1937) in Imai Seiichi, ed., *Showa no dōran*, Chikuma shobō, 1969, pp. 263–5.

94 Shibasaki, *Kindai Nihon*, p. 139.

95 Horikiri, rep. ed., *Maeda*, pp. 47–9; Saitō M. *et al.*, eds, *Amerika seishin*, pp. 78–9; and Cohen, Hirai, trans., 'Ajia mondai', pp. 421–2.

96 Horikiri, rep. ed., *Maeda*, p. 47.
97 ACIPR and ISIPR members, such as Carter, were also familiar to those involved in the institute, such as Count Kabayama. These ICPA members and Maeda also acted as JCIPR representatives in the negotiations over the Inquiry in 1938 and 1939. 'Takayanagi Kenzō kyōgiin yori no ri kaidan igo ni kansuru hōkoku', 4 September 1938, TYB/91/6, ACTU.
98 'Jinmon chōsho: Saionji Kinkazu', 16 March 1942, in Obi Toshito, ed., *Gendaishi shiryō*, vol. 3, Misuzu shobō, 1962, p. 483.
99 Miki had been working on education issues, and after July 1938, he became a central figure in its newly established cultural section. Baba, '1930 nendai', pp. 176–7. The paper was filed in the Takaki Yasaka's JCIPR's documents. Miki Kiyoshi, 'Shina jihen no sekaishiteki igi', printed by Showa kenkyūkai jimukyoku, 1938, TYB/87/43, ACTU.
100 'Jinmon chōsho: Ushiba Tomohiko', 8 May 1942, in Obi, ed., *Gendaishi shiryō*, vol. 3, p. 539.
101 Sakai, 'Showa kenkyūkai no higeki', p. 237.
102 Spaulding, 'Japan's new bureaucrats, 1932–45', pp. 63–4.
103 Usui, *Chūgoku*, p. 142.
104 'Tōa shin chitsujo seifu seimei, 3 November 1938', reprinted in Rekishigaku kenkyūkai, ed., *Nihonshi shiryō*, vol. 5, Iwanami shoten, 1997, pp. 82–3.
105 Miwa Kimitada, 'Ajia shugi no rekishiteki kōsatsu', in Hirano Ken'ichirō, ed., *Nihon bunka no henyō*, Kōdansha, 1973, pp. 447–50; and Miwa Kimitada, '"Tōa shin chitsujo"', in Miwa Kimitada, ed., *Saikō Taiheiyō sensō zenya: Nihon no 1930 nendai ron toshite*, Sōseiki, 1981, pp. 196–7.
106 Iriye Akira, 'Nichibei sensō kara Nichibei dōmei made', in Hosoya Chihiro and Honma Nagayo, eds, *Nichibei kankeishi*, Yūhikaku, 1993, first published in 1982, pp. 80 and 82; and Akira Iriye, *Power and Culture: The Japanese–American War, 1941–1945*, Cambridge, MA: Harvard University Press, 1981, Chapter 3.
107 When the General Headquarters of the Allied Forces ordered the dissolution of *Tōa dōbunkai*, Konoe resigned from the chair. He could not bear the thought that he would be directly involved in the end of the organization. Kōyūkai, ed., *Tōa dōbun shoin*, p. 31.
108 Ozaki Hotsumi, 'Tōa shinchitsujoron no genzai oyobi shōrai: Tōa kyōdōtairon o chūshin ni', first published in *Tōa mondai* in April 1939, reprinted in Ozaki Hotsumi, *Ozaki Hotsumi zenshū*, vol. 2, Keisō shobō, 1977, p. 350.
109 'Jinmon chōsho: Saionji Kinkazu', 2 June 1942, in Obi, ed., *Gendaishi shiryō*, vol. 3, p. 552. According to Miwa, however, Nakayama claimed that the main text was written by Major Horiba Kazuo at the General Staff Office. Miwa, '"Tōa shin chitsujo"', p. 213.
110 Matsumoto's memoir noted that he did not leave Shanghai until the end of December because of illness. He also denied involvement in writing the draft when he was examined by a prosecutor in Ozaki's espionage case in July 1942. Matsumoto S., *Shanhai jidai*, vol. 3, p. 315; and 'Jinmon chōsho: Matsumoto S., 9 July 1942, in Obi, ed., *Gendaishi shiryō*, vol. 3, p. 601.
111 Miwa, "Tōa shin chitsujo", p. 219.
112 Sabey, 'The Genyōsha', p. 320.
113 Yabe, *Konoe*, vol. 1, pp. 575–6, 584–7 and 590–2.
114 Konoe, 'Shin Nihon', p. 239.
115 Tobe, 'Gaimushō kakushinha no taibeisaku', p. 69.
116 Konoe, 'Jūshin', p. 265.
117 Baba, '1930 nendai', p. 107.
118 Ozaki, 'Tōa shinchitsujoron', pp. 351–2; and Rōyama Masamichi, *Tōa to sekai*, Kaizō, 1941, p. 3. At the same time, however, Rōyama emphasized that this theory developed as his intellectual quest independent from government policies. Ibid., p. 2; and Baba, '1930 nendai', pp. 185–7.

119 Shimizu Ikutarō, 'Miki Kiyoshi to Showa kenkyūkai', *Chūō kōron: Rekishi to jimbutsu*, April 1974, p. 63.
120 Saitō M. *et al.*, eds, *Amerika seishin*, p. 80.
121 Miki Kiyoshi, 'Shina jihen no sekaishiteki igi', pp. 1–10, TYB/87/43, ACTU.
122 Miki Kiyoshi, 'Shin Nihon no shisō genri', in Miki Kiyoshi, *Miki Kiyoshi zenshū*, vol. 17, Iwanami shoten, 1968, pp. 509 and 512–13.
123 On 'cooperativism' (*kyōdō shugi*) see Tetsuo Najita and H.D. Harootunian, 'Japanese revolt against the West: political and cultural criticism in the twentieth century', in Peter Duus, ed., *The Cambridge History of Japan*, vol. 6, Cambridge: Cambridge University Press, 1991, first published in 1988, p. 738.
124 Baba, '1930 nendai', pp. 108, 110 and 176 and Shiozaki Hiroaki, 'Showa kenkyūkai to Miki Kiyoshi no kyōdō shugi', *Nihon rekishi*, July 1993, p. 33.
125 Miki, 'Shin Nihon no shisō genri', pp. 514–16.
126 Rōyama, *Tōa*, pp. 5–6, 7 and 8.
127 Miki Kiyoshi, 'Shin Nihon no shisō genri: zokuhen', in Miki Kiyoshi, *Miki Kiyoshi zenshū*, vol. 17, pp. 535–6.
128 Rōyama, *Tōa*, p. 10.
129 Ibid., pp. 26–7. Miwa argues that this was a deliberate choice. Miwa Kimitada, *Nihon; 1945 nen no shiten*, Tokyo daigaku shuppankai, 1986, pp. 155–8.
130 Rōyama, *Tōa*, p. 1.
131 Ibid., pp. 29, 33 and 38.
132 Miki, 'Shin Nihon no shisō genri', pp. 510 and 518.
133 Ibid., pp. 528–9 and 530–3.
134 Rōyama, *Tōa*, p. 38.
135 Ibid., pp. 14–16.
136 Ozaki Hotsumi, '"Tōa kyōdōtai" no rinen to sono seiritsu no kyakkanteki kiso', published first in *Chūō kōron* in January 1939, reprinted in Ozaki Hotsumi, *Ozaki Hotsumi zenshū*, vol. 2, p. 316.
137 Ibid., pp. 311, 313 and 318.
138 Ibid., p. 315; and Ozaki, 'Tōa shinchitsujoron', p. 354.
139 Ozaki, '"Tōa kyōdōtai"', pp. 312–13.
140 Ozaki, 'Tōa shinchitsujoron', p. 355. Johnson notes that Ozaki's argument was regarded by post-war Japanese academics as a significant step to 'free the whole study of Asian politics in Japan from the cultural and literary *gestalt*' (emphasis in original). Johnson, *An Instance of Treason*, p. 112.
141 Ozaki, '"Tōa kyōdōtai"' p. 315.
142 Baba, '1930 nendai', p. 205.
143 Takeuchi Yoshimi, *Nihon to Ajia*, Chikuma shobō, 1966, p. 304.
144 Tsurumi S., *Tenkō*, pp. 14–15. Takeuchi questions the existence of alternatives in the 1930s, and emphasizes the ambiguity between resistance and submission. Takeuchi Yoshimi, 'Kindai no chōkoku' (first published in 1959) reprinted in Yoshimoto Takaaki, ed., *Nashonarizumu*, Chikuma shobō, 1964, pp. 384, 394, 398, 402, 405 and 407. Barshay suggests exploring limitations in the context of total war. Andrew E. Barshay, *State and Intellectual in Imperial Japan: The Public Man in Crisis*, Berkeley: University of California Press, 1998, pp. 29 and 31–2.
145 Takeuchi, *Nihon to Ajia*, p. 304.
146 Shōda Tatsuo, *Jūshin tachi no Showashi*, vol. 2, Bungei shunjūsha, 1981, p. 77.

9 Redefining the international order: the Pacific War and the IPR, 1940-5

1 Knock, *To End All Wars*, p. 272.
2 Akira Iriye, *The Cambridge History of American Foreign Relations*, vol. III, Cambridge: Cambridge University Press, 1993, p. 188.

3 Itō Takashi, *Konoe shin taisei: Taisei yokusankai eno michi*, Chūō kōronsha, 1983, pp. 115–16.

4 Saionji Kinkazu, 'Kizoku no taijō', in Imai, ed., *Shōwa no dōran*, p. 291; and 'Jinmon chōsho: Saionji Kinkazu', 31 March 1942 and 23 June 1942 in Obi Toshito, ed., *Gendaishi shiryō*, vol. 3, Misuzu shobō, 1962, pp. 497 and 597.

5 'Tōa shin chitsujo seifu seimei, 3 November 1938', reprinted in Rekishigaku kenkyūkai, ed., *Nihonshi shiryō*, vol. 5, p. 83.

6 Baba, '1930 nendai', p. 162.

7 Itō Takashi, *Konoe shin taisei*, pp. 109, 197 and 199–200.

8 Shimanaka Yūji, ed., 'Kaisō roku [of Rōyama Masamichi]: senzen no bu', in Keiō gijuku daigaku hōgakubu seiji gakka, Nakamura Katsunori kenkyūkai, ed., *Tokyo teidai Shinjinkai kenkyū nōto*, no. 10, [Editor], 1988, p. 110.

9 Maruyama Masao, 'The ideology and dynamics of Japanese fascism', in Maruyama Masao, *Thought and Behaviour in Modern Japanese Politics*, London: Oxford University Press, 1963, p. 33.

10 Nakamura Takafusa, 'Ryū Shintarō to tōsei keizai', *Chūō kōron: Rekishi to jinbutsu*, April 1974, p. 73 and Itō Takashi, 'Shin taisei undō to wa nanika', *Chūō kōron: Rekishi to jinbutsu*, April 1974, p. 42.

11 Nakamura, 'Ryū Shintarō', pp. 71–2. Business circles especially denounced Ryū Shintarō's economic policies as communist because they advocated the separation of capital and management, and restriction of profit.

12 Baba, '1930 nendai', p. 122.

13 Tsurumi S., *Tenkō*, pp. 231–2.

14 Fletcher, *Search*, pp. 52 and 86.

15 Matsumoto S., *Shanhai*, vol. 3, pp. 158–60.

16 Saionji, 'Kizoku', pp. 270–81. He noted that a British diplomat in Shanghai was enthusiastically promoting a peaceful solution.

17 Matsumoto S., *Shanhai*, vol. 3, pp. 262–72.

18 'Jinmon chōsho: Saionji Kinkazu', 30 March and 29 March and 2 June 1942, in Obi, ed., *Gendaishi shiryō*, vol. 3, pp. 489, 549 and 551. Matsumoto's memoirs do not mention any involvement of Matsuoka.

19 Matsumoto S., *Shanhai*, vol. 3, pp. 293–303, 311 and 314.

20 Matsumoto S., *Shōwashi*, p. 105; and Saionji, 'Kizoku', pp. 285–9.

21 These works include R.J.C. Butow, *The John Doe Associates*, Stanford: Stanford University Press, 1974; Nihon kokusai seiji gakkai, ed., *Taiheiyō sensō eno michi*, vol. 7, Asahi shinbumsha, 1963; Okumura Fusao, *Nichibei kōshō to Taiheiyō sensō*; Maeno shoten, 1970; Shiozakai Hiroaki, *Nichieibei sensō no kiro*, Yamakawa shuppansha, 1984; and Sudō Shinji, *Nichibei kaisen gaikō no kenkyū: Nichibei kōshō no hatten kara Haru nōto made*, Keiō tsūshin, 1986.

22 Sudō, *Nichiibei*, pp. 62–5.

23 Ibid., pp. 170–1.

24 'Shōnin jinmon chōsho: Yamamoto Kumaichi', 9 May 1942, in Obi, ed., *Gendaishi shiryō*, vol. 3, p. 541.

25 'Jinmon chōsho: Saionji Kinkazu', 31 March 1942, pp. 498–502.

26 Sudō, *Nichibei*, pp. 185–6.

27 Ibid., pp. 369 and 371.

28 Matsumoto S., *Shanhai*, vol. 1, pp. 173–5, and vol. 2, p. 285.

29 Yabe, *Konoe*, vol. 1, p. 579.

30 ISIPR, ed., *War and Peace in the Pacific*, London: the RIIA, 1943, p. 2.

31 'Sengo no heiwa kikō juritsu ni kansuru kokusai jimukyoku kikaku no chōsa keikaku ni tsuite, zai Nyūyōku Matsuo Matsuhei shi yori no hōkoku, 22 January 1941'; and Carter to Takaki, 10 January 1941, Takaki to Carter, 21 January 1941, TYB/102/32, 34, 35, ACTU.

32 Department of State, *Postwar Foreign Policy Preparation, 1939–1945*, Washington, DC: Department of State Publications, 1949, pp. 19–22, 41–2, 53, 56 and 58.

33 Carter to Fosdick, 20 November 1940, RFnA/1.1/200/351/4177, RA.
34 Ibid.
35 Note of JMP [Packard], 7 November 1940, RFnA/1.1/200/351/4177, RA. This support and a sense of commitment continued during World War II, and even in the difficult decade of the 1950s. Resolution, 23 June 1950, RFnA/1.1/200/351/4179, RA.
36 Field to Walker, 21 November 1938, RFnA/1.1/200/351/4176, RA.
37 R.L. Wilbur, 'The American Council and the war', 17 December 1941, RFnA/1.1/200/351/4178, RA.
38 Lockwood to Carter (n.d., but probably some time in mid-November 1941), PRC, Box 165/ACIPR 1942, BLCU.
39 Yui Daizaburō, *Mikan no senryō kaikaku*, Tokyo daigaku shuppankai, 1990, first published in 1989, pp. 91–2.
40 ISIPR, ed., *War and Peace*, pp. 38–9. The OWI also initiated research projects involving anthropologists on Japan such as Ruth Benedict and John Embree.
41 Yui, *Mikan*, pp. 53 and 86–9.
42 Iriye, *Power and Culture*, pp. 149–52 and 209–10.
43 Sudō, *Nichibei*, pp. 203–6.
44 Frederick Field, *From Right to Left: An Autobiography*, Westport, CT: Lawrence Hill, 1983, p. 125.
45 Resolution, 2 December 1942, RFnA/1.1/200/351/4179, RA.
46 Department of State, *Postwar*, pp. 75, 78, 80, 82, 83, 107, 120, 152 and 153.
47 Yui, *Mikan*, p. 78.
48 Cleeve to Carter, 30 March 1940 and 22 April 1940, PRC, Box 42/RIIA 1939 and Carter to Cleeve, 6 May 1940, PRC, Box 42/RIIA 1939, BLCU. Christopher Thorne, 'Chatham House, Whitehall, and Far Eastern issues, 1941–1945', *International Affairs*, vol. 54, no. 1, January 1978, pp. 1–29.
49 William Forsyth, 'The pre-war Melbourne group of the Australian Institute of International Affairs: some personal recollections', *Australian Outlook*, vol. 28, no. 1, April 1978, p. 44; and John Legge, *Australian Outlook: A History of the Australian Institute of International Affairs*, St Leonards, NSW: Allen & Unwin, 1999, Chapter 4.
50 Nihon gaisei kyōkai to Takaki [(n.d.) TYB/103/31, ACTU.
51 Ushiba to Takaki, 20 March 1943, 29 March 1943, 1 April 1943, 19 April 1943, 21 April 1943, 29 June 1943 and 17 August 1943; and Ishii to Takaki, 1 May 1943, TYB/104, ACTU.
52 Warren Cohen, *The Chinese Connection: Roger S. Greene, Thomas W. Lamont, George E. Sokolsky and American–East Asian Relations*, New York: Columbia University Press, 1978, pp. 277–8.
53 Sudō, *Nichibei*, p. 337.
54 Field, *From Right to Left*, p. 83. 'Interview of Walker and Stevens with Carter and Field, 4 October 1934', RFnA/1.1/ 200/350/4175, RA.
55 Hugh Borton, Saitō M. trans., 'Nihon kenkyū no kaitakushatachi', in Hosoya and Saitō M., eds, *Washinton taisei*, pp. 552–3 and 564–5.
56 'Report on education, 1935', included in the letter, Field to Mason, 12 November 1935, RFnA/1.1/200/350/4174, RA.
57 'Minute of round table on education', 31 October 1931 (at the IPR conference of 1931), TYB/58/8, ACTU.
58 Borton, 'Nihon kenkyū', p. 564.
59 Ibid., p. 565 and annual meeting (of the ACIPR), 18 December 1936, PRC, Box 1/ACIPR 1936, BLCU.
60 Borton, 'Nihon kenkyū', pp. 558–9 and 561–3.
61 Ibid., p. 565.
62 Carter to Fosdick, 20 November 1940, RFnA/1.1/200/351/4177, RA.

63 Yui, *Mikan*, pp. 76 and 89.
64 Resolution, 2 December 1942, RFnA/1.1/200/351/4179, RA.
65 'The IPR in war time', 11 August 1942, RFnA/1.1/200/350/4179, RA.
66 Carter to Fosdick, 20 November 1940, RFnA/1.1/200/351/4177, RA.
67 Hooper, ed., *Remembering*, p. 24.
68 Fourteen out of seventeen British participants (excluding secretaries) were current or former office holders in 1942, and thirteen out of twenty in 1945. The figure for the American group was fifteen out of twenty-five in 1942, and eight out of twenty-eight in 1945. For Canada, it was three out of fifteen in 1942, and six out of fourteen in 1945; and for China it was six out of ten in 1942, and eight out of nineteen in 1945. France only sent four in 1942, but twelve in 1945, and a half of each year's representatives were officials, mostly with a colonial background. Most of the representatives of the Netherlands Indies in this period were members of the Board for the Netherlands Indies, Surinam and Curacao, based in the United States. Australia and New Zealand did not send many participants, but they included a few diplomats. Thailand, the Philippines and India also sent a few, but officials accounted for the most of these groups. Hooper, ed., *Remembering*, pp. 26 and 38. 'Part VI: conference membership', in ISIPR, ed., *War and Peace*, pp. 154–162; and 'Appendix III: conference membership', in IPR, ed., *Security in the Pacific*, New York: The ISIPR, 1945, pp. 149–61.
69 Watt to Hodgson, 1 December 1943, M1942; 6, AA.
70 Christopher Thorne, *Allies of a Kind: the United States, Britain and the War against Japan, 1941–1945*, London: Hamish Hamilton, 1978, pp. 212–3 and 540.
71 'Report of the council of the NSW branch to the 14th annual meeting for the year ending June 30th 1943', 26 July 1943, AIIA Papers, GC.
72 Watt to Hasluck, 28 December 1943, M1942; 6, AA.
73 Thorne, *Allies*, p. 542.
74 Ōkubo Genji, 'Oboegaki: Herbert Norman no shōgai', in Ōkubo Genji, trans. and ed., *Herbert Norman zenshū*, vol. 4, Iwanami shoten, 1978, p. 583.
75 Gary Allinson, 'E.H. Norman on modern Japan: towards a constructive assessment', in Roger Bowen, ed., *E.H. Norman: His Life and Scholarship*, Toronto: University of Toronto Press, 1984, pp. 100 and 105.
76 Maruyama Masao, 'Mumei no mono eno aichaku: Herbert Norman no koto', *Mainichi Shimbun*, April 18–19, 1957. Bowen, R., *Innocence is not Enough*, pp. 53 and 65; and Roger Bowen, 'Cold War, McCarthyism and murder by slander: E.H. Norman's death in perspective', in Bowen, ed., *E.H. Norman: His Life*.
77 Ōkubo, 'Oboegaki', p. 581.
78 In May, Norman was discussing his research trip to Tokyo with Carter. Norman to Carter, 4 May 1938 and Carter to Norman, 7 May 1938, PRC, Box 123/ACIPR, 1933–8, BLCU. Ōkubo, 'Oboegaki', p. 583.
79 Maruyama Masao, 'Tsuisō', in Ōkubo Genji tsuitōshū kankōkai, ed., *Tsuisō Ōkubo Genji* [Editor], 1987, pp. 128–30.
80 These include *Nihon ni okeru kindai kokka no seiritsu*, Jiji tsūshinsha, 1947; *Herbert Norman zenshū*, vols. 1–4, Iwanami shoten, 1978; *Wasurerareta shisōka*, vols 1–2, Iwanami shoten, 1950; and *Nihon no heishi to nōmin*, Iwanami shoten, 1958.
81 John Dower, 'E.H. Norman, Japan and the use of history', in John Dower, ed., *Origin of the Modern Japanese State: Selected Writings of E.H. Norman*, New York: Pantheon Books, 1975, pp. 37 and 38; and John Dower 'E.H. Norman to jiyū shugiteki gakumon no gendaiteki kiki', *Shisō*, vol. 4, no. 634, 1977, p. 127.
82 E.H. Norman, *Japan's Emergence as a Modern State*, New York: ISIPR, 1940, p. 209.
83 Ibid., p. 204.
84 Ibid., p. 206.
85 Dower, *Empire*, pp. 109 and 215–16.
86 Konoe, 'Jūshin', pp. 263–4.

87 Ōkubo Genji, 'Kaidai', in Herbert Norman, Ōkubo Genji, trans. and ed., *Herbert Norman zenshū*, vol. 1, Iwanami shoten, 1977, pp. 370 and 373–4.
88 Carter to Fosdick, 20 November 1940, RFnA/1.1/200/351/4177, RA.
89 ISIPR, ed., *War and Peace*, pp. 42–3.
90 Thomas A. Bisson, *America's Far Eastern Policy*, New York: ISIPR, 1945, pp. 152–5.
91 Yui, *Mikan*, pp. 149–59 and 184–6. Sansom, however, was sceptical of the capability of 'liberals'.
92 Iriye, *Power and Culture*, pp. 151–3.
93 Yui, *Mikan*, pp. 61–2, 70, 87–88 and 194–203.
94 ISIPR, ed., *Security in the Pacific*, pp. 25–45.
95 Dower, 'Use of history', pp. 39–40.
96 Sudō, *Nichibei*, p. 313. This is an interesting contrast to the view of American 'Far Eastern' specialists of Konoe in 1939. See Chapter 8.
97 Norman's criticism was probably intensified after he knew that Konoe had been appointed as the head of the study group for the new constitution in 1945. E.H. Norman, Ōkubo Genji, trans., 'Sensō sekinin ni kansuru oboegaki, 5 November 1945: Konoe Fumimaro', in Herbert Norman, Ōkubo Genji, trans. and ed., *Herbert Norman zenshū*, vol. 2, Iwanami shoten, 1978, pp. 343–6, Ōkubo Genji, 'Kaidai', in ibid., pp. 453–5, Dower, 'Use of history', p. 27 and Yui, *Mikan*, p. 233–4.
98 Yui, *Mikan*, pp. 230–41 and 243–4. Their activities during the Occupation period are beyond the scope of this book, and have been analyzed in other works. Iokibe Makoto, *Beikoku no senryō seisaku*, vols. 1–2, Chūō kōronsha, 1985; and John Dower, *Embracing the Defeat: Japan in the Wake of World War II*, New York: Norton & Company, 1999.
99 Iriye, *Power and Culture*, pp. 98–9.
100 Iriye, *American Foreign Relations*, vol. III, pp. 197–8.
101 Yui, *Mikan*, p. 98.
102 Ibid., pp. 95–6 and 99–100.
103 JBK to JHW, 3 March 1942, RFnA/1.1/200/350/4179, RA.
104 ISIPR, ed., *War and Peace*, pp. 74–76.
105 Thorne, *Allies*, p. 213.
106 ISIPR, ed., *War and Peace*, p. 25.
107 Yui, *Mikan*, p. 112 and Thorne, *Allies*, pp. 223–4.
108 Ibid., p. 24.
109 ISIPR, ed., *War and Peace*, p. 56.
110 Ibid., p. 57.
111 Ibid., p. 49.
112 Ibid., p. 25.
113 Ibid., pp. 56–8.
114 Ibid., p. 49.
115 Department of State, *Postwar*, pp. 170–3.
116 ISIPR, *Security in the Pacific*, p.104.
117 Ibid., p. 10.
118 Ibid., pp. 124–6.
119 Thorne, *Allies*, p. 404.
120 ISIPR, *Security in the Pacific*, p. 128.
121 Ibid., pp. 89, 91–2 and 129.
122 Ibid., p. 76.
123 Ibid., p. 94.
124 Ibid., p. 114.
125 Ibid., pp. 111–12.
126 Ibid., pp. 102–3.

Postscript

1 Rōyama was purged in 1947, and was rehabilitated in 1950. He started to work for UNESCO in 1952. Maeda was purged in 1946, and was rehabilitated in 1950. He worked for the ILO from 1950 and UNESCO from 1952. Nasu was purged in 1947, and was rehabilitated in 1950. He worked for the ILO, UNESCO and the United Nations from 1951. Matsumoto was rehabilitated in 1950. In 1954–63, he was a committee member of the Japanese UNESCO association, and in 1957 attended the UNESCO conference in Paris as a Japanese representative.
2 John Dower, 'Peace and democracy in two systems: external policy and internal conflict', in Andrew Gordon, ed., *Postwar Japan as History*, Berkeley, CA: University of California Press, 1993, p. 11.
3 William Wallace, 'Between two worlds: think-tanks and foreign policy', in Christopher Hill and Pamela Beshoff, eds, *Two Worlds of International Relations: Academics, Practitioners and the Trade in Ideals*, London: Routledge, 1994, pp. 157–60; Louis T. Wells Jr, 'The multinational business enterprise: what kind of international organization?', in Keohane and Nye, eds, *Transnational Relations*, pp. 97–114; and Peter D. Bell, 'The Ford Foundation as a transnational actor', in ibid., pp. 116 and 126–8.
4 Laura Hein and Mark Selden, 'The lessons of war, global power, and social change,' in Hein and Selden, eds, *Censoring History*, pp. 21–3.
5 Even in the 1990s, this elitism is still evident in various INGOs. For example, see R.L. Sundquist's comment, cited in Richard Higgott and Diane Stone, 'The limits of influence: foreign policy think tanks in Britain and the USA', *Review of International Studies*, vol. 21, 1994, p. 14.

Appendix 1: IPR conferences

1 Because the topics of the Round Tables and Forums for the first conferences account for twenty seven, this list is a summary of these topics. From the second conference, the topics are listed as they are in the proceedings unless specified.
2 Because the proceeding of 1933 conference was summarized under the categories of, not issues, but countries, the main papers' titles are listed here to indicate the contents of the Round Table discussions.
3 Details of the following conferences are based on the information in Yamaoka Michio, 'Daisankai Taiheiyō kaigi (1929 nen) to Nihon no taiō,' *Kenkyū shirizu*, vol. 28 (May, 1991), p.193.

Appendix 2: participants at the IPR conferences, 1927–47

1 The figure is based on the lists in the conference proceedings.
2 Number of participants in total.

Appendix 3: office holders

1 Lists here are based on the information in the proceedings of the conferences and correspondences, and therefore the precise dates of changes of positions are at times unidentifiable.
2 The USA, Honolulu based.
3 In May 1928, *News Bulletin* [of the IPR] was renamed as *Pacific Affairs*.

4 The USA, East coast based.
5 Lists here are also based on the information in the proceedings of the conferences and correspondences, and therefore, this list should be taken as a guidance, rather than the fact.
6 The USA, West coast based.
7 The exact year is unidentifiable.

Select bibliography

Place of publication in Japan is Tokyo unless otherwise indicated.

Proceedings of the IPR conferences, 1925–47 (chronological order)

IPR, ed., *Institute of Pacific Relations: Honolulu Session June 30 to July 14, 1925: History, Organization, Proceedings Discussions and Addresses*, Honolulu: IPR, 1925.

Condliffe, John B., ed., *Problems of the Pacific: Proceedings of the Second Conference of the Institute of Pacific Relations, Honolulu, Hawaii, July 15 to 29, 1927*, Chicago: University of Chicago Press, 1928.

Condliffe, John B., ed., *Problems of the Pacific 1929: Proceedings of the Third Conference of the Institute of Pacific Relations, Nara and Kyoto, Japan, October 23 to November 9, 1929*, Chicago: University of Chicago Press, 1930.

Lasker, Bruno and Holland, William, eds, *Problems of the Pacific 1931: Proceedings of the Fourth Conference of the Institute of Pacific Relations, Hangchow and Shanghai, China, October 21 to November 2*, Chicago: University of Chicago Press, 1932.

Lasker, Bruno and Holland, William, eds, *Problems of the Pacific, 1933: Economic Conflict and Control: Proceedings of the Fifth Conference of the Institute of Pacific Relations, Banff, Canada, 14 – 26 August, 1933*, London: Oxford University Press, 1934.

Holland, William, Mitchell, Kate, Moore Harriet and Pyke, Richard, eds, *Problems of the Pacific, 1936: Aims and Results of Social and Economic Policies in Pacific Countries: Proceedings of the Sixth Conference of the Institute of Pacific Relations, Yosemite National Park, California, 15 – 29 August 1936*, London: Oxford University Press, 1937.

Mitchell, Kate and Holland, William, eds, *Problems of the Pacific, 1939: Proceedings of the Study Meeting of the Institute of Pacific Relations, Virginia Beach, Virginia, November 18 to December 2, 1939*, New York: IPR, 1940.

IPR, ed., *War and Peace in the Pacific: A Preliminary Report of the Eighth Conference of the Institute of Pacific Relations on Wartime and Post-war Cooperation of the United Nations in the Pacific and the Far East, Mont Tremblant, Quebec, December 4–14, 1942*, New York: the ISIPR, 1943.

IPR, ed., *Security in the Pacific: A Preliminary Report of the Ninth Conference of the Institute of Pacific Relations, Hot Springs, Virginia, January 6–17, 1945*, New York: ISIPR, 1945.

IPR, ed., *Problems of Economic Reconstruction in the Far East: Report of the Tenth Conference of the Institute of Pacific Relations, Stratford-on-Avon, England, September 5–20, 1947*, New York: ISIPR, 1949.

Japanese version of the proceedings in 1927–36 (chronological order)

Inoue, Junnosuke, ed., *Taiheiyō mondai*, Nihon hyōronsha, 1927.

Nitobe, Inazō, ed., *Taiheiyō mondai: 1929 nen Kyoto kaigi*, Taiheiyō mondai chōsakai, 1930.

Nasu, Shiroshi, ed., *Shanhai ni okeru Taiheiyō kaigi*, Iwanami shoten, 1932.

Nihon kokusai kyōkai, ed., *Taiheiyō mondai: Dairokkai Taiheiyō kaigi hōkoku*, Nihon kokusai kyōkai, 1937.

Others

Akami, Tomoko, 'Frederic Eggleston and Oriental Power, 1925–1929', in Paul Johns and Vera Mackie, eds, *Relationships: Australia and Japan, 1850s to 1950s*. Melbourne: University of Melbourne History Monograph no. 28, 2001.

―― '1920 nendai niokeru Ōsutoraria no Taiheiyō ishiki to Taiheiyō mondai chōsakai, 1920–1930', *Ōsutraria kenkyū*, vol. 5, December 1994, pp. 58–63.

―― 'Post-League Wilsonian internationalism and the Institute of Pacific Relations, 1925–1945', *Shibusawa kenkyū*, no. 11, October 1998, pp. 3–35.

―― 'The "new" discourse of international politics and a new generation of foreign experts in Australia in 1919–1929', in Chūkyō daigaku shakai kagaku kenkyūsho Ōsutoraria kenkyūbu, ed., *Nichi Gō no shakai to bunka, Part II*, Seibundō, 1999.

―― 'The Liberal Dilemma: Internationalism and the Institute of Pacific Relations in Japan, Australia and the USA, 1919–1942', PhD thesis, Australian National University, 1996.

―― 'The rise and fall of a "Pacific sense": the experiment of the Institute of Pacific Relations, 1925–1930', *Sibusawa kenkyū*, vol. 7, October 1994, pp. 2–37.

Allen, Gwenfread E., *Bridge Builders: The Story of Theodore and Mary Atherton Richards*, Honolulu, publisher unknown, 1970.

Allinson, Gary, 'E.H. Norman on modern Japan: towards a constructive assessment', in Roger Bowen, ed., *E.H. Norman: His Life and Scholarship*, Toronto: University of Toronto Press, 1984.

Asada, Sadao, *Ryōtaisen kan no Nichibei kankei: Kaigun to seisaku kettei katei*, Tokyo daigaku shuppankai, 1993.

―― 'Washinton kaigi o meguru Nichibei no seisaku kettei katei no hikaku: hito to kikō', in Hosoya Chihiro and Watanuki Jōji, eds, *Taigai seisaku kettei katei no Nichibei hikaku*, Tokyo daigaku shuppankai, 1977.

―― 'Washinton kaigi to Nihon no taiō: "kyū gaikō" to "shin gaikō" no hazama', in Iriye Akira and Aruga Tadashi, eds, *Senkanki no Nihon gaikō*, Tokyo daigaku shuppankai, 1984.

Baba, Shūichi, '1930 nendai niokeru Nihon chishikijin no dōkō: Showa kenkyūkai no shisō to kōdō', *Shakai kagaku kiyō, 1969*, June 1969, pp. 67–207.

Bacon, Robert, and James B. Scott, eds, *Men and Policies: Addresses by Elihu Root*, Cambridge, MA: Harvard University Press, 1924.

Bisson, Thomas A., *America's Far Eastern Policy*, New York: ISIPR, 1945.

Borton, Hugh, Saitō Makoto trans., 'Nihon kenkyū no kaitakushatachi', in Hosoya Chihiro and Saitō Makoto, eds, *Washinton taisei to Nichibei kankei*, Tokyo daigaku shuppankai, 1978.

Bowen, Roger, *Innocence is not Enough: The Life and Death of Herbert Norman*, Vancouver: Douglas & McIntyre, 1986.

The British League of Nations Union, *The Covenant of the League of Nations and the Geneva Protocol*, London: [The British] League of Nations Union, n.d.

Brown, Nicholas, 'Australian intellectuals and the image of Asia, 1920–1960', *Australian Cultural History*, no. 9, 1990, pp. 80–92.

Burgman, Thomas, 'Nitobe Inazō as Under-Secretary General of the League of Nations, 1920–1926', *The Journal of International Studies*, Institute of International Relations, Sophia University, Tokyo, no. 14, January 1985, pp. 77–93.

Carr, E.H., *The Twenty Years' Crisis, 1919–1939: An Introduction to the Study of International Relations*, London: Papermac, 1993, first published in 1939, second edition in 1946.

Carter, William, 'Memories of Edward C. Carter by W.D. Carter: Addendum 1', (unpublished manuscript) 8 May 1986.

—— 'Some memories of Edward C. Carter by his son' (unpublished manuscript), 17 April 1986.

Chernow, Ron, *The House of Morgan: An American Banking Dynasty and the Rise of Modern Finance*, New York: Touchstone, 1990.

Cohen, Warren, Hirai Atsuko, trans., 'Ajia mondai to Amerika minkan dantai', in Hosoya Chihiro *et al.*, eds, *Nichibei kankeishi: Kaisen ni itaru jūnen*, vol. 3, Tokyo daigaku shuppankai, 1971.

Condliffe, John B., *Reminiscences of the Institute of Pacific Relations*, Vancouver, BC: Institute of Asian Research, University of British Columbia, 1981.

Davidann, Jon T., 'Colossal illusions: US–Japanese relations in the Institute of Pacific Relations, 1919–1938', *Journal of World History*, vol. 12, no. 1, spring, 2001 pp. 155–82.

DeBenedetti, Charles, *Origins of the Modern American Peace Movement, 1915–1929*, New York: KTO Press, 1978.

Department of State, *Postwar Foreign Policy Preparation, 1939–1945*, Washington, DC: Department of State Publications, 1949.

Dirlik, Arif, 'The Asia–Pacific idea: reality and representation in the invention of a regional structure', *Journal of World History*, vol. 3, no. 1, spring, 1992, pp. 55–79.

Dower, John, 'E.H. Norman, Japan and the use of history', in John Dower, ed., *Origin of the Modern Japanese State: Selected Writings of E.H. Norman*, New York: Pantheon Books, 1975.

—— *Empire and Aftermath: Yoshida Shigeru and the Japanese Experience, 1878–1954*, Cambridge, MA: Harvard University Press, 1979.

—— 'Ōkubo Genji: the unfinished agenda', in Ōkubo Genji tsuitōshū kankōkai, ed., *Tsuisō Ōkubo Genji*, [Editor], 1987.

Duncan-Hall, H. and J.B. Condliffe, *What of the Pacific?: A Searchlight on its Problems*, Honolulu, 1925.

Eggleston, F., Frederic, 'Australia and the Pacific', [Melbourne] *Herald*, 23 December 1929 and 25 January 1930.

Elkin, A.P., *Pacific Science Association: Its History and Role in International Cooperation*, Honolulu: Bishop Museum Press, 1961.

Fairbank, John, 'William L. Holland and the IPR in historical perspective', *Pacific Affairs*, vol. 52, no. 4, winter, 1979–1980, pp. 587–590.

Field, Frederick, *From Right to Left: An Autobiography*, Westport, CT: Lawrence Hill, 1983.

Fletcher, W. Miles III, *The Search for a New Order: Intellectuals and Fascism in Prewar Japan*, Chapel Hill: University of North Carolina Press, 1982.

Forsyth, William, 'The pre-war Melbourne group of the Australian Institute of International Affairs: some personal recollections', *Australian Outlook*, vol. 28, no. 1, April 1978, pp. 44–9.

Fujisawa, Chikao, 'Kokusai shugi no kiso kannen', *Kokusai chishiki*, vol. 8, no. 9, 1928, pp. 20–36.

Gaimushō, ed., *Nihon gaikō monjo: Nihon gaikō tsuikairoku, 1900–1935,* Gaimushō, 1983.

—— ed., *Nihon gaikō monjo,* Showaki I, Part II, vols 1 and 4, Gaimu shō, 1988 and 1991.

Grew, Joseph C., *Ten Years in Japan,* New York: Simon and Schuster, 1944.

Haller, Mark H., *Eugenics: Hereditarian Attitudes in American Thought,* New Brunswick, NJ: Rutgers University Press, 1963.

Hara, Kakuten, *Gendai Ajia kenkyū seiritsushiron,* Keisō shobō, 1984.

Hein, Laura, and Mark Selden, eds, *Censoring History: Citizenship and Memory in Japan, Germany and the United States,* Armonk, NY: M.E. Sharpe, 2000.

Holland, William, 'Source materials on the Institute of Pacific Relations: bibliographical note', *Pacific Affairs,* vol. 58, no. 1, spring, 1985, pp. 91–7.

Hooper, Paul F., *Elusive Destiny: The Internationalist Movement in Modern Hawaii,* Honolulu: University of Hawaii Press, 1980.

—— ed., *Remembering the Institute of Pacific Relations: The Memoirs of William L. Holland,* Ryūkei shōsha, 1995.

Horikiri, Zenjirō, rep. ed., *Maeda Tamon: Sono bun sono hito,* Maeda Tamon kankōkai, 1963.

Hosoya, Chihiro, 'Nihon no Eibeikan to senkanki no Higashi Ajia', in Hosoya Chihiro, ed., *Nichiei kankei shi 1917–1949,* Tokyo daigaku shuppankai, 1982.

Inoki, Masamichi, ed., *Nihon seiji gaikōshi shiryōsen,* Yūshindō, 1973.

The Institute of Politics, *Its First Decade,* Williamstown, MA: The Institute of Politics, 1931.

IPR, *Report of the International Secretariat to the Pacific Council, 1933–1936,* [New York]: IPR, 1936.

Iriye, Akira, *After Imperialism: The Search for a New Order in the Far East, 1921–1931,* Cambridge, MA: Harvard University Press, 1965.

—— *The Cambridge History of American Foreign Relations,* vol. III, Cambridge: Cambridge University Press, 1993.

—— *Power and Culture: The Japanese—American War, 1941–1945,* Cambridge, MA: Harvard University Press, 1981.

Ishibashi, Tanzan, *Ishibashi Tanzan hyōron senshū, 1884–1973,* Tōyō keizai shimpōsha, 1990.

Ishii, Kikujirō, 'Taiheiyō mondai chōsakai tono gappei ni tsuite', *Kokusai chishiki,* vol. 15, no. 12, December 1935, pp. 77–80.

Ishii, Mitsuru, *Nagao Hampei den,* Kyōbunkan, 1937.

Itō, Takashi, *Konoe shin taisei: Taisei yokusankai eno michi,* Chūō kōronsha, 1983.

—— '"Kyokoku icchi" naikakuki no seikai saihensei mondai: Showa 13 nen Konoe shintō mondai kenkyū no tameni', *Shakai kagaku kenkyū,* vol. 24, no. 1, 1972, pp. 56–130.

—— *Showa shoki seijishi kenkyū: Rondon kaigun gunshuku mondai o meguru shoseiji dantai no taikō to teikei,* Tokyo daigaku shuppankai, 1991, first published in 1969.

Johnson, Charmers, *An Instance of Treason: Ozaki Hotsumi and the Sorge Spy Ring,* Stanford, CA: Stanford University Press, 1990, expanded edition, first published in 1964.

Kajima, Morinosuke, ed., *Nihon gaikōshi,* vol. 12, Kajima kenkyūsho shuppankai, 1971.

Kanzaki, Kiichi, 'Taiheiyō mondai to Kokusai renmei: Renmei wa Ōshū renmei taru bekarazu', *Kokusai chishiki,* vol. 6, no. 6, June 1926, pp. 51–7.

Kasza, Gregory J., *The State and the Mass Media in Japan, 1918–1945,* Berkeley, University of California Press, 1988.

Katagiri, Nobuo, 'Senkanki Taiheiyō jidai no anzen hoshō imegi', *Kokusai seiji,* no. 102, February 1993, pp. 82–98.

—— 'Taiheiyō mondai chōsakai to Chōsen daihyōken mondai: Chōsen gurūpu no dattai, 1925–1931', *Hōgaku kenkyū,* vol. 59, no. 4, April 1986, pp. 45–76.

—— 'Taiheiyō mondai chōsakai to imin mondai: daiikkai Hawai kaigi o chūshin toshite, part 2', *Hōgaku kenkyū*, vol. 58, no. 7, July 1985, pp. 37–56.

—— 'Taiheiyō mondai chōsakai to imin mondai: dainikai Hawai kaigi o chūshin toshite', *Hōgaku kenkyū*, vol. 65, no. 2, February 1992, pp. 155–84.

—— 'Taiheiyō mondai chōsakai to Manshū mondai', *Hōgaku kenkyū*, vol. 52, no. 9, 1979, pp. 48–81.

—— 'Taiheiyō mondai chōsakai (IPR) to seijiteki seiryoku kinkō oyobi heiwateki chōsei mondai: dai rokkai Yosemite kaigi o chūshin toshite', *Shakai kagaku tōkyū*, no. 125, September 1997, pp. 251–300.

—— 'Taiheiyō mondai chōsakai (IPR) to Taiheiyō no heiwa kikan mondai: daigokai Banfu kaigi ni okeru Takaki Yokota an o chūshin toshite', *Kenkyū shirizu*, no. 35, August 1996, pp. 101–32.

Katzenstein, Peter J. and Takashi Shiraishi, eds, *Network Power: Japan and Asia*, Ithaca: Cornell University Press, 1997.

Kazumata, Masao, 'Nichibei imin mondai to kokunai mondai: kokusaihō ni okeru kokunai mondai riron shutsugen no tancho', in Ueda Toshio, ed., *Kindai Nihon gaikōshi no kenkyū*, Yūhikaku, 1956.

Kendle, John, *The Round Table Movement and Imperial Union*, Toronto: University of Toronto Press, 1975.

Keohane, Robert O. and Joseph S. Nye Jr, eds, *Transnational Relations and World Politics*, Cambridge, MA: Harvard University Press, 1972.

Kimura, Masato, *Shibusawa Eiichi: Minkan keizai gaikō no sōshisha*, Chūō kōronsha, 1991.

Knock, Thomas J., *To End All Wars: Woodrow Wilson and the Quest for a New World Order*, New York: Oxford University Press, 1993.

Ko Sakatani shishaku kinen jigyōkai, ed., *Sakatani Yoshirō den*, Ko Sakatani shishaku kinen jigyōkai, 1951.

Kobayashi, Tatsuo, 'Pari heiwa kaigi to Nihon no gaikō', in Ueda Toshio, ed., *Kindai Nihon gaikōshi no kenkyū*, Yūhikaku, 1956.

Konoe, Fumimaro, 'Jūshin to yo', in Imai Seiichi, ed., *Showa no dōran*, Chikuma shobō, 1969.

—— 'Shin Nihon no sugata o shimese', *Bungei shunjū*, 9 September 1934, reprinted in Bungei shunjū, ed., *"Bungei shunjū" ni miru Showashi*, Bungei shunjūsha, 1988.

Korhonen, Pekka, 'The Pacific Age in world history', *Journal of World History*, vol. 7, no. 1, spring, 1996, pp. 41–70.

Kōyūkai, ed., *Tōa dōbun shoin daigaku shi*, Kōyū kai, 1955.

Kuehl, W.F., ed., *Biographical Dictionary of Internationalists*, London: Greenwood Press, 1983.

Lattimore, Owen, and Isono Fujiko, *China Memoirs: Chiang Kai-shek and the War against Japan*, University of Tokyo Press, 1990.

Legge, John, *Australian Outlook: A History of the Australian Institute of International Affairs*, St Leonards, NSW: Allen & Unwin, 1999.

Levin, N. Gordon Jr, *Woodrow Wilson and World Politics: America's Response to War and Revolution*, New York: Oxford University Press, 1968.

Link, Arthur S., ed., *The Papers of Woodrow Wilson (PWW)* vols 45, 54–7, Princeton, NJ: Princeton University Press, 1984–1987.

—— and William M. Leary, Jr, eds, *The Diplomacy of World Power: The United States, 1889–1920*, Edinburgh: Edward Arnold, 1970.

Masuda, Hiroshi, *Ishibashi Tanzan kenkyū: "Shō Nihon shugisha" no kokusai ninshiki*, Tōyō keizai shimpōsha, 1990.

Matsumoto, Shigeharu, *Shanhai jidai*, vol. 1–3, Chūō kōronsha, 1974–5.

—— *Showashi no ichishōgen*, Mainichi shinbumsha, 1986.

Matsuzawa, Hiroaki, 'Jiyū shugi ron', *Iwanami kōza, Nihon tsūshi*, vol. 18, Iwanami shoten, 1994.

Miki, Kiyoshi, *Miki Kiyoshi zenshū*, vol. 17, Iwanami shoten, 1968.

Mitani, Taichirō, '"Tenkanki" (1918–1921) no gaikō shidō', in Shinohara Hajime and Mitani Taichirō, eds, *Kindai Nihon no seiji shidō: Seijika kenkyū II*, Tokyo daigaku shuppankai, 1965.

—— *Taisho demokurashiron: Yoshino Sakuzō to sono jidai*, Chūō kōronsha, 1974.

Miwa, Kimitada, 'Ajia shugi no rekishiteki kōsatsu', in Hirano Ken'ichirō, ed., *Nihon bunka no henyō*, Kōdansha, 1973.

—— *Matsuoka Yōsuke: Sono ningen to gaikō*, Chūō kōronsha, 1971.

—— '"Tōa shin chitsujo" sengen to "Daitōa kyōeiken" kōsō no dansō', in Miwa Kimitada, ed., *Saikō Taiheiyō sensō zenya: Nihon no 1930 nendai ron toshite*, Sōseiki, 1981.

Nagatomi, Morinosuke, 'Gendai no chōkokkateki rengō undō no ichi shimyaku to shite no Pan-Ajia undō', *Kokusai chishiki*, vol. 6, no. 10, October 1926, pp. 2–13.

Nakami, Mari, 'Taiheiyō mondai chōsakai to Nihon no chishikijin', *Shisō*, no. 728, February 1985, pp. 104–27.

Nakamura, Takafusa, 'Ryū Shintarō to tōsei keizai', *Chūō kōron: Rekishi to jinbutsu*, April 1974, pp. 66–74.

Newman, Robert, *Owen Lattimore and the "Loss" of China*, Berkeley: University of California Press, 1992.

Nish, Ian, *Japan's Struggle with Internationalism: Japan, China and the League of Nations, 1931–1933*, London: Kegan Paul International, 1993.

Norman, E. Herbert, Ōkubo, Genji, trans. and ed., *Herbert Norman zenshū*, vols 1, 2 and 4, Iwanami shoten, 1977–8.

—— *Japan's Emergence as a Modern State*, New York: ISIPR, 1940.

Obi, Toshito, ed., *Gendaishi shiryō*, vol. 3, Misuzu shobō, 1962.

Ogata, Sadako, 'Kokusai shugi dantai no yakuwari', in Hosoya Chihiro *et al.*, eds, *Nichibei kankeishi: Kaisen ni itaru jūnen*, vol. 3, Tokyo daigaku shuppankai, 1971.

Ōkubo Genji tsuitōshū kankōkai, ed., *Tsuisō Ōkubo Genji* [Editor], 1987.

Ōshiro, George, *Nitobe Inazō: Kokusai shugi no kaitakusha*, Chūō daigaku shuppansha, 1992.

Osmond, Warren, *Frederic Eggleston: An Intellectual in Australian Politics*, Sydney: Allen and Unwin, 1985.

Ozaki, Hotsumi, *Ozaki Hotsumi zenshū*, vol. 2, Keisō shobō, 1977.

Ozawa, Yūsaku, 'Sawayanagi Masatarō no shokuminchi kyōikukan', in Sawayanagi Masatarō, *Sawayanagi Masatarō zenshū*, Bekkan, Kokudosha, 1979.

Quigley, Carroll, *The Anglo-American Establishment: From Rhodes to Cliveden*, New York: Books in Focus, 1981.

—— *Tragedy and Hope: A History of the World in Our Time*, New York: Macmillan, 1966.

Rekishigaku kenkyūkai, ed., *Nihonshi shiryō*, vol. 5, Iwanami shoten, 1997.

Robinson, Edgar E. and Paul C. Edwards, eds, *The Memoirs of Ray Lyman Wilbur, 1875–1949*, Stanford: Stanford University Press, 1960.

Roden, Donald, *Schooldays in Imperial Japan: A Study in the Culture of a Student Elite*, Berkeley: University of California Press, 1980.

Rōyama, Masamichi, *Nihon seiji dōkōron*, Kōyō shoin, 1933.

—— *Tōa to sekai*, Kaizō, 1941.

Sabey, J.W., 'The Gen'yōsha, the Kokuryūkai and Japanese Expansionism', PhD thesis, University of Michigan, 1972.

Said, Edward, *Orientalism: Western Conceptions of the Orient*, London: Penguin Books, 1991, first published in 1978.

Saionji, Kinkazu, 'Kizoku no taijō', in Imai Seiichi, ed., *Showa no dōran*, Chikuma shobō, 1969.

Saitō, Makoto, 'Nihon ni okeru kokusaigaku no senkusha I: Takaki Yasaka', *Kokusaigaku kenkyū*, no. 1, 1987, no. 19.

—— 'Sōseiki Amerika kenkyū no mokuteki ishiki: Nitobe Inazō to "Beikoku kenkyū"', in Hosoya Chihiro and Saitō Makoto, eds, *Washinton taisei to Nichibei kankei*, Tokyo daigaku shuppankai, 1978.

—— *et al.*, eds, *Amerika seishin o motomete: Takaki Yasaka no shōgai*, Tokyo daigaku shuppankai, 1985.

Sakai, Saburō, 'Showa kenkyūkai no higeki', *Bungei shunjū*, October 1964, pp. 234–45.

Sawada, Setsuzō, 'Nihon ni okeru heiwa shisō no hatten', *Kokusai chishiki*, vol. 5, no. 11, November 1925, pp. 15–22.

Schulzinger, Robert, *American Diplomacy in the Twentieth Century*, New York: Oxford University Press, 1994.

—— *Wise Men of Foreign Affairs: The History of the Council on Foreign Relations*, New York: Columbia University Press, 1984.

Shibasaki, Atsushi, *Kindai Nihon to kokusai bunka kōryū: Kokusai bunka shinkōkai no sōsetsu to tenkai*, Yūshindō kōbunsha, 1999.

Shibusawa Eiichi denki shiryō kankōkai, ed., *Shibusawa Eiichi denki shiryō (SEDS)*, vols. 34–37, Shibusawa Eiichi denki shiryō kankōkai, 1960–1961.

Shibusawa, Masahide, *Taiheiyō ni kakeru hashi: Shibusawa Eiichi no shōgai*, Yomiuri shimbunsha, 1970.

Shiozaki, Hiroaki, *Kokusai shinchitsujo o motomete: RIIA, CFR, IPR no keifu to ryōtaisenkan no renkei kankei*, Fukuoka: Kyushu daigaku shuppankai, 1998.

—— 'Showa kenkyūkai to Miki Kiyoshi no kyōdō shugi', *Nihon rekishi*, July 1993, pp. 18–37.

Shotwell, James T., *At the Paris Peace Conference*, New York: Macmillan, 1937.

Shoup, Laurence H. and William Minter, *Imperial Brain Trust: The Council on Foreign Relations and United States Foreign Policy*, New York: Monthly Review Press, 1977.

Smith, Henry D. II, *Japan's First Student Radicals*, Cambridge, MA: Harvard University Press, 1972.

Spaulding, Robert M., 'Japan's new bureaucrats, 1932–45', in George M. Wilson, ed., *Crisis Politics in Prewar Japan: Institutional and Ideological Problems of the 1930s*, Sophia University, 1970.

Steigerwald, David, *Wilsonian Idealism in America*, Ithaca: Cornell University Press, 1994.

Stone, Diane, *Capturing the Political Imagination: Think Tanks and the Policy Process*, London: Frank Cass, 1996.

Sudō, Shinji, *Nichibei kaisen gaikō no kenkyū: Nichibei kōshō no hatten kara Haru nōto made*, Keiō tsūshin, 1986.

Takaki, Yasaka, 'Taiheiyō kankei chōsakai no seiritsu nituite', *Gaikō jihō*, vol. 42, no. 501, October 1925, pp. 58–67.

Tanaka, Stefan, *Japan's Orient: Rendering Pasts into History*, Berkeley: University of California Press, 1993.

Thomas, John, *The Institute of Pacific Relations: Asian Scholars and American Politics*, Seattle: University of Washington Press, 1974.

Thorne, Christopher, *Allies of a Kind: the United States, Britain and the War against Japan, 1941–1945*, London: Hamish Hamilton, 1978.

—— 'Chatham House, Whitehall, and Far Eastern issues, 1941–1945', *International Affairs*, vol. 54, no. 1, January 1978, pp. 1–29.

—— *The Limits of Foreign Policy: The West, the League and the Far Eastern Crisis of 1931–33*, New York: Capricorn Books, 1973.

Tobe, Ryōichi, 'Gaimushō kakushinha no taibeisaku', *Gaikō jihō*, no. 1273, 1990, pp. 66–80.

—— 'Gaimushō "kakushinha" to gunbu', in Miyake Masaki, ed., *Showashi no gunbu to seiji, 2*, Daiichi hōki shuppan, 1983.

Toshino, Inosuke, ed., *Iwanaga Yūkichi kun*, Iwanaga Yūkichi kun denki hensan iinkai, 1941.

Tsurumi, Shunsuke, *Tenkō kenkyū*, Chikuma shobō, 1976.

Tsurumi, Yūsuke, *Chūdō o ayumu kokoro*, Shinshakai, 1927.

—— 'Shin jiyū shugi no tachiba yori', *Kaizō*, vol. 10, no. 5, May 1928, pp. 24–31.

Usui, Katsumi, *Chūgoku o meguru kindai Nihon no gaikō*, Chikuma shobō, 1983.

Watabiki, Misao, 'Taiheiyō kaigi yori dattai seyo', *Nihon oyobi Nihonjin*, no. 226, June 1931, pp. 22–9.

White, Lyman C., *International Non-Governmental Organizations: Their Purpose, Methods, and Accomplishments*, New Brunswick, NJ: Rutgers University Press, 1951.

—— *The Structure of Private International Organizations*, Philadelphia, PA: George S. Ferguson Company, 1933.

Wilson, Sandra, 'The Manchurian Crisis and moderate Japanese intellectuals: the Japan Council of the Institute of Pacific Relations', *Modern Asian Studies*, vol. 26, no. 3, 1992, pp. 507–44.

Woodrow, Wilson, *The New Freedom*, London: J.M. Dent and Sons, 1916.

Woods, Lawrence, *Asia–Pacific Diplomacy: Nongovernmental Organizations and International Relations*, Vancouver: University of British Columbia Press, 1993.

—— 'Canada and the Institute of Pacific Relations: lessons from an earlier voyage', *Canadian Foreign Policy/La Politique Étrangère du Canada*, vol. 6, no. 2, winter, 1999, pp. 119–38.

Yabe, Teiji, *Konoe Ayamaro* (Fumimaro), vol. 1, Kōbundō, 1952.

Yamakawa, Tadao, 'Dairokkai Taiheiyō kaigi ni tsukite', *Kokusai chishiki*, vol. 16, no. 11, November 1936, pp. 1–27.

Yamaoka, Michio, *Ajia Taiheiyō jidai ni mukete: Sono zenshi to shite no Taiheiyō mondai chōsakai to Taiheiyō kaigi*, Hokuju shuppan, 1991.

—— 'Senzenki Nihon Taiheiyō mondai chōsakai to kokusai jimukyoku tono tairitsu: "Inkuaiari" mondai o chūshin toshite', *Shakai kagaku tōkyū*, no. 121, March 1996, pp. 465–511.

—— 'Taiheiyō mondai kenkyūkai ni okeru Nichibei kankei iinkai no katsudō', *Shakai kagaku tōkyū*, no. 105, December 1990, pp. 99–128.

Yanaihara, Tadao, *Pacific Islands Under Japanese Mandate*, London: Oxford University Press, 1940.

Yui, Daizaburō, *Mikan no senryō kaikaku*, Tokyo daigaku shuppankai, 1990, first published in 1989.

Zimmern, Alfred, 'Democracy and the expert', *Political Quarterly*, vol. 1, 1930, pp. 7–25.

—— *The Prospects of Democracy and other Essays*, London: Chatto and Windus, 1929.

Zumoto, Motosada, 'Japan and the Pan-Asiatic movement', *News Bulletin [of the IPR]*, January 1927, p. 15.

—— 'Kyoto kaigi no atoshimatsu', *Gaikō jihō*, vol. 53, no. 602, 1 January 1930, pp. 291–6.

Index

Abe, Nobuyuki 241
about this book: focus 1; hope for 16; IPR
archives, use of 3; sources, limits on 3–4
ACIPR (American Council of the IPR):
Anglophile sentiments in 187; Carter a
central figure 169; demands of Pacific
War on 257; educational objectives of
255–7; ISIPR and the 120; Pacific
Council, Philippine group and 142;
Philippine independence 184–5; strength
and independence of 131; 'united
nations' approach of 249; virtual
integration with ISIPR 252–3; wartime
cooperation 252–4, 257; weakness of
West coast within 175
ACNJA (American Committee for Non-
Participation in Japanese Aggression)
222, 254–5
agency, non-state see non-state agency
AIAA (Australian Institute of International
Affairs) 177–8
Akagi, Hidemichi 108
Alexander, Wallace 40, 55, 175, 176
Allen, Ian 138
Amerasi 211
American Asiatic Association 54
American Council of Learned Societies
(ACLS) 255
America's Far Eastern Policy (Bisson, T.A.) 211,
264
Amō, Eiji 194–5, 205, 206, 208
Anezaki, Masaharu 73, 103, 104
Anglo-American relations: Anglo-American
solidarity 42–5; Anglo-Saxon bloc, 138;
conflicting views from the US on postwar
reconstruction policies 259, 264, 267–9;
US cooperation with (at Paris
Conference) 26; *see also* Britain and the
United States
anti-Japanese immigration act of the US
(*Hainichi iminhō*): 40–2, 69, 110–12; *see
also* immigration
Aoki, Setsuichi 114
APEC (Asia-Pacific Economic Cooperation
forum) 5

appeasement, 'peaceful adjustment' and
213–14
Arita, Hachirō 27, 150, 205, 220
Asia: new powers in 22–5, 56; redefinition of
236; *see also* East Asia
Asianism 64–5, 67, 144, 233
Associated Press 202
Atherton, Frank: address to IPR Honolulu
Conference (1925) 93; Davis resignation,
dissuasion of 128; grant applications 50;
Hawai'i base of 79; ISIPR move to New
York, objection to 176, 183; ISIPR
Treasurer 118; JARC member 55; loss of
Pacific-centred perspective 175; major
promoter of IPR 2, 47; Orientalism of
186; USSR visit 96
Atlantic Charter 240, 266, 267, 268
Australia: American regional leadership,
view on 91; Commonwealth delegations
at Paris Conference 26–7; Davis
resignation, view on 138; foreign policy
discretion, lack of 88, 90; Hawai'i, view
on 173; IPR and dissemination of
knowledge to 15; ISIPR New York move,
view on 176; pledged financial
contribution to IPR 154; political
equality, sense of? 93–4; racial equality,
opposition to 23; relationship with states,
closeness discussed 258–9; strategic view
of the Pacific 189; YMCA domination of
group 117
Axis Pact *see* Tripartite Pact

Baba, Shūichi 235, 238
Baker, Newton 26, 171, 207, 213, 222
Banff Springs Conference (1933) 171, 192–4,
194, 196, 199, 283
Batchelder, Charles 54, 104
BCRC (British Commonwealth Relations
Conference) 187–8
Benitez, Conrado 100–1
Berlin Pact (1940) 250; *see also* Tripartite Pact
Bisson, Thomas A. 211–12, 264
Blakeslee, George 46, 54, 118, 120, 165, 253,
259, 262

352   *Index*

United Nations 5–6, 277; *see also* United
Nations, Charter of the
United Nations, Charter of the 5–6, 24; *see
also* Dumbarton Oaks, New World Order
United News Agency *see Dōmei tsūshin*
United States: America as Star of Hope, 69;
American ideals, 41; American
internationalism 4–5; American order
and the JCIPR 65–70; American post-
League internationalism 33–4; American
world order, redefinition of 172; Anglo-
American solidarity 42–5; anti-Japanese
immigration act (1924) 69, 111–12;
British cooperation with (at Paris
Conference) 26; emergence as dominant
power 15–16; financial contribution to
IPR 154; great power at Paris
Conference 22; immigration policy 111–
12; independent internationalism of 34;
Japanese peace negotiations (1941) 245–
8; nativism in 41; Pacific Community and
the 34–8; Pacific region and the 65–70;
see also Anglo-American relations,
Monroe Doctrine, Pacific Community,
US, US–Japan relations
Universal Declaration of Human Rights 272,
281
Uramatsu, Samitarō 164
Urice, Jay A. 49, 52, 54
US anti-Japanese immigration act; *see* anti-
Japanese immigration act of the US
Ushiba, Tomohiko 200, 211, 216–17, 229–30,
241, 243–8, 254
US–Japan Commerce and Navigation Treaty
245
US–Japan relations: America as Star of
Hope for JCIPR members 69; American
naval strength, concern for 72–3;
American order and the JCIPR 65–70;
area of possible conflict between US and
Japan; assessment (1936) of Washington
Treaties 208; Japanese concerns
regarding US 38; JCIPR and war 238–9;
peace negotiations between US and
Japan (1941) 245–8; US anti-Japanese
immigration act (1924) 40–2, 69, 111–12;
US, interaction with 35, 36; Versailles–
Washington system and 59–62; *see also*
Japan, United States
US–Japan Security Treaty 279
USSR 12, 39, 170, 173, 201, 208

Versailles Treaty 26; *see also* Paris Peace
Conference (1919)
Versailles–Washington system: challenge to
the 62–5; dominant international order,
support for 59–62; *see also* post-League
order
Vietnam War 278

Virginia Beach study meeting (1939) 224–5,
257–8, 283

Walker, Sydnor 251
Wang Zhaoyao (Wang Chao-yao) 244
Washington Conference 34–42; *see also*
Versailles–Washington system
Watt, Alan 258
Welles, Sumner 253, 267
Westphalian sovereignty *see* state
sovereignty
Whyte, Frederick 90–1, 156
Wickersham, George 41, 55, 221
Wilbur, Ray 46, 50–2, 54, 56–7, 78, 101, 106,
109, 118, 120, 129, 144–5, 175, 216, 251–
2
Wilde, Oscar 63
Wilson, George G., 54
Wilson, Woodrow 1, 7, 17, 19–21, 23, 33, 44
Wilson Club (*Uiruson kurabu*) 84–5
Wilsonian internationalism: dominant in
IPR 4; focus of book 1; ideals,
institutionalization of 8; ideology and 5–
6; 'liberal democracy', nature of 6–7;
'Liberalism' and 5–7; nationalism and
the nation-state 6–7; Post-League (of
Nations) internationalism 7–8; utopian
ideal and 5, 8; World War II and
enthusiasm for 240; *see also*
internationalism, post-League
internationalism
Wright, Quincy 111, 209, 215

Yale Club meeting 46–7, 53, 54–8
Yamada, Sanzō 70
Yamakawa, Tadao 206, 207, 208–9
Yamanaka, Atsutarō 165
Yamasaki, Keiichi 129
Yanaihara, Tadao 197–8, 220
Yarnell, Harry 268
YMCA International 25–6, 46–8, 50, 52, 73,
117–18, 128, 169
Yokota, Kisaburō 161–2, 165, 194–5, 196,
197, 198
Yonai, Mitsumasa
Yosemite Conference (1936) 176, 200–18,
283
Yoshida, Shigeru 10, 20, 27, 60
Yoshino, Sakuzō 75, 84
Yoshizawa, Kenkichi 157, 158, 163, 192, 200,
207–9, 215
Yui, David Z.T. 118, 129, 148

Zaibatsu, power of 263–5
Zhang Xueliang (Chang Hsueh-liang) 157
Zhang Zuolin (Chang Tso-lin) 147, 151, 157
Zimmern, Alfred 14, 24, 28, 29, 146
Zumoto, Motosada 67, 68, 73, 78, 143–4